The proliferation of studies on the 'body' (and subjects in close relation) is an obvious, even startling, feature of the literature of the social sciences and humanities in recent years. Such an explosion of interest makes the lack of a standard study of the 'body' and the major religions of the world the more surprising. In setting out to remedy this omission, *Religion and the body* aims above all to highlight the distinctive and *unfamiliar* ways in which diverse religious traditions understand the 'body', and, in doing this, to raise to greater consciousness some of the assumptions and problems of contemporary attitudes to it.

This volume brings together essays by established experts in the history of religion, the social sciences, and philosophy. Part I is devoted to an analysis of current secularized discourses on the 'body', and to exposing both their anti-religious and their covertly religious content. Parts II and III provide essays on traditional 'Western' and 'Eastern' religious attitudes to the 'body'. Each contributor focusses on some (especially characteristic) devotional practices or relevant texts; each carefully outlines the total context in which a distinctive religious attitude to 'bodiliness' occurs.

CAMBRIDGE STUDIES IN RELIGIOUS TRADITIONS 8

RELIGION AND THE BODY

CAMBRIDGE STUDIES IN RELIGIOUS TRADITIONS

Edited by John Clayton (University of Lancaster), Steven Collins (University of Chicago) and Nicholas de Lange (University of Cambridge)

RELIGION AND THE BODY

EDITED BY

SARAH COAKLEY

Mallinckrodt Professor of Divinity, Harvard University

CAMBRIDGE
UNIVERSITY PRESS

PUBLISHED BY THE PRESS SYNDICATE OF THE UNIVERSITY OF CAMBRIDGE
The Pitt Building, Trumpington Street, Cambridge, United Kingdom

CAMBRIDGE UNIVERSITY PRESS
The Edinburgh Building, Cambridge CB2 2RU, UK   www.cup.cam.ac.uk
40 West 20th Street, New York, NY 10011–4211, USA   www.cup.org
10 Stamford Road, Oakleigh, Melbourne 3166, Australia
Ruiz de Alarcón 13, 28014 Madrid, Spain

First published 1997
First paperback edition published with corrections 2000

Typeset in Baskerville 11/12.5 pt [VN]

A catalogue record for this book is available from the British Library

Library of Congress cataloguing in publication data

Religion and the body / edited by Sarah Coakley.
p.   cm. – (Cambridge Studies in Religious Traditions; 8)
Includes bibliographical references.
ISBN 0 521 36669 0 (hardback)
1. Body, Human–Religious aspects. I. Coakley, Sarah, 1951– .
II. Series.
BL604.B64R44 1997
291.2'2–dc20   96–6474   CIP

ISBN 0 521 36669 0 hardback
ISBN 0 521 78386 0 paperback

Transferred to digital printing 2003

Contents

Illustrations

Contributors

TALAL ASAD received his university education in Britain. He is now Distinguished Professor of Anthropology at the City University of New York, and previously taught at Johns Hopkins University, at the New School for Social Research, New York, and at Hull University. His most recent book is *Genealogies of Religion* (1993).

SARAH COAKLEY has theology degrees from Cambridge and Harvard. She is now Mallinckrodt Professor of Divinity, Harvard Divinity School, and previously taught at Oriel College, Oxford, and at Lancaster University. She is the author of *Christ without Absolutes: A Study of the Christology of Ernst Troeltsch* (1988), *God, Sexuality and the Self: An Essay 'On the Trinity'* (forthcoming), and co-editor with David A. Pailin of *The Making and Re-making of Christian Doctrine* (1993).

STEVEN COLLINS is Professor and Chairman in the Department of South Asian Languages and Civilizations, University of Chicago. He is the author of *Selfless Persons: Imagery and Thought in Theravāda Buddhism* (1982), and *Nirvāṇa and other Buddhist Felicities* (1998).

WENDY DONIGER (formerly Wendy Doniger O'Flaherty) trained as a dancer before taking two doctorates in Sanskrit and Indian Studies at Harvard and Oxford. She has taught at Harvard, Oxford, the University of London, and the University of California at Berkeley, and is now the Mircea Eliade Professor of the History of Religions at the University of Chicago. She is the author of many books, including *Women, Androgynes, and Other Mythical Beasts* (1980), *Dreams, Illusion and Other Realities* (1984), and *Other People's Myths: The Cave of Echoes* (1988). She has also edited and translated many texts, including *Hindu Myths* (1975), *The Rig Veda* (1981), and (with Brian K. Smith) *The Laws of Manu* (1991). Her most recent book is *Splitting the Difference: Gender and Myth in Ancient Greece and India* (1999).

LOUIS JACOBS was educated at Manchester Talmudical College and University College, London, and has been Rabbi of the New London Synagogue since 1964. More recently he was visiting Professor of Jewish Studies at Lancaster University. He is the author of a number of books, including *A Jewish Theology* (1973), *Principles of Jewish Faith* (1964[1], 1988[2]), *The Talmudic Argument* (1985), *Structure and Form in the Babylonian Talmud* (1991), *Religion and the Individual: A Jewish Perspective* (1992), and *The Jewish Religion: A Companion* (1995).

ANDREW LOUTH is Professor in the Department of Theology at the University of Durham. He was previously Professor of Cultural History at Goldsmiths' College, University of London, and before that taught for fifteen years at Worcester College, Oxford. He is best known for three of his books, *The Origins of the Christian Mystical Tradition: From Plato to Denys* (1981), *Denys the Areopagite* (1989), and *The Wilderness of God* (1991). His most recent work is *Maximus the Confessor* (1996).

MARY MIDGLEY taught philosophy at the University of Newcastle, until she took early retirement in order to have more time to write. She has been a visiting lecturer at Cornell University, and at Trent University, Ontario. She is the author of a number of books, including: *Beast and Man* (1980), *Heart and Mind: The Varieties of Moral Experience* (1981), *Women's Choices: Philosophical Problems Facing Feminism* (with Judith Hughes, 1983), *Wickedness* (1984), *Science as Salvation: A Modern Myth and its Meaning* (1992), and *Utopias, Dolphins, and Computers: Some Problems in Philosophical Plumbing* (1996).

ELEANOR NESBITT read Classics and Theology at Cambridge, and holds a doctorate in Sikhism from the University of Warwick. She has taught in both India and Britain and is currently Senior Research Fellow in the Warwick Religions and Education Unit, University of Warwick. Her publications include *Hindu Children in Britain* (with Robert Jackson, 1993), and *Sikhs in Britain: An Annotated Bibliography* (with Darshan Singh Tatla, 1994).

MICHAEL PYE studied Modern Languages and Theology at Cambridge, and has spent a number of years in Japan between 1961 and the present. He has taught Religious Studies at Lancaster and Leeds Universities in England, and is currently Professor of Comparative Religion at the University of Marburg, Germany. His publications include *Skilful Means, A Concept in Mahāyāna Buddhism* (1978), *Emerging from Meditation* (translations from Tominaga Nakamoto, 1990), and other writings both on Japanese religion and more general questions of comparative religion.

MICHAEL SASO has degrees in Philosophy and Chinese Studies from the Universities of Gonzaga, Yale, and London (SOAS). He has spent many years researching and practising Taoism and other Chinese religions in mainland China, and is now Director at the Institute of Asian Studies, Chinese Academy of Social Sciences, Beijing. He was previously Professor at the University of Hawaii. He is the author of a number of books, including *Taoism and the Rite of Cosmic Renewal* (1972), *The Teachings of Taoist Master Chung* (1978), *Blue Dragon White Tiger: Taoist Rites of Passage* (1990), and *Tantric Art and Meditation* (1990).

ANNEMARIE SCHIMMEL was educated in Germany, earning her first doctorate at the youthful age of nineteen. She taught Islamic Studies, especially Sufism, in Germany and Turkey, before becoming Professor of Indo-Muslim Culture at Harvard University, a post she held for twenty-five years. She has written more than ninety books, including the classic *Mystical Dimensions of Islam* (1975), has done many translations of poetry and prose texts from Arabic, Persian, Turkish, Pashto, Sindhi, etc., and has also written her own poetry in both German and English.

DAVID TRIPP was educated at Cambridge, Leeds, and Heidelberg Universities. He is a Methodist minister and liturgical specialist who has taught at Lincoln Theological College, Notre Dame University Indiana, and The Queen's College, Birmingham. His publications include *The Renewal of the Covenant in the Methodist Tradition* (1969), contributions to *The Study of Liturgy* (1978, revised edition 1992), and he has edited and translated (with N. S. F. Alldrit) *The Latin and French Inscriptions of Lincoln Minster* (1990).

BRYAN S. TURNER was trained in sociology at the University of Leeds. He has held professorial positions in Australia, the Netherlands, and Great Britain, and fellowships at La Trobe University, Bielefeld University, and the London School of Economics. He is now Professor of Sociology in the Department of Social and Political Sciences, University of Cambridge. His many books include *Weber and Islam* (1974), *Marx and the End of Orientalism* (1978), *Religion and Social Theory* (1983; revised edition 1991), *The Body and Society* (1984), *Regulating Bodies* (1992), and *Max Weber from History to Modernity* (1992).

KALLISTOS WARE is Spalding Lecturer in Eastern Orthodox Studies, Oxford University, and Bishop of Diokleia (in the Orthodox Archdiocese of Thyateira and Great Britain). He is the author of *The Orthodox Church* (1963, revised 1993), *Eustratios Argenti: A Study of the Greek Church under Turkish Rule* (1964), and *The Orthodox Way* (1979). He is co-editor of the English translations of *The Festal Menaion,* (1969), *The Lenten Triodion* (1978) and *The Philokalia* (1979).

ALAN WILLIAMS read Classics and Oriental Studies at Oxford, and took his doctorate in Iranian Studies at SOAS, London. He was previously lecturer in Religious Studies at the University of Sussex, and is now lecturer in Comparative Religion at the University of Manchester. He is the author of *The Pahlavi Rivāyat Accompanying the Dādestān ī Dēnīg* (2 vols., 1990), and of numerous articles on Zoroastrianism.

PAUL WILLIAMS studied Philosophy and Religion at Sussex University and took his doctorate in Buddhist Studies at Oxford University. He is currently Reader in Indo-Tibetan Studies, and Co-director of the Centre for Buddhist Studies at Bristol University. His recent publications include *Mahāyāna Buddhism: The Doctrinal Foundations* (1989), and *A Tibetan Madhyamaka Defence of the Reflexive Nature of Awareness* (1995).

Preface

The idea for a book on 'religion and the body' goes as far back as
1987, when I was a Lecturer in the Department of Religious Studies at
Lancaster University. I was that year responsible for organizing a
large conference at Lancaster entitled 'The Body: A Colloquium on
Comparative Spirituality'. A total of 29 papers (including 3 pa-
per/demonstrations) were offered at the conference,[1] and enthusiastically received by a diverse audience of religionists, theologians, philosophers and social scientists. It was clear, however, that the 'interests'
and methodologies of the participants were far from unified. The
social scientists had one narrative to tell about the 'body', whilst
feminists, Eastern religionists, Christian theologians and Western philosophers had others. Whether they were even discoursing about the
same phenomenon under the rubric of 'body' was a matter of some
intense debate at the conference itself – though without any very clear
resolution at the time. It was obvious, however, that a compendium
volume clarifying some of these conflicted methodological issues, as
well as providing basic coverage on attitudes to the 'body' in the great
religious traditions, was much needed.[2] But it was also clear that a
volume such as this would have to be forged from the outset on a

[1] A book of abstracts of the paper was published by the Department of Religious Studies, Lancaster,
for the conference (8–11 July 1987). Only one paper from the original conference (that of Steven
Collins) appears in this volume in anything like its original form. Seven of the shorter
communications from the conference were later published in *Religion* 19 (1989), 197–273, and form
a useful adjunct group to the contributions in this book.
[2] Since the original Lancaster conference three books have appeared from SUNY Press with
obvious relevance to our topic and some overlapping interest: Yuasa Yasuo, *The Body: Toward an
Eastern Mind-Body Theory* (Albany, NY, 1987); ed. Thomas P. Kasulis (with Roger T. Ames and
Wimal Dissanayake), *Self as Body in Asian Theory and Practice* (Albany, NY, 1993); and ed. Roger T.
Ames (with Wimal Dissanayake and Thomas P. Kasulis), *Self as Person in Asian Theory and Practice*
(Albany, NY, 1994). These important books are commented upon by a number of the contributors
in this volume; they do not however cover the same range of religious traditions treated here.

clear set of agreed principles, rather than operating with the variety of
perspectives presented at the original conference. The rationale for
this enterprise, as it has finally taken shape, is explained in the
Introduction.

The project that has resulted owes a good deal to the work of
Ulrike Hellen (with whom I initially conducted negotiations at Cambridge University Press), and to her successor Alex Wright. I thank
them both for their support, patience, and technical assistance. As
contributions were commissioned and arrived in first draft, they were
vetted by up to four specialist readers in each case; and, since all these
specialists – busy and eminent scholars – gave their time freely and
generously, I owe them a great debt of gratitude. I must also thank
the contributors themselves for their patience and goodwill during this
time-consuming process of writing and rewriting. All the essays that
appear in this volume have been specially written for it, with one
exception, that of Annemarie Schimmel's piece, which was originally
published as 'Eros – Heavenly and Not so Heavenly – in Sufi
Literature and Life', in Afaf Lutfi al-Sayyid-Marsot, ed., *Society and the
Sexes in Medieval Islam*, Malibu, CA: Undena Publications, 1979,
119–46. The essay is reproduced here with kind permission of the
author and publisher.

The initial conception, and subsequent editorial production, of this
book have spanned a period when I myself have moved in quick
succession from Lancaster to Oxford to Harvard. I am therefore
indebted to a number of different people for their secretarial assistance. I must mention in this connection Wendy Francis and Janice
Parkes at Lancaster, for their invaluable help with the original conference; and Maggie Stanley at Harvard, who has done characteristically
intelligent work with final retyping of parts of the manuscript. My two
recent research assistants at Harvard, Francis Caponi, OSA, and
David Kyuman Kim, have also done much to smooth the final path
to publication; and Wolfhart Heinrichs and Alma Giese kindly provided technical and bibliographical assistance with the reformatting of
Annemarie Schimmel's article. In addition, Jennifer Cross has done
sterling work on the index. I must also record my indebtedness to the
Luce Foundation, for a Henry Luce III Fellowship in the academic
year 1994–5, which has enabled me to complete this project as well as
others.

Finally, I want to record my special gratitude to my former colleagues at the Department of Religious Studies, Lancaster University

(some of them now dispersed elsewhere), especially to John Clayton, Mary Douglas, Paul Heelas, John Milbank, and Paul Morris, who did much to inform the vision of this book from the outset, and whose wit and wisdom is (to some derivative extent) perhaps still reflected in it. To them I dedicate the volume in its final shape.

Sarah Coakley
Corpus Christi, 1995

In preparation for the paperback edition of this volume I have taken the opportunity to correct a few minor typographical errors and to update the details given about the contributors at the beginning of the book. The flow of publications on the 'body' has not abated since 1995; but the essays in this volume have been left in their original form, as challenges to further comparative and interdisciplinary work yet to be undertaken.

Sarah Coakley
St. Giles, 1999

CHAPTER I

Introduction: religion and the body

Sarah Coakley

A book that invites comparisons between religious traditions does well to declare its 'interests' at the outset. This is true, firstly, because the nervousness about ethnocentric imposition of Western categories on the 'other' in matters of culture and religion has currently become so intense in some quarters as to make any sort of comparisons across traditions inherently suspect.[1] Hence, secondly, the project of providing parallel essays on a topic of shared (perhaps even universal) interest is open to the scornful objection of a spurious dispassion. It is thus the task of this brief introduction to lay bare the editorial interests and aims of this collection, and to declare what it hopes to achieve and illuminate, as well as what lies beyond its particular scope and intentions.

In clarifying these goals I shall not (as is common in editorial introductions) provide a précised version of each of my contributors' essays in advance. Rather I shall highlight the ways in which the *ordering* of the book's contents is intended to lead the reader from the known to the (relatively) unknown: from an analysis of our current Western (and 'secularized') obsessions with the 'body' (Part I); through a deepening understanding of the 'Western' religious traditions that have spawned this (Part II) – and are still, I shall argue, to some extent ironically replicated in it; to the lesser-known territories of 'Eastern' religious traditions on the 'body' (Part III), themselves increasingly becoming the targets of consumerist Western syncretism.

From this it will be clear that the organization of the volume is unashamedly contemporary and Western in its starting-point, an admission, however, that does not detract from the care with which the scholars whose work appears in Parts II and III have, to the best of their abilities, attempted to 'bracket the familiarity' of current 'body' dis-

---

[1] See eds. Clifford and Marcus 1986, for an expression of radical doubt about the possibility of ethnographic objectivity in fieldwork observation; and Said 1978, for an exposé of the projections involved in Western views of the 'East'.

cussions in their treatment of religious traditions less immediate to contemporary Western attention. When they do import categories or methodologies from these discussions into their exposition (structuralist, symbolic, or Foucaultian accounts of 'bodiliness', for instance), the intellectual genesis – and contestability – of these accounts will have already been made clear from the analysis in Part I. In this way the volume can profitably be read as a dialectic between the Parts, as well as a systematic unfolding from Part I to Part III. The final editorial objects (and novelties) of the exercise, however, are these: the clarification, first, of the specificity, oddity, and even repressed *religiosity* of the current secularized debates about 'bodies'; the complexification and contextualization, second, of the (now often misconstrued and derided) 'Western' religious heritages that have formed their backcloth; and the analysis, third, of religious 'bodily' practice within metaphysical frameworks beyond the traditional purview of Western eyes.

If this initial division reflects a series of demarcations that are now becoming rapidly outmoded, it is advised; it is precisely the further intent of this book to throw these demarcations into question – to raise implicit questions about the spiritual and philosophical impoverishment of our current 'body' obsessions, and yet also about the superficiality of consumerist 'magpie' raids on Eastern religious bodily practice. The frantic assemblage of fragments of wisdom from Eastern religious traditions in our culture so often serves a wholly unquestioned narcissistic quest for gratification and pleasure, or a more insidious and pervasive 'denial of death'.[2]

WHO OR WHAT IS THE BODY?

This initial statement of intent, however, with its admission of an element of 'hermeneutical circularity', has to contend with a more fundamental methodological objection. The notable explosion of thought and literature on the subject of the 'body' in the last decades[3] has begged a question of definition which is not so easily grasped, let alone answered. It is as if we are clear about an agreed cultural obsession – the 'body' – but far from assured about its referent. As Judith Butler has recently put it (Butler 1993, ix), 'I tried to discipline myself to stay on the

---

[2] See Becker 1973, for an influential analysis of this 'denial of death'.
[3] Some idea of this will be gleaned from the bibliographies appended to each of the essays in this volume. For further such bibliographies, see Barbara Duden's 'A Repertory of Body History', in ed. Feher 1989, Part III, 471–554; McGuire 1990; and Csordas 1990.

subject, but found that I could not fix bodies as objects of thought . . . Inevitably, I began to consider that perhaps this resistance was essential to the matter in hand.' Or, as put from a rather different methodological perspective, by Mary Douglas (1966, 122, my emphasis): 'Just as it is true that everything symbolizes the body, so it is equally true that the body symbolizes *everything else*.' But why, then, are 'bodies' simultaneously so ubiquitous and yet so hard to get our 'hands' around?

The cumulative answer to this question emerges from the analyses of Part I, but can be stated summarily here. A naive approach to ethnography or 'comparative' religion might still imagine that bodies provide us with an Archimedean point, a 'natural' datum of uncontentious physicality upon which religious traditions have then spun their various interpretations.[4] Structuralists still harbour this language of the 'natural';[5] and it has a surprisingly persistent mythological power even in the thought of those who have ostensibly forsworn it.[6] But the question that presses in a post-modern age is this: if we can no longer count on a universal 'grand narrative' to undergird the enterprises of religious and cultural studies, then does not the 'body', too, become subject to infinitely variable social constructions? Indeed the 'body' comes to bear huge, and paradoxical, philosophical weight in post-modern thought: just as its Enlightenment partner, the 'mind/soul' of Cartesianism, is seen off with almost unexamined vehemence,[7] so, simultaneously, what is left (the 'body') becomes infinitely problematized and elusive.[8] It is all that we *have*, but we seemingly cannot grasp it; nor are we sure we can control the political forces that regiment it.[9] Devoid now of religious

[4] This issue is discussed in more detail by Talal Asad, below. To adopt a (finally) relativistic line on this issue is not of course to suggest anything approaching incommensurability on matters 'bodily' between cultures and religions, especially when different religions (as in India) share many cultural assumptions in common. Further, work such as Ekman's (1982) on transcultural facial expressions suggests strong points of similarity across cultures in the expression of basic emotions, even allowing for significant 'constructed' differences.

[5] See the opening of Wendy Doniger's essay, below; and Douglas' *Natural Symbols* (Douglas 1970), whose central thesis however undercuts the possibility of a pristine 'natural' state *prior* to symbolization.

[6] See Keat 1986, for instance, for fascinating evidence that Foucault himself still worked with the idea of a 'natural' (unrepressed) body.

[7] See Simpson 1993 and McGuire 1990 for two recent disavowals of the effects of Cartesianism on their respective social sciences (sociology and anthropology). In Coakley 1992 I have tried to ask more probing questions, however, about the ultimate roots of this disaffection with Descartes, and what social and political programme it in turn bespeaks.

[8] On this point see Bryan Turner's chapter below, and also his adjunct piece in eds. Featherstone, Hepworth, and Turner 1991, 1–35.

[9] This is of course a central paradox in Foucault's work: are our 'bodies' deterministically controlled by state intervention, or is there sufficient (individual) agency in us to repel such intervention? On this paradox, and especially its implications for feminist use of Foucault, see McNay 1992.

meaning or of the capacity for any fluidity into the divine, shorn of any expectation of new life beyond the grave, it has shrunk to the limits of individual fleshliness; hence our only hope seems to reside in keeping it alive, youthful, consuming, sexually active, and jogging on (literally), for as long as possible.[10]

As the chapters in Part I of this volume show, then, there is no one regnant definition of 'body' now available to us. Yet each is, in its way, already laden with ideological freight. In testing what is at stake in any such discussion, therefore, it is always worth asking: what is it (on this particular view) that the 'body' is *not*? What is the lurking x-factor 'beyond'? Even if Cartesian *mind*/body dualism is supposedly decried, other disjunctions and contrasts may replicate it. In materialist philosophy of mind, for instance, the 'body' may be everything else except the brain;[11] in feminist analyses of pornography and cultural manipulation it represents the female that males seek to control;[12] in both Freudian and Foucaultian accounts of sexuality it becomes the site of either forbidden or condoned pleasures, rather than the more-or-less unconscious medium of all human existence;[13] and in popular magazine discussions of slimming and fitness it still stands for the rebellious fleshliness that has to be controlled and subdued from some other place of surveillance.[14] Despite the legion cries for *greater* 'embodiedness', for a notion of self *as* body,[15] the spectres of religious and philosophical 'dualism' die hard.

WHY IS THE 'BODY' SO MUCH ON OUR 'MIND'?

It is for this reason that the pre-Enlightenment religious background to our current *aporias* on the 'body' is so significant a point of reflection. The task of Part II is to provide some guidance in the complex task of charting

[10] For a recent fascinating analysis of the 'consuming' body, see Falk 1994. For the cult of fitness, see especially Glassner 1989, and the discussion by Bryan Turner, below.
[11] See, for example, Daniel Dennett's celebrated thought-experiment about a 'brain in a vat' with its (disconnected) 'body' dead underground, in Dennett 1981, 310–23; and compare Mary Midgley's discussion of philosophy and the 'body', below.
[12] See, for example, Bordo 1993; eds. Jaggar and Bordo 1989; and Dworkin 1989.
[13] The remarks by Starobinski (1982, 38), also quoted in n. 12 of Talal Asad's chapter below, are apposite here: he speaks of the 'considerable narcissistic component of contemporary Western culture' which causes an 'infatuation' with the 'body' (in this self-conscious, sexualized, sense) wholly different from the self's naive (and unselfconscious) 'bodiliness'.
[14] This point is made with particular power by Susan Bordo (1993), who shows how women ironically internalize a ('male') hatred of their own ('female') flesh in slimming and its pathological outcome, anorexia.
[15] See, *inter alia*, Csordas 1990 (the 1988 Stirling Award Essay) for a discussion of the need for a more 'embodied' vision of the self in anthropology, an account that draws on the philosophy of Merleau-Ponty and the anthropology of Bourdieu.

traditional 'Western'[16] attitudes to bodily devotion, and thereby to lay the dust on a number of potent mythologies about this heritage, mythologies that continue to lurk influentially even when questioned and corrected by careful scholarship.[17] Current sociological and feminist accounts of the 'body', especially, tend to proceed with a jaundiced (but undifferentiated) vision of the 'Christianity' that their theorizing has replaced: its alliance with 'bourgeois capitalism' in a 'religious (if hypocritical) condemnation of sexual pleasures' (Turner in eds. Featherstone, Hepworth, and Turner 1991, 19), its perception of the sexual body as 'gross' and 'instinctual',[18] or, more generally, its 'blanket of oppression and violence against bodiliness'.[19] But it is far from clear that any of these generalizations (true as any truisms may be) can stand the test of a *nuanced* reading of the complex different strands of thought about 'bodiliness' and its meanings in Jewish and Christian traditions of the pre-Enlightenment era.

It is no coincidence, of course, that contemporary social historians of our 'body'-obsessed culture have turned back, with such evident passion, to watershed periods of change in Western culture (the twelfth to thirteenth and eighteenth centuries, in particular) when profound political upheavals found their correlate, as today, in fascinating shifts in body metaphors and symbolizations.[20] But the best of these studies do

[16] I use inverted commas here because of the obvious contestability of the term 'Western' when used, in this volume, to include Eastern Orthodox views of the 'body', but to exclude, for example, Islam. The decision to draw these (ultimately artificial) lines arose from the desire to provide as complete a comparative account as possible of traditional Christian views of the 'body', and to throw them into contrast with the vision of its 'Christian' past spawned by current social science literature. It was this that also led to allocating three chapters to the Christian tradition, and only one to others – a decision taken in full consciousness of the (relative) imbalance of space given to Christianity here, for the reasons already given.

[17] A number of such 'truistic' generalizations were widely vocalized at the original 'Body' conference in 1987, but I trust will have finally been laid to rest by this and other volumes (most notably Brown 1988, in regard to early Christianity). I include in this category: (i) the view that Judaism (*tout court*) is 'positive' about the 'body' whilst Christianity is 'negative'; (ii) the correlative view that Christianity was also thus 'positive' in its early manifestation, until 'Greek' 'dualism' infected it; (iii) the view that strict sexual mores or ascetical practices are necessarily 'negative' towards the 'body'; and (iv) the even more fatuously generalized perception that 'Eastern' religions are more 'positive' about the 'body' than 'Christianity'. It will be clear from these remarks, and from the book as a whole, that I regard the epithets 'positive' and 'negative', when applied to views of the 'body', as wholly question-begging unless carefully contextualized.

[18] From Bordo (1993, 4), writing as a secularized Jew of 'Christian thought' on the 'body'.

[19] A quotation from the feminist theologian and ethicist Grace Jantzen (1988, 31), discussing the 'dualism' of the 'religion of the west' (ibid., 30).

[20] For the twelfth and thirteenth centuries, see most recently Bynum 1995, but also the debates spawned by the earlier discussion of the (so-called) twelfth-century 'invention of the individual' (see especially Morris 1972). For the eighteenth and nineteenth centuries, see the work of Laqueur (Laqueur 1990, and eds. Gallagher and Laqueur 1987), which charts the *novelties* of the perception of male and female 'bodies' and sexuality achieved at the Enlightenment and in its aftermath. The comparative lack of application of similar ('body'-related) methods and questions to the

not merely import our own current obsessions about sexual pleasure, gender, and social constructionism; rather they painstakingly unpick the nexus of 'body' associations that we may all too easily have repressed, in our desire to see off both 'dualism' and death.[21]

If Part II succeeds in its goals, then, it will throw into a new light the cultural specificity, and still lurking religiosity, of our present 'bodily' interests (as outlined in Part I). For these interests arise from particular post-*Christian* and post-*Enlightenment* twists in 'body'-history: the loss of belief in a 'true body' (*verum corpus*) as both transcendent and socially binding;[22] the simultaneous demise of belief in an eschatological 'body' – the perfected 'body' of the life beyond;[23] the destablizing of a unified, forensic notion of responsible 'selfhood' in twentieth-century Western thought;[24] the anxieties caused by medical power and intervention in contemporary society, as well as by the limitations of that power (symbolized potently by the AIDS epidemic);[25] the riddles of personal identity that arise from the capacity to swap body-parts;[26] the manifold challenges of secular feminist theory and feminist theology: the questioning of an identification of woman with the (despised and subordinated) 'body', or of the hegemony of 'masculinist' reason over the 'body';[27] the assertion of women's medical rights over their own 'bodies', and the exposure of the falsifying pressures of consumerism on women's self-image;[28] the rediscovery and exploration of (female) 'thinking through the body';[29] the canvassing of 'gay rights' and the

Reformation and its political upheavals is somewhat puzzling (though see, for example, Roper 1989, for transformations in women's status and opportunities in the Reformation in Augsburg; and David Tripp's programmatic discussion, below).

[21] On this point, see especially Bynum's survey essay, Bynum 1991.

[22] On this, see Andrew Louth's discussion of medieval Western eucharistic theology, below (and also plate 3, for a pictorial illustration of the 'true body' in this sense).

[23] Bynum's analysis (Bynum 1995) of the intense interest in the reassemblage of bodily parts at the resurrection evidenced in early scholasticism, makes a fascinating contrast with today's discussion of personal identity and the medical transplantation of bodily parts (in which thoughts of eschatology play no part).

[24] See Douglas' essay 'Thought Style Exemplified: the Idea of the Self', in Douglas 1992, 211–34, in which Douglas explores the erosion of a Lockean 'forensic' notion of the self as responsible agent under the impact of modern psychoanalytic categories of the 'unconscious'.

[25] See both Bryan Turner's and Talal Asad's discussion of these themes, below. For reflection on cultural 'exclusion' techniques which have bearing on the fear occasioned by AIDS in our present society, see Douglas 1991.

[26] On this issue see especially the much-debated Parfit 1984.

[27] See, *inter alia*, ed. Suleiman 1986 and Bordo 1993 (for women's 'bodily' self-images); and Lloyd 1984 (for an analysis of the 'Man of Reason' in Western philosophy).

[28] See, for example, Martin 1987; eds. Jacobus *et al.* 1990; and (again) Bordo 1993.

[29] See Gallop 1988; and (somewhat differently, from the perspective of French feminist response to Freud and Lacan) Irigaray 1985a and 1985b.

arguments of 'queer theory';[30] and last, but far from least, the grave anxieties caused by the redrawing of the 'body'-map of the political world: the uncertainties about what is now 'Left' and what 'Right', what friend and what foe.

It is no wonder that these 'body' matters so exercise us; for the quest seemingly encoded in them is for a unifying, and *socially cohesive*,[31] point of reference that will give mortal flesh final significance. It is no wonder that 'body' studies can be published only as *Fragments*,[32] since there is no longer a eucharistic presence to 'gather them on the mountains'. And yet, whilst the Western resources for religious orientation have been largely abandoned, ironic, secularized ghosts from that past continue to haunt us. What have elsewhere been called the 'cultural contradictions' of contemporary life (Bell 1976) are no less evident in matters of the 'body': the 'body' is sexually affirmed, but puritanically punished in matters of diet or exercise; continuously stuffed with consumerist goods, but guiltily denied particular foods in aid of the 'salvation' of a longer life; taught that there is nothing *but* it (the 'body'), and yet asked to discipline itself from some other site of control; flaunted everywhere, yet continuously disappearing on the cybernet.[33]

Do we see here the perverse replication of a (desacramentalized) Christian asceticism, or is it the last smile on the face of a *Cartesian* Cheshire cat?[34]

---

[30] See especially Butler 1990 and 1993.

[31] See Mary Douglas' observation (repeated often elsewhere) that 'doctrines which use the human body as their metaphor . . . are likely to be specially concerned with social relationships' (Douglas 1970b, 71; cited in Gager 1982, 347).

[32] See ed. Feher 1989, for contemporary 'fragments'; the allusion to eucharistic fragments gathered together by Christ at the (eschatological) banquet ·is from the early Christian document, the *Didache*, section 9.

[33] Bryan Turner discusses some of these 'contradictions' on the 'body', below. On the last point (the 'disappearance' of the 'body' in the computerized world), see Taylor and Saarinen 1994: in the section 'Body Snatching', 8+9, the question is put, 'Where do I meet my body in the net?', and the comment made: 'Why has the body become the preoccupation of so many in our culture? . . . In virtual worlds, the body disappears or is displaced by a so-called artificial prosthesis. As the materiality of experience vanishes, the need to reaffirm it grows intense.'
    I am grateful to my (1993) teaching assistant Kimerer LaMothe for an illuminating discussion that helped me clarify the nature of some of these 'bodily' contradictions.

[34] The philosopher of mind John Searle has recently suggested (in eds. Warner and Szubka 1994, 279) that mainstream contemporary philosophers of mind have been lured to the 'physicalist' extreme by a profound resistance to the *religious* implications of the alternatives. And yet they are also 'deeply committed' to the 'traditional vocabulary and categories' ('dualism', 'materialism', 'physicalism', etc.), which Cartesianism spawned: 'They use these words with neither embarrassment or irony.' In another context (that of feminist analysis of consumerist visions of the 'body'), Susan Bordo (1993b, 266) comments on how our bodies are now meant to be infinitely malleable or 'plastic' to our desires (through surgery, dieting, and other forms of intervention): 'In place of God the watchmaker, we now have ourselves, the master sculptors of that plastic . . . [which

RELIGIONS AND THE BODY

It will be clear by now that this editorial introduction is not free of value-laden, indeed religious, assumptions; but then nor is any attitude to 'bodiliness', as it has been my task so far to underscore. The contributors to Parts II and III of this volume, however, were not invited to toe any particular ideological or theological line. Rather they were asked to choose some limited number of (especially characteristic) 'bodily' *practices* or attendant mythologies from the tradition they represented; and then to face the question explicitly: can we assume that we know what the 'body' (so-called) means in this different cultural and religious context? To throw light on the complexity and cultural embeddedness of this question, the essayists were asked to make reference to adjunct matters of 'bodily' interest, to throw light on the *total* significance of the religious practices in question: attitudes to food, authority, sexual relations, nakedness, pleasure and pain, medicine and healing, and the use of 'body' metaphors at *micro-* and *macro-*levels in the religious society. The question being pressed here was: *how*, exactly, do corporeal 'practices' mediate social meanings and even transform them (or *vice versa*)? – a matter not always sufficiently attended to, perhaps, in the heady rush to utilize Bourdieu's vogue categories of 'practice' and 'habitus'.[35]

Inevitably some essayists chose to range wider in the choice of their material than others (the editorial whip has its limits!); and the restriction of the focus of this book to literate religions was a decision made with some regret. But the (first) cumulative effect of this collection should at least be to give *pause* to the idea that 'bodily' practices from other religious and ritual contexts can be taken over merely for the purposes of undemanding relaxation and restoration. Particular body practices imply (no less particular) metaphysical and cultural commitments, and may indeed finally induce them. As Thomas P. Kasulis has remarked (Yuasa 1987, 7, my emphasis), 'Religious beliefs are embodied *through* religious practices. In fact the practices may be said to precede the beliefs'. In other words, devotional 'practice' is no optional frill attendant on metaphysical theories acquired somewhere else; rather it is the very

---

bespeaks [a] disdain for material limits, and [an] intoxication with freedom, change and self-determination.'

[35] See Bourdieu 1977. Kleinman and Kleinman (1994, 708) comment: 'Pierre Bourdieu . . . repeatedly invokes a dialectic between habitus and social structures as the source of social incorporations into the body almost as an article of faith. That resonant model of a connection between the corporeal and the social, which has gained the support of many anthropologists, is left largely unanalysed by Bourdieu and other theorists, however – the equivalent in social theory of psychosomatic medicine's "mystical leap" between mind and body.'

medium of such belief, ultimately transcending the thought/action divide.[36] Or to put it conversely, in Talal Asad's acute observation, the inability 'to enter into communion with God' may well be 'a function of untaught bodies'.[37] One of the notable features of 'taught' religious bodies, indeed, is the relative lack of interest shown by them in self-conscious theorizing about the *nature* of the 'body'; immersion in ritual or meditative practice, it seems, allows these anxious questionings in large part to fall away. The individual 'body' has found its place in a divine drama, and can cease from its anxious self-examination.

The essays by religionists gathered in this volume form a *praeparatio* for the infinitely complex task of 'comparative' study between (and within) traditions on the 'body'. But this can only proceed piecemeal, and with the sort of careful attention to context to which this book as a whole has aspired. To move from careful exegetical and phenomenological accounts (the stuff of this book) to detailed comparisons across religious boundaries, however, is a demanding matter in which crass generalizations have little legitimate place, and for which separate monographs are required.[38] The discerning reader of this volume, none the less, will note recurring themes of connection (all of them somewhat alien to the contemporary secularized mind), as the essays unfold: the intense ambiguity of the individual body as locus both of potential sanctification and of defilement, and the careful regulation of points of entry and exit; the transformative and fluid capacities of human bodies to pass into the divine (sometimes at various levels), and of divine bodies to appear in the flesh; the reverence accorded to physical objects representing divine bodies; the stories of divine actors as *foci* for the playing out of the ambiguities of the body; the denial and chastening of naive bodily satisfactions for the sake of a transformed and transindividual state; and the correlation of bodily meditations with societal and cosmic effects.[39]

[36] This point is made forcefully (in relation to ritual theory) in Bell 1992. Similar lines of argument are found in Csordas 1990 and McGuire 1990.

[37] See Talal Asad's essay below, and also his illuminating (and related) discussion of medieval attitudes to pain and asceticism in Asad 1993, chs. 3 and 4.

[38] Some of this work has been helpfully started in Yuasa 1987 and ed. Kasulis 1993.

[39] Some of these productive points of comparison are also suggested in the long review article Sullivan 1990. Sullivan ends that article with the rhetorical question (ibid., 99): 'Since the body is so often demonstrated to be a primary instrument of knowledge, and since the understanding of the body can vary markedly from one culture and epoch to another, we may have to add to our customary list of hermeneutical reflections yet another question: What kind of challenge is our own bodily existence to the study of religion?' This current volume should not only raise that question, but also – and perhaps more pressingly – its obverse: What kind of challenge is the study of religion (and the 'body') to our own bodily existence?

I am grateful to Lawrence Sullivan for a useful discussion of these matters.

None of these (superficially stated) points of connection between traditions, however, can be sustained without attention to the form of culture that attends them. As Mary Douglas' work has so insistently reminded us, it is a society of a particular sort that guards its personal apertures with care, and likewise a society of a particular sort that provides a strong community sense of self, transcending the individual.[40] The nostalgic longing for such reassuring boundedness and security in matters 'bodily' is perhaps what (unconsciously) drives our own culture's obsession with the matter; but to choose such 'hierarchical' options would now be 'counter-cultural',[41] making (literally) all the difference in the 'world'.

If this volume serves to highlight such points of connection and contrast, even in a preliminary way, it will have performed its function, and paved the way for a more richly informed interdisciplinary discussion of the many 'bodies', secular and religious, that press upon us.

BIBLIOGRAPHY

Asad, T. (1993), *Genealogies of Religion*, Baltimore and London: Johns Hopkins University Press.
Becker, E. (1973), *The Denial of Death*, New York: Free Press.
Bell, C. (1992), *Ritual Theory, Ritual Practice*, New York: Oxford University Press.
Bell, D. (1976), *The Cultural Contradictions of Capitalism*, London: Heinemann Educational.
Bordo, S. (1993a), *Unbearable Weight: Feminism, Western Culture, and the Body*, Berkeley: University of California Press.
  (1993b), '"Material Girl": The Effacements of Postmodern Culture', in ed. C. Swichtenberg, *The Madonna Connection*, Boulder, CO: Westview Press, 265–90.
Bourdieu, P. (1977), *Outline of a Theory of Practice*, Cambridge University Press.
Brown, P. (1988), *The Body and Society: Men, Women and Sexual Renunciation in Early Christianity*, New York: Columbia University Press.
Butler, J. (1990), *Gender Trouble*, New York: Routledge.
  (1993), *Bodies that Matter: On the Discursive Limits of 'Sex'*, New York: Routledge.
Bynum, C. W. (1991), 'Bodily Miracles in the High Middle Ages', in ed. T. Kselman, *Belief in History: Innovative Approaches to European and American Religion*, Notre Dame, IN and London: University of Notre Dame Press, 68–106.

---

[40] See again Douglas 1966 and 1970a; and, for 'cosmic effects' and the body in more detail, see Douglas 1990.
[41] For this use of the category 'hierarchy', and its lack of attraction in an individualistic 'enterprise culture', see Douglas 1992. In this volume Douglas suggests a new fourfold typology of visions of self-and-culture: 'hierarchy', 'enclave', 'enterprise/individualism', and 'isolate'.

(1995), *The Resurrection of the Body in Western Christianity, 1200–1336*, New York: Columbia University Press.

Clifford, J .and Marcus, G. E. (eds.) (1986), *Writing Culture: The Poetics and Politics of Ethnography*, Berkeley: University of California Press.

Coakley, S. (1992), 'Visions of the Self in Late Medieval Christianity', in ed. M. McGhee, *Philosophy, Religion and the Spiritual Life: Royal Institute of Philosophy Supplement*, Cambridge University Press, 89–103.

Csordas, T. J. (1990), 'Embodiment as a Paradigm for Anthropology', *Ethos* 18, 5–47.

Dennett, D. (1981), *Brainstorms: Philosophical Essays on Mind and Psychology*, Cambridge, MA: MIT Press.

Douglas, M. (1966), *Purity and Danger: An Analysis of Concepts of Pollution and Taboo*, London: Routledge and Kegan Paul.

(1970a), *Natural Symbols: Explorations in Cosmology*, London: Barrie and Jenkins.

(1970b), 'Social Preconditions of Enthusiasm and Heterodoxy', in ed. R. F. Spencer, *Forms of Symbolic Action: Proceedings of the 1969 Annual Meeting of the American Ethnological Society*, Seattle and London: American Ethnological Society, 69–80.

(1990), 'The Body of the World', *International Social Science Journal*, 125, 395–9.

(1991), 'Witchcraft and Leprosy: Two Strategies of Exclusion', *Man* 26, 723–36.

(1992), *Risk and Blame: Essays in Cultural Theory*, London and New York: Routledge.

Dworkin, A. (1989), *Pornography*, New York: Dutton.

Ekman, P. (1982), *Emotions in the Human Face*, Cambridge University Press.

Falk, P. (1994), *The Consuming Body*, London: Sage Publications.

Featherstone, M., Hepworth, M., and Turner, B. S. (eds.) (1991), *The Body: Social Process and Cultural Theory*, London: Sage Publications.

Feher, M., with Naddaff, R., and Tazi, N. (1989), *Fragments for a History of the Human Body, Zone 3* (Part I), *Zone 4* (Part II), and *Zone 5* (Part III), New York: Urzone Inc.

Gager, J. G. (1982), 'Body-Symbols and Social Reality: Resurrection, Incarnation and Asceticism in Early Christianity', *Religion* 12, 345–63.

Gallagher, C., and Laqueur, T. (eds.) (1987), *The Making of the Modern Body: Sexuality and Society in the Nineteenth Century*, Berkeley: University of California Press.

Gallop, J. (1988), *Thinking Through the Body*, New York: Columbia University Press.

Glassner, B. (1989), 'Fitness and the Postmodern Self', *Journal of Health and Social Behavior* 30, 180–91.

Irigaray, L. (1985a), *Speculum of the Other Woman*, Ithaca, NY: Cornell University Press.

(1985b), *This Sex Which is Not One*, Ithaca, NY: Cornell University Press.

Jacobus, M., Fox Keller, E., and Shuttleworth, S. (eds.) (1990), *Body/Politics: Women and the Discourses of Science*, New York: Routledge.

Jaggar, A., and Bordo, S. (eds.) (1989), *Gender/Body/Knowledge: Feminist Reconstructions of Being and Knowing*, New Brunswick: Rutgers University Press.

Jantzen, G. (1988), 'Ethics and Energy', *Studies in Christian Ethics* 1, 17–31.

Kasulis, T. P. (ed.), with Ames, R. T., and Dissanayake, W. (1993), *Self as Body in Asian Theory and Practice*, Albany, NY: SUNY Press.

Keat, R. (1986), 'The Human Body in Social Theory: Reich, Foucault and the Repressive Hypothesis', *Radical Philosophy* 42, 24–32.

Kleinman, A., and Kleinman, J. (1994), 'How Bodies Remember: Social Memory and Bodily Experience of Criticism, Resistance, and Delegitimation Following China's Cultural Revolution', *New Literary History* 25, 707–23.

Laqueur, T. (1990), *Making Sex: Body and Gender from the Greeks to Freud*, Cambridge, MA: Harvard University Press.

Lloyd, G. (1984), *The Man of Reason: 'Male' and 'Female' in Western Philosophy*, Minneapolis, MN: University of Minnesota Press.

McGuire, M. (1990), 'Religion and the Body: Rematerializing the Human Body in the Social Sciences of Religion', *Journal of the Scientific Study of Religion* 29, 283–96.

McNay, L. (1992), *Foucault and Feminism*, Cambridge: Polity Press.

Martin, E. (1987), *The Woman in the Body*, Boston: Beacon Press.

Morris, C. (1972), *The Discovery of the Individual, 1050–1200*, London: SPCK.

Parfit, D. (1984), *Reasons and Persons*, Oxford: Clarendon Press.

Roper, L. (1989), *The Holy Household: Women and Morals in Reformation Augsburg*, Oxford University Press.

Said, E. W. (1978), *Orientalism*, New York: Pantheon.

Simpson, J. H. (1993), 'Religion and the Body: Sociological Themes and Prospects', in ed. W. H. Swatos, Jr., *A Future for Religion? New Paradigms for Social Analysis*, London: Sage Publications, 149–64.

Starobinski, J. (1982), 'A Short History of Body Consciousness', *Humanities in Review* 1, 22–40.

Suleiman, S. (ed.) (1986), *The Female Body in Western Culture*, Cambridge, MA: Harvard University Press.

Sullivan, L. E. (1990), 'Body Works: Knowledge of the Body in the Study of Religion', *History of Religions* 30, 86–99.

Taylor, M. C., and Saarinen, E. (1994), *Imagologies: Media Philosophy*, London: Routledge.

Warner, R., and Szubka, T. (eds.) (1994), *The Mind–Body Problem: A Guide to Current Debate*, Oxford: Basil Blackwell.

Yuasa, Y. (1987), *The Body: Toward an Eastern Mind–Body Theory*, ed. T. P. Kasulis, Albany: SUNY Press.

PART I:

Contemporary Western perspectives: secularism and the body

The body in Western society: social theory and its perspectives

Bryan S. Turner

INTRODUCTION: EMBODIMENT

In recent years the human body has emerged as a central focus of research and theory in sociology and anthropology. No doubt this growing academic interest reflects broader social changes in which the body has become increasingly the target of consumerism, political surveillance, and scientific research. Within sociology and history, this heightened interest is also a reflection of the influence of the social philosophy of Michel Foucault (Lemert and Gillan 1982; Smart 1985), of growing interest in French social theory generally (Boyne 1986), and of the decline of various streams of structuralist philosophy, including structuralist Marxism (Kurzweil 1986). For example, for Foucault, the centrality of the body to modern systems of discipline and control was seen to be an effect of the growing sophistication of social regulation, which has been brought about by the social combination of knowledge and power in the medical institutions of Western societies (Foucault 1973), and more generally by the dispersal of techniques of discipline through the factory and the school (Foucault 1977). Foucault's extensive influence in contemporary social theory, history writing, discourse analysis, and feminist theory has produced a large literature on surveillance and regulation of populations and bodies, alongside a sociology of the body, sexuality, and populations (O'Neill 1985; Turner 1992). Of course, there is also a highly developed anthropological literature on the human body, especially on the symbolic and classificatory role of the body.

Within a broader theoretical perspective there are basically four views of the body in modern social theory. First, following Foucault, the body is an effect of deeper structural arrangements of power and knowledge. Secondly, the body is a symbolic system which produces a set of metaphors by which power is conceptualized. Thirdly, the body can only be understood as a consequence of long-term historical changes in human society. In short the body has a history. These three approaches have one thing in common: they challenge any assumption about the ontological coherence of the body as a universal historical phenomenon. The fourth approach derives partly from the philosophical anthropology of Maurice Merleau-Ponty; this approach is concerned to analyse the body in the context of the lived experience of everyday life. It is with this question mark over the ontological coherence of our being-in-body that I wish to start this chapter by an examination of phenomenology.

While Foucault's work was in many respects highly innovative and radical in its implications for both natural and social science, it is possible to identify a variety of earlier perspectives on human embodiment which have also contributed to the development of a new intellectual scene. Merleau-Ponty's *Phenomenology of Perception* was particularly important in developing a new framework for the understanding of the phenomenology of embodiment which provided a radical and profound critique of the division between mind and body which was the legacy of Descartes' positivism (Merleau-Ponty 1962). For Merleau-Ponty, the relationship between the person and the body is never like the relationship between a person and the environment, and we cannot think of our fingers, for example, as human versions of technical instruments such as scissors and knives. Our relationship to our body is always an internal and direct one, and therefore in Merleau-Ponty's philosophy the body was crucial to the understanding of perception, existence, and sociality (Mallin 1979). Merleau-Ponty's work was significantly influenced by the phenomenology of Husserl and by Heidegger's transformation of the debate surrounding Being. The study of the body in French theory was also importantly influenced by the existentialist philosophy of writers like J. P. Sartre (Sartre 1957). The roots of these developments in French social theory have to be sought (via Martin Heidegger's *Time and Being*) in the nineteenth-century rejection of Hegelian systematic philosophy, the romantic critique of industrialism, and in the development of German 'life-philosophy' (Stauth and Turner 1988). In German social theory, it is possible to identify a left-wing critique of the regulation of the body and sexuality in the interests of ascetic capitalist production in the work of Herbert Marcuse (1955), and a neglected critique from the romantic, aesthetic philosophy of Ludwig Klages and the circle of writers around Stefan George (Huch 1973).

These developments in philosophical phenomenology have far-reaching implications for sociology, anthropology, and social theory.

One immediate consequence is that we need a radical revision of scientific approaches to sickness (Turner 1987). For instance, these phenomenological perspectives have been brilliantly illustrated by the medical studies of O. W. Sacks in his highly perceptive inquiries into migraine (1970) and Parkinson's Disease (1976). The implication of these inquiries is that disease is never simply an external attack on our biochemical organism, but rather a subjectively profound and symbolically significant variation in our embodiment.

While sociologists have drawn considerable inspiration from the work of Foucault and Merleau-Ponty, in anthropology similar developments have taken place in the analysis of human embodiment and body symbolism under the influence of writers like Mary Douglas, whose *Purity and Danger* (Douglas 1970) brought about a conceptual revolution in the anthropological perspective on body pollution and rituals of purification. Unlike the phenomenology of the French tradition, however, Douglas has been less interested in the idea of the 'lived body' than in the body as a code or metaphor of socio-cognitive mappings of reality – an issue which she further explored in *Natural Symbols* (1973). Of great importance also was the work of Marcel Mauss who through the notion of 'body techniques' drew attention to the cultural shaping of the body and the use of the body in social action (Mauss 1979). Mauss argued persuasively that walking, sitting, and other everyday activities were not the natural or direct outcome of the body as an organism within nature, but that even our most basic bodily activities should be regarded as techniques which are learnt and culturally shaped. In short, they are an ensemble of practices rather than a fixed, 'natural' legacy.

What are the implications of these various lines of inquiry within the social sciences, history and philosophy into our understanding of the body? The first and rather obvious implication is that we cannot take 'the body' for granted as a natural, fixed and historically universal datum of human societies. The body has many meanings within human practice, and can be conceptualized within a variety of dimensions and frameworks. For example, we are by now familiar with the various metaphors of the body as symbol for or statement about social and political relations. In Christian iconography, the church was often depicted in the Middle Ages as a lactating mother (as in Giovanni Pisano's *Ecclesia lactans* from the early fourteenth century). Within human cultural history, the body has been frequently used as a metaphor of both social stability and social instability. There appears to be an intimate connection between the exterior order of the socio-political world and the equilibrium of the human body, so that instabilities within the body are thought to reflect instabilities within the wider social system. For example, Robert Burton in *The Anatomy of Melancholy* (first published in 1621) regarded the instabilities of the body in the development of melancholy as merely a reflection of the general disease of human society which had fallen from grace (Fox 1976). The disordered body exhibited a disjointed discourse of social decay, and it was the role of the doctor to provide an interpretation of the 'scandal of disease' (Baross 1981). In a similar fashion, the body of the king has often been regarded as the symbol or metaphor of sovereignty, so that an attack upon the king's body was equivalent to a violent assault on the society as a whole. The symbolism and rituals which surrounded the scaffold in human history have reflected the notion that the monarch had two bodies, a mortal and finite body, but also a sovereign, abstract, and immortal body which was the symbol or vehicle for political authority (Kantorowicz 1957). There is therefore a close relationship between medical theories of illness and disease and political theories of the government of society, since disease within the human body has been frequently associated with political and social disorder. In this respect medical theories are simultaneously political theories (Turner 1982). We frequently express the character of illness as a struggle by military metaphors, suggesting that the body has been invaded by alien forces (Sontag 1978). In summary, illness is always a metaphor of other more general and profound social processes.

We can further understand the complexity of the body in human culture by considering the language by which we describe the presence and nature of the body in human interaction. The argument here is that the body and the possession of bodies can be seen as a convention of language. Behind this argument there is also the modern revolution in structural linguistics in which it is argued that 'reality' is always the effect of discursive conventions. Reality is apprehended and produced by discursive practices, and in particular as a result of the authority of certain metaphorical devices. In feminist theory, often powerfully influenced by the psychoanalytic philosophy of Jacques Lacan, writers like Kristeva and Irigaray have studied the notion of the female body as absence or lack. This philosophical perspective points to the metaphoricity of the body. The history of medical science is a history of changing metaphors in which the body appears as a collection of pumps, canals, engines, machines, and so forth (Turner 1982). In everyday language, we often refer, for example, to the body as if it were an external, objective thing or environment. We speak about having bodies or about how people carry their bodies, or about being bodies, but following the phenomenological tradition it would be equally sensible to speak about the ways in which we *do* our bodies, since we are embodied.

Within the German philosophical tradition, there has been a traditional focus on the idea of a 'lived body'. To have a body involves body-work because the body needs constant attention, but this attention has primarily expressive and symbolic significance. We can speak about doing our bodies, but at a deeper level it also makes sense to talk about *being* a body. Our bodies (their presentation and representation) express the self because the loss of face (signified by blushes and other threatening outcomes) is a loss of self (Goffman 1969). Any loss of control over our bodies is socially embarrassing, implying a loss of control over ourselves. The mutilation of the body is the primary mutilation of the self. Hence ceremonies of humiliation centre on the degradation of the body by rituals of stripping, beating, and undressing (Garfinkel 1956).

A further implication of these sociological perspectives is that the body, rather than being a naturally given datum, is a socially constructed artefact rather like other cultural products. The body (its image, its bearing, and representation) is the effect of innumerable practices, behaviours, and discourses which construct and produce the body as a culturally recognizable feature of social relations. For example, according to Foucault (1980) we cannot take the gendered nature of the body for granted, since the sexually constructed character of the body is in part an outcome of political and governmental intervention. As a consequence of medical and administrative changes in the nineteenth century, Foucault argued that it is impossible for one body to have two sexes, since for administrative purposes hermaphroditism implies the separation of sexes within the body. Because the single-gendered-body is (from this point of view) an effect of state administration, political radicalism and artistic opposition to social regulation has often been associated with a fantasy world around the figure of the androgyne (Buci-Glucksmann 1984).

The consequence of this view is to challenge any foundationalist concept of the body as a feature of nature which is unproblematic (Berthelot 1986). Against such a view, it would appear to be commonsensically proper to argue that, while the body may be socially constructed, we cannot ignore the physiological, biological, and chemical grounding of the body in the world of nature. However, this commonsensical position is not so easy to maintain on closer inspection. For example, our bodies change significantly over time so that the body which I inhabited as a young person is no longer the same body which I will inhabit in old age. It is not mere science fiction to imagine a future society in which the state owned or managed enormous genetic banks by which 'bodies' are constantly replenished, repaired, and replaced. Such a system is likely to provide at least one solution to epidemics such as AIDS. This problem of ageing and body replacement raises many philosophical problems as to the identity of the person within the body, while also raising difficulties about what it means to have one body or the same body over time. Furthermore, with the development of modern medical technology, it is possible for an individual in one lifetime to acquire many new parts for the body either from other bodies or from manufactured, artificial substitutes. This again brings to the foreground some well-known philosophical problems about the person, the body, and consciousness in the definition of the self.

THE BODY AS FLESH

I have so far attempted to make the body problematic as a feature or aspect of cultural analysis within comparative sociology. In particular, I have attempted to challenge the taken-for-granted assumption that the body is a natural feature of reality which is essentially unidimensional and historically continuous. While I have relativized the body, I nevertheless want to suggest that there are some enduring cultural themes in the relationship between the body and religion. At least in the West (during the classical and Christian eras) the body has been seen to be a threatening and dangerous phenomenon, if not adequately controlled and regulated by cultural processes. The body has been regarded as the vehicle or vessel of unruly, ungovernable, and irrational passions, desires, and emotions. The necessity to control the body (its locations, its excretions, and its reproduction) is an enduring theme within Western philosophy, religion, and art. While commentators have frequently suggested that this fear of the body has its origins in Christian culture, the body was also regarded as a threat to public stability, the continuation of government, and the maintenance of a civilized public realm. There were a number of themes in Greek society which paralleled the later Christian contraction of sexuality:

A certain association of sexual activity and evil, the norm of procreative monogamy, the condemnation of relations with the same sex, the exultation of continence. (Foucault 1984a, 21).

These sexual norms in classical Greek culture were associated with the importance of self-mastery (*enkrateia*), which was seen to be an appropriate technology for all moral subjects. Within Greek life, moral virtue was associated with free men who regulated the public world to the exclusion of women, young boys, and slaves. Within this Greek tradition, the relationship between man and wife was not focussed on sexual activity but rather on relations of authority in terms of the regulation of domestic space. Because sexual pleasure threatened self-mastery, it had been regulated or at least excluded from the public world. These forms of separation and exclusion involved ascetic practices appropriate to a good citizen. Women, slaves, and boys were socially and ethically subordinate to free-men, because they were the objects rather than the subjects of sexual encounters. This was the basis of extensive discussions of homosexuality in classical Greece. While Foucault (1984b) identified an ethic of sexual austerity in the early Roman Empire, he also noted certain changes under the principate in which there was a stronger emphasis on the sexual pleasures of married life in which love played a part in cementing a social bond between men and women. There evolved a sexual code which had certain similarities to that of Christianity; this classical sexual ethic in Roman times was associated with a certain introspectiveness and privatization of life.

With the growing importance of Christianity as a dominant culture within the West, there was an intensification of the ascetic attitude towards the body, since, as a consequence of the Christian theology of evil, the body became more central to the characterization of man as a fallen creature. Perhaps the Christian ambivalence towards the body is nowhere better summarized than in the idea of 'flesh':

'Flesh' is full of paradox. The flesh stands at the threshold of death and life: consider the similarity between the act of love and the sacrifice. Both reveal the flesh. Sacrifice replaces the ordered life of the animal with a blind convulsion of its organs . . . Flesh is the extravagance within us set up against the law of decency. Flesh is the born enemy of people haunted by Christian taboos. (Bataille 1981, 92)

Although Christianity inherited from the Greek and Roman world the vision of reality as a system split between reason and desire, between the mind and body, between Apollo and Dionysus, the Christian monastic tradition in particular gave this view of the body a darker meaning, seeing the flesh as the metaphor of fallen man and the irrational rejection of God. This passionate body required the discipline of diet, meditation, and constraint. The Western religious tradition 'had long told women that physicality was particularly their problem' (Bynum 1991, 146). Man was to woman what spirit was to matter. Of course, the theological elaboration of Mary's spirituality complicated this picture, but basically the duty to master the flesh remained. It was the Christian's duty to master this threatening nature (this wilderness within order) to maintain the life of the soul and of the mind.

We can regard this attempt to regulate the body as a version or an aspect of a more general ethic of world mastery; furthermore, I shall treat ethical world mastery as the essential project of modernity, that is, the imposition of instrumental reason over nature and social relations. In their famous study of the Enlightenment, Adorno and Horkheimer (1979, 231) noted that Europe has two separate histories:

A well known, written history and an underground history. The latter consists in the fate of the human instincts and passions which are displaced and distorted by civilization.

They suggested that the development of Western society had brought about a profound denial of human emotionality in order to establish a regime of regulation and control. In particular, they saw this denial of the body as one consequence of Christian ascetic theology which regarded the flesh as a source of evil. But they also recognized that instrumental rationality, asceticism, and individualism had deep roots in classical civilization. Adorno and Horkheimer were reluctant to ac-knowledge any relationship between their critical theory and the romantic work of writers like Ludwig Klages and Friedrich Nietzsche who were associated with the German conservative tradition. However, the death-of-God problem in Nietzsche and Klages' notion of the 'cosmic eros' (Klages 1981) shaped German critical philosophy in many directions (Stauth and Turner 1988). There is also a close relationship between Max Weber's emphasis on rationalization as the core feature of modernization and the argument in the critical theory of the Frankfurt School that the modern project is the unfolding of instrumental rationality.

In Weber's sociology, there is the central thesis that rationalization as calculation owed a great deal to the theology and practice of the Protestant sects, which in turn laid the cultural foundations for the emergence of asceticism, control, and capitalist accumulation. Rational-ization involved the secularization of culture and the decline of magic, the intellectualization of life through the imposition of science, the calculation and regulation of bodies in the interests of greater efficiency, and finally the rise of a market society in which the calculation of the values of commodities is independent of traditional culture and religious institutions. We can treat the rationalization project as an ethic of world mastery involving the control of the flesh (sexuality and human passions), the subordination of the mind (by training and education), in order to exclude the threat of madness, the regulation and taming of nature in order to bring an exclusion of wilderness from social reality, and finally the taming and training of the outer world of alien societies through a project of colonization. The ethic of world mastery as a project of modernity involved the evolution of techniques of regulation (a government) of bodies through the use of dietary practices and other medical regimens. The ethic of world mastery also required a management of the mind, through the use of the Protestant confessional, the religious diary, and the spirituality of prayer and other religious exercises (Hepworth and Turner 1982). The conquest of nature within the ethic of world mastery produced the new empiricism and positivism of Baconian science which sought to control and conquer nature through experiment, and the discovery of natural laws in the interests of social expansion and the regulation of untrammelled nature. Finally, the colonial projects of the seventeenth century can be seen within the same framework as an expression of a new concern with mastery over nature and over other races. The early fascination with cannibalism in seventeenth-century anthropology was an important step in the Western construction of Otherness, outside the pale of civilization and reason. Otherness was encapsulated in the figure of Caliban in Shakespeare's *The Tempest*, a play which summarized the discourse of contrasting natures in the idealization of the admired Miranda.

The emergence of a modern ethic of control corresponds to the emergence of a philosophical project for rational understanding which links together the philosophical inquiries of Hobbes, Descartes, Locke, and Kant (Bernstein 1985). The expansion of European colonialism created, at least at the political level, the origins of global society within which philosophical universalism could flourish. It was on the basis of this colonial world that philosophers could, with a certain sense of security and confidence, speculate about the essential and fundamental questions of truth and rationality. Truth had become global and hence universal. Social systems which diverged from these central notions of truth and reason were explicable as mere deviations from rational human culture, deviations associated with lesser colonial people. These deviations gave rise eventually to anthropology and Orientalism which sought to explain alien belief systems (Turner 1978). Colonialism and rational philosophy stand in an ambiguous relationship, whereby philosophy as it were turns a blind eye to the exploitation which makes philosophy possible:

There were two races by nature: the greater and the lesser. The liberation of the European individual took place in the context of a general, cultural transformation which increased the gap among the 'free' people all the more on the internal plane as the physical compulsion from outside declined. The exploited body was defined as 'evil', and the spiritual occupations in which the higher people were free to indulge were asserted to be the greatest good. This process made possible the supreme cultural achievements of Europe, but the suspicion of the trickery which was apparent from the outset heightened the love/hate relationship with the body which permeated the thinking of the masses over the centuries, and found its authentic expression in the language of Luther. (Adorno and Horkheimer 1979, 232)

Against this world of order and stability, there were opposed various negative realms which had to be excluded from thought. The first was madness itself as the antipode of reason. In order for the project of reason to begin, Descartes had to remove the possibility of madness as a threat to rationality, recognizing only dreams and illusions as deviations from reason (Foucault 1971). While madmen were being excluded from society through the creation of new prisons and asylums, so also was madness excluded from the world of reasonableness. If madness haunted the world of rationality, the world of nature was threatened by monsters and pathologies. The anomaly was a confusion in nature threatening the order of things from outside. Within society the great disorder to the regular control of bodies and passions was the illegitimate union of men and women giving vent to their uncontrolled lusts. In the world of Baroque fantasy, illegitimacy, monsters, and madness were conjoined in such plays as *Titus Andronicus* and in the dark figures of *King Lear*.

These three problems of madness, illegitimacy, and anomaly came together in the figure of woman, who within the medico-moral legacy of Galen and Aristotle was typically regarded as an anomalous and monstrous creature, or a secondary creation. In the Western world, this medical code was often combined with Christian creation mythology to provide a powerful denigration of women. The problem of the woman in Christian theology had its origins in the Adamic myth in which Eve was the source of human evil and sorrow because of her original disobedience. The notion that women are morally dangerous was also a legacy from Judaism mediated through the Essene sects in which the Coming Kingdom required strict sexual regulation of its members. These early negative views of women were further developed in Pauline theology in which it was argued that, while reproduction and marriage were necessary evils, they should be divorced from physical pleasure and enjoyment, since the only justification for marriage was the reproduction of the human race (Ariès and Béjin 1986). Any sociological analysis of the body and spirituality must therefore address the question of women's bodies, the theology of sexuality, and the structural organization of the sexual division of labour within society. It is only by understanding the cultural presentation of women's bodies in social space that we can ultimately begin to understand the problem of sexuality and spirituality in human societies.

The relationship of Christianity to sexuality and, more specifically, Christian attitudes towards women are more diverse and complex than this generalization suggests. Caroline Bynum's research on the female mystical tradition in medieval religion has been very important for historians and sociologists. In her collection of essays on *Fragmentation and Redemption* (1991), Bynum shows that any interpretation of female spirituality must be set in the context of the enormous emphasis which medieval theologians and philosophers placed on the continuity of the body (the absence of fragmentation) for the continuity of the self (the redemption of the soul). Thus physical resurrection of the whole body was a basic assumption of mainstream medieval religious thought.

Women were condemned for their physical natures, but in the twelfth and thirteenth centuries female mystics were more apt to somatize their experiences of the divine. In the struggle against heresy (such as the dualism of the Cathars), the bodily miracles of women were used by the church as powerful counter-blasts to the doctrines of the unfaithful and the ungodly. Religious ecstacy among women was used as a method of legitimizing the role of women in society. Mariology was a powerful theological tool for such arguments. Christ had no human father and his body came from Mary. Out of these conditions, there had developed the view that both the church (*ecclesia*) and humanity (*humanitas*) were female.

PATRIARCHY, ECONOMICS, AND THE DEVELOPMENT OF MODERN SOCIETY

Women's sexuality has been regarded as problematic within a patriarchal society, because it is necessary to guarantee the legitimate reproduction of men in order to secure the economic basis of society. In short, to understand women's sexuality we need to understand the distribution of property within societies, regulated typically through the patriarchal structure of the household. Changes in the relation between women and the household reflect changes in the pattern of economic production, and it is these basic processes within the economy and the household which provide economic parameters for an analysis of human sexuality, and attitudes towards sexuality. However this argument is not an economically reductionist one, since it assumes a complicated interaction between economic, political, and cultural dimensions in the development of human societies.

By patriarchy I mean a system of political authority, based upon the household, in which dominant property-owning males control and regulate the lives of subordinate members of the household, regardless of their sex or age. Therefore, in a patriarchal system, young males are as much subject to patriarchal authority as women, and subordinate members of a household would include the brothers and other male relatives of dominant male householders. This primitive system of patriarchy became linked eventually to monarchical power, since there was an obvious parallel between the authority of husbands and that of the monarch over his people. In turn this husband/monarch system of power was related to divine fatherly rule on the part of a benevolent God. This theory of patriarchal authority was given articulate expression in the English case by Sir Robert Filmer in *Patriarcha, A Defence of the Natural Power of Kings Against the Unnatural Liberty of the People*, written around 1640 and published finally in 1680. Filmer's argument about the divine authority of husbands and monarchs was an argument against social-contract theories as represented by writers like Thomas Hobbes and Spinoza, and therefore the patriarchal conception was an anti-individualistic theory of political power (Schochet 1975). This defence of the divine powers of the king has to be seen in the context of seventeenth-century absolutism in which the king's body, especially in the French court, was increasingly wrapped in liturgical symbols, indicating its sacred qualities (Giesey 1987).

The existence of patriarchy predated the seventeenth century, being located in a system of private property around the principle of primogeniture as the basis of inheritance; it is however interesting to keep in mind the fact that patriarchal theory was in some respects an articulate critique of an emerging system of individualistic culture in relation to the development of capitalist markets in the seventeenth century in England and Holland. The original system of patriarchy arose in association with the problem of paternity, that is, the problem of securing a flow of property between generations within a single household or single economic unit in accordance with the principle of male inheritance and dominance. This control of wealth through kinship relations depended upon the regulation and control of wives and children. It was through this combination of patriarchy, private property, and paternity through legitimate male heirs, that in pre-modern societies women were characteristically seen as a potential or real threat to the social solidarity of primary kinship groups. In such a society there could be no absolute or clear guarantee that the children born to women actually belonged biologically to the group. Given the widespread presence of an incest taboo, men could not take wives from within the circle of their primary kinfolk, and the necessity to marry out and to bring women into the group created uncertainty as to the actual paternity of children. In a situation of economic scarcities, the social cohesion of the household under a system of patriarchy depended upon, or was enhanced by, the absence of sexual rivalries and political disputes over property, paternity, and legitimacy.

In feudalism, the social accumulation of property in land within the family rested upon a system of successful marriage alliances, and the continuity of household property between the patriarchal father and his offspring. This system of feudal property was at least in part backed up by a strong doctrine of sexual behaviour in medieval Catholic theology and practice. Religious teaching on female chastity, virginity, filial piety, and social duty provided the necessary normative basis for this economic and political system of dominance and control. Given the military and political instability of feudal societies, the social conditions for maximum fertility were always insecure and could not guarantee male succession on the basis of legitimate reproduction. The system of regular confession of women, the sacraments of marriage and birth, and strong household regulation of women, created a confessional culture geared to the regulation of female sexuality (Asad 1993; Hepworth and Turner 1982).

There were, however, often many conflicts between an ecclesiastical model of marriage and lay practice, since landowners wanted to repudiate their barren wives and to create new marital unions in order to secure their property through the birth of male children (Duby 1978). Indeed there emerged in this situation a dual form of sexual relations, in which marriage was exclusively associated with the necessities of reproduction and economic arrangements, while romantic attachments and love had to be formed and developed outside the legitimate marriage alliance. The whole tradition, therefore, of the Romance of the Rose and Courtly Love, which had its social location in this pattern of patriarchal reproduction, was the product of landless youth from the nobility who could not form stable marriage unions because of their exclusion from land and property. It is not surprising that the principal themes of Courtly Love poetry placed an emphasis upon courtesy, humility, adultery, and the religion of love (Lewis 1936). Desire and romantic passion were channelled through the oppositional poetry and mythology of the young knight without land or social attachment.

While Marxist sociologists have often focussed upon the profound changes in human society in the transition from feudalism to capitalism, in reality these two modes of production did not necessarily lead to a revolution in the close relationship between private property in productive resources, patriarchy, and the traditional household. At least in the English case, early capitalism depended upon kinship relations to secure the distribution of property and to finance future investments. In short, the patriarchal landlord gave way without too much historical interruption to the patriarchal capitalist owner of enterprises within a modern market society. Competitive or early capitalism depended upon primogeniture to concentrate wealth in the hands of heads of household who were now capitalist owners of property. The young sons of these owners of capitalist enterprises had to be prepared to conserve the wealth of the family within stable marriage arrangements in order to avoid the economic disasters of divorce, separation, and barren wives. Without secure lines of inheritance through the male, it was impossible to secure the future of enterprises. Therefore, in early capitalism there was the necessity for a strong moral or religious regulation of sexuality in order to secure these basic economic conditions.

However, the capitalist enterprise also required the development and training of a disciplined and productive labour force; asceticism was now important, not so much for the training of monks, but for the training of a disciplined and productive body. Since labour power was the source of values in commodities, the working-class population became the target of a variety of disciplines and calculating processes designed to secure the maximum profitability of products. For example, this productive and disciplined body was the target of Taylorism and factory discipline. This discipline of the body was associated in the second half of the nineteenth century with the development of institutions, rituals, and knowledge which made the body useful, disciplined, and reliable; these included the expansion of primary education, the Boy Scout movement, the creation of cycling clubs for both men and women, the growth of new theories of domestic hygiene, the creation of special holidays, the attack on alcoholism, the growth of social housing, and the movement to establish workers' garden plots.

We can regard these social and cultural changes as a medicalization of the body in which religious notions of diet and asceticism were gradually replaced by secular medical perspectives and regimens. The secularization of the body was therefore associated, not only with the growth of scientific theories of diet and moral management, but also with a rapid expansion of the medical profession, which came to specialize in the disorders of the middle class. We can see this movement in terms of a transition from a concern with the interior body and its passions to a regulation of the exterior body by a new conception of domestic culture associated with the urban middle class and its medical problems (Donzelot 1979). The medical categorization of the hysterical woman was connected with male anxiety about the introduction of women into new professional and quasi-professional occupations, especially in nursing and education (Foucault 1979). Male anxiety was also associated with a new form of women's complaints, especially the agoraphobic syndrome which emerged around the 1870s (de Swaan 1981). As women began to leave the safety of the household in the late nineteenth century to seek new forms of urban improvement, women were seen to be susceptible to the problems of false self-regard. In the new urban centres, dangers of infatuation, insult, and abduction become prominent. Female agoraphobia expressed the anxiety of husbands with respect to their patriarchal control over the domestic household, but also paradoxically symbolized the wife's dependence on the security and social status of a secure bourgeois domestic life style.

While in the nineteenth century women's position in society was still subordinate as a consequence of the continuity of patriarchal authority, women's social position was transformed in the early twentieth century as a result of their employment in the labour market during war-time emergency, by changes in the legal status of women, by feminist politics, and by new political arrangements, especially the franchise. I have argued elsewhere (Turner 1984) that the concept of patrimonial or patriarchal authority no longer adequately expressed the social position of women with the development of new forms of capitalism. This change in the status of women was associated with changes in the character of property and household, with the development of new divorce legislation, with the sexual liberation of women, and by the development of new techniques of contraception. The decline of objective patriarchy gave rise to a new form of conflict between men and women which might be described as 'patrism'.

We may define patrism as a system of authority where the objective power of men declines with changes in the household, creating a system of intense inter-personal conflict between men and women over the distribution of resources. Whereas patriarchy generally had the backing of law, politics, and custom, patrism is associated with the development of women as citizens with a legal capacity to defend their equality before the courts. While women objectively continued to experience poor wages, inadequate employment, and other economic disadvantages, in legal and formal terms they had access to law, to parliamentary and democratic processes, and to the rights of a fully fledged citizen within the public arena. The social decline of traditional patriarchy and the emergence of patrism as a system of unresolved conflict may also be associated with the erosion of the nineteenth-century nuclear family. In the twentieth century, household structures have become more diversified and complex as the nuclear family declined with changing population patterns. The household in contemporary society assumes a variety of forms, including the single-parent household, the nuclear family, the homosexual couple, the development of communal or collective joint-households, and various other impermanent and experimental relationships. Women continue to be exploited in these new domestic structures, but the old system of patriarchal authority associated with the traditional household appears to have disappeared or at least declined significantly. These social changes imply also profound transformations of the traditional structure of religio-political relations: God/Monarch/Father and Church/State/Family.

Many of these changes in the family and sexuality have been analysed by Anthony Giddens (1992) in his *The Transformation of Intimacy*. Giddens argues that the democratic revolution, which occurred in the political arena in the late nineteenth century, has now also taken place within the private sphere, especially in terms of relations of intimacy between men and women. The romantic ideal, the feminist movement, and the emphasis on emotive satisfaction have created a wave of rising expectations in sexual and intimate partnerships. Marriage depends more on the satisfaction of intimacy than on the property bond or on children. Rising divorce rates, empty marriages, and a pattern of serial monogamy have been the social consequences of this cultural revolution. The conventional Christian marriage which ideally emphasized trust and friendship might be compatible with the sexual revolution, but the idea of permanent monogamy may not be. The new ideals of intimacy in any case came from lesbian couples, according to Giddens, not from conventional norms.

The liberation of women is brought about by the collapse of the traditional patriarchal nuclear household, but the disappearance of this household is also a consequence of demographic changes and, more importantly, with changes in the pattern of economic ownership of production. There has been a widespread 'depersonalization' of property with the development of so-called 'institutional ownership', by banks, governments, international corporations, and insurance companies. In technical terms the decline of family capitalism (Bell 1960) means that there is an institutional differentiation of the human person, the economic subject and the legal relations of ownership. Quite simply, the ancient relationship between the family, the household, and the economy has been broken by the growth of new forms of investment, production, and distribution. The consequence of this economic change is that the regulation of women's sexuality is no longer a precondition of the capitalist economy, because institutionalized capitalism can operate on the basis of a variety of sexual codes and does not require the union of asceticism and property ownership. On the contrary, modern capitalism seems to be highly compatible, not only with a great diversity of sexual codes, but with various forms of promiscuity and hedonism as the basis of consumption and advertising. By the 1950s, production and reproduction had become separated, leaving a space for extensive sexual experimentation.

It is possible to conceptualize these changes in terms of an extensive rationalization of capitalism. In the first stages of capitalism, there is a rationalization of production and productive technology. This productive rationalization required a disciplined labour force, intensive surveillance of workers, and a rational system of factory production. This early stage of capitalism was associated with the development of religious asceticism, and there was a natural convergence between capitalist systems of production and the Protestant emphasis on regulation and discipline (Weber 1930). Capitalism was further developed by the rationalization of distribution and supply, which was made possible by a number of technical developments such as refrigeration. The rationalization of distributive systems contributed significantly to the emergence of world capitalism. In the post-Second World War period, we can argue that capitalism was further developed and rationalized by improvements in the nature of credit and consumption. The development of supermarkets, television advertising, credit schemes, and computerized banking have extended the market and created a mass society based upon mass consumption. The McDonaldization of society (Ritzer 1992) involves the application of Fordism and Taylorism to the fast-food industry. McDonaldization has now been applied to a variety of consumption patterns.

In the 1970s it was commonly argued in sociology that contemporary industrial society rested upon a series of tensions which were described by Daniel Bell (1976) as the cultural contradictions of capitalism. One major contradiction was that, within the workforce and the marketplace, there was an emphasis on discipline, regulation, and asceticism as norms suitable for rational production, while, in terms of consumption and the household, there was a distinctive emphasis on hedonism as a perspective appropriate for continuous and uninterrupted consumption. New technologies, new productive processes, and new systems of information had created new possibilities for commercialized recreation and extensive leisure. The development of an information society had led some writers to think about modern society as a post-industrial civilization (Bell 1974). Asceticism and discipline, along with the patriarchal nuclear family and a life-cycle dominated by work and career, had become increasingly inappropriate in such a society. The implications of these changes for religion were equally important.

The development of consumerism was associated with a certain secularization of society, because consumer culture opened up endless opportunities for experimentation with innovative and deviant life styles and personal images separated from the church or from a religious perspective. Consumption within the modern world also had important implications for the nature of the body:

Within a consumer culture the body is proclaimed as a vehicle of pleasure: it is desirable and desiring and the closer the actual body approximates to the idealized images of youth, health, fitness and beauty, the higher its exchange value. Consumer culture permits the unashamed display of the human body. (Featherstone 1982, 21–2)

Whereas the traditional religious/medical model of dieting sought to bring about the regulation of the interior body in order to control passion by purgation, diet, and restraint, the new consumer culture seeks to enhance the surface of the body and to emphasize its sexual desirability.

There is at the level of popular culture a definite emphasis on aesthetics as a justification for life, which finds its mirror-image in the philosophical debate about the ethical as the aesthetic. There is also a new subjectivism of the self, with the development of a representational personality whose value is linked to its commercial status within the world of consumer goods (Lasch 1978). On the one hand, there are various pressures towards the regulation and control of individuals through state bureaucracies resulting in an administered society, but there are also other pressures towards a greater emphasis on the subjective individuality of the person within a diversified market-place. While there are these contradictory forces, there appears to be little room within contemporary capitalism for the Weberian personality of conventional capitalism combining asceticism, activism, and achievement motivation.

Social theorists like Anthony Giddens (1992) and Ulrich Beck (1992) have argued that the characteristic feature of high modernity is the reflexive self, that is, the self in modernity is conceptualized as a project. The self is a project which is to be made, constructed, and endlessly refashioned through the life-cycle. However, it is also the case that the body is a project in high modernity. Like the reflexive self, the modern body can be refashioned by face-lifts, by breast augmentation, by diet and jogging, and for women, if necessary, by weight-lifting. Transsexualism and transvestitism are now a familiar feature of the middle-class scene. For some writers on the sociology of the body, in modern society the self *is* the body (Synnott 1992; Shilling 1992). These developments represent a definite reversal of the traditional Christian pattern in which the flesh was subordinated in the interests of the soul.

Within contemporary capitalism there are various social processes which have brought about radical changes, not only in the nature of production and consumption, but in the character of the actors themselves. These changes are so profound that some writers wish to suggest that we have moved from a modern society to a post-modern society (Lyotard 1986). Post-modernism is associated with the fragmentation of life-worlds, reflected in the disappearance of both high culture and mass consumerism. We no longer have fashion but fashions which emerge out of the highly diversified and decentralized character of consumption and individual style. This fragmentation of life-worlds and experience is also reflected in the perspectivism of contemporary philosophy, social science, and the art world, where it is difficult to find a secure foundation for a coherent notion of truth and rationality. Within the world of mass media, it is further argued that the old distinction between the imaginary world of television and the real world of politics has disappeared. We live in a world of symbolic simulation where we have an inflationary system of symbols and signs (Baudrillard 1981 and 1983). Indeed within this perspective, modern industrial society has moved from the dominance of the production of commodities to the dominance of the production of the sign. For the theorists of post-modernism, this fragmentation of the world, the dominance of the sign, and the emergence of global simulation, mean the end of philosophy as an account of a single system of reason, and indeed the end of the project of modernization.

There is currently much dispute over the problem of whether to regard post-modernism as the negation of modernism or simply its extension, and there is certainly much criticism of writers like Lyotard and Baudrillard (see Rojek and Turner 1993). However, in this chapter I shall treat the world of post-modernity as indeed merely the final outcome of changes in industrial capitalism which had their origins in the expansion of mass consumption in the 1950s and 1960s. Thus Bell, writing in the 1970s on the cultural contradictions of the modern world, noted that:

The world of hedonism is the world of fashion, photography, advertising, television and travel. It is a world of makebelieve in which one lives with expectations, for what will come rather than what is. And it must come without effort. It is no accident that the successful new magazine of the previous decade was called *Playboy*. (Bell 1976, 70)

We can regard post-modernism as the cultural logic of late capitalism in which there has been a profound pluralization and fragmentation of the life-world, reflected in the perspectivism and simulation of the world of contemporary media products and consumer life style (Jameson 1984). While there is a fragmentation of everyday life brought about by the diversity of the market-place, there is also a tendency towards a global culture, where, with the developments of a system of world communication and extensive mass markets, separate nation-states may be subject to common cultural processes (Robertson 1987).

RELIGION IN THE POST-MODERN AGE

These changes in the social structure of Western societies, which I have described in the long transition from early feudalism to late capitalism, have obviously had major implications for religious practice, belief, and symbolism. I have argued, with special reference to the nature of dominant ideologies in feudalism, that, in Western society, there developed a strong relationship between the status of women, the religious view of the body, property ownership, and patriarchy, whereby the religious ideology served as the social cement of Western civilization. I have attempted to avoid a unidimensional view of religion and patriarchy by recognizing the impact of female mysticism and the cult of Mary on official teaching and practice. With the collapse of traditional patriarchy and the evolution of modern patrism, the changing status of women in society has been reflected in, amongst other things, the religious conceptualization of God and the social division of labour within the church between the (primarily male) priestly leadership and the (primarily female) lay membership. It would be possible to trace the changing status of men and women in terms of changes in the religious conceptualization of God in the Western Christian tradition. The old patriarchal God of traditional fundamentalism gave way initially to a more 'democratic' vision of God as friend and confidant. In turn this notion of the male God in Christianity has been challenged by feminist theology (see Gross 1977), which is associated with the rise of patrism. The changing character of woman in Western society continues to challenge the patriarchal presuppositions of Abrahamic theology which had its original location within a pastoralist economy and with a strong patriarchal tradition. In so far as Christianity is committed to the idea of a personal God, it has been difficult to imagine how this concept of personality could be degendered to give expression to a social equality between men and women. Fundamentalist movements in the late twentieth century may be interpreted as reactions to the uncertainty and potential instability of a post-modern age. Once more the fantasy of the androgyne in modern literature has been used as a critique of both capitalism and Christianity in the work of writers like Walter Benjamin (Buci-Glucksmann 1984).

The long-term erosion of the connection between property, primogeniture, and patriarchy has also had important implications for the body, spirituality and sexuality. I have attempted to conceptualize this transition in terms of a shift from an early emphasis on the interior regulation of the body to control sexuality through such practices as diet, to a new view of the body in which the external presentation of ourselves within the consumer market-place puts a special emphasis on the style and form of the external body. This change in emphasis may also be connected with a secularization of the body, since the old religious controls over passion have been replaced by scientific (specifically medical) controls over the family, and sexuality. In a 'risk society' (Beck 1992), the uncertainties and hazards of everyday life may require more detailed and sophisticated forms of personal regulation and surveillance.

The social function of the church and religious doctrine have been largely overtaken by medical practice and medical authority, since what defines the good-life in contemporary societies is the healthy life as conceptualized by the medical profession. Whereas in traditional systems diet and exercise attempted to regulate the passions, within modern medical systems jogging, dieting, and abstinence serve to guard us against infections and illness with the aim of promoting longevity. The social history of 'holy anorexia' (Bell 1985) is a powerful illustration of the secularization of religious disorders into diseases. Contemporary medical practices are also part of a preventive medical system organized by the state to bring about an economy within the welfare system. These overt goals have apparently little to do with traditional religious values of personal restraint to bring about an equilibrium of the body as the basis of a stable society.

Changes in the character of the market and the expansion of consumption have resulted in a pluralization of style, life-world, and outlook. The emergence of a pluralistic cultural system has major implications for the nature of religious practice and spirituality. This pluralism in culture leads to a market situation in religion where within a global and cosmopolitan environment modern people can choose religious styles and beliefs rather like they choose commodities (Berger and Luckmann 1967). However, cosmopolitanism in religious life styles is also connected with a sense of the artificiality of these choices which in a certain way devalues traditional, life-long commitments to religion based upon training, faith, and conversion. Within the post-modern life style we do not simply choose things; we *know* that we choose them. These changes have radical implications not just for Christianity, but also for Islam (Ahmed 1992; Gellner 1992).

In the post-modern world, along with a growing artificiality of life style and the fragmentation of the life-world, the body comes increasingly into social dominance. While the working-class body of the late nineteenth century was constituted as a decaying sick or alcoholic body (the target of innumerable government surveys and inquiries), the body of the twentieth century has been produced as the desirable hedonistic and playful body. Particularly with the growth of mass leisure, nudism, mass holidays, and diverse leisure pursuits, the body emerges as a playful object, the vehicle of pleasure, the site of endless consumer battles. Writing in the 1970s, therefore, Baudrillard (1970) noted that the body as a space of desire had become an object of salvation which has in its ideological functions replaced the soul.

By the late 1980s, however, it became clear that the body was also caught within the paradigms of other negative or oppositional moral discourses. With the contemporary crisis brought about by AIDS and the revival of certain forms of fundamentalism in opposition to post-modernism, there is emerging the idea that the body must be regulated, restrained, and controlled, since, as the vehicle of new epidemics, it threatens the political and economic continuity of, not only African, but also many Western societies. The state, in a society where the church as a social institution has receded from the public arena, constantly inter-venes to control and regulate the production and reproduction of human life itself. Given the rapid development of modern biotechnology, the moral, political and social problems raised by artificial reproduction of human bodies has drawn the state into the arena previously dominated exclusively either by the medical profession or in an earlier period by the clergy. Through legislation and other forms of moral discourse, the state has become, however inadequately, committed to the provision of meanings and purposes for birth, death, human reproduction, ageing, and illness. That is, the state is forced to consider various telic issues which are concerned with 'the ends of man' (Parsons 1978). However, by becoming involved with the regulation of society, the state to some extent demonstrates that what we take to be the 'natural' world is in fact socially constituted or fabricated by human action. The naturalness of the life-world is furthermore undermined by such processes:

In other words, at one and the same time the ostensibly secular state has moved into hithertofore sacred realms and the 'client adherence' of modern states has in various ways become conscious of the 'fabricated' nature of the state-run society. The modern state 'invites' religious encroachment, precisely but not wholly because it is increasingly concerned with matters traditionally associated with the religious domain. (Robertson and Chirico 1985, 225)

Around this struggle over the body, the state is drawn into moral and religious battles associated with the very definition of life itself, and, since the body is now the target of various warring parties, the state provides a minimum of political integration for the social order in an attempt to guarantee the continuity of the reproduction of life. This contradictory set of forces within society brings the secular state constantly into the domain of moral and religious questions, where the traditional functions of the natural-law tradition and Christianity have been questioned or undermined by the very differentiation and fragmentation of life associated with the emergence of consumerism. Within this context, the body is constantly seen to be itself a fabricated or constructed phenomenon, the plaything of consumerism, or the artificial product of biomedical technology. It is a project, and to some extent, therefore, an artifice.

CONCLUSION: RATIONALIZATION AND SECULARIZATION OF THE BODY

In this historical commentary on the sociology of the body, a variety of approaches have been identified and discussed. In my opening statement, four separate approaches to the analysis of the body in the social sciences were conceptualized. Although there is much theoretical diversity in the sociology of the body, there is also considerable consensus around the view that the body is central to discourses of power, especially to those medical and religious traditions which represent the body as a metaphor of social (especially gender) relationships. The body provides an ambiguous set of metaphors for social problems and conflicts, but it also provides a discourse for joy and ecstasy. In this chapter, therefore, I have focused on those anthropological and sociological traditions which attempt to understand the history of the body in the context of changes in culture, political power, and economic relations. More precisely, I have been concerned with the rise and fall of religions, asceticism, and the medicalization of social relations.

In this discourse of the body as flesh, the body is the ultimate origin of idolatry, which must be regulated by religious practices, by the medical regimen, by the penitentiary, and, ultimately, by the discipline of torture. Sexuality is, within this tradition, the final folly, betraying reason to the short-term pleasures of the body. We can consequently approach the history of Western culture as, in Weber's terms, the unfolding of an ethic of world mastery that starts with the control of the flesh and ends with the control of the self. In the history of diet, medical regiments, athletics, the gymnasium, gastronomy, etiquette, domestic science, the anatomy theatre, the penitentiary, eugenics, the medical sciences of reproduction and gerontology, we find a vast panoply of beliefs, institutions, and structures which we may call by the convenient term 'civilization' (Elias 1978). These practices of civilization are also the conduits along which pass the historical processes of secularization, medicalization, and regimentation. Modern societies are, as a consequence, caught between two contradictory processes which both produce and regulate the body, while also freeing it for the hedonistic pleasures of modern consumerism. The modern professions, which involve a combination of power and knowledge operating under the auspices of the state, have contributed to the regularization and control of the body. The modern world is a place of biopolitics which requires and achieves a certain surveillance of the person through the regimentation of the body. However, there are other forces which through consumerism allow a certain liberation of the body as the vehicle of hedonism and desire. These two forces are part of the profound set of cultural contradictions within modern capitalism.

BIBLIOGRAPHY

Adorno, T., and Horkheimer, M. (1979), *Dialectic of Enlightenment*, London: Verso.

Ahmed, A. (1992), *Postmodernism and Islam*, London: Routledge.

Ariès, P., and Béjin, A. (eds.) (1986), *Western Sexuality, Practice and Precept in Past and Present Times*, Oxford: Basil Blackwell.

Asad, T. (1993), *Genealogies of Religion. Discipline and Reasons of Power in Christianity and Islam.* Baltimore and London: Johns Hopkins University Press.

Baross, Z. (1981), *The Scandal of Disease*, University of Amsterdam, Academe Proefschrift.

Bataille, G. (1981), *Eroticism*, London: Marion Boyars.

Baudrillard, J. (1970), *La Société de Consommation*, Paris: SGPP.

(1981), *For a Critique of the Political Economy of the Sign*, St. Louis: Telos Press.

(1983), *Simulations*, New York: Semiotexte.

Beck, U. (1992), *Risk Society*, London: Sage.

Bell, D. (1960), *The End of Ideology*, New York: Collier.

(1974), *The Coming of Post-Industrial Society*, New York: Basic Books.

(1976), *The Cultural Contradictions of Capitalism*, New York: Basic Books.

Bell, R. M. (1985), *Holy Anorexia*, Chicago and London: University of Chicago Press.

Berger, P.L., and Luckmann, T. (1967), *The Social Construction of Reality*, London: The Penguin Press.

Bernstein, R. (1985), *Philosophical Profiles: Essays in a Pragmatic Mode*, Cambridge: Polity Press.

Berthelot, J. M. (1986), 'Sociological Discourse and the Body', *Theory Culture and Society* 3/3, 155–164.

Boyne, R. (1986), 'The Domain of the Third: French Social Theory into the 1980s', *Theory Culture and Society* 3/3, 7–24.

Buci-Glucksmann, C. (1984), *La Raison Baroque, de Baudelaire à Benjamin*, Paris: Editions Galilee.

Bynum, C. W. (1991), *Fragmentation and Redemption: Essays on Gender and the Human Body in Medieval Religion*. New York: Zone Books.

de Swaan, A. (1981), 'The Politics of Agoraphobia', *Theory and Society* 10, 359–85.

Donzelot, J. (1979), *The Policing of Families*, New York: Pantheon.

Douglas, M. (1970), *Purity and Danger: An Analysis of Concepts of Pollution and Taboo*, Harmondsworth: Penguin Books.

(1973), *Natural Symbols*, Harmondsworth: Penguin Books.

Duby, G. (1978), *Medieval Marriage, Two Models from 12th Century France*, Baltimore and London: Johns Hopkins University Press.

Elias, N. (1978), *The Civilizing Process*, vol. 1, Oxford: Basil Blackwell.

Featherstone, M. (1982), 'The Body in Consumer Culture', *Theory, Culture and Society* I, 18–33.

Foucault, M. (1971), *Madness and Civilization*, London: Tavistock.

(1973), *The Birth of the Clinic*, London: Tavistock.

(1977), *Discipline and Punish, The Birth of the Prison*, London: Tavistock.

(1979), *History of Sexuality*, vol. 1, London: Tavistock.

(1980), *Herculine Barbin: Being the Recently Discovered Memoires of a 19th Century French Hermaphrodite*, Brighton: Wheatsheaf Press.

(1984a), *L'Usage des Plaisirs*, Paris: Gallimard.

(1984b), *Le Souci de Soi*, Paris: Gallimard.

Fox, R. A. (1976), *The Tangled Chain, The Structure of Disorder in the Anatomy of Melancholy*, Berkeley: University of California Press.

Garfinkel, H. (1956), 'Conditions of Successful Degradation Ceremonies', *American Journal of Sociology* 61, 420–24.

Gellner, E. (1992), *Religion and Postmodernity*. London: Routledge.

Giddens, A. (1992), *The Transformation of Intimacy, Sexuality, Love and Eroticism in Modern Societies*, Cambridge: Polity Press.

Giesey, R. E. (1987), 'The King Imagined', in ed. Baker, K. M., *The French Revolution and the Creation of Modern Political Culture, Volume 1, The Political Culture of the Old Regime*, Oxford: Pergamon Press, 41–61.

Goffman, E. (1969), *The Presentation of Self in Everyday Life*, London: Allen Lane.

Gross, R. M. (eds.) (1977), *Beyond Androcentrism: New Essays on Women and Religion*, Montana: Scholars Press.

Hepworth, M., and Turner, B. S. (1982), *Confession, Studies in Deviance and Religion*, London: Routledge and Kegan Paul.

Huch, R. (1973), *Alfred Schuler, Ludwig Klages und Stefan George, Erinnerungen an Kreise und Krisen der Jahrhundertwende in München-Schwabing*, Amsterdam: Castrum Peregrin Press.

Jameson, F. (1984), 'Post-modernism or the Cultural Logic of late Capitalism', *New Left Review* 146, 53–92.

Kantorowicz, E. H. (1957), *The King's Two Bodies*, University of Princeton Press.

Klages, L. (1981), *Vom Kosmogonischen Eros*, Bonn: Bouvier.

Kurzweil, E. (1986), 'The Fate of Structuralism', *Theory Culture and Society* 3/3, 113–26.

Lasch, C. (1978), *The Culture of Narcissism: American Life in an Age of Diminishing Expectations*, New York: W. W. Norton and Co.

Lemert, C. C., and Gillan, G. (1982), *Michel Foucault, Social Theory and Transgression*, New York: Columbia University Press.

Lewis, C. S. (1936), *The Allegory of Love*, London: Oxford University Press.

Lyotard, J.-F. (1986), *The Postmodern Condition. A Report on Knowledge*, Manchester University Press.

Mallin, S. B. (1979), *Merleau-Ponty's Philosophy*, New Haven and London: Yale University Press.

Marcuse, H. (1955), *Eros and Civilization, a Philosophical Inquiry into Freud*, Boston: Beacon Press.

Mauss, M. (1979), *Sociology and Psychology, Essays*, London: Routledge and Kegan Paul.

Merleau-Ponty, M. (1962), *Phenomenology of Perception*, London: Routledge and Kegan Paul.

O'Neill, J. (1985), *Five Bodies, the Human Shape of Modern Society*, Ithaca and London: Cornell University Press.

Parsons, T. (1978), *Action Theory and Human Condition*, New York: Free Press.

Ritzer, G. (1992) *The McDonaldization of Society*, London: Sage.

Robertson, R. (1987), 'Globalization Theory and Civilization Analysis', *Comparative Civilizations Review* 17, 20–30.

Robertson, R., and Chirico, J. (1985), 'Humanity, Globalization and World-Wide Religious Resurgence: A Theoretical Explanation', *A Sociological Analysis* 46, 210–42.

Rojek, C., and Turner, B. S. (eds.) (1993), *Forget Baudrillard*, London: Routledge.

Sacks, O. W. (1970), *Migraine*, Berkeley: University of California Press.

(1976), *Awakenings*, Harmondsworth: Penguin Books.

Sartre, J. P. (1957), *Being and Nothingness*, London: Methuen.

Schochet, G. J. (1975), *Patriarchalism and Political Thought*, New York: Basic Books.

Shilling, C. (1992), *The Body and Social Theory*, London: Sage.

Smart, B. (1985), *Michel Foucault*, Chichester: Ellis Horword, London: Tavistock.

Sontag, S. (1978), *Illness as Metaphor*, New York: Vintage Books.

Stauth, G., and Turner, B. S. (1988), *Nietzsche's Dance, Reciprocity, Resistance and Resentment in Social Life*, Oxford: Basil Blackwell.

Synnot, A. (1992), *The Body Social*, London: Routledge.

Turner, B. S. (1978), *Marx and the End of Orientalism*, London: Allen and Unwin.

(1982), 'The Government of the Body, Medical Regimens and the Rationalization of Diet', *British Journal of Sociology* 33, 254–69.

(1984), *The Body and Society: Explorations in Social Theory*, Oxford: Basil Blackwell.

(1987), *Medical Power and Social Knowledge*, London: Sage.

(1992), *Regulating Bodies: Essays in Medical Sociology*, London: Routledge.

Weber, M. (1930), *The Protestant Ethic and the Spirit of Capitalism*, London: Allen and Unwin.

CHAPTER 3

Remarks on the anthropology of the body

Talal Asad

I

Anthropologists have long been interested in ideas about the body. Thus in nineteenth-century anthropology the centrality of the notion of 'race' involved detailed studies of the bodies of 'primitives'. European imperialism made possible, and evolutionary theories of progress encouraged and fed on, the detailed description and classification of types of European and non-European bodies. These taxonomies were elaborated well into the twentieth century[1] as signs of a world political order which contained its own universal justification and its grand historical momentum. But, ever since Nazi theories and practices of race fastened onto European populations, notions of biological destiny have been met with scepticism (see, for example, Proctor 1988).

Yet it was in the context of the idea of natural selection that Charles Darwin's *The Expression of the Emotions in Man and Animals* (1872) was conceived and written, and that it became the work that stimulated studies of the body as a medium of voluntary and involuntary communication. By the 1950s, American anthropologists had developed a systematic field of inquiry – called 'kinesics' – connected to linguistics but focussed on body communication (Birtwhistell 1968). The identification of expressions that are universal (innate and essentially unchanging) as opposed to those that are culture-specific (learnt and therefore changeable) has always been a primary task in a field that emerged directly out of nineteenth-century ideas of humanity's biological destiny.

But from the end of the nineteenth century there appeared studies of the 'symbolic' aspects of the body in 'primitive cultures', separated from biology in method, and more directly related to the concept of culturally determined thought: the cosmological significance of death, the struc-

---

[1] Physical anthropology was an integral part of Indian Census information throughout the period of British Rule.

ture of sacrifice, the categorical pre-eminence of the right hand, rites of passage, etc. (Hertz 1960; Hubert and Mauss 1964; van Gennep 1960). These anthropological themes came to be regarded as 'symbolic' not because they concerned problems of human communication (kinesics was never part of 'symbolic anthropology'), but because it was assumed that the study of primitive representations[2] would tell us something profound about the human mind.[3]

However, the recent, more generalized, interest in 'the body' is not merely a popularization of concerns that anthropologists have always had. I subscribe to the view that this rapidly growing preoccupation with 'the body' is itself linked to a noticeable ideological development in contemporary life: the urge to aestheticize modern life. The body as *image* – in advertisement photographs, on television, and in the flesh – whether named or unnamed, famous or ordinary, is one aspect of that tendency.

The salience of symbolic studies of the body has been precisely their focus on *representations of the body* and on *the body and its parts as representations*. This remark applies to Mary Douglas' influential writings,[4] as it does to most of the contributors to collections on what has come to be called 'The Anthropology of the Body', such as Benthall and Polhemus (1975), Blacking (1977), and Polhemus (1978). In spite of the fact that Mauss' 1935 essay 'Techniques of the Body' is often cited, problems about the formation of the body have received less attention than those relating to its representation. This neglect is the consequence not merely of an intellectual division of labour, but also of a theoretical stance that I believe to be mistaken. For, although the two sets of problems have tended to be addressed relatively independently of each other, they are inextricably linked in complicated ways. To appreciate this requires us to

---

[2] Although the word 'primitive' is no longer fashionable in anthropology, 'symbolic' studies usually retain the same preoccupation with 'non-rational' or 'non-scientific' representation-cum-signification as the earlier studies. Compare, for example, the title of Needham's well-known text-book, *Symbolic Classification* (1979), which deals with the same themes as the classic by Durkheim and Mauss, 'On Some Primitive Forms of Classification: Contribution to the Study of Collective Representations' (1903), translated with an introduction by Needham as *Primitive Classification* (1963).

[3] One strand in the emergence of the anthropological preoccupation with representation-cum-signification as the way to understand the human mind may be traced in the eighteenth- and nineteenth-century history of the notion 'symbol' as it displaced the previous idea of 'allegory'. The implications of this displacement for a reformulated epistemology to be found in the writings of romantic authors and literary critics is sketched out in de Man 1983. See also Gadamer 1975, and Honour 1979.

[4] 'Just as it is true that everything symbolizes the body', she has written, 'so it is equally true that the body symbolizes everything else'. (1966, 122).

distinguish (something 'symbolic anthropologists' do not always do) between the representative and semantic functions of language, and then to question the ambitious idea that the study of symbolism provides us with an important understanding of 'the human mind': the idea that the (disembodied) mind confronts 'the world' through the interface of 'symbols'. True, signs are necessary to the social processes by which the human body (external and internal) is cultivated. But signs are not *sui generis*; they are intrinsic to the social practices of human bodies,[5] and acquire their interpreted sense and reference as part of the historicity of those practices. But equally important, the body's knowledge of the real world is not always dependent on signs.

The concern with decoding body symbols has also been central to classical anthropological approaches to ritual. This concern follows naturally from the long-established definition of ritual as symbolic or expressive action, as opposed to action that is technical or instrumental (cf. Radcliffe-Brown 1939, 143). For many anthropologists this meant that a clear separation had to be made between the social meaning of rites and the psychological states of participating bodies.

It was in this context that Evans-Pritchard wrote (1965, 44): 'Only chaos would result were anthropologists to classify social phenomena by emotions which are supposed to accompany them, for such emotional states, if present at all, must vary not only from individual to individual, but also in the same individual on different occasions and even at different points in the same rite.' The meaning given to the word 'emotion' here is evidently something like *sensations*, i.e. feelings that are not only spontaneous and ephemeral, but essentially internal and unique to each body. In this view by a leading British anthropologist the possibility is not envisaged that when sensations become the objects of (ritual) signs they thereby necessarily change their character.[6]

There were anthropologists, of course, who addressed themselves to the systematic connections between social representations and individual bodies in the context of ritual. Victor Turner, for example, insisted that ritual symbols should also be analysed as 'a set of evocative devices

---

[5] Or as Voloshinov said of language: 'The actual reality of language-speech is not the abstract system of linguistic forms, not the isolated monologic utterance, and not the psychophysiological act of its implementation, but the social event of verbal interaction implemented in an utterance or utterances' (1973, 94).

[6] Evans-Pritchard's empiricist psychology may be contrasted with Collingwood's argument (1938) that when sensations are captured in thought (i.e. language) they cease to be fleeting, private, and non-directional. Collingwood's writings were admired and occasionally cited by Evans-Pritchard, so it is surprising to find that neither he nor his followers at Oxford ever engaged Collingwood's views on emotions and thought.

for rousing, channelling and domesticating powerful emotions' (1969, 42–3). But Turner's depth-psychology approach assumed that emotions were bodily drives which needed to be managed ('domesticated') by archetypal symbols, and he described how this process worked in particular African communities whose rites he had examined in impressive detail. In other words Turner regarded 'the body' (especially its innate impulses and feelings) as essentially non-cultural. Culture (as the variable domain of studied thought, speech, and gesture) and body (as the source of individual feelings and universal desires that were potentially disruptive of culture) remained conceptually distinct.

A more recent survey (Lutz and White 1986) points out that newer trends in the anthropological study of the emotions are attempting to shift their attention from the 'body' (seen as the domain of psychobiology) to 'culture' and language. However, these shifts are less radical than may appear at first sight, because they simply reproduce the existing duality. The authors seem uncomfortably aware of this, for, although on the one hand they assert that the newer researches 'hold the seeds of a basic reconceptualization', they warn against such studies leading to 'their own impoverishment unless links can be forged between the often dichotomized worlds of the rational and irrational, public and private, individual and social' (1986, 429).[7]

The year after Lutz and White wrote their survey, two medical anthropologists, Scheper-Hughes and Lock, published a thoughtful essay entitled 'The Mindful Body' in which they too set out to question the dualities that underlie much contemporary thinking on the subject. The article deals interestingly in turn with 'the individual body' (lived experiences of the body-self), 'the social body' (representational uses of the body), and 'the body politic' (the social control of bodies, individual and collective), and it concludes with a plea for 'a new epistemology and metaphysics of the mindful body' that will replace the Cartesian dualisms which they see as dominating Western thought.

My view is that, while this philosophical revolution may eventually come about, there are, within classic anthropological literature, questions about the body that can still be profitably explored. Among them are questions posed by Mauss.

---

[7] Incidentally, with the decline of structuralism, it has become quite common for anthropologists to criticize the use of dichotomous categories. But it is worth stressing that there is nothing *essentially* wrong with them. The absurdity lies only in assuming that all dualities have the same logical status, or in insisting that all thought can be reduced to dualities. It cannot *always* be wrong to counterpose 'mind' to 'body', or 'reason' to 'emotion', or 'life' to 'death' regardless of context.

Mauss was the first anthropologist to discuss the complex ways in which
the human body was socially invested. His seminal essay 'Techniques of
the Body' contains insights relating to the study of embodied behaviour
that have not yet been fully absorbed. Douglas has perhaps come closest
to doing so, but her own commitment to 'symbolic analysis' has
prevented her from appreciating the far-reaching character of Mauss'
concerns. Thus in her widely read book entitled *Natural Symbols*,
published before Mauss's essay was translated into English, she summarized and popularized its concerns as follows:

> Marcel Mauss, in his essay on the techniques of the body (1935), boldly asserted
> that there can be no such thing as natural behaviour. Every kind of action
> carries the imprint of learning, from feeding to washing, from repose to
> movement and, above all, sex. Nothing is more essentially transmitted by a
> social process of learning than sexual behaviour, and this of course is closely
> related to morality . . . Mauss saw that the study of body techniques would have
> to take place within a study of symbolic systems. He hoped that the sociologists
> would co-ordinate their approaches with those of the perception theory as it was
> being developed then by Cambridge psychologists . . . But this was as far as he
> got, in this gem of an essay, to suggesting a programme for organising the study
> of 'l'homme total' . . . Mauss's denial that there is any such thing as natural
> behaviour is confusing. It falsely poses the relation between nature and culture.
> Here I seek to identify a natural tendency to express situations of a certain kind
> in an appropriate bodily style. In so far as it is unconscious, in so far as it is
> obeyed universally in all cultures, the tendency is natural. It is generated in
> response to a perceived social situation, but the latter must always come clothed
> in its local history and culture. Therefore the natural expression is culturally
> determined. (Douglas 1970, 65 and 68–9)

But, in fact, Mauss' essay does not really deal with the nature–nurture
problem. It is true that he does say, with reference to something as
mundane as walking, that 'This was an acquired, not a natural, way of
walking' and that 'there is perhaps no "natural way" for the adult' (1979,
102). Yet his interest is not primarily in emphasizing the cultural
variation of bodily expressions (even in 1935 such an argument would
have been banal). Mauss aims to explore the dynamic constitution of
embodied behaviour which he wanted to conceptualize as *apt* behaviour.
He does not operate in this essay with the culture/nature opposition,
which was later popularised by Lévi-Straussian structuralism and which
became central to much of Douglas' own work.

   Mauss insisted that 'The body is man's first and most natural instrument. Or more accurately, not to speak of instruments, man's first and most natural technical object, and at the same time technical means, is his body' (1979, 104). By talking about 'body techniques' he sought to focus attention on the fact that if we conceptualized human behaviour in terms of learned capabilities, we might see the need for investigating how these were linked to authoritative standards and regular practice:

Hence I have had this notion of the social nature of the '*habitus*' for many years. Please note that I use the Latin word . . . *habitus*. The word translates infinitely better than '*habitude*' [habit or custom], the '*exis*', the 'acquired ability' and 'faculty' of Aristotle (who was a psychologist) . . . These 'habits' do not vary just with individuals and their imitations; they vary especially between societies, educations, proprieties and fashions, prestiges. In them we should see the techniques and work of collective and individual practical reason rather than, in the ordinary way, merely the soul and its repetitive faculties. (1979, 101)

This concept of *habitus*[8] is not about the body as symbol of something, or about things that symbolize the body. Of course it presupposes human communication regarding models of appropriate/inappropriate behaviour, but the concept of *habitus* invites us to analyse 'the body' as an assemblage of embodied aptitudes not as systems of symbolic meanings. Hence Mauss' concern to talk about 'those people with a sense of the adaptation of all their well-coordinated movements to a goal, who are practised, who "know what they are up to"' (1979, 108), implying a bodily *competence* at something, a sense which he named by the Latin *habilis* because the French *habile* did not quite convey what he was getting at. I argue that Mauss wanted to talk as it were about the way a professional pianist's *practised hands* remember and play the music being performed, not about how the symbolizing mind 'clothes a natural bodily tendency' with cultural meaning.

In effect, Mauss was attempting to define an anthropology of *practical reason*.[9] The human body is not to be viewed simply as the passive recipient of 'cultural imprints', still less as the active source of 'natural expressions' that are 'clothed in local history and culture', but as the *self-developable* means for achieving a range of human objects – from styles of physical movement (for example, walking), through modes of

---

[8] Bourdieu (1977) was later to popularize the word *habitus* for theoretical purposes that are not those of Mauss. This may explain why Mauss is not given credit by Bourdieu for having originated the concept.

[9] Akin to the sense given that term by Kant, which relates to the objective conditions of self-determining action. Kant, of course, used the term to describe the bourgeois concept of moral practice; Mauss deals with a much wider range of practices.

emotional being (for example, composure), to kinds of spiritual experience (for example, mystical states).

It is the final paragraph of Mauss' essay that carries what are perhaps the most far-reaching implications for an anthropological understanding of the body. Beginning with a reference to Granet's remarkable studies of Taoist body techniques, he goes on: 'I believe precisely that at the bottom of all our mystical states there are body techniques which we have not studied, but which were studied fully in China and India, even in very remote periods. This socio-psycho-biological study should be made. I think that there are necessarily biological means of entering into "communion with God."' (1979, 122) Thus the possibility is opened up of inquiring into the ways in which embodied practices (including language-in-use) form a precondition for varieties of religious experience.[10] The inability to 'enter into communion with God' becomes a function of untaught bodies.

Whatever may be the intellectual appeal of a phenomenology of the body, it seems to me that Mauss' approach runs counter to the assumption of primordial bodily experiences.[11] It encourages us to think of such experience not as an autogenetic impulse, but as a mutually constituting relationship between body-sense and body-learning.[12] Such a position fits well with what we know of even something as basic and universal as body pain. For anthropological as well as psychological research reveals that the perception of pain threshold varies considerably according to traditions of body training, and also according to the pain history of individual bodies (Melzack and Wall 1982; Brihaye,

[10] In my own work (Asad 1987) I have attempted to explore this question with reference to medieval Christian monastic discipline. I deal there with how bodily attitudes were cultivated, but also with how sexuality (libido) was differently managed among Benedictines (who recruited children) and Cistercians (who recruited adults only) in the education of Christian virtues. In the one case this involved trying to direct the body's experience; in the other, to reconvert the experienced body. My suggestion was that not only the force and direction of universal desire but desires themselves (specific Christian virtues) may be historically constituted.

[11] The appeal of that position is exemplified in an article by Jackson which provides many shrewd criticisms of 'symbolic and semiotic' analyses of the body. It assumes, however, that bodily awareness is at once primordial and universal: 'While words and concepts distinguish and divide, bodiliness unites and forms the grounds of an empathic, even universal, understanding. This may be why the body so often takes the place of speech and eclipses thought in rituals' (1983, 341).

[12] In his fascinating essay on the modern history of cenesthesia (inner perception of our bodies), Starobinski distinguishes critically between the self's naive, taken-for-grantedness of its body, and (following Freud) the ego's intentional awareness of its body. 'In a conscious awareness of the body', argues Starobinski, 'the aesthetic element of cenesthesia is in the nature of an instinctual satisfaction undeniably confused with primary physiological information. It is a variation on "turning round upon the subject's own self". There is nothing very bold in drawing the only superficially banal conclusion that the present infatuation with the different modes of body consciousness is a symptom of the considerable narcissistic component characteristic of contemporary Western culture' (1982, 38).

Loew, and Pia 1985). Thus, from Mauss' perspective, an experience of the body becomes an experienced body. And the more experienced the human body, the less its dependence on language. Which is not to deny, of course, that an experienced body is always sited in specific relations – even if these are changing, or contradictory – with itself and with other bodies, animate and inanimate, past and present.

III

Does the anthropological view that 'the body' is socially constructed expose us to the dangers of relativism? It depends, I think, on precisely what the anxiety is that underlies this familiar question.

Of course it is always possible that an anthropologist may wrongly attribute his or her own preoccupations and concepts to the people being reported on – as may the historian, the psychologist, or anyone else for that matter. In principle (so it may be maintained) such accounts are always disputable, and therefore there is no serious problem here.[13] But there *is* one, of course, and it concerns the relation of any report to the reality it seeks to recount. For, so long as this problem is posed in terms of reading ethnographic texts, it seems to me it is irresolvable in any definitive sense: the possibilities of interpretation, and counter-interpretation, are endless. Anthropologists may dispute, among themselves or with those whose lives they have tried to narrativize, about the interpretation of what they have written. Disputes may result in convincing one's colleagues, or even one's ethnographic subjects, of the validity of one's account; but there is no assurance that the next generation will be equally persuaded. For conviction (like scepticism) is, as everyone knows, a guarantee of nothing but a state of mind.

Philosophical anxiety about relativism arises in the context of abstracted representations of other bodies and consequent questions about how the representations are related to what they purport to describe. But we cannot specify in advance what arguments will always secure assent regarding the accuracy of the description – not even commitment to the idea of the body as a universal biological datum. Indeed, if our worry is over communicating with members of other cultures about their experience, I cannot see how accepting the idea of the body as a universal datum solves anything. Because, if experience is essentially a matter of pure physiological sense data, then even two persons from the same culture will have a problem talking about it. On the other hand, if

---

[13] Although in the case of some ethnographies independent evidence may be extremely difficult to obtain, a reanalysis of the account offered can be fruitful for developing counter-arguments.

experience is – as Mauss suggested – a function of teachable bodies, then cultural differences are not an insurmountable barrier to communication (communication must not, in any case, be confused with identification), but a reason for trying to understand the practices, the ways of living, that are presupposed by different experiences.

I want to end with some general comments from the direction of practice regarding the universalism of the body. In recent years we have begun to witness new methods of genetic engineering which are largely confined, at present, to the domain of industrial agriculture (Yanchinski 1985; Goodman, Sorj, and Wilkinson 1987). It is clear that, whatever else they signify, the technique of incorporating DNA segments from one organism into the DNA of another undermines at least some long-standing assumptions about biological universalism versus cultural changeability.

At the same time, understanding the modern world as a process of global *interventions* suggests that the social construction of the human body is, if not universal, at any rate universalizable. Within and across modern states and economies there are powerful inducements to individuals everywhere to relate to their bodies aesthetically, so that ideally each individual is encouraged to become self-conscious about 'the inalienable right' to represent, re-create, and pleasure 'one's own' body.

It is not simply how the anthropologist represents other bodies that matters, but what the powers to which he/she belongs do to them. It is precisely here, and not with regard to philosophical relativism, that our anxieties about the body should focus.

BIBLIOGRAPHY

Asad, T. (1987), 'On Ritual and Discipline in Medieval Christian Monasticism', *Economy and Society* 16/2, 159–203.
Benthall, J., and Polhemus, T. (eds.) (1975), *The Body as a Medium of Expression*, London: Allen Lane.
Birtwhistell, R. L., '*Communication without Words*', *Ekistics* 25/151, 439–44.
Blacking, J. (1977), *The Anthropology of The Body*, London: Academic Press.
Bourdieu, P. (1977 [1972]), *Outline of a Theory of Practice*, Cambridge University Press.
Brihaye, J., Loew, F., and Pía, H. W. (eds.) (1985), *Pain: A Medical and Anthropological Challenge*, New York: Springer-Verlag.
Collingwood, R. G. (1938), *The Principles of Art*, London: Oxford University Press.
Darwin, C. (1872), *The Expression of the Emotions in Man and Animals*, London: J. Murray.

de Man, P. (1983), 'The Rhetoric of Temporality', in *Blindness and Insight: Essays in the Rhetoric of Contemporary Criticism*, Minneapolis: University of Minnesota Press.

Douglas, M. (1966), *Purity and Danger: An Analysis of Concepts of Pollution and Taboo*, London: Routledge and Kegan Paul.

(1970), *Natural Symbols: Explorations in Cosmology*, London: Barrie and Rockliffe.

Durkheim, E., and Mauss, M. (1963), 'On Some Primitive Forms of Classification: Contribution to the Study of Collective Representations' (1903), in ed. R. Needham, *Primitive Classifications*, London: Cohen and West.

Evans-Pritchard, E. E. (1965), *Theories of Primitive Religion*, London: Oxford University Press.

Gadamer, H.-G. (1975 (1960)), *Truth and Method*, trans. by G. Barden and J. Cumming, New York: Seabury Press.

Goodman, D., Sorj, B., and Wilkinson, J. (1987), *From Farming to Biotechnology: A Theory of Agro-Industrial Development*, Oxford: Blackwell.

Hertz, R. (1960), 'The Collective Representation of Death' (1907), and 'The Pre-eminence of the Right Hand' (1909), in *Death and The Right Hand*, trans. by R. and C. Needham, London: Cohen and West.

Honour, H. (1979), *Romanticism*, London: Allen Lane.

Hubert, H., and Mauss, M. (1964 [1898]), *Sacrifice: Its Nature and Functions*, trans. by W. D. Halls, London: Cohen and West.

Jackson, M. (1983), 'Knowledge of the Body', *Man*, N.S., 18/2, 327–45.

Lutz, C., and White, G. M. (1986), 'The Anthropology of Emotions', *Annual Review of Anthropology*, vol. 15, 405–36.

Mauss, M. (1979), 'Techniques of the Body' (1935) in *Sociology and Psychology: Essays*, trans. by B. Brewster, London: Routledge and Kegan Paul.

Melzack, R., and Wall, P. (1982), *The Challenge of Pain*, Harmondsworth, Middlesex: Penguin Books.

Needham, R. (1979), *Symbolic Classification*, Santa Monica, CA: Goodyear.

Proctor, R. (1988), 'From Anthropologie to Rassenkunde in the German Anthropological Tradition', in ed. G. W. Stocking, *Bones, Bodies, Behaviour: Essays in Biological Anthropology*, Madison, WI: University of Wisconsin Press.

Polhemus, Ted (ed.) (1978), *Social Aspects of the Human Body*, Harmondsworth, Middlesex: Penguin Books.

Radcliffe-Brown, A.R. (1952), 'Taboo' (1939), in *Structure and Function in Primitive Society*, London: Cohen and West.

Scheper-Hughes, N., and Lock, M. M. (1987), 'The Mindful Body: A Prolegomena to Future Work in Medical Anthropology', *Medical Anthropology Quarterly*, N.S. 1/1, 6–41.

Starobinski, J. (1982), 'A Short History of Body Consciousness', *Humanities in Review* 1, 22–40.

Turner, V. (1969), *The Ritual Process: Structure and Anti-Structure*, London: Routledge and Kegan Paul.

van Gennep, A. (1960 [1909]), *The Rites of Passage*, trans. by M. B. Vizedom and G. L. Caffee, London: Routledge and Kegan Paul.

Volosinov, V. N. (1973), *Marxism and the Philosophy of Language*, New York: Seminar Press.

Wilkinson, J. (1987), *From Farming to Biotechnology: A Theory of Agro-Industrial Development*, Oxford: Basil Blackwell.

Yanchinski, S. (1985), *Setting Genes to Work: The Industrial Era of Biotechnology*, Harmondsworth: Penguin Books.

CHAPTER 4

The soul's successors: philosophy and the 'body'

Mary Midgley

THE SURPRISING PERSISTENCE OF MIND

What does our secular and scientific culture think today about the relation between mind and body? The question may sound old-fashioned; when, according to the majority secularist view, there is obviously nothing *but* a body, why should it relate to anything? If certain confusions do result from Descartes' having sliced human beings down the middle, many people feel that the best cure is just to drop the immaterial half altogether.

The early Behaviourists said this explicitly;[1] mind and consciousness were simply myths. Philosophically, this attitude is still very widespread. Amputation of the 'mind' is to be performed by reductive techniques, translating whatever needs to be said about minds into statements about bodies. Eventually, these remarks will be checkable by laboratory experiments. The philosophers who favour this programme are known as Physicalists.[2] Sometimes they promote it with brutal zest, sometimes quite apologetically and kindly.

Whether this proposal could ever make sense anywhere is uncertain.[3] (Proposals about translation always sound better as grand abstract projects than they do when people try to work them out in detail.) But certainly the thing cannot be acceptably done in our culture *at large* today, for moral reasons. It clashes with the moral position which is central to the very attitude that calls for this scientific reduction. It offends against individualism.

[1] See, e.g. Skinner 1953.
[2] For an early influential form of physicalism, see Smart 1969. Introductory textbooks on the philosophy of mind (such as Teichman 1988) provide useful accounts of current variations on the physicalist theme, as well as giving an overview of successive fashions in the philosophy of mind in this century: from early behaviourism and physicalism, through linguistic behaviourism, to mind/brain identity theories.
[3] A detailed account of this debate is provided by the contributors in eds. Warner and Szubka 1994 (which includes a number of 'dualist' detractors from reductive forms of physicalism). Taliaferro (1994) has recently provided a painstaking (and critical) analysis of different forms of materialism from a theistic standpoint.

When the sages of the Enlightenment deposed God and demystified Mother Nature, they did not leave us without an object of reverence. The human soul, renamed as the individual[4] – free, autonomous, and creative – succeeded to that post, and has been confirmed in it with increasing sureness ever since. Though it is not expected to be immortal, it is still our pearl of great price. Thus, paradoxical as it may seem, our 'materialist' culture takes for granted an entity that its 'physicalist' philosophers have by and large rejected.

Can we then, without offence, describe this awe-striking object reductively and indirectly, as a mere function of the body? Scarcely. Freedom and independence from the compulsions of that body are seen as crucial to its special value. The individual, according to one influential view spawned by the Enlightenment, is essentially a will using an intellect. This individual is still widely conceived as the eighteenth-century sages conceived it, as active reason, asserting itself in a battle against passive feeling, which is seen as relatively subhuman – a merely animal affair, emanating from the body. The dignity of the will rests on controlling and conquering that feeling.[5]

The dominance of this model has been serious philosophical business, but it cannot be dealt with only by citing academic philosophy. Indeed, as this model wanes in attractiveness to professional philosophers, its general cultural appeal appears, ironically, the more prevalent. Big conceptual schemes like this work at every level in our lives. The conceptual framework is indeed its skeleton, but skeletons do not go about nude. Concepts are embodied in myths and fantasies, in images, ideologies and half-beliefs, in hopes and fears, in shame, pride, and vanity. Like the great philosophers of the past who helped to shape our tradition, we need to start from there.

THE NEED TO TAKE SIDES

The mind/body division evokes the general human tendency to dramatize conflicts. If asked 'what does a human being consist in?' theorists readily pick out two elements which seem to oppose each other, because such opposition is striking, and indeed often does need our

---

[4] 'Individualism' is a term with a variety of meanings (on which see Lukes 1973); here I am employing it to denote a distinctive (philosophical) view of the self spawned by the Enlightenment and emphasizing the supreme value of personal autonomy and (libertarian) freedom.
[5] For a succinct, but highly revealing, feminist account of *different* Enlightenment visions of the 'man of reason' (and his attitudes toward will, feeling, and body), see Lloyd 1984.

attention. This is not the only way to start thinking about human personality, but it has been very active in our tradition. Paul the Apostle, following Plato, wrote that 'the flesh lusts against the spirit and the spirit against the flesh, so that ye cannot do the thing which ye would' (Galatians 5:17), and the idea became a moral commonplace.

The notions of both mind and body have therefore been shaped, from the start, by their roles as opponents in this drama. Without this, the sharp division between them may lose much of its point. 'Perhaps', one might want to say, 'a human being is a whole and acts as a whole, in spite of these inner conflicts. Never mind for the moment what may happen after death; in this life what matters is to look beyond conflicts to the integration of the personality.'

Indeed, the notion that mind opposes body, when baldly stated, may sound rather puritanical today. Yet the idea that such a drama is essential to human dignity is still powerful. The actions by which the will is to show its independence may indeed now be different ones. We praise a bold adultery rather than a martyrdom. But this is not really a concession to the flesh. What is admired is the boldness.[6] The ideal of asserting one's own will rather than doing what comes naturally is as strong as ever. The force of this model can be seen in a hundred theoretical battles. It appeared notably in the violent objection to 'biological determinism' which greeted the sociobiologists' suggestion that human motivation might owe something to genetic causes (see Midgley 1980, opening chapters).

There were certainly other things badly wrong with sociobiological thinking (see Midgley 1979), but this particular complaint was bizarre. Why should biological causes be specially objectionable among the many sorts of causes which – on any view – set the scene for human action? Why were genetic influences more offensive than social conditioning, whose presence nobody doubted? Was it really supposed that hormones did not affect our moods, or that babies started life with no feelings and no tendency to develop any particular sort of feeling? Was our whole emotional and imaginative life then sheer imitation, a set of behaviour-patterns imprinted from outside on passive material by our society? Or, if we occasionally escaped from those influences, were we always performing some existential miracle of self-assertion, without source in the world around us? Had genius (for instance) no roots in the individual physical constitution? Do our *bodies* play no part in our

---

[6] This particular view of the will arguably owes more to Nietzsche than to earlier (Enlightenment) figures. See my more specific discussion of Nietzsche below.

personal lives except as an inert vehicle, a dough, or occasionally an impediment?

These are, I think, positions which no one would accept today on their own merits. Yet many people of good will have thought them both factually true and morally necessary. Their appeal flows from powerful imaginative patterns used by the sages of the Enlightenment. Those patterns have served us well, but they are now reaching the limits of their usefulness.

Enlightenment thinking was not, any more than any other style of thinking, wholly impartial, detached, rational, and impersonal. It was, in fact, as practical, as local, as much coloured by particular political and social programmes, and by the private quirks of its inventors, as any other body of thought. Since we have by now taken in much of what is good in it, we need to attend sharply now to these foreign bodies.

THE SOLITARY WILL (AND THE FORGOTTEN BODY)

The central question is about personal identity, about what 'I' essentially am. The view of Enlightenment rationalism about this was badly flawed. Crudely – and we have to be crude here to bring the matter out into the open – this notion showed the essential self as consisting in reason. That meant an isolated will, guided by an intelligence, arbitrarily connected to a rather unsatisfactory array of feelings, and lodged, by chance, in an equally unsatisfactory human body. Externally, this being stood alone. Each individual's relation to all others was optional, to be arranged at will by contract. It depended on the calculations of the intellect about self-interest and on views of that interest freely chosen by the will.[7]

This is, fairly clearly, not an uncontentious or *obvious* picture of the human condition. How came it to be widely accepted? The answer is, of course, that it was devised largely for particular, quite urgent, political purposes connected with civic freedom and the vote. The social-contract conceptual scheme was a tool, a wire-cutter for freeing us from mistaken allegiance to kings, churches, and customs. Like other such tools, this way of thinking was carefully not used in places which did not suit those purposes. In particular, it was originally applied only to men, and any later attempts to extend it to women aroused painful indignation and

---

[7] This is, of course, a generalization about developments in the Enlightenment period. For more detailed accounts of different leading philosophers' perceptions of the self (and the will) in political context, see Moller Okin 1980; Elshtain 1981; and Lloyd 1984.

confusion. Each man – each voter – was conceived as representing and defending his household. There was no question of its other members needing to speak for themselves.

WHY THE CASE OF WOMEN MATTERS: WOMEN AND THE BODY

This is not a perverse or irrelevant point. It is no trifling matter that the whole idea of an independent, inquiring, choosing individual, an idea central to Western thought, has always been essentially the – somewhat romanticized – idea of a male. It was so developed by the Greeks, and still more by the great libertarian movements of the eighteenth century (see Moller Okin 1980). It was no accident that their cry was for 'the rights of man' and for 'one man, one vote'. For implicit in these developments was a covert identification of the 'individual' will with the male, and of the neglected body (and feeling) with the female. Rousseau himself, the great architect of modern social-contract thinking and champion of individual freedom, denied firmly that any such ideas could be extended to women. 'Girls', he explained

should early be accustomed to restraint, because all their life long they will have to submit to the most enduring restraints, those of propriety . . . They have, or ought to have, little freedom . . . As a woman's conduct is controlled by public opinion, so is her religion ruled by authority . . . Unable to judge for themselves, they should accept the judgment of father and husband as that of the church. (Rousseau 1966, Book v, 332)

So wrote the man who owed his whole career to the devoted, intelligent, educated encouragement of Mesdames de Warens, d'Épinay, and others, in the book (*Émile*) whose main theme is the need for complete freedom in the education of boys. As for equality, that too, he said, was solely a male affair. 'Woman is made to submit to man and to endure even injustice at his hands' (ibid., 359).

At the end of the eighteenth century, Mary Wollstonecraft pointed out that this was odd, and suggested in her *Vindication of the Rights of Women* that Rousseau's ideals should extend to both sexes (Wollstonecraft 1975). Horace Walpole voiced the general fury by calling her 'a hyaena in petticoats'. And, throughout the nineteenth century, proposals to educate and enfranchise women continued to produce similar frenzy. They were not just opposed as troublesome and inconvenient, but as monstrous – a view supported by amazingly feeble arguments.

THE LIE IN THE SOUL

It surely emerges that the original, sex-linked idea of a free and independent individual had not been thoroughly thought through. Despite its force and nobility, that idea contained a deep strain of falsity. The trouble is not just that the reason why it should apply only to one half of the human race was not honestly considered. It is that the supposed independence of the male was itself false. It was parasitical, taking for granted the love and service of non-autonomous females – and indeed, usually of the less enlightened males as well (for these it was who provided for the needs of 'bodily' life). It pretended to be universal when it was not.

Mutual dependence is central to all human life. The equivocal, unrealistic dismissal of it does not just inconvenience women. It distorts morality by a lop-sided melodrama. It causes the virtues that we need for giving and receiving love and service (and indeed for catering for everyday 'bodily' needs) to be uncritically downgraded, while those involved in self-assertion are uncritically exalted – except, of course, when they are displayed by women. The point is not just that heroic male virtues are getting exalted over 'passive' female ones. It is that, in truth, both sexes need, and can practise, all the virtues. Though there are real (some would still say 'natural') differences between men and women (see Midgley 1988), they do not have this drastic moral consequence. The official, wholly separate, ideal of manhood as disembodied will is a distorted one. It damages men's lives as well as women's. The supposed gender-division of moral labour is, and always was, a lie.

Mary Wollstonecraft's protest was maddening to her contemporaries because it was so plainly justified. She was not changing the rules. The individualistic tradition, being supposedly radical and universal, did indeed demand to be extended to females. But it had been so shaped that it could not be. It rested on an unreal, stereotyped notion of the relation between gender and the virtues. Though stark, honest realism had always been the watchword of the rationalist tradition, on this matter it was riddled by evasion, bias, and self-deception.

To put the point another way: 'feminism' is not the name of some new doctrine, imported into controversies arbitrarily and for no good reason. That name stands for the steady, systematic correction of an ancient and very damaging bias. Virism has always reigned unnoticed. Correcting it is not a single, simple move. It demands different emphasis in different places because the bias has worked unevenly.[8] Like other corrections, feminism might hope in the end to become unnecessary and so to put itself out of business. But that end is at present a long way off.

NIETZSCHE, SARTRE, AND THE PRIVATIZATION OF MORALITY

The kind of bad faith just mentioned has been specially crippling in the strain of extreme individualism that is generally seen as belonging to the Left – the near-anarchistic strain that descends from Rousseau through Nietzsche and Heidegger to Sartre, and to a wide variety of present-day egoistic individualism, as well as the more right-facing kinds expressed in monetarism and sociobiology (see Easlea 1981). Modern feminists, unfortunately, initially put a lot of confidence in this tradition, and did not at once subject Nietzsche to anything like the well-deserved acid bath that they gave Freud.[9] (Sartre's influence, transmitted through Simone de Beauvoir, probably protected him.) It is worth reflecting on how this strand of tradition significantly (if indirectly) has bearing on the mind/body problem.

What Nietzsche did was to move the good will, which Kant had placed at the centre of morals, from a social to a solitary habitat. For Kant, the good will was the rational will. It respected all other rational beings, and agreed to moral laws which they too could find reasonable. It was united with them in the 'Kingdom of Ends' – not, of course, an actual state, but an ideal, imagined community in which all could in principle agree on values.

Nietzsche, though deeply impressed with Kant's assertion of the dignity of the will, rejected this communalism. On the one hand he was far too sceptical about moral reasoning to suppose rational agreement possible. On the other, he – himself a solitary – was merely disgusted by Kant's ideal of social harmony and communal virtue:

A word against Kant as moralist. A virtue has to be *our* invention, our more personal defence and necessity; in any other sense it is merely a danger . . . 'Virtue', 'duty', 'good in itself'; impersonal and universal – phantoms, expressions of decline, of the final exhaustion of life, of Konigsbergian Chinadom. The profoundest laws of preservation and growth demand the reverse of this; that each one of us should devise his own virtue, his own categorical imperative. (Nietzsche 1969, *The Anti-Christ*, sec. 11, 121)

[8] This point is made most sharply by Spelman (1988) in her critique of an 'essentialist' vision of women's needs and goals.
[9] However, for a brilliant recent exposé of the dangers to feminism of an overhasty alliance with 'Nietzschean' post-modernism, see Lovibond 1989.

This, he said, would naturally lead any enlightened person to live alone, despising his contemporaries, and rejecting all claims by others on fellowship or compassion, feelings which he regarded as shameful weakness. Nietzsche advertised this ideal strongly as a virile one, and buttressed it by a great deal of spiteful misogyny in the style of Rousseau and Schopenhauer. He did not, apparently, see that solitude might as easily be a refuge for weakness as an assertion of strength, nor that childish boasting about one's own superiority makes this interpretation rather likely.

Nietzsche was, of course, in many ways an impressive and serious thinker. But he was an astonishingly uneven and unselfcritical one. His chosen solitude made it hard for him to spot defects in his thought, and – exactly as happened with Rousseau – in that protected environment his neuroses, flourishing like green bay-trees, often seized his pen and distorted his metaphysics.

It is not possible to make literal, explicit sense of the idea of many private, personalized moralities, all quite separate from each other. Nietzsche may indeed not have meant us to take it literally, for he always worked through rhetoric and often laughed at systematic theorists. But, since he has become a recognized sage, people do take it literally. Fantasies like this are, of course, quite as influential as completed systems, and Nietzsche certainly meant them to be influential.

The respectful way to treat him is not to put all his views politely in a museum, but to do as he did himself and point out sharply which of the things he said have living value, and which are – like this one – poppycock. (For further discussion of Immoralism, see Midgley 1984, chapter 2, and Midgley 1990.)

This Nietzschean moral fantasy is surely the source of Sartre's similar suggestions that we need, in some sense, to create or invent our own values. Values might in principle be anything. 'One can', he says, 'choose anything, but only if it is upon the plane of true commitment'. Someone might, he adds, object that

'your values are not serious, since you choose them yourselves'. To that I can only say that I am very sorry that it should be so, but if I have excluded God the Father, there must be somebody to invent values. (Sartre 1948, 54)

So what happens (as the philosopher Philippa Foot once asked) if I choose that the only value shall be not-treading-on-the-lines-of-the-paving-stones, or perhaps sneezing-every-ten-minutes (see Foot 1954)? Would this then become a value? Certainly it is not one at the present, but then that is just why I have had to invent it. If I show true commitment – devote my life to doing these things – will that constitute these as my invented values? Or does commitment perhaps also involve vigorous efforts to convert others to doing them too?

The interesting question is, what is wrong with this example? Plainly, we would not in fact see it as an instance of moral freedom, but of obsession – that is, of being made *unfree* by an arbitrary compulsion, extraneous to the personality. What is the difference? Philippa Foot pointed out that, though perhaps anything could, in principle, be said to have value, not everything can be so described intelligibly. The question always arises, what kind of value does it have? When people praise something that we do not see the point of, we ask for that point, and often we are given it. This is necessary, not just to convince others, but for our own satisfaction. The sneezer or paving-stone-avoider might explain their precepts as religious rituals, or perhaps as promoting health. But they would have to make it clear why they were so, and they would depend, both for satisfying themselves and for convincing anyone else, on a pre-existing, shared understanding of the sort of value that health or religion themselves have. Language is not private. What makes the point intelligible is a background range of values and ideals, furnished partly by our culture, but also, more deeply, by our common species-repertoire.

Kant, in fact, was not being silly in emphasizing the communal background needed for morality. No doubt he was too narrow in his ideas of what was actually moral conduct, and also too confident about the role of reasoning – as opposed to feeling – in producing agreement. But he was right that background agreement was necessary, and that new, free thinking must be intelligibly related to what it grew out of. Moral insights are not explosions, interrupting all previous thought. They are organic growths, continuing existing lines. However startling they may be, they always arise from a community, and they always aspire to go on and influence a community.

How seriously were these professions of solipsistic moral independence actually meant? They have certainly been of enormous use to adolescents at the stage of life when they need to develop away from their homes. (At that point it may sometimes even be necessary to forget for the moment one's dependence on others.) They also have a particular value in public situations such as Sartre's – that of the French Resistance during the Second World War – where outside circumstances force a sudden, drastic change in the moral options open to people. But at other times it is hard to see what they could amount to.

In actual life, both Sartre and Nietzsche were men of principle, who in fact took a great deal of trouble to justify their actions to others, and sometimes vigorously to promote particular public causes. In doing this, they used the common moral vocabulary without embarrassment, and appealed to existing notions of value. They did indeed show originality in making new moral suggestions, in a way which can well be described as refining or extending or reshaping values. But what could it mean to invent a new one? And if this were somehow done, how could it appear as the work of the will rather than of the imagination? More significantly, for our present purposes, what had become of the 'body'?

WHICH WAY IS LEFT?

The whole idea of centering human personality on the (disembodied) will is, I think, imaginative and moral propaganda rather than a piece of dispassionate psychological analysis. It is an image designed to move people from certain current positions, an image which ought never to have been let harden into a metaphysical doctrine about what a human being essentially is. Up to a point, no doubt, all such ideas are coloured in this way. That is why it is essential to understand what their message is – how they are intended to work. Politically, this exaltation of the individual will has in the past been popular on the 'Left' in so far as Leftness means innovation, because the will was needed in order to break free from the emotional bonds of convention. Besides, demands for individual freedom – of a modest, political sort, not extreme Sartrean internal freedom – are another mark of Leftness.

The Right/Left antithesis is, however, confused and unhelpful on this topic, as on many others. It is not clear where, on that political spectrum, we should place the unspoken creed which runs, 'I believe only in the independent, creative individual. The one certain human duty is to avoid interfering with that individual, and it is a duty demanded particularly from women.' If there is such a spectrum, its ends run round behind and join each other.

On the recognized Right, the ideal of a free spirit as a heroic individual, poised above the multitude, has been very powerful. Nietzsche liked it, but its most eloquent proponent was Carlyle, who is worth hearing on our present topic. After his wife's death, Carlyle told Tyndall broken-heartedly 'how loyally and lovingly she had made herself a soft cushion to protect him from the rude collisions of the world'.

How could someone whose lifelong theme was heroism, and who held great audiences spellbound by celebrating it, make such a claim and such an admission? Why did he need his 'cushion'? Clashes between ideals never bothered Carlyle much, since he thought consistency rather a fiddling consideration anyway. But he also had a real advantage here over many theorists of his time and ours in that he had never claimed to subscribe to the ideals of liberty, equality, and fraternity. Could people who did subscribe to them take the same line about women? It might seem hard, but most of them managed it. As Mill remarked:

The social subordination of women stands out, an isolated fact in modern social institutions . . . a single relic of an old world of thought and practice exploded in everything else, but retained in the one thing of most universal interest; as if a gigantic dolmen, or temple of Jupiter Olympius, occupied the site of St. Paul's and received daily worship, while the surrounding Christian churches were resorted to only on fasts and festivals. (Mill 1970, 21)

Women (that is) were still called on to remain hierarchical, feudal, emotional, 'bodily', and biological, in order to make it possible for the men to become totally free, equal, autonomous, intellectual, and creative.

IMAGES IN MANY MIRRORS

As far as this *political* proposal goes – which, of course, is not the central point of the present chapter – that game is surely now up. Too many women have noticed the absurdity of the demand, and are impolite enough to mention it. They cannot all be put down by being called 'hyaenas in petticoats'. Politically speaking, then, the choice now is between promoting everybody, equally, to the position of the Hobbesian or Sartrean solitary individual, or rethinking the notion of individuality radically from scratch. It is cheering to see that feminists are now proving very critical of the moves toward the first solution, which were rather common a decade or two back.[10] Undoubtedly, the rethinking option is the one we shall have to try. Much good feminist writing now is devoted to attempting it,[11] and it is, of course, what I am trying to forward in this

[10] For a particularly clear discussion of the brands of feminism that have succeeded its initial (individualistic and 'liberal') form, see Jaggar (1983), who promotes a form of 'socialist' feminism.
[11] For feminist writers who have turned to explore the *specific* moral attributes and gifts of women, see, for example, Gilligan 1982; Noddings 1984; Ruddick 1989. Grimshaw (1986, especially chs. 5 and 6) provides a useful philosophical account of the *tension* in feminism between the (individualistic) quest for autonomy on the one hand, and the interest in caring and 'relatedness' on the other, and offers astute criticism of both these tendencies when presented in unguarded or extreme form.

chapter. But the way forward is by no means clear or unambiguous.[12]

Then why (you are still wondering) do I persist in talking about the relations between the sexes instead of getting down directly to the mind/body problem? I answer: *because mind/body problems, being queries about ourselves, never do present themselves to us directly.* They are always seen reflected indirectly in some mirror or other, and the distortions of the particular mirror are crucial to understanding them. They always appear in our lives in terms of myth, and the current myths are shot through with dramas about gender.

Consider, for instance, these remarks from Sartre, when, in his exaltation of the will, he has occasion to denounce physical matter as alien to it, and therefore to our essential being. We could hardly hope for a more explicit connection of the physical or bodily and the 'feminine'. He describes the material world as 'viscous', clinging to us in order to entrap us:

The For-Itself is suddenly *compromised.* I open my hands, I want to let go of the slimy and it sticks to me, it draws me, it sucks at me . . . It is a soft, yielding action, a moist and feminine sucking . . . it draws me to it as the bottom of a precipice might draw me . . . Slime is the revenge of the In-Itself. A sickly-sweet, feminine revenge . . . The obscenity of the feminine sex is that of everything which 'gapes open'. It is an *appeal to being,* as all holes are . . . Beyond any doubt her sex is a mouth and a voracious mouth which devours the penis. (Sartre 1966, 776–7, 782; discussed by Easlea 1981, 40, 58)

This shows how extraordinarily easy it is, when trying to talk about the whole human condition, to project one's fantasies onto this vast screen, and how dominant, among such fantasies, is the kind of conflict which readily presents itself both as one of reason versus feeling and also as one between the sexes. Certainly, this is an unguarded passage, not the sort of thing that would appear in sober Anglo-American philosophical journals. Of course I have chosen it for that reason. But these bizarre statements about the isolation of the will are useful just because they are unguarded. We have grown so used to the greyer, more moderate forms that they pervade our thinking and are hard to notice. For instance, R. M. Hare's highly respectable, academic, 'prescriptivist' account of morals (Hare 1952) could be argued to have at its root a notion of individual moral freedom not wholly unlike Sartre's existentialist one (despite all the differences). Could it therefore be that it owes its success

[12] Not only is there the negotiation to be made between the goals of autonomy and relatedness (see n. 11), but also between post-modern trends in philosophy (in some ways apparently liberating for women) and critical feminist assessments of them. For debate on the latter issue, see ed. Nicholson 1990.

to the fact that its readers had, at some imaginative level, already accepted the more colourful existentialist account? The point I have been raising here is what 'package' of assumptions goes along with such a view? What unspoken prejudices about 'bodiliness' and femaleness? These questions are always worth probing.

THE APOTHEOSIS OF THE INTELLECT

So far, I have been dealing chiefly with the notion of the essential self as the will. The will has, however, always been thought of as accompanied by, and using, the intellect. 'Reason' in the eighteenth-century sense included both; indeed, as Kant put it, the will simply is practical reason. Today, this idea has branched away from straightforward exaltation of the will to produce a rival diagnosis of personal identity as centring on the scientific intellect.

This is now a powerful idea, especially where people interested in artificial intelligence want to blur the differences between people and computer programs. Space allows me only a single example of this syndrome, and for reasons already given I choose a lurid one, which is, however, backed by some highly respected scientists. (I have discussed it elsewhere: see Midgley 1992.)

It has for some time been proposed that *Homo Sapiens* should colonize space, and should, for convenience in this project, transform himself mechanically into non-organic forms. This project is now held to look increasingly feasible, on the grounds that computer software is the same whatever kind of hardware it runs on, and that minds are only a kind of computer software. Thus, as the eminent Princeton physicist Freeman Dyson puts it:

It is impossible to set any limit to the variety of physical forms that life may assume . . . It is conceivable that in another 10^{10} years life could evolve away from flesh and blood and become embodied in an interstellar black cloud . . . or in a sentient computer . . . (Dyson 1979, 453)

Our successors can thus not only avoid ordinary death, but also survive (if you care to call it surviving) the heat-death of the universe, and sit about exchanging opinions in an otherwise empty cosmos. This, Dyson thinks, would restore the meaning to life, which has otherwise been drained from it by the thought that final destruction is unavoidable. Could fear and hatred of the flesh go further? J. D. Bernal, a founding father of this movement, expressed it well:

As the scene of life would be more the cold emptiness of space than the warm, dense atmosphere of the planets, the advantage of containing no organic material at all . . . would be increasingly felt . . . *Bodies at this time would be left far behind* . . . Bit by bit, the heritage in the direct line of mankind – the heritage of the original life emerging on the face of the world – would dwindle, and in the end disappear effectively, being preserved perhaps as some curious relic. (Bernal 1929, 56–7, my emphasis).

Reason, in fact, can at last divorce the unsatisfactory wife he has been complaining of since the eighteenth century, and live comfortably for ever among the boys playing computer-games in the solitudes of space. Is that not touching?

CONCLUSION

Of course the cult of the cerebral has milder, less frantic aspects and did not originally require such aberrations. But it has hypertrophied, and today it generates them. The individual will and intellect are exalted in a way that can make any interference with them – even that of the other features of the organism they belong to – seem an outrage.

Moral solipsism is on offer. It is not just that rational choice is exalted high above the emotions. It has also been sharply separated from them, treated as the central, necessary part of the personal identity while the emotions are a chance, extraneous matter. This analysis is not just inhumane, it is incoherent. Choice and thought cannot be separated from feeling and imagination; they are all aspects of personality. Exalters of choice and of the intellect are not free from feeling; they are unconsciously led by one set of feelings rather than another – often to very strange and disagreeable places (see Dent 1984). The division between mind and body, conceived as essentially one between reason and feeling, is not necessary. There is no set of perforations down the middle of a human being directing us to tear at this point.

Contemporary philosophers have noted this in a variety of very useful discussions.[13] Unlike the popular mythologies we have been examining, recent philosophy of mind has done its best to see off the disembodied hero of the Enlightenment: its preference remains, overwhelmingly, for a 'materialist' account of the mind/body relation, however subtly enunciated.[14] What is ironic, however, about this ostensible rejection of

[13] *Compendia* of contemporary views on the matter of personal identity which remain useful are ed. Perry 1975 and ed. Rorty 1976. Taliaferro's more recent (1994) survey of current opinions goes on to argue for an 'integrative dualism' that will (he contends) avoid this 'perforation' factor.

[14] This is evident from the selection of essays in eds. Warner and Szubka 1994, despite the care taken to include a full range of opinions.

'dualism' by most contemporary philosophers of mind, is the persistence in their thinking of shades of the Enlightenment ghost they thought they had routed. For, when they discourse about the 'mind/body' relation, they rarely consider anything in that 'body' below the level of the neck. Either they focus exclusively on the mind's relation to the brain, or, more generally, on its relation to the physical world *tout court.*[15] Flesh and bones (and, unsurprisingly, women's minds) are still relatively neglected subjects in the field.

BIBLIOGRAPHY

Bernal, J. D. (1929), *The World, The Flesh and the Devil*, London: Kegan Paul.

Dent, N. J. H. (1984), *The Moral Psychology of the Virtues*, Cambridge University Press.

Dyson, F. (1979), 'Time Without End; Physics and Biology in an Open Universe', *Reviews of Modern Physics* 51, 447–60.

Easlea, B. (1981), *Science and Sexual Oppression*, London: Weidenfeld and Nicolson.

Elshtain, J. Bethke (1981), *Public Man, Private Woman: Women in Social and Political Thought*, Princeton University Press.

Foot, P. (1954), 'When is a Principle a Moral Principle?' *Belief and Will: Aristotelian Society supplementary volume* XXVIII; London: Harrison, 95–110.

Gilligan, C. (1982), *In A Different Voice*, Cambridge, MA: Harvard University Press.

Grimshaw, J. (1986), *Feminist Philosophers*, London: Harvester Wheatsheaf.

Hare, R. M. (1952), *The Language of Morals*, Oxford: Clarendon Press.

Jaggar, A. (1983), *Feminist Politics and Human Nature*, Brighton: Harvester.

Johnson, M. (1987), *The Body in the Mind: The Bodily Basis of Meaning, Imagination and Reason*, University of Chicago Press.

Kant, I. (1948), *The Moral Law* (sometimes also called *Groundwork of the Metaphysics of Morals*), trans. by H. J. Paton, London: Hutchinson.

Lloyd, G. (1984), *The Man of Reason: 'Male' and 'Female' in Western Philosophy*, Minneapolis: University of Minnesota Press.

Lovibond, S. (1989), 'Feminism and Postmodernism', *New Left Review* 178, 5–28.

Lukes, S. (1973), *Individualism*, Oxford: Basil Blackwell.

Midgley, M. (1979), 'Gene-Juggling', *Philosophy*, 54, 439–58.

(1980), *Beast and Man*, London: Methuen.

[15] This is in some ways fully understandable, given the intricacies (and apparent mysteries) of the mind's relation to brain-function, and the prevalent scepticism about the mind's independent status over against the 'natural' world at all. None the less it is striking how little attention is given in the literature of analytic philosophy of mind to the fleshliness of (individual) bodies. A partial exception to this rule is found in the work of John Searle (see, for example, Searle 1982, especially chs. 3 and 4), in his *detailed* attention to the relation between human intentionality and physical movements; and another quite different, corrective is suggested by Johnson (1987) in his examination of the bodily basis of the role of imagination in philosophical reasoning. For specifically *feminist* critiques of prevalent views of 'reason', see the useful recent survey article and bibliography, Rooney 1994. Not a great deal of feminist attention has yet been given, however, to the more technical debates of analytic philosophy of mind.

(1984), *Wickedness*, London: Routledge.

(1988), 'On Not Being Afraid of Natural Sex Differences', in eds. M. Griffiths and M. Whitford, *Feminist Perspectives in Philosophy*, London: Macmillan, 29–41.

(1990), *Can't We Make Moral Judgments?* Bristol Classical Press.

(1992), *Science as Salvation: A Modern Myth and its Meaning*, London: Routledge.

Mill, J. S. (1970), *The Subjection of Women*, London and Cambridge, MA: MIT Press.

Moller Okin, S. (1980), *Women in Western Political Thought*, London: Virago.

Nicholson, L. J. (ed.) (1990), *Feminism/Postmodernism*, New York: Routledge.

Nietzsche, F. (1969), *Twilight of the Idols and The Antichrist*, trans. by R. J. Hollingdale, Harmondsworth: Penguin.

Noddings, N. (1984), *Caring: A Feminine Approach to Ethics and Moral Education*, Berkeley: University of California Press.

Perry, J. (ed.) (1975), *Personal Identity*, Berkeley: University of California Press.

Rooney, P. (1994), 'Recent Work in Feminist Discussions of Reason', *American Philosophical Quarterly* 31, 1–21.

Rorty, A. (ed.) (1976), *The Identities of Persons*, Berkeley: University of California Press.

Rousseau, J. J. (1966), *Émile, or On Education*, trans. by B. Foxley, London and New York: Dent and Dutton.

Ruddick, S. (1989), *Maternal Thinking: Toward a Politics of Peace*, New York: Ballantine.

Sartre, J. P. (1948), *Existentialism and Humanism*, trans. by Philip Mairet, London: Methuen.

(1966), *Being and Nothingness*, trans. by Hazel E. Barnes, New York: Washington Square Press.

Searle, J. R. (1983), *Intentionality*, Cambridge University Press.

Skinner, B. F. (originally 1953; 1983), *Science and Human Behavior*, New York: Macmillan.

Smart, J. C. C. (1969), *Philosophy and Scientific Realism*, London: Routledge and Kegan Paul.

Spelman, E. V. (1988), *Inessential Woman: Problems of Exclusion in Feminist Thought*, Boston: Beacon Press.

Taliaferro, C. (1994), *Mind and the Consciousness of God*, Cambridge University Press.

Teichman, J. (1988), *Philosophy and the Mind*, Oxford: Basil Blackwell.

Warner, R., and Szubka, T. (eds.) (1994), *The Mind–Body Problem*, Oxford: Basil Blackwell.

Wollstonecraft, M. (1975), *Vindication of the Rights of Women*, Harmondsworth: Pelican.

PART II

The Western religious inheritance: Judaism and Christianity on the body

CHAPTER 5

The body in Jewish worship: three rituals examined

Louis Jacobs

In this chapter the relationship is examined between body and soul as expressed in three Jewish rituals – the sabbath rituals, the death and burial rites, and the priestly blessing – with a view to uncovering some of the nuances of this relationship in Judaism in general. It is hoped that in the process the lie will be given to the caricature of Judaism as a religion with its stress above all on the physical body in its relationship to the divine. Any neat distinction, say, between Christianity, supposedly concerned primarily with the soul, and Judaism, supposedly concerned primarily with the body, must be rejected if only because of the complexity of the issue. There is no single, official view in Judaism (and, I imagine, the same is true of Christianity) on this and on similar extremely involved topics. Modern scholarly investigation has succeeded in demonstrating that religions have a history in which ideas, forms, and rituals have developed in response to changing social, economic, political, and even climatic conditions, and that the particular temperament of religious teachers has also had its effect. These facts go a long way to explaining why no article on the body is found in the standard Jewish encyclopedias; nor has any monograph been published on Jewish attitudes to the body. The task of the historian of Jewish ideas and rituals is to try to collate stray references in diverse sources, produced over lengthy periods of time, so as to produce some kind of systematic picture, being fully aware that in the very process he is imposing categories not really present in the sources.

Here is not the place for anything like a history of Jewish thought on the body through the various stages of Jewish civilization; but a brief, preliminary and tentative overview cannot be dispensed with altogether if the rituals we are examining are accurately to be understood.

The minds of Old Testament scholars have been much exercised in discovering whether the Biblical authors ever entertain the notion of body and soul as two distinct entities that have become conjoined, or

71

whether, for these authors, there is only a single entity, what we (but not the biblical authors themselves) call the human being or human person. In the second creation narrative (Genesis 2:7) the formation of Adam is described as: 'And the Lord God formed man of the dust of the ground, and breathed into his nostrils the breath of life; and man became a living soul.' But the original Hebrew, *nefesh ḥayyah*, translated as 'living soul', certainly has no reference to the soul as a separate entity – this is ruled out, in any event, by the context. The nearest in our language to what is implied is rather 'a living person'. Similarly, in the parallel to Genesis it is said of the death of the body: 'Then shall the dust return to the earth as it was; and the spirit shall return unto God who gave it' (Ecclesiastes 12:7). It is true that the later Jewish tradition reads into this latter verse the idea that at the death of the body the soul leaves to return to God, residing with Him for ever, but it is a moot point whether the author of Ecclesiastes himself was thinking of an immortal soul which leaves its temporal abode, the body, when the latter dies. It has often been noted that, while it would be too much to say that the Old Testament knows nothing at all of an immortal soul, belief in the Hereafter generally is only faintly implied; possibly because, in the early biblical period, at least, the other world was the domain of the gods against the worship of whom the biblical authors so strongly protest.

Under the influence of Greek thought, ideas such as the complete distinctiveness of body and soul and conflict between the two did emerge in Judaism, especially in the Greek-speaking community of Alexandria, the foremost representative of which is Philo, whose eschatology is confined to the immortality of the soul and who knows nothing of the later Rabbinic doctrine of bodily resurrection at the end of time. The most pronounced element, however, in subsequent Jewish thought is that of the Talmudic rabbis (Philo is not mentioned at all in the traditional Jewish sources until as late as the sixteenth century). The Rabbinic views, much closer to religious poetry than to precise, theological statement, are found in the Mishnah (edited around the year CE 200); the Jerusalem Talmud (edited around CE 400); and the Babylonian Talmud (edited around CE 500). In the Talmudic/Rabbinic literature the dichotomy between body and soul is everywhere present but the holistic implications of many of the earlier, biblical passages are also, though somewhat paradoxically, acknowledged, as the following typical passages demonstrate:

1. Rabbi Eleazar son of Rabbi Zadok said: 'To what are the righteous compared in this world? To a tree standing wholly in a place of purity, but its bough overhangs to a place of impurity; when the bough is lopped off, it stands entirely in a place of purity. Thus the Holy One, blessed be He, brings suffering upon the righteous in this world, in order that they may inherit the World to Come . . . And to what are the wicked compared in this world? To a tree standing wholly in a place of impurity, but its bough overhangs a place of purity; when the bough is lopped off, it stands entirely in a place of impurity. Thus the Holy one, blessed be He, provides them with goodness in this world, in order to destroy them, consigning them to the nethermost rung.' (*Kiddushin* 40b)

2. Antoninus said to Rabbi Judah the Prince: 'The body and soul can both free themselves from judgement. The body can plead: It is the soul that has sinned since the moment it left me I am like a dumb stone in the grave. And the soul can say: It is the body that has sinned since from the day I departed from it I fly in the air like a bird.' He replied: 'Let me tell you a parable. A human king had a beautiful orchard containing splendid figs. He appointed two watchmen over the orchard, one lame, the other blind. The lame man said to the blind man: "I see splendid figs in the orchard. Take me up on your shoulders and we can get them to eat." The lame man bestrode the blind and they got hold of the figs and ate them. When the owner of the orchard asked them what had happened to the figs, the lame man protested: "Have I feet with which to walk?" and the blind man protested: "Have I eyes with which to see?" What did the owner do? He placed the lame man on the shoulders of the blind man and judged them together. So will the Holy One, blessed be He, bring the soul, place it in the body, and judge them together'. (*Sanhedrin* 91a–b)

The medieval Jewish thinkers, influenced by Greek thought in its Arabic garb, went far beyond the idea of the lameness of the soul and the blindness of the body to stress the struggle, rather than the co-operation between the two, with the corollary that a strong dose of denial of bodily pleasures is essential to the religious life. The greatest of the medieval thinkers, Maimonides (1135–1206), writes that the destruction of the soul is in direct proportion to the building up of the body (*Commentary to the Mishnah*, Kapah, 22). Bahya Ibn Pakudah (twelfth century), while advocating for his contemporaries a balanced attitude towards asceticism, can still admire the world-losers, the hermits and ascetics (*Duties*, IX, ed. Hyamson 1962, 288–337). In the Talmud a great variety of views is found on the question of asceticism. In the very same Talmudic passage (*Taanit* 11a) two conflicting opinions are recorded. According to one rabbi, the Nazirite is a holy man because he denies himself wine and the man who fasts, denying himself all food and drink, is an even holier man.

According to the other rabbi, the Nazirite is a sinner because he denied himself God's gift of wine, and the man who fasts, denying himself all food and drink, is an even greater sinner. In the Jerusalem Talmud (*Kiddushin* 66d) there occurs the astonishing anti-ascetic saying that a man will be obliged to give an account before God for every legitimate pleasure he denied himself. Even the ascetically inclined among the Jewish pietists, and they were many, followed the Rabbinic injunction to offer thanks to God in the form of a benediction for every bodily pleasure they enjoy (Singer 1962, 385–90). The popular seventeenth-century book, *Meah Berakhot* ('One Hundred Blessings'), as its name implies, is a list of such blessings to be recited daily.

In both the Rabbinic and the philosophical traditions the many *mitzvot* ('precepts') of the Torah to be carried out by bodily activity are binding upon Jews. The Talmudic homily (*Makkot* 22b) that there are 248 positive precepts, corresponding to the 248 parts of the human body, and 365 negative precepts, corresponding to the days of the solar year, became a powerful slogan for Jewish piety; the Jew who kept the 613 precepts was held to be sanctifying his body and his years. For the rabbis of the Talmud, observance of the *mitzvot* is not a means to an end but the end itself – obedience to the will of God. The philosophers, on the other hand, tended to see the *mitzvot* as the means to what, for the philosophers, is the true aim of religion, contemplation on the divine truths. The rabbis, too, demand proper concentration (*kavvanah*) when carrying out the *mitzvot* and they condemn mere mechanical observance, but the *kavvanah* demanded is simply: 'I do this for the sake of God who has commanded it.' The rabbis were not primarily interested in why God commanded this or that. It was sufficient that He had so commanded. Not so the philosophers who were mightily concerned with 'the reasons for the *mitzvot*', arguing that to carry out certain acts merely because God had so commanded, without asking why, would result in less than enthusiastic observance; would constitute a poor defence of Judaism as a rational faith; and would tend to treat God as a tyrant who issues arbitrary dictates (Heinemann 1949, 10–11). Yet, for all their attempts at explanation, the philosophers had to admit that many of the details of the *mitzvot* remained opaque. As Maimonides (*Guide*, III, 26) puts it:

Know that wisdom rendered it necessary that there should be particulars for which no cause can be found; it was, as it were, impossible in regard to the law that there could be nothing of this class in it. In such a case the impossibility is due to the circumstances that when you ask why a *lamb* should be prescribed instead of a *ram*, the same question would have to be asked if a *ram* had been prescribed instead of a *lamb*. But one particular species had to be chosen, The same holds for you asking why *seven lambs* and not *eight* have been prescribed. For a similar question would have been put if *eight* or *ten* or *twenty* had been prescribed. (trans. Pines 1914, 509)

For Maimonides, then, the ordered rules and regulations of the sacrificial system – and the same would hold good for all the other *mitzvot* – are the necessary means to the general aim of intellectual and moral perfection. But, once rules have become necessary, it is futile to ask why these details in particular since one cannot have rules without them being detailed and such details are, indeed, quite arbitrary. It was left to the Kabbalists to develop a system in which every detail of the *mitzvot* is highly significant because it represents one or other of the divine processes on high.

The Kabbalah is the theosophical system which arose in Provence in the twelfth century to reach its culmination in Spain in the book Zohar, which first saw the light at the end of the thirteenth century. A more elaborate version of the Kabbalah was produced in Safed by Isaac Luria (1534–1572), known as the *Ari* ('The Lion'). In both the Zoharic and the Lurianic systems, bodily acts of worship have a highly charged mythological significance in that the human body is a pale reflection of the divine corpus. Long before the rise of the Kabbalah, the work *Shiur Komah* ('The Measurements of God's Stature') sought to describe the mystical dimensions of God's 'body' (Scholem 1974, 16–18). *Tikkuney ha-Zohar*, the work that supplements the Zohar proper, states that each 'limb' of the king is a *mitzvah*, i.e., the *mitzvot* represent the divine corpus (No. 30, ed. Margaliot, 1978, 74a).

Basic to the Kabbalah is the idea that there are two aspects of the Deity – God as He is in Himself and God in manifestation. The former is known as *En Sof* ('The Limitless') and is the impersonal Ground of Being, known only to Itself and utterly beyond all human comprehension. The latter is the revelation of *En Sof* through the *Sefirot*, the powers or potencies in the Godhead, of which there are ten. These, in descending order, are: (1) *Keter* ('Crown'), the divine will; (2) *Hokhmah* ('Wisdom'); (3) *Binah* ('Understanding'); (4) *Hesed* ('Love'); (5) *Gevurah* ('Power'); (6) *Tiferet* ('Beauty'); (7) *Netzah* ('Victory'); (8) *Hod* ('Splendour'); (9) *Yesod* ('Foundation'); (10) *Malkhut* ('Sovereignty'). The *Sefirot* proceed from *En Sof* by a process of emanation and are, in a favourite Kabbalistic simile, like bottles of various colours into which transparent water is poured, the water taking on the colour of the bottle into which it is poured. The *Sefirot* represent the body of God, that is, they are the cosmic forces that are the counterparts on high of the human body on earth. *Ḥesed*, for example, is God's right arm which assumes in this world a human right arm and which is the ultimate source of all human love.

Here lies the significance of the body and bodily actions according to the Kabbalah. The 'image of God' in which man is created (Genesis 1:26–7) means for the Kabbalists that the human body mirrors forth the Godhead. The idea of the image of God referring to the actual physical body of man is not unknown in earlier sources. The Midrash (Leviticus Rabbah 34:3), for example, tells of the sage, Hillel, who, on his way to the bath house, said to his disciples that he was going to carry out a *mitzvah*. 'Is it a religious obligation to bathe?', they asked. 'Yes', replied Hillel, 'If the statues of kings erected in theatres and circuses are regularly scoured and washed by the person appointed to look after them, how much more, I, who has been created in God's image and likeness.' But this whole idea comes to mean for the Kabbalists that the human body mirrors forth the *Sefirot* and can influence them by the actions it performs. When human beings, at the end of a great chain of being reaching back to the *Sefirot*, perform acts of virtue, they send beneficent impulses on high to promote harmony among the *Sefirot* and then the divine grace can flow unimpeded through all creation. Conversely, when humans are vicious they send baneful impulses on high to disturb the harmony of the *Sefirot* and arrest the flow of the divine grace.

It follows that every detailed act in the performance of the *mitzvot* has its correspondence in the Sefirotic realm and each detail contributes to the formidable task of literally holding up the heavens. The body is significant precisely because it alone can provide the cosmic energy required if the divine purpose in creation is to be realized. Unlike the rationalists, the Kabbalists do see in every detail of the *mitzvot* a way of influencing the upper worlds. Some of the hymns composed by the Kabbalists to invoke the *Sefirot* 'read like the hymns of a mystery religion' (Scholem 1967, 143).

A further refinement is found in the Lurianic Kabbalah, where the doctrine runs that at one stage in the emanation process, as the infinite light of *En Sof* poured into the vessels of the *Sefirot*, the vessels, too weak to sustain the overpowering light, were shattered under the impact, with the result that, even after their reconstitution, there were 'holy sparks' imprisoned among the demonic forces, the *kelippot* ('shells'). Every virtuous act helps towards the rescue of the 'holy sparks' from their imprisonment by the dark powers.

In the Hasidic movement, which arose in the eighteenth century, the doctrine of the 'holy sparks' receives further elaboration. It is not only through the performance of the *mitzvot* that the 'holy sparks' are rescued. Every bodily act performed in the spirit of holiness – eating, drinking, sex, even smoking a pipe – has the effect of releasing the 'holy sparks' from their prison. In Hasidism 'serving the Creator with the body' means not alone that the body be engaged in the perform-ance of the *mitzvot*, but that ordinary physical acts, neutral in them-selves, become vehicles for the sacred if carried out for the glory of God.

Before turning to the three rituals, it has to be added that these and all other Jewish rituals became codified. The major Codes are: *Mishneh Torah* of Maimonides; *Tur* of Jacob ben Asher (d. 1340); and *Shulḥan Arukh* of Joseph Karo (1488–1575), the last, once it had received the glosses of Moses Isserles of Cracow (d. 1572), becoming the standard Code for observant Jews. Karo and Isserles introduced here and there rituals of Kabbalistic origin, and so did their commentators, especially Abraham Gombiner (d. 1683) in his *Magen Avraham*. There is, in addition, a special Code devoted entirely to the Kabbalistic meaning of the rituals – *Shulḥan Arukh ha-Ari*. Local custom also has a voice in these matters, for example, in the different forms adopted by the Sephardim – Jews hailing from Spanish countries – and Ashkenazim – German and French Jews. We can now look at the rituals and observe how the above actually operates.

THE SABBATH

The body is engaged positively in a large number of sabbath rituals, but the very institution of the Sabbath, with its requirement that there be total cessation of all creative manual labour on the day, constitutes in itself worship with the body, albeit by negation. In the Rabbinic tradition, the biblical injunctions to refrain from 'work' on the Sabbath (Exodus 20:8–11; 35:2–3; Deuteronomy 5:12–15) are understood as re-ferring not to all physical actions, but only to those which involve creative manipulation of the material world. The Mishnah (*Shabbat* 7:2) spells it out:

The main classes of work are forty save one; sowing, ploughing, reaping, binding sheaves, threshing, winnowing, cleansing crops, grinding, sifting, kneading, baking, shearing wool, washing or beating or dyeing it, spinning, weaving, making two loops, weaving two threads, separating two threads, tying a knot, loosening a knot, sewing two stitches, tearing in order to sew two stitches, hunting a gazelle, slaughtering or flaying or salting it or curing its skin, scraping it or cutting it up, writing two letters, erasing in order to write two letters, building, pulling down, putting out a fire, lighting a fire, striking with a hammer and taking out something from one domain to another.

Thus what is forbidden is evidently acts involved in the preparation of food, clothing, and housing. Naturally these are types of creative labour that were the norm in second-century Palestine when the Mishnah was compiled. The idea behind it all seems to be that God is acknowledged as the Creator by refraining on this day from that which is, on the other days of the week, a divine gift to man, his creative talent (see Genesis 2:1–3 and Exodus 20:11).

While the body is to be restrained from working on the Sabbath, the satisfaction of bodily needs and appetites on the day is enjoined as a religious duty. The prophetic injunction (Isaiah 58:13) to 'call the Sabbath a delight' forms the basis of the Rabbinic idea of *oneg shabbat* ('Sabbath delight'), defined by Maimonides in his Mishneh Torah (1983, *Shabbat* 30:7–8) on the basis of Talmudic statement, as the enjoyment on the Sabbath of special juicy dishes and good wine. The Talmud (*Berakhot* 31b) states that while it is forbidden to fast on the Sabbath, yet if a man has had a bad dream which disturbs him he is allowed to fast on the sacred day in order to counteract its baneful effects. Nevertheless, he must undertake another fast as a penance for having offended against the principle of Sabbath delight. The Talmud (*Shabbat* 118a) also states that, unlike on weekdays when it is normal to partake of only two meals each day, on the Sabbath one should partake of three meals, one on Friday night (when the Sabbath begins), one at lunchtime and one on Sabbath afternoon.

Sabbath delight thus involves a degree of indulgence of the body. Rashi (1040–1105), the famous French commentator, understands the Talmudic notion (*Betzah* 16a) of the 'additional soul' with which a man is said to be endowed on the Sabbath as: 'A heart with an extended capacity for tranquility and joy, open to enlargement, so that he is able to eat and drink without feeling ill.' This attitude has been captured exquisitely in Heine's pen portrait of the poor packman Moses Lump who works hard during the day to earn his meagre living:

But when on Friday evening he comes home, he finds the candlestick with seven candles lighted, and the table covered with a fair white cloth, and he puts away his pack and his cares, and he sits down to table with his squinting wife and yet more squinting daughter, and eats fish with them, fish which has been dressed in beautiful white garlic sauce, sings therewith the grandest psalms of David, rejoices with his whole heart over the deliverance of the children of Israel out of

Egypt, rejoices, too, that all the wicked ones who have done the children of Israel hurt, have ended by taking themselves off, that King Pharaoh, Nebuchadnezzar, Haman, Antiochus, Titus, and all such people, are well dead, while he, Moses Lump, is yet alive, and eating fish with his wife and daughter; and I can tell, Doctor, the fish is delicious and the man happy. (Roth 1960, 26)

For the Kabbalists, such an approach, admirable enough for ordinary folk, is far too pedestrian. The Zohar (ii, 88b) understands the 'additional soul' in its literal sense; on the Sabbath the *Shekhinah* (in the Zohar this represents the personification of the female principle in the Godhead, the *Sefirah* called *Malkhut*) is present at the table. Based on this passage, the Lurianic Kabbalists see one of the *Sefirot* being especially present at the first meal, another at the second, and another at the third. In Hasidism the three sacred meals are partaken of in the presence of the Zaddik, the spiritual leader and saint, who tastes a little of each dish, the remainder being distributed to his followers so that some of his close attachment to God might be carried over to them through the food he has tasted and blessed. The third meal has special numinous qualities because at this meal the Zaddik delivers his homilies, his Torah; it being believed by the Hasidim that at this awesome moment the *Shekhinah* speaks through the throat of the Zaddik (Wertheim 1960, 151–3; 167–9).

The Talmud (*Bava Kama* 32b) speaks of welcoming the Sabbath as Israel's bride; but for the Kabbalists the Sabbath represents the *Shekhinah*, the *Sefirah Malkhut*, while Israel is the *Sefirah Tiferet*, the male principle in the Godhead. The Safed mystics used to dress in white on the eve of the Sabbath and go out to welcome the Sabbath/*Shekhinah*. The poem composed for the purpose by Solomon Alkabetz (d. 1576) is now recited on Friday night in synagogues all over the world, when, during the evening prayers, the whole congregation turns towards the door to welcome the Sabbath with the words of the poem, 'Come my friend, to meet the bride: let us welcome the presence of the Sabbath', sung in a melody of hope and yearning (Singer 1962, 146–7).

The Friday-night meal at the beginning of the Sabbath is a family occasion. The table is covered with a white cloth on which are set two candles, two whole loaves of bread, corresponding to the double portion of manna on the Sabbath (Exodus 16:5), and a goblet of wine over which the *kiddush* ('sanctification') is recited in which God is praised as Creator and for giving the Sabbath to Israel. Since the kindling of fire cannot be done on the Sabbath itself, the candles are lit just before Sabbath begins by the mistress of the house who covers her eyes with her hands while she prays for her family. The Midrash (Genesis Rabbah 8:8) sees the duty of kindling the Sabbath lights as devolving particularly on women, because when Eve was responsible for Adam's sin she extinguished 'the light of the world'. The husband recites the verses in Proverbs (31:10–31) in praise of the 'woman of worth', referring to his wife, although in the Kabbalah these verses were introduced in praise of the *Shekhinah*, the female principle, united with Her Spouse, *Tiferet*, the male principle in the Godhead. From this union souls are born.

This is why Friday night is the special time for marital relations. The Talmud (*Ketubot* 62b) quotes the third-century Babylonian teacher, Samuel, as saying that scholars are obliged to make love to their wives on Friday night; in context, this is because they are often away from home studying during the rest of the week. But in another Talmudic passage (*Bava Kama* 82a) it is implied that this duty is not confined to scholars, presumably because other people, too, can be preoccupied during weekdays. Here it is said that Ezra introduced the practice of eating garlic, presumed to be an aphrodisiac, on the eve of the Sabbath. The Kabbalists built on this to construct the Friday-night union into a sacred ritual, mirroring forth the 'Sacred Marriage' on high, a ritual to be carried out, so far as possible, as a mystical rite to be engaged in without pleasure or passion (Vital 1890, 10). It is difficult to know how far the Kabbalists were able to succeed in banishing pleasure and passion from the act. Karo, in his *Shulhan Arukh*, section *Orah Hayyim* (280:1) follows earlier authorities in extending the concept of Sabbath *delight* so as to include the marital act. Jacob Emden (1697–1776), in his extraordinarily detailed guide to marital relations on the Sabbath, writes that, while a man should not speak lewdly to his wife, he should speak loving words to her to make her happy and responsive to his caresses (Emden 1904, 159).

The *havdalah* ('division') ceremony takes place when the Sabbath ends on Saturday night (Singer 1962, 292–94). Over a cup of wine the benediction is recited in which God is praised for making a distinction between holy and profane, between light and darkness, between Israel and other nations, between the Sabbath and the six working days. Sweet spices are smelled in order to restore the soul saddened by the departure of the 'additional soul' of the Sabbath. Since fire cannot be kindled on the Sabbath but is now permitted, a taper is lit over which God is praised for giving man the precious gift of fire and light. The order of the *havdalah* rituals is first the wine, representing the sense of taste; then the spices, representing the sense of smell; then the light, the sense of sight; and, finally, the mind is brought into play in reflection on the meaning of the rite as a whole. Thus, at the beginning of the new week, the Jew resolves

Plate 1   Illustration in a seventeenth-century Jewish devotional work (the *Meah Berakhot*) showing the use of the five senses in worship.

to elevate his bodily senses from taste to smell to sight, each more refined and more subtle than the other, and to have them controlled by his intellect (Gaguine 1955, 470).

The curious custom is still followed of looking at the fingernails by the light of the *havdalah* taper. Karo (298:3) simply states that it is the custom to gaze at the palms and the fingernails, but Isserles adds: 'One should gaze at the nails of the right hand while holding the cup of wine in the left hand and one should bend the fingers towards the palm so that one looks at the palm and the nails at the same time and sees the inside of the fingers.' Some see in all this an echo of ancient forms of divination (see Finesinger 1937–8). The Kabbalists see it as part of the distinction between the upper world, represented by the flesh of the palm, and the demonic powers, represented by the nails (Ginsburg 1989, 271–2). There is a further custom of extending afterwards the hands towards the light, said to denote that the hands, held back from work during the Sabbath, can now freely be employed.

DEATH AND BURIAL RITES

Attitudes towards a dead body differ widely in the history of Judaism. In the Bible a corpse is a severe source of ritual contamination. Anyone who has been in contact with a corpse must undergo the rite of sprinkling with the ashes of the red heifer before being allowed to enter the sacred camp (see Numbers 19). The priests were forbidden to come into contact with a corpse other than that of a near relative (Leviticus 21:1–4). This latter is still the rule for observant Jews. A *kohen*, a descendant of the ancient priests (hence the name Cohen), does not enter a house in which there is a corpse and does not walk near the graves in the cemetery. There was a view, however, in the Middle Ages, that the bodies of the saints do not contaminate. The French scholars known as the Tosafists, authors of glosses to the Talmud, quote (*Ketubot* 103b) a Rabbi Hayyim Kohen who said that if he had been present at the funeral of the great teacher, Rabbenu Tam (d. 1171), he would have participated in the burial since the body of a saint does not contaminate. While this view still prevails in some circles, the weight of opinion is against it (see Langauer 1977). Legends are told of Jewish saints whose corpses suffered no decomposition and emitted a sweet fragrance, the reward of their holy life while in the body.

The Mishnah (*Yadaim* 5:6) records a debate between the Sadducees and the Pharisees on the strange Pharisaic law that a scroll of the Torah renders the hands unclean, i.e., the hands have to be ritually washed before handling sacred food. Why, asked the Sadducees, should sacred scripture contaminate and yet the works of Homer do not contaminate? The Pharisees reply that scripture is treated as a taboo for the same reason that a corpse is a source of contamination, not because it is abhorrent, but, on the contrary, to prevent it being treated in an overfamiliar way. The comparison with scripture is also found in the Talmudic statement (*Moed Katan* 25a) that those present at the death must rend their garments as if they had witnessed the burning of a Scroll of the Torah.

In any event, the corpse has to be treated with respect, though the author of a popular compendium on the laws of death and burial (Tykocinski 1960, 64–74) goes too far in suggesting that because of the comparison with the scroll of the Torah a corpse possesses a degree of sanctity. In most Jewish communities the preparations of the corpse for burial are carried out by the members of a special society known as the *ḥevra kaddisha* ('Holy Brotherhood') to which only the most learned and most pious members of the community are allowed to belong. On the basis of the Talmudic rule (*Hullin* 11b) that it is forbidden to mutilate a corpse, Orthodox law frowns on autopsies and the dissection of corpses, though in some circumstances, where lives can be saved as result, for instance, organ transplants are permitted.

Many of the practices in connection with death and burial are due to Kabbalistic influences and, naturally in these matters, superstitions have crept in, for instance, that the water in the vicinity of a death must be poured out. This practice is not found in Jewish sources earlier than the thirteenth century, but it has been noted that the practice was followed by Christians in France and Germany at a still earlier date so that borrowing seems plausible. A Jewish interpretation given to the practice is that the Angel of Death may have let fall into the water a drop from the poison on the sword with which he slays (Trachtenberg 1970, 176). The practice of watching over a corpse is mentioned in the Talmud (*Berakhot* 18a), but there the reason is in order to keep the rats away. Later on the reason given was to frighten off the demons who are attracted to a dead body (Trachtenberg 1970, 175). The Kabbalistic treatise, *Maavar Yabok* ('Ford of Yabok') by Aaron Berachiah of Modena was first published in Mantua in 1623, but the rites and ceremonies of death and burial mentioned in the book are still largely followed in the more traditional Jewish communities. The book contains a vivid eschatological scheme according to which the soul has three parts: *nefesh*, the lowest, *ruaḥ*, the next highest, and *neshamah*, highest of the three. The *nefesh* remains in the body and suffers with the body in the grave. The *ruaḥ* is punished for its sins, but twelve months after its departure from the body it is allowed to enter the 'Lower Garden of Eden'. The *neshamah* departs at once for the 'Higher Garden of Eden'. These complex relationships between the three parts of the soul and between them and the body are variously interpreted by the Kabbalists (Scholem 1974, 333–6).

The Mishnah (*Shabbat* 23:5) refers to the practice of washing the corpse before burial, but eventually there developed an elaborate rite of purification known as the *tohorah*, 'purification' (Rabbinowicz 1967, 39; Levine 1985, 300–12). The procedure followed is to place the corpse on its back on a flat board. It is then held upright while approximately four and a half gallons of water are poured over it. The hair is washed and combed and the nails trimmed. The medieval German work, *Sefer Hasidim* ('Book of the Pious') bases the *tohorah* on the verse in Ecclesiastes (5:15): 'as he came so shall he go', understanding it to mean, as he was bathed when he came into the world so is he to be bathed when he departs from the world (par. 560, ed. Margaliot 1973, 370). The corpse is then dressed in shrouds made of linen or cotton. These are usually a cap, a shirt, breeches, a neckcloth, a surplice, and a girdle. It can be seen that the shrouds resemble the garments worn by the priests in the Temple (Exodus 28:40–3). At the burial, as the coffin is lowered into the grave, all present declare: 'May he/she come into his/her place in peace.' For a female all these rites are carried out by women members of the *hevra kaddisha*.

The nearest relatives of the deceased (father, mother, brother, sister, son, daughter, husband, wife) rend their garments before the funeral. This is known as the *keriah* ('rending') and is referred to in the Bible (for example, in Genesis 37:34). The *keriah* is performed with the mourners standing upright, symbolic of their faith in God which allows them to face grief without becoming prey to despair. Nowadays, except for the very pious, the *keriah* is done on a token item of clothing such as a necktie or cardigan (Klein 1979, 279).

THE PRIESTLY BLESSING

The biblical source for the priestly blessing is the book of Numbers (6:23–7): 'And the Lord spake unto Moses saying, Speak unto Aaron and his sons, saying, Thus ye shall bless the children of Israel, saying unto them, The Lord bless thee, and keep thee; The Lord make His face shine upon thee, and be gracious unto thee; The Lord lift up His countenance upon thee, and give thee peace. And they shall put my name upon the children of Israel and I will bless them.' In Temple times the priests blessed the people daily as part of the Temple service. After the destruction of the Temple, the priestly blessing is recited in the synagogue at the section in the liturgy containing references to worship in the Temple but, in many communities, only on the festivals. In Temple times the priests recited the blessing from a special platform, the *dukhan*;

hence the popular Yiddish expression for the rite, *duchaning*, 'platform-ing'. The full rite is given in the standard prayer books (Singer 1962, 324–5).

At the suitable place in the liturgy, the cantor recites: 'Our God and God of our fathers, bless us with the threefold blessing of the Law written by the hand of Moses thy servant, which was spoken by Aaron and his sons, THE PRIESTS', reciting the last two words in a loud voice in order to invite the priests to proceed to bless. As above, the *kohanim* ('priests') are men who claim descent by family tradition from the ancient priesthood. Before they ascend to take their place for the blessing in front of the holy Ark, the priests remove their shoes (see Gold 1981; Sperling n.d., 54–6). The hands of the priests are washed by the Levites in the congregation (men believed to be descended from the ancient Levites, people called Levy or Levine, for example). The Zohar (III, 146b) observes that the priest requires further sanctity to his own to be added before he can become worthy to recite the blessing, hence the washing of his hands by the Levites. If no Levite is present, the hands of the priests are washed by a first-born, who also possesses a special degree of sanctity (Gombiner, 128,7). The priests then station themselves in front of the Ark to await the cantor's invitation, at which they turn their faces to the congregation, raise their hands, and recite the blessing. Before reciting the blessing the priests say: 'Blessed art thou, O Lord our God, King of the universe, who hast sanctified us with the sanctity of Aaron and hast commanded us to bless thy people Israel in love.'

A good deal is made of the positioning of the hands of the priests. The custom as stated in the *Tur* (128) is for the ten fingers of the priest to be positioned in such a way that five apertures are formed. This is based on a Midrashic comment on the verse: 'gazing through the lattices' (Song of Songs 2:9), God sending His blessing, as it were, through the openings between the fingers of the priests. Gombiner (128,9) records a custom (this not usually followed) of the priests, before reciting the blessing, drawing in the air with their fingers the four Hebrew letters of the Tetragrammaton. The Kabbalist, Shabbetai Sheftel Horowitz (d. 1619) in his *Shefa Tal* (6) notes that there are fifteen Hebrew words in the priestly blessing. There are 14 joints of the hand – 3 on each of the 4 fingers and 2 on the thumb – representing 14 of the words, while the final word *shalom*-, 'peace', is represented by the palm of the hand. In the Zohar (III, 146b) the ten fingers of the priest represent the ten *Sefirot*, the right hand being raised a little above the left so that love should prevail over the 'left side' of rigorous judgement (Zohar, III, 145a). A further symbolic interpretation in the Zohar (III, 145b) is that the priest represents *Hesed* and the blessing itself the *Shekhinah, Malkhut*, the priest bringing down the divine grace from one to the other so that it might flow through all creation.

The Talmud (*Hagigah* 15a) states that the eyes of the man which gaze on the hands of the priests while they are reciting the blessing will become dim, which Rashi (*Megillah* 24b) says is because the *Shekhinah* rests on their hands. The Tosafists to the passage say that this only applied in Temple times, when a special divine name, kept secret by the priests, was used for the blessing. Nevertheless, even nowadays, it is discouraged to gaze at the hands of the priests. The idea that the *Shekhinah* rests on the hands of the priests is stated in the Zohar (III, 147a), where it is said that although no man can actually behold the *Shekhinah* while he is still in the body, yet one should still refrain from gazing at the hands of the priests in reverence for the *Shekhinah*.

The Talmud (*Berakhot* 32b) quotes the verse: 'And when ye spread forth your hands, I will hide mine eyes from you . . . your hands are full of blood' (Isaiah 1:15), to yield the thought that if a priest had been guilty of homicide, according to some, even of manslaughter, he must never again raise his hands to recite the priestly blessing.

CONCLUSIONS

Although the Sabbath rituals, the death and burial rites and the priestly blessing have no direct connection with one another – it would not have been too difficult to choose other examples for our purpose – yet these three in particular are all good examples of how Jewish religious practices give expression to the inevitable tensions that exist between the striving for spirituality and the need to keep religion earthbound in some measure by means of physical activity. In these practices performed by the body or on behalf of the body the spiritual side is never overlooked. Earth is rarely seen, except by the Jewish mystics, as crammed with heaven, but neither is the heavenly dimension ignored. There is much truth in Max Kadushin's description of Rabbinic Judaism as 'normal mysticism' (Gillman 1990, 122).

Sabbath delight involves eating and drinking and other forms of physical pleasure, but it is all in the spirit of sanctity and spiritual awareness through the symbols of light and fragrance and the love of God. The Talmud (*Berakhot* 57b) can state without irony that the Sabbath is a foretaste (the Talmud actually says a sixtieth) of the World to Come, which itself is referred to in the tradition as the 'Sabbath'. Nothing can be more earthbound than a dead body, yet, in the burial rites, it is treated with reverence and prepared (at least according to the conventional view) for its eventual resurrection, even though a thinker like Nahmanides thinks of the resurrected body as so refined that it has become itself a kind of soul, and even though Maimonides holds that the resurrection will be only temporary, the soul alone enjoying eternal bliss (Jacobs 1973, 312–15). In the priestly blessing it is material well-being that is promised and bodily movements attend the blessing, yet behind the whole notion of blessing lies the mystery of divine providence with God as the lover who gazes at his beloved through the lattices.

Naturally, since Judaism is not monolithic, there are various shades of emphasis. The Sabbath delight of a Moses Lump is quite different from what the Kabbalists understand by the concept. And it would be pointless to deny that on the popular level the burial rites imply that somehow the body is still alive, and that many believe the *Shekhinah* to be present in a quasi-physical sense when the priests recite their blessing, so that to look at them is to go blind. How could it be otherwise in view of the many forms of Jewish religious expression?

It should be added that this chapter describes rituals practised by Orthodox Jews, some of which, like the priestly blessing, have been abandoned by Reform Jews. Nor is this an essay in comparative religion, though many a parallel can easily be found in the practices of other religions. The priestly blessing, to give only the most obvious illustration, has been taken over by the Christian Church; the Christian priest becoming the 'kohen' of the 'New Israel'.

The blend of the physical and the spiritual in these rituals can be found often in Judaism. Is Judaism 'religious materialism', as it has been called, or is it a religion of pure spirituality; does Judaism place the emphasis on the body or on the soul; is the Jewish religion this-worldly or other-worldly? The only possible answer, from the historical point of view, is that both ways of looking at it are true. There is no avoiding the paradox expressed so cogently in the section of the Mishnah (*Avot* 4:17) known as 'Ethics of the Fathers': 'One hour of repentance and good deeds in this world is better than all the life of the World to Come and yet one hour of spiritual bliss in the World to Come is better than all the life of this world.' Eternity finds its expression in time and time is an expression of eternity.

BIBLIOGRAPHY

Aaron Berachiah of Modena (1896), *Maavar Yabok*, Vilna.

Bahya Ibn Pakudah (1962), *Hovot ha-Levavot* ('Duties of the Heart'), ed. and trans. by M. Hyamson, Jerusalem, New York.

Emden, J. (1904), *Siddur Bet Yaakov*, Lemberg.

Finesinger, S. (1937–8), 'The Custom of Looking at the Fingernails at the Outgoing of the Sabbath', in *Hebrew Union College Annual*, 12–13, 347–65.

Gaguine, S. (1955), *Keter Shem Tov*, London.

Gillman, N. (1990), *Sacred Fragments; Recovering Theology for the Modern Jew*, New York.

Ginsburg, E. K. (1989), *The Sabbath in the Classical Kabbalah*, Albany.

Gold, A. (1981), *The Priestly Blessing*, Brooklyn.

Gombiner, A. *Magen Avraham*, in *Shulhan Arukh*, var. eds.

Heinemann, I. (1949), *Taamey ha-Mitzvot*, Jerusalem.

Horowitz, S. S. (1712), *Shefa Tal*, Hanover.

Jacobs, L. (1973), *A Jewish Theology*, London.

(1992), *Religion and the Individual: A Jewish Perspective*, Cambridge.

Kadushin, M. (1952), *The Rabbinic Mind*, New York.

Klein, I. (1979), *A Guide to Jewish Religious Practice*, New York.

Langauer, E. (1977), 'Contamination of Priests at the Graves of the Saints' (Heb.) in *Noam* 21, 184–232.

Levine, A. (1985), *Zikhron Meir*, Toronto.

Maimonides, M. (1883), *Mishneh Torah*, Warsaw.

(1963), *Commentary to the Mishnah* (Heb.) ed. J. Kapah, Jerusalem.

(1914), *Moreh Nevukhim*, trans. S. Pines, Vilna.

(1974), *Guide for the Perplexed*, Chicago University Press.

Meah Berakhot ('One Hundred Benedictions') (1687), Amsterdam.

Midrash Rabbah, ed. Vilna, 1911; English trans. H. Freedman and M. Simon, Soncino, London, 1977.

Mishnah, ed. H. Albeck, Tel-Aviv (1959); English trans. H. Danby, Oxford University Press.

Rabbinowicz, H. (1967), *A Guide to Life: Jewish Laws and Customs of Mourning*, New York.

Rashi: Standard Commentary to Talmud by Rabbi Shlomo Yitzhaki, in all editions of the Babylonian Talmud.

Roth, L. (1960), *Judaism, A Portrait*, London.

Scholem, G. (1967), *On the Kabbalah and Its Symbolism*, London.

(1974), *Kabbalah*, Jerusalem.

Sefer Hasidim (1973), ed. R. Margaliot, Jerusalem.

Shulhan Arukh, Joseph Karo and Moses Isserles, var. eds.

Shulhan Arukh ha-Ari, Isaac Luria, Munkacs, n.d.

Singer, S. (1962), *Authorised Daily Prayer Book*, London.

Sperling, A. I., *Taamey ha-Minhagim*, Jerusalem, n.d.

Talmud, Babylonian, Vilna, 1936; English trans. I. Epstein, I. Soncino, London, 1948.

Talmud, Jerusalem, Krotoschin, 1866.

Tikkuney ha-Zohar, ed. R. Margaliot, Jerusalem, 1978.

Tosafists, medieval glosses to the Talmud, in most eds.

Trachtenberg, J. (1970), *Jewish Magic and Superstition*, New York.

Tur, Jacob ben Asher, var. eds.

Tykocinski, Y. M. (1960), *Gesher ha-Ḥayyim*, Jerusalem.

Vital, H. (1890), *Etz Ḥayyim*, ed. Warsaw.

Wertheim, A. (1960), *Halakhot ve-Halikhot ba-Ḥasidut*, Jerusalem.

Zohar, ed. R. Margaliot, Jerusalem, 1964; English trans. H. Sperling and M. Simon, Soncino, London, 1949.

CHAPTER 6

'My helper and my enemy': the body in Greek Christianity

Kallistos Ware

'WHAT IS THIS MYSTERY IN ME?'

'He is my helper and my enemy, my assistant and my opponent, a protector and a traitor': so John Climacus (seventh century), Abbot of Sinai, sums up his attitude towards his own body. He and his body seem to have a love–hate relationship with each other: 'How can I hate him when my nature disposes me to love him? How can I break away from him when I am bound to him for ever? How can I escape from him when he is going to rise with me? . . . I embrace him. And I turn away from him. What is this mystery in me?' (Climacus 1982, 185–6).

Here Climacus displays towards his own physicality an attitude that is deeply ambivalent. He regards the body as an occasion of sin and temptation, an obstacle and hindrance in the spiritual life. Yet he is no dualist. He acknowledges the body as God's creation, and therefore in itself good. He sees his physicality as an essential and enduring element in his personhood, and he looks beyond the separation of body and soul at death to their future reintegration at the resurrection on the last day: 'he is going to rise with me'. Even in this present life, he insists, we should not seek simply to save our souls, but our aim is 'a body made holy' (Climacus 1982, 74).

Climacus' bafflement is shared by many others in the Christian East. Why are they so puzzled? In attempting an explanation, we need to remember that, alike in Eastern and in Western Christendom, there has never been a single universally accepted doctrine of human personhood. The seven ecumenical or general councils, which met between 325 and 787 and which (next to the Bible) constitute for Greek Christianity the final doctrinal authority, made no formal definitions concerning human nature or the human body. As Peter Brown has shown in his brilliant survey *The Body and Society* (Brown 1989), our human physicality was in practice understood by early Christians in a wide variety of ways. There are no simple answers. In what follows, for reasons of space we shall deal only with the Greek Orthodox tradition and, to a lesser extent, with that of Russian Orthodoxy. If we were to take into account the other traditions of the Christian East as well – Syrian, Coptic, Ethiopian, Armenian, Indian, among others – the picture would be even more complicated.

Two factors in particular help to explain the ambivalence of John Climacus and others like him. First of all, the doctrine of the Fall has to be taken into account. When an author speaks of the human body in negative terms, to what level of existence is he referring – the unfallen or the fallen? Is he talking about the body in its natural state, as originally created by God? Or does he have in view the body as we know it in our present experience, in its *contra*-natural condition subject to the consequences of original sin (however that is to be understood)? Any specific statement concerning the body requires to be read in context. When, for example, Climacus calls his body 'helper' and 'protector', presumably he is thinking of the body in its true and natural state; when he speaks of it as 'opponent' and 'traitor', he surely means the body in its state of fallen sinfulness – what Paul the Apostle termed 'this body of death' (Romans 7:24).

Secondly, the ambivalence arises in part because Greek Christianity is heir to a double inheritance: to the Hebraic–biblical tradition, which is strongly holistic in its understanding of the human person, and to the Hellenic–Platonist approach, which – without being strictly dualist, except in rare instances – makes a firm differentiation between soul and body. This Platonist influence accounts for an unresolved tension in many Greek Christian texts, although it certainly does not provide a full explanation for the distinctive character of early Christian teaching on the body and sexuality.

Let us look in more detail at this twofold background. The Old Testament envisages the human person, not as a combination of two separate entities, body and soul, but as a single, undivided unity. The Hebrew conception of personhood is embodied and physical: I do not *have* a body, I *am* my body – I am 'flesh-animated-by soul'. When the later strata of the Old Testament begin to refer (somewhat hesitantly) to life after death, it is understood in terms, not of the immortality of the soul, but of the resurrection of the body (Isaiah 26:19; Daniel 12:2). Within the Hebrew approach there is no place for the Greek notions of the soul's pre-existence and its transmigration from one body to another. When ideas of this kind appear in a late text such as Wisdom 8:20, this is to be explained by direct Hellenic influence.

In contrast to the holistic approach of the Old Testament, the Platonic view of personhood is expressed in separatist categories. 'The soul is man', states a Platonic text (*Alcibiades* I, 130c); and, within the soul, it is only the highest of its three aspects, the intelligent or intellectual part (*logistikon, nous*), that possesses immortality. In this present life, it is true, the soul needs to make use of the body, with its various instincts and desires, including the sexual urge. The body and its impulses are not evil, even though they need to be kept under control (see the analogy of the charioteer in Plato's *Phaedrus*, 246ab, 253c–254b). But, while not evil, at the same time these bodily impulses are extrinsic to genuine personhood. The true person is to be envisaged as an intellect or mind, temporarily imprisoned in a material body and aspiring to freedom; the body (*sōma*) is a tomb (*sēma*). The intellect alone is eternal; it pre-existed the body and will survive the body's dissolution. Our ultimate future hope, as Platonism sees it, is an existence stripped of all physicality.

Plato's teaching is modified by Aristotle, who is in some ways less separatist. The Stoics for their part are thoroughly unitary in their anthropology, adopting a standpoint not very different from that of the Old Testament. Later Platonism, however, remains pessimistic in its view of the body. Plotinus (AD 205–69/70), the founding father of Neoplatonism, 'seemed ashamed of being in a body', according to his disciple and biographer Porphyry. He would not allow anyone to paint his portrait, for he considered his physical appearance a matter of no importance; and he refused to disclose the date of his birthday, holding that the entry of his soul into a body was cause for mourning rather than celebration (Porphyry, *Life of Plotinus*, 1–2). The Hellenizing Jew Philo (d. CE 45) takes a yet more gloomy view, not only terming the body a 'foul prison house' (*The Migration of Abraham*, 9) but even condemning it – in a way that Plato and Plotinus would not have done – as 'evil *by nature*' (*Allegorical Interpretation of the Laws*, III, 71).

The unitary standpoint of the Hebrew Scriptures continues to prevail in the New Testament. In particular, the spiritual value of the human body is firmly underlined by the central event on which the Christian faith is founded: God's flesh-taking or incarnation. 'The Word became flesh' (John 1:14): in order to save humanity, God did not simply appear on earth, but he took up into himself our human nature in its entirety, including a human soul and a human body. 'What we have seen with our eyes, what we have looked at and touched with our hands . . . that is what we declare to you' (1 John 1:1–3): salvation is visible, palpable, embodied. Jesus Christ the Saviour was born physically from a woman (Galatians

4:4); although his birth was from a virgin mother (Matthew 1:18–25), it was none the less a real birth. He lived out on earth a genuinely physical existence, involving hunger, thirst and exhaustion (Matthew 21:18; Mark 4:38; John 4:6; 19:28). In his physical body he was transfigured in glory on the mountain (Matthew 17:1–8), and in his physical body he underwent suffering and death on the Cross, rising again on the third day from the dead. The gospel narratives insist upon the physicality of his resurrection body: 'Touch me and see', says the risen Christ; 'for a ghost does not have flesh and bones, as you see that I have' (Luke 24:39). In this way the body plays an altogether central role in the Christian salvation-story. *Caro salutis est cardo,* insists the North African Tertullian (*c.* 160–*c.* 225): 'The flesh is the pivot of salvation' (*On the Resurrection,* 8). In the words of Origen (*c.* 185–*c.* 254), 'The whole human person would not have been saved unless the Lord had taken upon him the whole human person' (*Dialogue with Heraclides*: Oulton and Chadwick 1954, 442).

A holistic approach to the person is strikingly evident in the letters of the apostle Paul (Robinson 1952, 17–33; but note the qualifications in Gundry 1976, 29–80, 135–56). So far, at any rate, as his anthropology is concerned, Paul is exactly what he himself claims to be, 'a Hebrew of the Hebrews' (Philippians 3:5). Nowhere does he make a direct contrast between soul and body, except possibly in 1 Thessalonians 5:23: 'May your spirit and soul and body be kept sound and blameless.' But even here his intention is not to enumerate systematically three 'parts' or 'components' of the human person, but simply to insist on the completeness of personal preservation by God. When Paul does choose to assert a contrast, this is not between body (*sōma*) and soul (*psychē*), but between flesh (*sarx*) and spirit (*pneuma*). The two sets of terms are by no means interchangeable. 'Flesh' in Paul's usage signifies, not the bodily or physical aspect, but total humanity – soul and body together – in so far as it is separated from God and in rebellion against him. By the same token 'spirit' designates, not the soul, but human personhood in its entirety – body and soul together – when it is living in obedience to God and in communion with him. Thus the terms 'flesh' and 'spirit' indicate, not components of the person, but relationships embracing personhood in its totality. 'Flesh' is the *whole* person as fallen, 'spirit' the *whole* person as redeemed. As Paul sees it, the mind can become 'fleshly' or 'carnal' (Colossians 2:18), just as the body can become 'spiritual' (1 Corinthians 15:44). When he lists the 'works of the flesh' (Galatians 5:19–21), he includes such things as 'quarrels', 'envy', 'party intrigues', which have no special connection with the body.

While Paul's view of the flesh is sombre, his estimate of the body is highly affirmative. 'Present your bodies as a living sacrifice to God', he writes (Romans 12:1). 'Your body is a temple of the Holy Spirit . . . Glorify God in your body' (1 Corinthians 6:19–20). That is exactly why sexual promiscuity is so deplorable – not because the body and its sexuality are unclean but because they are potentially holy: 'Your bodies are members of Christ' (1 Corinthians 6:15). This vital Pauline distinction between *sarx* and *sōma* has unfortunately been overlooked by all too many Christian preachers and moralists in later times, and so they have assumed that his strictures about the flesh apply to the body as such. The pastoral consequences have been depressing.

As well as applying the term *sōma* to the human body, Paul employs it also for the bread received in the Eucharist and for the community of the church, referring to both of these things as 'the body of Christ'. So he says of the Eucharist, 'The bread that we break, is it not a communion in the body of Christ?' (1 Corinthians 10:16). Similarly he envisages the church on the analogy of the human body, describing it as a unity-in-diversity formed from many limbs or members: 'Just as the body is one and has many members, and all the members of the body, though many, are one body, so it is with Christ . . . Now you are the body of Christ and individually members of it' (1 Corinthians 12:12,27). He sees these two senses of the term 'body of Christ' – the eucharistic and the ecclesial – as directly connected: 'We who are many are one body, for we all partake of the one bread' (1 Corinthians 10:17). It is through sharing at the Eucharist in the sacramental body of Christ that we are incorporated into Christ's body the church; the Eucharist creates the unity of the church. This Pauline conception of the church as essentially a eucharistic society, which only becomes truly itself through the act of holy communion, has been taken up and developed by modern Orthodox theologians, both Russian and Greek (Afanassieff 1963, 58–82; Zizioulas 1985, 143–69).

Here, then, in Paul's usage are three interconnecting levels of meaning in the term 'body'. It denotes equally the physical body of the worshipper, the sacramental body that each receives in holy communion, and the social or ecclesial body into which each is incorporated through participating in the Eucharist. It is the second of these three levels, the eucharistic body, that links together the first level with the third, mediating between the physical body and the body corporate. Eucharistic communion causes Christians to belong, as members of the church, not merely to an exterior organization, but to a living organism that is genuinely 'embodied'. To express this 'embodied' awareness, contemporary Orthodox writers often employ the Russian term *sobornost*, meaning 'catholicity', 'conciliarity', 'togetherness' – that is to say, the inner wholeness whereby many different individuals, without forfeiting personal freedom, come to feel, think and act as one (Florovsky in ed. Mascall 1934, 55–8).

While the New Testament reaffirms in this way the Hebraic view of the intrinsic goodness and the spirit-bearing potentialities of the human body, there is also to be found in its pages a new emphasis, not evident in the Old Testament; and this is the particular value that is attached to sexual continence. While there were ascetic movements both in first-century Judaism and in the Greco-Roman world, the New Testament advocates celibacy in a way that was not in general characteristic of either Judaism or Hellenism. Christ is recorded as saying, 'There are some who have made themselves eunuchs for the sake of the kingdom of heaven: let anyone accept this who can' (Matthew 19:12). Paul expresses a definite preference for celibacy rather than marriage (1 Corinthians 7:7,38), and in the Apocalypse a special place in heaven is assigned to the virgins 'who have not defiled themselves with women' (Revelation 14:4).

At the same time New Testament writers clearly insist that marriage is in no way sinful: 'Let marriage be held in honour by all, and let the marriage bed be kept undefiled' (Hebrews 13:4). When virginity is preferred, this is for positive reasons: it is felt to afford a greater freedom to serve God (1 Corinthians 7:32–4), and it is viewed in eschatological terms, as an anticipation of the state of the righteous in the age to come (Luke 20:35–6). Paul's particular reason for advocating celibacy is because he expects the second coming of Christ in the immediate future (1 Corinthians 7:29), not because he feels any revulsion for sexuality as such (Pagels 1990, 17). As the years passed, however, and these eschatological hopes receded, the New Testament passages concerning virginity came to be understood in a somewhat different way.

'EVEN THE SEED IS HOLY'

What, then, did Greek Christians – heirs both to the Bible and to Hellenic philosophy – make of their double inheritance? The society in which they were living was characterized by an increasingly rigid hierarchical structure and by an ever sharper differentiation of social roles. During the period from the Emperor Diocletian (284–305) to the Emperor Justinian (527–65), hereditary serfdom was becoming widespread, with peasants tied more and more closely to the soil, while in the cities sons were often compelled to follow the occupation of their fathers. This is what Mary Douglas classifies as 'strong grid' and 'strong group'. Bearing in mind her thesis concerning the correlation between the two bodies, the social and the physical, this would lead us to expect a corresponding rigidity and constraint in bodily and especially sexual behaviour (Douglas 1973, 93–112). And this indeed is precisely what we find. The Roman Empire from the first and second centuries onwards was marked by a growing moral strictness, amounting to what has been termed *la déroute du corporel*, a veritable 'rout of the body' (Brown 1989, 441). But it would be a mistake to attribute this increasing rigorism exclusively to Christian influence, for it was already in evidence before Christianity had become a dominant factor in society at large. Christianity, however, with its exaltation of virginity and its severe condemnation of all sexual relationships outside marriage, certainly reinforced the existing tendency of the age.

The high point in the Christian disparagement of the body in fact occurs relatively early in church history, during the later part of the second century. Encratite groups at this time, especially in Syria, condemned marriage and required baptized Christians to abstain altogether from sexual activity. The Gnostics went further than this, endorsing Philo's view that the body is 'evil by nature'; according to the followers of Basilides, 'There is salvation for the soul alone, since the body is by nature perishable' (Irenaeus, *Against the Heresies*, I, xxiv, 5). But such extreme opinions were repudiated by the main body of Christians. Against the Encratites, it was insisted – as the New Testament itself clearly affirms – that marriage is a state blessed by God; indeed, the Greek East goes further here than the Latin West, for it has always admitted married men to the priesthood, while permitting them to continue living a full married life. In response to the Gnostics, Irenaeus of Lyons (d. *c.* 200) upholds a holistic, Hebraic standpoint. In his view the whole human person, body and soul together, is made in God's image (cf. Genesis 1:26), and he has much to say about the resurrection of the body on the last day. Using the word 'flesh' not in the Pauline sense but as a term for human physicality, he writes: 'The flesh is to be interpenetrated by the power of the spirit, in such a way that it is no longer simply carnal but becomes truly spiritual through its communion with the spirit . . . Just as the flesh is liable to corruption, so it is also capable of attaining incorruptibility' (Fragment 6, in *Patrologia Orientalis*, 12:738).

Something of the complexity in the early Christian evidence can be appreciated if we compare Origen with his immediate predecessor at Alexandria, Clement (d. *c.* 215). Both are Christian Platonists, although Clement also incorporates Stoic ideas in his teaching on human nature. Origen defines the human person in typically Platonic fashion as 'a soul using a body' (*Against Celsus*, VII, 38). The body is no more than an instrument or tool of the soul, while the divine image is reflected in the latter alone. The soul existed before the body, and only entered an embodied state after it had fallen into sin; it was 'bound to the body as a punishment' (*On First Principles*, I, viii, 1). This does not mean that Origen sees the body as evil; for in his theological system punishment is always reformative, not retributive, and so God has given us a body in order to heal the soul and bring about its restoration. Evil originates not from matter or from the body, but from the misuse of our free will (*Against Celsus*, IV, 65–6). It remains true, however, that for Origen the body is not a part of essential personhood; we were originally created by God as intellects without a body.

Clement sees the body in a far more positive light. The body is the 'soul's consort and ally', and it is only 'through the body' that we can attain our destined end (*The Pedagogue*, I, 13 (102, 3)). Clement does not envisage the soul as pre-existing the body (indeed, Origen's teaching on this point was later condemned by the fifth Ecumenical Council at Constantinople in 553). Moreover, so far from linking the divine image with the soul alone, Clement associates it also with the body and even with human sexuality: 'The human person is the image of God by virtue of the fact that, human though we are, we co-operate with God in the birth of other human beings' (*The Pedagogue*, II, 10 (83, 21)). Formed in the divine image, humans are co-creators with God, and sexuality is one of the expressions of our God-given creativity. 'Among those who are sanctified', states Clement, 'even the seed is holy' (*Stromateis*, II, 6; Oulton and Chadwick 1954, 62).

Later Greek Fathers, however, tend to be a good deal less favourable than Clement in their assessment of sexuality. Athanasius and Gregory of Nyssa in the fourth century, and Maximus the Confessor in the seventh, even take the view that marital union has been approved by God only because of the Fall. Had Adam and Eve continued in paradise in an unfallen state, there would have been no sexual intercourse between them. It does not follow from this that human sexuality as such is sinful; on the contrary, it is something ordained by God. It is not, however, part of the Creator's primary and original plan, but was devised by him specifically with the Fall in view, which in his foreknowledge he anticipated. Yet this somewhat derogatory view of sexuality is explicitly repudiated by other Christian writers, such as Irenaeus in the East and Augustine of Hippo (354–430) in the West. Irenaeus sees Adam and Eve as sexual beings even before the Fall. There was in fact no sexual intercourse in the Garden of Eden, he says, because initially the two of them were still children; but, had they not disobeyed God, they would in due course have grown up to sexual maturity in paradise and procreated offspring (*Against the Heresies*, III, xxii, 4; cf. Brown 1989, 400). For Irenaeus and Augustine, then, the physical bond of marriage and the social order of the family have their roots firmly in the primary, unfallen state of humankind.

Maximus, despite his frequent use of Platonist language and his reservations about sexuality, in fact adopts a model of human personhood that is holistic rather than separatist. He thinks of the human being as microcosm and mediator. We are each of us a 'second cosmos', reflecting in ourselves the complexity of the whole universe – 'a laboratory that contains everything in a comprehensive way' – and it is our human vocation to mediate between all the divided extremes in the created order. Within ourselves we are to draw all things to unity, overcoming the divorce between matter and spirit, between earth and heaven (Thunberg 1965, 100–52; Nellas 1987, 211–16). Now it is clearly impossible for us to fulfil this mediatorial task unless we accept as an integral part of ourselves the body through which we relate to our material environment. Rejecting our body, we reject also our God-given role as mediators (Ware 1987, 197–201).

Outside Gnosticism, then, what we find in Greek Christianity is not an outright rejection of the body, but at the most an ambivalence, an unresolved tension. While the fundamental goodness of the body is always upheld, in practice it is often viewed in a negative light. In particular, from at least as early as the third century, there is a tendency to revive within a Christian context the regulations laid down in the Old Testament concerning the ritual impurity of women during menstruation (Leviticus 15:19–24). Although some early Christian texts maintain that women are free to receive communion at all times, regardless of their bodily condition, the more common view is that they should not communicate during their monthly periods (Brown 1989, 146, 433). Within the Orthodox Church today this prohibition is still enforced widely, although not universally. In the early sources similar restrictions are also applied to males, who are usually discouraged from communicating if they have undergone an emission during sleep in the previous night (Ward and

Russell 1980, 135); significantly, however, the ruling is phrased less strictly than are the prohibitions relating to women. In theory such regulations might spring, not from a hatred of the body, but from a reverence for the power and mystery of sexuality. But in practice they have frequently been understood, by women and men alike, to mean that anything connected with procreation involves defilement.

A parallel ruling in the Christian East forbids married couples to have intercourse in the night before communion (Brown 1989, 256). Once more, this does not necessarily imply that sexuality is sinful. Such abstinence can be seen simply as part of the preparation for receiving the Eucharist, on a level with the pre-communion fast from food. Yet the prohibition stands in marked contrast to the Jewish viewpoint, which sees the Sabbath night as a particularly appropriate occasion for husband and wife to make love.

A suspicion of the body, and more especially of women's bodies, is a recurrent feature of monasticism from the fourth century onwards: 'a woman's body is fire', state the Sayings of the Desert Fathers. But the evidence does not always point in one direction only. Elsewhere the *Apophthegmata* express a more relaxed and humane attitude. 'Meeting some nuns on the road, a monk turned aside. But the abbess said to him, "If you were a perfect monk, you wouldn't even have noticed we were women"' (Ward 1975, 6–7). Monks and nuns have always shown a particular reverence for the bodies of the sick and the poor, a theme much emphasized by Basil of Caesarea (d. 379) and John Chrysostom (d. 407) (Brown 1989, 289–90, 309–12). It is particularly reassuring to find, in one of the earliest and most influential of all Greek monastic texts – *The Life of Antony*, traditionally attributed to Athanasius (d. 373) – a surprisingly positive view of the body. When Antony the hermit emerged after twenty years shut up in a fort, his friends 'were amazed to see that his body had maintained its former condition, neither fat from lack of exercise, nor emaciated from fasting and combat with demons, but he was just as they had known him before his withdrawal . . . He was altogether balanced, as one guided by reason and abiding in a natural state.' Although Antony lived to be more than a hundred, 'his eyes were undimmed and quite sound, and he saw clearly; he lost none of his teeth – they had simply become worn down to the gums because of the old man's great age. He remained strong in both feet and hands' (*The Life of Antony*, sections 14 and 93; Pettersen 1989, 438–47). There is no trace of dualism here; physical austerities have not destroyed Antony's body but restored it to a healthy and natural state. Asceticism, rightly understood,

is a struggle not *against* but *for* the body; in the words of the Russian
Orthodox theologian Sergei Bulgakov (1871–1944), 'Kill the flesh, so as
to acquire a body' (Bloom 1967, 41).

In common with almost all Greek Christian sources, *The Life of Antony*
displays a fear of the naked body (Athanasius 1980, §60). But there are
some monastic texts in which even this is not to be found. Symeon the
New Theologian (949–1022) records with approval the attitude of his
teacher Symeon the Studite:

> He was not afraid of the limbs of anyone,
> Or to see others naked and to be seen naked himself.
> For he possessed the whole Christ, and was himself wholly Christ.
> And always he regarded all his own limbs, and the limbs of everyone else,
> Individually and collectively, as being Christ himself.

Symeon the New Theologian develops the point with startling detail: my
hand is Christ, he says, my foot is Christ – even my penis is Christ. To
anyone scandalized by his forthrightness, he responds: 'Do not accuse
me of blasphemy, but accept these things and worship Christ who made
you as you are' (*Hymns*, xv, 141–211). Such an explicit endorsement of the
body in all its functions is altogether exceptional in Greek Christianity;
but Symeon is doing no more than to follow out to the end the logic of
Irenaeus' teaching concerning paradise and Maximus' vision of the
human person as microcosm and mediator.

'UNFATHOMABLE DEPTHS': THE HEART AS UNIFYING CENTRE

One way in which the Christian East emphasizes the unity of the human
person, soul and body together, is through the term 'heart' (*kardia*). In the
Bible this signifies much more than just the feelings or emotions (which
are on the whole located lower down, in the belly, entrails, or guts). The
heart is regarded, in both the Old and the New Testament, as the focal
point of moral action, the seat of intelligence and wisdom. It represents
the spiritual centre of the human subject in its totality, the place where
we find our personal unity and where at the same time we experience
divine grace: in Paul's words, 'God has sent the Spirit of his Son *into our
hearts*' (Galatians 4:6).

Although the richness of the Semitic usage is lacking in many Greek
Christian texts, there are also occasions when the heart is given its full
biblical value (Guillaumont 1952, 2281). A notable example occurs in the
Homilies attributed to Macarius, a late fourth-century text written in
Greek, although Syrian in background. Here the heart is seen as a
unifying symbol for total personhood:

The heart governs and reigns over the whole bodily organism; and when grace possesses the pasturages of the heart, it rules over all the members and the thoughts. For there, within the heart, is the intellect, with all the thoughts of the soul and all its expectation; and in this way grace penetrates also to all the members of the body . . . Within the heart are unfathomable depths . . . The heart is Christ's palace: there Christ the king comes to take his rest, with the angels and the spirits of the saints, and he dwells there, walking within it and placing his kingdom there. (*Homilies*, xv, 20, 32–3)

For Macarius the heart is thus the point of convergence and interaction within the human person as a whole. It is the means whereby grace permeates our body, and at the same time it is the centre in which the intellect resides. Macarius does not posit a head–heart contrast but, like the American Indian Ochwiay Biano in his conversation with C. G. Jung, he considers that we think with our heart (Jung 1967, 276). 'Within the heart are unfathomable depths', and its true fullness is hidden from us: it extends below into the unconscious, and it is the domain where unspoken thoughts and desires lurk in darkness; at the same time it reaches upwards into the abyss of God.

Using heart in this all-embracing Hebraic sense, John Climacus writes: 'I cried out with my whole heart – that is, with my body and soul and spirit' (Climacus 1982, 281). When later Byzantine writers refer to 'prayer of the heart', 'discovering the place of the heart', 'entering the heart', they are reading into the word 'heart' a similar range of meaning. 'Prayer of the heart' is not merely 'affective' prayer but prayer of the entire person, including the body – not merely the prayer that is said by human efforts but the prayer that God's Spirit is praying within the person. To 'enter' or 'discover' the heart therefore signifies the total reintegration of human personhood in God.

The heart is in this way the hidden core of the self, the *temenos* or inner shrine. It is the secret place of meeting between body and soul, between soul and spirit, between the unconscious and the conscious, between the created and the uncreated. Here surely is a fitting symbol to express a holistic anthropology. Within a spirituality of the heart, the body acquires its true religious significance.

THE PHYSICALITY OF WORSHIP

'Christianity is a liturgical religion', says Georges Florovsky (1893–1979). 'Worship comes first, doctrine and discipline second.' How then is the Greek Christian understanding of the body expressed in worship? What practical use do we make of our physicality when praying?

(1) The body participates in worship first of all through a wide range of *symbolical actions*. Eastern Christians face towards the East; they mark themselves with the sign of the Cross (Christians in the Orthodox world do this with far greater frequency than Western Christians); they make deep bows, and sometimes prostrations to the ground.

(2) The body is also involved in the spiritual life through *fasting and abstinence*, which continue to play an important part in the daily experience of Eastern Christians up to the present day. Wednesdays and Fridays in almost all weeks throughout the year are fast days; there are also a seven-week fast before Easter, a forty-day fast before Christmas, and two shorter fasts in the summer. In principle 'fasting' means abstinence from meat, from dairy products (eggs, milk, butter, and cheese), and on many days also from fish, wine, and olive oil; but in practice today the regulations are often interpreted flexibly, especially among Orthodox Christians in the West. Married couples are required to abstain from sexual intercourse during the night preceding a fast day, and throughout the longer fasts; but here again there is flexibility over the application of the rules. If fasting is enjoined, this is not because there is anything intrinsically sinful about eating (or about sexual intercourse within marriage). The fast is in order to render eating sacramental, so that it becomes an expression of thanksgiving to God for the gift of food and a means of communion with other humans, instead of being simply the selfish satisfaction of physical needs. Similarly the abstinence of married couples has as its aim not the suppression but the purification of sexuality.

(3) The two chief Christian sacraments or 'mysteries' (as they are termed in Greek), *baptism and the Eucharist*, obviously involve the body in a direct way. At their baptism people are washed with water, in the Eucharist they eat bread and wine. In both cases the Orthodox Church seeks to preserve undiminished the materiality of the sacramental signs. Except in cases of emergency, baptism is performed by immersion. It is not enough to pour a little water over the candidate's forehead, but it must flow over the whole body – a symbolical drowning, 'a furious devout drench', to borrow Philip Larkin's phrase. In the same way at the Eucharist the Orthodox Church uses not wafers but leavened bread, similar to the bread eaten daily in the home.

'Those who receive the Eucharist with faith are made holy in both body and soul', states Clement of Alexandria (*The Pedagogue*, II, 2 (20, 1)): eucharistic eating, as a physical act, transforms and sanctifies the body. Whereas in ordinary eating food is changed into the person who consumes it – fish, bread, and milk become human flesh and blood – here the reverse happens: we become what we eat, and through holy communion our bodies are changed into the members of Christ's body. So Symeon the New Theologian writes, in a post-communion thanksgiving to Christ:

> This my defiled tabernacle, subject to corruption,
> Has been united to your all-pure body
> And my blood has been mixed with your blood.
> I know that I have been united also to your Godhead
> And have become your most pure body,
> A member shining with light, holy, glorious, transparent . . .
> Altogether ashamed and hesitant, I am at a loss
> Where to sit down and what to touch,
> Where to rest these limbs that have become your limbs,
> In what works or actions to employ
> These members that are terrible and divine (*Hymns*, II, 11–29)

(4) *Anointing* of the body with oil is frequent in the Christian East. Olive-oil is not only a normal ingredient in the *cuisine* of Greek Christians, but also an accepted part of their worship. At baptism there is first a pre-baptismal anointing with ordinary olive-oil, and then after the immersion there is a post-baptismal anointing with a special consecrated oil (mixed with aromatic substances) known as *myron* or chrism; this 'chrismation', as it is termed, corresponds to Western confirmation. The chrism is marked in the form of the Cross on forehead, eyes, nostrils, lips, ears, breast, hands, and feet: the whole body is involved. The sick are anointed sacramentally with oil in the service known in Greek as *Euchelaion* or 'Oil of Prayer'. As the priest performs the anointing, he uses the words 'For the healing of soul and body', implying a holistic standpoint: there is no clear line of demarcation between bodily illness and sickness of the soul, and so the two are healed together. Thus the *Euchelaion* is held to confer not only physical healing (if that is God's will), but also the forgiveness of sins. An anointing with oil frequently forms part of the Vigil Service on Saturday evenings and the eves of feasts, especially in the Russian tradition; and pilgrims are anointed with oil from the lamp burning before the saint's shrine.

(5) Another sacramental gesture that involves the body is the *laying-on of hands*. This takes place both at ordinations and in the Orthodox rite of confession. In the ancient practice, to signify a transfer of guilt the penitent at confession laid his hand on the neck of the priest; today, to

symbolize Christ's gift of forgiveness, a reverse gesture occurs with the priest placing his stole and then his hand on the penitent's head (Hausherr 1990, xxv).

(6) At *funerals* the coffin is left open and all approach to give a last kiss to the departed, a ceremony already mentioned around 500 by Dionysius the Areopagite (*The Ecclesiastical Hierarchy*, vii, 2). The dead body is an object of love, not of abhorrence. Cremation is normally forbidden in the Orthodox Church, for the same reasons as in Judaism: because of the reverence for the physical body and the belief in its ultimate resurrection.

All five bodily senses have in this way a part to play in worship: not only sight and hearing, but taste (at the Eucharist), touch (through anointing, through the laying-on of hands, through kissing the dead body, and also through kissing the holy icons in church and at home), and even smell (through the aromatic substances in the chrism, and through the burning of incense both in church and in the home).

(7) There is one 'mystery' in which the body is involved with particular immediacy, and that is *marriage*. Elsewhere the 'matter' of the sacrament is a substance – such as water, bread, wine, or oil – that is blessed or consecrated, and then applied to or consumed by the bodies of the worshippers. In marriage, on the other hand, the sacramental 'matter' that receives God's blessing is the actual body itself of the man and woman who are entering into matrimony.

The attitude of the Greek Fathers towards marriage, as already noted, is often less than totally affirmative. It is seen as inferior to celibacy, and sometimes associated specifically with the fallen condition. While regarded as a state of life ordained by God and blessed by the church, it tends to be viewed in predominantly physiological terms. Sexual intercourse within marriage is felt to be justified when used for the purpose of child-bearing, but it is not normally commended as a way in which the couple express their mutual love. This physiological emphasis, perhaps derived from Stoicism, is apparent already in the middle of the second century. 'We do not marry except in order to raise up children', says Justin Martyr (d. *c.* 165); 'otherwise we abstain from marriage and observe total celibacy' (*First Apology*, 29; Richardson 1953, 260). It is not easy to find in Greek Christianity a parallel to the remarkable statement of the Jewish *Zohar*, 'The pleasure of cohabitation is a religious one, giving joy also to the Divine Presence (*shekinah*)' (Scholem 1963, 35). The standpoint of Gregory Palamas (1296–1359) is very different: 'The pleasure experienced in procreating children within the lawful bond of marriage should most definitely *not* be termed a divine gift of God, for it is fleshly, the gift of nature and not of grace, even though nature was created by God' (*Triads*, 1, i, 22).

It is therefore surprising to find that a negative view of marriage and sexuality is not in fact to be found anywhere in the service for a first marriage (Evdokimov 1985, 130–48). Nowhere is it implied that marriage is a second best, inferior to celibacy. Nowhere is it suggested that marriage is to be regarded as a remedy against sin, a way of controlling our unruly impulses (this is, however, stated in the special service prescribed for a second marriage following a divorce). Two reasons only are given for marriage, and they are both of them positive: the bearing and upbringing of children, and shared love between husband and wife. Sexuality is seen, not just from a physiological viewpoint, but also in terms of personal relationships. Petitions are said for 'the gift of children', 'the fruit of the womb', but the prayers speak with equal emphasis about 'mutual love in the bond of peace', 'a bond of affection that cannot be broken'. No attempt is made to single out one of these two things rather than the other as the primary aim of marriage, but they are mentioned together. Adopting a holistic perspective the service speaks about 'concord of *soul and body*'.

In assessing the attitude of the Christian East towards the role of the body in marriage, we need to give particular attention to the text of the marriage rite. For each single person who has read Gregory of Nyssa or Maximus the Confessor, there must be a thousand who have listened to the prayers of the marriage service, not just once but repeatedly. In shaping the 'Orthodox' mind, these prayers have had an influence incomparably greater than that of any individual author, however eminent.

(8) The body has its part not only in liturgical worship but in *private prayer*. This is evident above all in the so-called 'physical method' employed by the Byzantine Hesychasts (i.e., persons who seek *hesychia* or inner stillness). From the fifth century onwards it has been customary in the Christian East to use a short invocation, frequently repeated, known as the 'Jesus Prayer'. Often this takes the form 'Lord Jesus Christ, Son of God, have mercy on me', but there are a number of variants. In Coptic sources dating from the seventh or eighth century this invocation of Jesus is linked with the rhythm of the breathing (Guillaumont 1974, 66–71). In the Greek tradition at the same period Climacus and Hesychius of Sinai possibly hint at a similar practice (Climacus 1982, 48–50), but the first clear description of the 'physical method' comes only in Greek writers of the late thirteenth and the fourteenth centuries, most notably

Plate 2   A hesychast at prayer (in the position of Elijah: see 1 Kings 18:42). From a
miniature in a twelfth-century ms. of John Climacus (Vatican Gr. 1754).

Nicephorus the Hesychast, Gregory of Sinai and Gregory Palamas
(Meyendorff 1964, 134–56; 1974, 55–63).

In its developed form the 'physical method' has three aspects:

(i) A particular *bodily posture* is recommended: the hesychast sits on a
low stool (contrast the normal position for prayer in the Christian East,
which is to stand), with his head bowed and his chin resting on his chest.
This is different from the 'lotus' position in Yoga, in which the back is
straight. As a Biblical precedent, the Byzantine hesychasts mention the
example of Elijah, who when praying 'put his face between his knees'
(1 Kings 18:42).

(ii) The *breathing* is regulated: its rhythm is slowed down and at the
same time co-ordinated with the words of the Jesus Prayer. In modern

Orthodox practice it is common to say the opening words of the Jesus Prayer, 'Lord Jesus Christ, Son of God', while breathing in, and the remainder – often with the words 'a sinner' added at the end – while breathing out. In a nineteenth-century Russian text, *The Way of a Pilgrim*, the invocation is linked with the beating of the heart (French 1954, 19–20, 102), but the Greek sources say nothing of this, and in contemporary Orthodoxy such a practice is seen as potentially harmful and is generally discouraged.

(iii) Simultaneously with the control of the breathing, the hesychast practises *inner exploration*, searching for the place of the heart. According to Nicephorus, he is to picture his breath entering through the nostrils and then passing down within the lungs until it reaches the heart; at the same time he is to make his *nous* or intellect descend with the breath, so that intellect and heart are united. On no account is he to extend this inner exploration to the regions below the heart. There are parallels here with techniques in Yoga and Sufism. Obviously the term 'heart' is being used in this context in both a literal and a symbolical sense: it signifies not only the physical organ but the spiritual centre of the total human person.

Here, then, is a tradition of prayer that seeks to assign full value to the body. So far from being merely a hindrance and cause of distraction, the body if properly disciplined can be a constructive helper. Defending this bodily technique, Gregory Palamas is careful to point out that it does not constitute the essence of inner prayer, but is no more than a useful accessory suited primarily for 'beginners'. At the same time, however, he considers that it rests on a sound biblical doctrine of the person as an undivided unity. 'Through our outward posture we train outselves to be inwardly attentive', he writes (*Triads*, 1, ii, 10): the outer affects the inner, and the body has dynamic energies which can be creatively harnessed in the work of prayer.

Not only in his defence of the physical method but in his theology as a whole, Gregory Palamas is for the most part highly affirmative in his view of the body (notwithstanding the comment on marriage quoted above). Following Irenaeus, he holds that it is not just the intellect or soul that is created in God's image, but the entire human person, including the body. He cites with approval the words of Maximus the Confessor, 'The body is divinized along with the soul' (*Triads*, 1, iii, 37). 'The flesh also is transformed', he writes (not using *sarx* here in the Pauline sense). 'It is raised on high together with the soul, and together it enjoys communion with God, becoming his domain and dwelling-place'

(*Triads*, 1, ii, 9). The body is directly involved in the vision of God. At Christ's transfiguration on Mount Tabor, the apostles beheld the uncreated light of the Godhead through their bodily eyes, and at the second coming the righteous will likewise gaze on Christ's eternal glory through the physical eyes of their resurrection body. Even in this present life the bodies of the saints sometimes shine outwardly with the same divine light that shone from Christ on Tabor. 'If in the age to come', says Palamas, 'the body will share with the soul in ineffable blessings, it must certainly share in them, so far as possible, here and now' (*The Tome of the Holy Mountain*, 6).

At an earlier point we noted, in the first centuries of Greek Christianity, two contrasting attitudes towards the human body: the Platonizing approach of Origen, which, without being dualist, none the less marginalizes the body; and the biblical anthropology of Irenaeus, which treats personhood as a single unity. Traversing eleven centuries and coming to Palamas it is noteworthy that the viewpoint which finally prevails is Biblical rather than Platonic, Irenaean rather than Origenist. In that double inheritance to which Greek Christians were the heirs, it is the biblical element that proves in the end the more influential. Jerusalem prevails over Athens. 'Our retrieval of mystery', it has been said, 'is dependent on our reinstatement of the body, with its rhythms and dreams and ways of knowing' (Taylor 1972, 45). With this claim the Christian East on the whole agrees. 'I am bound to him for ever', says St John Climacus. But that is not our misfortune; it is our opportunity.

BIBLIOGRAPHY

Afanassieff, N. (1963), 'The Church which presides in love', in eds. J. Meyendorff *et al.*, *The Primacy of Peter*, London: 57–110.
Athanasius (1980), *The Life of Antony*, trans. R. C. Gregg, The Classics of Western Spirituality, New York.
Bloom, Metropolitan A. (1967), 'Body and Matter in Spiritual Life', in ed. A. M. Allchin, *Sacrament and Image: Essays in the Christian Understanding of Man*, London: 33–41.
Brown, P. (1989), *The Body and Society. Men, Women and Sexual Renunciation in Early Christianity*, London.
    (1990), 'Bodies and Minds: Sexuality and Renunciation in Early Christianity', in eds. D. M. Halperin, J. J. Winkler, and F. I. Zeitlin, *Before Sexuality: The Construction of Erotic Experience in the Ancient World*, Princeton: 479–95.
Clement of Alexandria (1960–70), *The Pedagogue*, eds. H.-I. Marrou *et al.*, *Sources chrétiennes*, 70, 108, 158, Paris.

Climacus, John (1982), *The Ladder of Divine Ascent*, trans. C. Luibheid and N. Russell, The Classics of Western Spirituality, New York.

Dionysius the Areopagite ('Pseudo-Dionysius') (1987), *The Complete Works*, trans. C. Luibheid and P. Rorem, The Classics of Western Spirituality, New York.

Douglas, M. (1966), *Purity and Danger. An Analysis of the Concepts of Pollution and Taboo*, London.

(1973), *Natural Symbols: Explorations in Cosmology*, 2nd edn, London.

Evdokimov, P. (1985), *The Sacrament of Love*, New York.

Florovsky, G. (1934), '*Sobornost*: The Catholicity of the Church', in ed. E. L. Mascall, *The Church of God: An Anglo-Russian Symposium*, London: 53–74.

French, R. M. (trans.) (1954), *The Way of a Pilgrim*, London.

Gregory Palamas (1959), *Triads in Defence of the Holy Hesychasts*, ed. J. Meyendorff, Louvain.

(1966), *The Tome of the Holy Mountain*, eds. P. Christou *et al.*, *Writings of Gregory Palamas*, vol. 2, Thessalonica: 567–78.

Guillaumont, A. (1952), 'Le "coeur" chez les spirituels grecs à l'époque ancienne', *Dictionnaire de Spiritualité*, ii, Paris: 2281–8.

(1974), 'The Jesus Prayer among the Monks of Egypt', *Eastern Churches Review* 6:1, 66–71.

Gundry, R. H. (1976), *Sōma in Biblical Theology: with Emphasis on Pauline Anthropology*, Cambridge.

Hausherr, I. (1990), *Spiritual Direction in the Christian East*, with a foreword by K. Ware, Cistercian Studies Series 116, Kalamazoo.

Irenaeus (1965–82), *Against the Heresies*, eds. A. Rousseau, L. Doutreleau, and C. Mercier, *Sources chrétiennes*, 100, 152–3, 210–11, 263–4, 293–4, Paris.

Jung, C. G. (1967), *Memories, Dreams, Reflections*, Fontana Library, London.

Macarius (1921), *Homilies*, trans. A. J. Mason, London.

Meyendorff, J. (1964), *A Study of Gregory Palamas*, London.

(1974), *St. Gregory Palamas and Orthodox Spirituality*, New York.

Nellas, P. (1987), *Deification in Christ: Orthodox Perspectives on the Nature of the Human Person*, New York.

Origen (1953), *Against Celsus*, trans. H. Chadwick, Cambridge.

(1936) *On First Principles*, trans. G. W. Butterworth, London.

Oulton, J. E. L., and Chadwick, H. (eds.) (1954), *Alexandrian Christianity*, The Library of Christian Classics, vol. 2, London.

Pagels, E. (1990), *Adam and Eve, and the Serpent*, London: Penguin Books.

Pettersen, A. (1989), 'Athanasius' Presentation of Antony of the Desert's Admiration for his Body', in ed. E. A. Livingstone, *Studia Patristica* 21, 438–47.

(1990), *Athanasius and the Human Body*, Bristol.

Philo (1929), *Allegorical Interpretation of the Laws*, eds. F. H. Colson and G. H. Whitaker, Loeb Classical Library, vol. 1, London.

Philo (1932), *The Migration of Abraham*, eds. F. H. Colson and G. H. Whitaker, Loeb Classical Library, vol. 4, London.

Porphyry (1966), *Life of Plotinus*, ed. A. H. Armstrong, *Plotinus*, Loeb Classical Library, vol. 1, London.

Price, R. M. (1990), 'The Distinctiveness of Early Christian Sexual Ethics', *Heythrop Journal* 31, 257–76.

Richardson, C. C. (ed.) (1953), *Early Christian Fathers*, The Library of Christian Classics, vol. 1, London.

Robinson, J. A. T. (1952), *The Body. A Study in Pauline Theology*, London.

Rouselle, A. (1988), *Porneia: On Desire and the Body in Antiquity*, Oxford.

Scholem, G. G. (ed.) (1963), *Zohar: The Book of Splendor. Basic Readings from the Kabbalah*, New York: Schocken Books.

Sherrard, P. (1976), *Christianity and Eros*, London.

Symeon the New Theologian (1969–73), *Hymns*, ed. J. Koder, *Sources chrétiennes*, 156, 174, 196, Paris.

Taylor, J. V. (1972), *The Go-Between God. The Holy Spirit and the Christian Mission*, London.

Tertullian, (1960), *On the Resurrection*, ed. E. Evans, London.

Thunberg, L. (1965), *Microcosm and Mediator: the Theological Anthropology of Maximus the Confessor*, Lund.

Wallace-Hadrill, D. S. (1968), *The Greek Patristic View of Nature*, Manchester: 40–65.

Ward, Sister B. (trans.) (1975), *The Wisdom of the Desert Fathers: Apophthegmata Patrum from the Anonymous Series*, Oxford: Fairacres Publication 48.

Ward, Sister B. and Russell, N. (trans.) (1980), *The Lives of the Desert Fathers: the Historia Monachorum in Aegypto*, London/Oxford.

Ware, K. (1967), 'The Transfiguration of the Body', in ed. A. M. Allchin, *Sacrament and Image: Essays in the Christian Understanding of Man*, London: 17–32.

(1987), 'The Unity of the Human Person according to the Greek Fathers', in eds. A. Peacocke and G. Gillett, *Persons and Personality: A Contemporary Enquiry*, Oxford: 197–206.

Zizioulas, Metropolitan J. (1985), *Being as Communion: Studies in Personhood and the Church*, New York.

CHAPTER 7

The body in Western Catholic Christianity

Andrew Louth

To survey the significance of the body in Western Christianity before the Reformation is not to study an established tradition, but rather to try and trace a variety of attempts to locate and value the bodily in a society that was rarely settled but constantly subject to changing pressures. It is also to look at attitudes to the bodily that are based on very different presuppositions from our own, so much so that one is often given to doubt whether the understanding of the bodily in this society has any real continuity with any of the ways in which we relate to the bodily.

Western Catholic Christianity did not start in a vacuum, nor is its immediate background to be seen in the New Testament and behind that the Hebrew tradition of the Old Testament. In its origins Western Catholic Christianity is simply the Christianity of the Mediterranean world, predominantly Greek in language and thought-forms: it is only towards the end of the fourth century that we can begin to use the epithet 'Western' (and 'Latin') in any confident way. It is necessary, then, to begin with, to sketch in those features of the earlier 'undivided' Christian tradition that are necessary for an understanding of what was to become distinctively 'Western'.

A useful way of doing this, for our purposes, is to look briefly at the understanding of the human person, not in one or other of the early Christian writers, but in one of the works of the greatest and most influential of the classical Greek philosophers, Plato, his late cosmological dialogue, the *Timaeus*. This is not so much because the *Timaeus* was enormously influential for later understanding of the human person (though it was, and in fact was the only one of Plato's dialogues available in Latin translation, and then only in part, to the Western Middle Ages), but because its cosmology and anthropology were *typical* for conceptions of the body in late antiquity. Here are, as it were, the presuppositions that are so different from ours.

Two features of the *Timaeus* are important for our purposes. First of all, the cosmos is understood on the analogy of the human person, or conversely – and this is how it seemed to Plato – the human person is a copy, reflection, image of the cosmos, which is a living creature endowed with soul and reason (ζῷον ἔμψυχον ἔννουν: *Tim.* 30B). The cosmos is seen as a great body, the human being as a little body: and both owe their life and form to indwelling soul and reason. So the human body is seen against the background of the cosmos: it is both a part of it and an encapsulation of the whole (the all – τὸ πᾶν – as Plato often calls the cosmos). So to think of the human body (as a whole informed by reason, not as a mere piece of matter: that would be simply a corpse) is to think of something that is an analogy of the cosmos, a key to understanding the cosmos itself. The other feature of the *Timaeus* that needs to be remarked on is the account of the human body as such in the third part of the work (69A–92C). Here the body is seen as giving physical expression to the soul and undergirding its threefold nature as reason, psychological energy (θυμός) and desire (ἐπιθυμία). This physical expression takes place through the disposition of the four elements – fire, air, water, and earth – and the balance of the four humours (χυμοί), though in Plato's account in the *Timaeus* the doctrine of the humours is very much in the background. Health is a matter of the *balance* of the constituents, a balance that reflects (and effects) the proper balance that ought to exist between the three parts of the soul (a balance called justice, δικαιοσύνη, in the *Republic*: IV.441E–442B), and also the balance that exists in the cosmos: health is achieved 'by imitation of the form of the Universe' (88C). The notion that the body is an organism whose health is a matter of the balance of forces that can be identified as phlegm, blood, and so forth yields an understanding of the body that is much more accessible than the notions of modern medicine. In antiquity and the Middle Ages people could make much more use of their sense of the complexity of the body than we can of a much more accurate understanding of its complexity that has become a specialized preserve. Sexual activity, for instance, was not just an interpersonal matter: in it were mirrored the energies of the cosmos. As Peter Brown graphically puts it, the bodies of men and women of late antiquity 'were little fiery universes, through whose heart, brain, and veins there pulsed the same heat and vital spirit as glowed in the stars'.[1]

Christians expressed their understanding of the human person in the context of the kind of presuppositions to which the *Timaeus* bears witness.

---

[1] Brown, 1988, 17.

I want to point to two ways – one practical, one theoretical – in which this 'cosmic' understanding of the human person (and the human body) was given expression. The first, practical way concerns the position adopted by the body in prayer. Plato had already seen man's upright posture as having 'cosmic' significance: a notion that had become a commonplace. He spoke of the rational soul as 'housed in the top of our body' and of its 'raising us – seeing that we are not an earthly but a heavenly plant – up from the earth towards our kindred in heaven . . . for it is by suspending our head and root from that region whence the substance of our soul first came that the divine power keeps upright our whole body'.[2] The early Christians went further than this: like the Jews (and later the Muslims), they specified the direction one should face in prayer. The Jews turned to face Jerusalem (as Muslims turn to face Mecca), which they understood to be the centre of the earth (an idea preserved in many medieval maps).[3] Christians, probably in deliberate contrast, turned to face East, whence the sun rose and whence they expected the coming of the Messiah. Three treatises on prayer survive from the pre-Constantinian period – by Origen, Tertullian, and Cyprian – and for all these writers prayer is to be made by Christians, standing up, with hands raised, facing East, and, in the case of men, with heads uncovered.[4] Origen lays considerable stress on Eastward-facing prayer as symbolizing 'the soul looking towards where the true light arises', and insists that one should pray facing East even if it means facing a blank wall, for the orientation of a room is a matter of convention (θέσει), whereas it is by nature (φύσει) that the East takes precedence over the other points of the compass.[5] The use of the Stoic distinction between θέσις and φύσις is significant in that what is by nature is part of the structure of the cosmos, whereas what is by convention is merely a matter of human taste or contrivance. The custom of standing for prayer (on Sundays and during Pentecost) was given canonical authority by the First Ecumenical Council, held at Nicaea in 325 (canon 20). The custom of facing East for prayer influenced the orientation of churches (just as synagogues faced Jerusalem) from as early as we have evidence.[6] This concern for the position, and orientation, of the body in prayer is a practical expression of a sense of the cosmic significance of the body, and

[2] *Timaeus* 90AB: trans. by R. G. Bury, Loeb Classical Library, 1929, 245–7.
[3] See Nebenzahl 1986.
[4] Origen, *de Oratione* 31f.; Tertullian, *de Oratione* 14, 17 (prayer facing East is mentioned by Tertullian elsewhere, see *Apologia* 16.10; cf. also 30.7); Cyprian, *de Oratione Dominica* 4ff.
[5] Origen, *de Oratione* 32.   [6] See Moreton 1982.

of the cosmic significance of the redemption that was brought about through the resurrection. Such a notion of orientation provides the basis for a notion of sacred space, in which there is celebrated liturgically the restoration of the cosmos.

The other way in which Christians expressed a cosmic understanding of the human person is found in their understanding of cosmology. Plato in his *Timaeus* is agnostic about the 'whence' of the cosmos: it is beyond understanding, all he can do is tell a 'likely story' (εἰκὼς μῦθος: 29D). Later thinkers were more confident and, especially from the second century AD onwards, their understanding of cosmogony was governed by an anxiety to see this process as the derivation of the manifold from the simple and single. Such a movement from the One was profoundly ambivalent. For Plotinus it was, on the one hand, the overflow of the goodness of the One, a demonstration of superabundant generosity, but, on the other, it was an act of daring (τόλμα), an act of separation (τόμη – Plotinus avails himself of the play on words afforded by the Greek), of separation from the origin that seemed to be the original fault, the primal sin, which the soul's return to the One would overcome and absolve. It might seem that Christianity managed to separate out these two opposed motives, assigning overflow of goodness to creation and the primal sin to the Fall – God created everything and it was good, Adam sinned and brought about the Fall – but if we look more closely we see it is not as simple as that. Origen, for instance, envisaged a primal state of pure spiritual beings (with, perhaps, pure spiritual bodies) freely and perfectly contemplating the primal unity of God: but these beings turned away from God and fell; in their fall they became souls and were provided with bodies (or terrestrial bodies) and it is these fallen souls with their bodies that constitute the cosmos.[7] So the creation of the cosmos *is* the fall of the pre-existent souls. Or, put another way, there is a notion of a double creation, or two-stage creation: the first stage is the creation of spiritual beings, fashioned in the image of God, the second stage is the creation of the material cosmos of embodied souls, souls that have fallen away from God. And one feature of this cosmos of embodied souls is that these bodies manifest sexual differentiation: such distinction, such a manifestation of twoness (or the dyad), is a sign of the corporeal creation's having fallen away from primitive unity. Origen's idea of double creation was not original to him: he owed it to the Alexandrian Jewish philosopher Philo, the contemporary of Jesus and Paul. Although the precise form in

---

[7] Cf., for example, Origen, *de Principiis* 1.4.

which Origen expressed it, involving a primal state of eternally pre-existent souls, was not acceptable to later Christian orthodoxy, the notion of double creation was to have a deep influence on Greek patristic and Byzantine Christianity: it is found in several writers of the fourth century, most notably Gregory of Nyssa, and, perhaps even more significantly, in the greatest of the Byzantine theologians, Maximus the Confessor, who lived in the seventh century. This doctrine of double creation makes a distinction within creation between the first creation of spiritual beings in the image of God, and the creation of human beings, embodied and marked by sexual differentiation. For orthodox writers, both these stages are good (second creation is not identified with the Fall, as with Origen), but even so the first stage is more fundamentally good, for the second stage, marked as it is by duality (between soul and body, male and female), contains within itself the seeds of sinful division, and for Maximus, for example, the goal of the Christian life is not simply the overcoming of sin and its disruptive effects on humanity, but also the transcending of the duality manifest at the level of second creation, including that between male and female (it is perhaps not without significance that Plato, in the *Timaeus*, treats of sexual differentiation, sexual congress and procreation in an appendix: 90E–91D).

But such a doctrine of double creation was not simply a matter of ideas and theories: it had a powerful influence on ideals of Christian living in late antiquity. A striking feature of Christian life in that period is the enormous prominence of the ideal of virginity, or celibacy. Various justifications might be given for such an ideal, and Peter Brown makes clear the great variety of social strategies the ideal of virginity subserved.[8] Paul the Apostle extols celibacy on the grounds that it makes one free, free from worldly concerns and free for the Lord: the unmarried person is single-minded. The expectation of the imminent end of the world intensified such considerations (cf. 1 Corinthians 7:15–25). Something along these lines is presumably what Jesus meant by those who are 'eunuchs for the sake of the kingdom of heaven' (Matthew 19:12). But, when Jesus said to the Sadducees that 'when they rise from the dead, they neither marry nor are given in marriage, but are like the angels in heaven' (Mark 12:25), his words could be taken as suggesting a more fundamental justification for celibacy: the celibate anticipates the state of the resurrection, which is an angelic state, a state that does not admit of the distinction between the sexes, nor *a fortiori* has any place for marriage.

---

[8] Brown 1988, *passim*.

And here the doctrine of double creation provides powerful theoretical support. If the state of those risen from the dead is beyond the distinction of sex, then it is like man's first creation: the end is like the beginning. The celibate is seeking to return to his or her original, primal state. The eschatological justification for celibacy becomes *proto*logical: it is justified by humanity's first state. And that readily becomes *onto*logical: the celibate is seen as seeking to return to his original, *natural* state, he is becoming what, most deeply, he is. The Fall of man has brought about a state of affairs characterized by corruption and death (φθορά and θάνατος): marriage and the bearing of children contribute to the maintenance of this state of corruption and death. Children are born to die, the sexual act involves corruption (ἄφθορος, incorrupt, is used to designate a virgin, rarely in classical Greek, but commonly amongst the Greek Fathers): the virgin, the celibate, has thus withdrawn from the realm of human fallenness and is in search of man's primal, incorrupt condition. It is noted that the first mention of Adam and Eve's making love occurs in the biblical account *after* their exclusion from paradise (Genesis 4:1). This only confirms that marriage belongs to man's fallen state: in the Garden of Eden Adam and Eve were a virginal couple.

Such ideas – sketched here all too briefly – were enormously popular in early and patristic Christianity, and were not confined to the fringes of Christianity.[9] Sexual differentiation is not part of man's original state; marriage and child-bearing are aspects of the fallen human condition. Humanity's original condition transcended sexual differentiation: and that original human condition is often seen as precisely *man's*, i.e. male, so that Jerome derives the word *virgo* from *vir*, man (as opposed to woman).[10] Alternatively, a primal hermaphroditic condition was sometimes envisaged.

In these two ways (the practical matter of the position adopted by the body in prayer and the theoretical understanding of how the composite nature of the body and, linked with that, sexual differentiation, are but a part of the declension of the cosmos into the manifold) a Christian understanding of the body in a cosmic context can be seen. But I have singled out these two features because both of them are points where Augustine broke with already established Christian tradition, and where we can see the beginnings of a distinctively Western tradition.

His attitude to the question of bodily posture in prayer first emerges

---

[9] See Bianchi 1985, and especially A. Guillaumont's article, which deals almost exclusively with orthodox sources: ibid., 83–98.

[10] Jerome, Ep. 49.2.

clearly in one of the answers he made to various questions put to him by the priest Simplicianus early in his episcopate. The fourth question of the second book discusses posture in prayer apropos 2 Kings 2:18, where King David is said to sit down before the Lord.[11] Augustine points out that various postures for prayer are mentioned in Scripture: standing, kneeling, sitting, even lying down (cf. Ps. 6:7). Nothing therefore is prescribed as to bodily posture in prayer. What one should do when one is going to pray is to put oneself in that posture that is most conducive to the soul's desire to pray, but when the desire for prayer, *appetitus orandi*, stirs within one, then it does not matter what our bodily posture is. What is important for Augustine is one's interior state: exteriority is unimportant except in so far as it can hinder or foster one's interior state. Augustine could cite dominical support for such a stress on interiority (notably Matthew 6:5f., or more significantly perhaps Mark 7:20–3), but it is of a piece with the importance of interiority in his thought, something in which he was much influenced by Plotinus.

In another place, in his homilies on the Sermon on the Mount, we find Augustine discussing apropos the first petition of the Lord's Prayer the custom of praying towards the East. 'When we stand for prayer,' he says, 'we turn to the East, whence heaven arises', and he goes on to explain that this is simply symbolic, for God dwells everywhere. As a corporeal symbol, it is mainly valuable for the simple and unlearned, for whom it is better that they think that God dwells in heaven rather than on earth. But, he continues, when they learn that the soul is more excellent than even a heavenly body, they will think rather that God dwells in the soul than in any place. When further they learn how great a distinction there is between the souls of the righteous and the souls of sinners, they will think that God dwells in the soul of the just man, as in his holy temple: so 'he who prays [Our Father, who art in heaven] expresses the wish that the One he invokes may dwell within himself'.[12] Prayer facing East is then for Augustine a custom of the Church that expresses in a symbolic way for the very simple something that for the more advanced in the faith has no reference to the spatial or bodily at all. What is important for Augustine is inwardness: in that inwardness the importance of the body as part of the human person's reality as a reflection in miniature of the cosmos has faded away.

But equally Augustine breaks with the theoretical understanding of the cosmos we outlined above. This theory, or ideology, gave powerful

---

[11] Augustine, *Quaestiones ad Simplicianum* II.4.
[12] Augustine, *de Sermone Domini in Monte* II.5.18.

support to the ideal of virginity that was so popular from the fourth
century onwards. And, although Augustine's own conversion to Christianity was also a conversion to sexual continence, it was to be Augustine
who was to challenge most fundamentally this whole mythology of
virginity. To begin with, to be sure, Augustine shared this mythology,
embraced as it was by such as Ambrose and Jerome whom he revered. In
his early commentary on Genesis, directed against the Manichees, he
held that Adam and Eve were created to be a virginal couple: Eve was to
share with Adam in his praise of God and be his companion.[13] But
gradually, possibly in reaction against Jerome's shrill defence of virginity,[14] he came to reject such overemphasis on virginity. A beginning can
be seen in his treatise of 401, *de Bono conjugali*, and its development can be
traced through his literal Commentary on Genesis to his mature, and
vastly influential, *de Civitate Dei*. By book 9 of the Commentary on
Genesis (finished around 410), Augustine had abandoned the idea that
Eve was created as a companion for Adam (not, admittedly, on very
encouraging grounds: despite what Genesis says, Eve cannot have been
created as a companion for Adam, to assuage his solitude, for had that
been God's purpose, He would have created for Adam a friend, not a
woman): Eve was created to be Adam's wife and to bear children.[15]
Adam and Eve were not, and had never been intended to be, a virginal
couple: if they had not fallen, they would have made love and had
children in Paradise, though this would have taken place without lust.[16]
Sexual differentiation is part of the created order, and will characterize
the bodies of men and women in the Resurrection.[17] The doctrine of
double creation is thus abandoned by Augustine and is replaced by his
doctrine of creation and fall: what is created is unambiguously good, and
that includes physicality and sexuality; evil is a result of the Fall.

In breaking with the traditional cosmic view, Augustine alters the
focus in which the body is perceived. In the traditional view, the body, in
its composite complexity and its sexual differentiation, reflects in itself
the ambivalent move towards the manifold that is implied in the coming
into being of the cosmos. But the bodily, too, is the arena, as it were, in
which the reversal of this process of dissolution takes place. It is through a
body that the Word introduces into the cosmos a new principle that calls

---

[13] Augustine, *de Genesi contra Manichaeos* II.11.1.
[14] On this see, most recently, Markus 1991, 45–83.
[15] Augustine, *de Genesi ad litteram* IX.9.9.
[16] Cf., Augustine, *de Civitate Dei* XIV.22f. and 26.
[17] Cf., ibid., XXII.17.

humankind back to union with God: that movement towards God is celebrated and effected in the liturgy that takes place in a sacred space oriented towards the eachatological coming of the Messiah. It is in the body, through ascetic endeavour, that the dualities implicit in the fallen human condition are to be overcome (dualities that include the duality of sex). For Augustine all this is qualified by an understanding of the human person as a spiritual being defined by inwardness. The bodily is the outward, it is composite and differentiated, easier to grasp than the baffling simplicity of the spiritual: the Incarnation makes possible parables of spiritual truth that are easier to grasp, and which once grasped are to be interiorized. The bodily can hinder the spiritual: it can distract it, it can try to offer a kind of fake inwardness, the 'private', in which the spiritual self can lose itself. Asceticism can perhaps help, though Augustine is not very sanguine,[18] but the aim of asceticism is a kind of effortless interiority, in which the soul is at home in the body and in control: asceticism is not seen as addressing anything as fundamental as the resolution of duality, implicit in the traditional 'cosmic' view. His concern with inwardness is not, however, to be construed as some kind of *individualism*. This effortless interiority renders the body 'transparent', so to speak, and makes possible a community between souls that have been cut off from one another by the opacity of the fallen body. This possibility will only be realized in heaven where 'God will be so known by us and so present to our eyes that by means of the spirit he will be seen by each of us in each of us, seen by each in his neighbour and by each in himself',[19] but the hope of some adumbration of it here inspires his concern with the creation of community here on earth, especially in the religious communities in which he lived from his conversion to the end of his life. So his monastic rule begins: 'The chief motivation for your sharing life together is to live harmoniously in the house and to have one heart and one soul seeking God.'[20]

When we move beyond Augustine, we must be careful, I think, not to exaggerate his influence in the West. This is something Peter Brown tends to do, his deep empathy with the African father leading him to look back on late antiquity from a perspective that is Augustine's, with the result that Augustine too easily becomes the watershed between late antiquity and the Latin early Middle Ages and is too readily regarded as

---

[18] See Augustine, *Confessions* x.28ff.
[19] Augustine, *de Civitate Dei* xxii.29, cf. Ep. 92.2.
[20] *Regula S. Augustini, Praeceptum*, 1.2; trans. by G. Lawless, in Lawless 1987, 81. See also Markus 1991, ch. 11, 157–79 (especially 159–68), and White 1992, 185–217.

the determinative influence on medieval Latin Christianity.[21] Augustine's ideas, here as elsewhere, were highly original, but he was not the
only influence on the Latin West. Ambrose – 'the last of the Greek
Fathers before St Augustine', as Mme Lot-Borodine aptly dubbed him[22]
– and Cassian, who brought to the West the experience of the Desert
Fathers, especially Evagrius: both these were read and their influence
kept alive the traditional cosmic view of man and redemption. In the
ninth century, Eriugena, by his translations of Greek Fathers, as well as
by his own works, despite his own very considerable debt to Augustine,
provided a kind of window through which for the last time for many
centuries the West could gaze on the theological landscape of Byzan-
tium. And the Greek Fathers he translated – Gregory of Nyssa, Denys
the Areopagite, Maximus the Confessor – were precisely those who
worked out a Christian version of the ancient cosmic understanding of
humankind. Augustine's doctrine of inwardness did not drive away
understandings of sacred space, and, bound up with that, sacred time
(Augustine's own understanding of time, in *Confessions* XI, significantly
moves time away from the cosmos and locates it in the soul). Easter
followed the shifting coincidences of solar and lunar time, and people
cared passionately about how to calculate that coincidence (witness the
synod of Whitby in 664). Churches continued to be oriented towards the
East (indeed elaborate care was taken that altars should face the
direction from which the sun rose on the feast of the saint in whose
honour the altar was consecrated, and whose relics lay beneath it).
Sacred space was given contour and form through relics and the pilgrim
paths that led to them. The labyrinths in some French cathedrals
perhaps bear witness to conceptions of sacred space as it was understood
in the twelfth century that are now quite lost to us.[23]

However, it is, perhaps, possible to point to ways in which Augustine's
understanding of inwardness produced changes in the apprehension of
the body from the twelfth century onwards. Why it is that there is such a
delayed effect of Augustine's ideas is too big an issue to discuss here, but it
is certainly connected with the renewed interest in theology, provoked
by the Cathedral Schools and the new universities, that we find in the
twelfth century. On any theological topic Augustine had something to
say and so found those 'more pensive readers' to whom Peter Brown
refers[24] in greater abundance than earlier. There is other evidence, too,

[21] See my review of Brown (1988) in *Journal of Theological Studies*, N.S. 41 (1990), 231–5.
[22] Quoted by H. de Lubac in Lubac 1949, 146.
[23] See Doob 1990.   [24] Brown 1988, 433.

of a revival of Augustinian theology in the twelfth century: the doctrine of original sin, for example, which only re-emerges in its Augustinian form then.[25] If the body comes to be seen as the outward, through which the inward expresses itself, then, for instance, the body of Christ will be understood in a different way. For Athanasius of Alexandria, in the fourth century, the body of Christ was a part of the cosmos, vulnerable and subject to death, in this way sharing in the corruption and death that the Fall of man had introduced into the cosmos. By means of that body, the Word of God became *inward to the cosmos*[26] and thus was able to become subject to corruption and death and thereby overcome them. Athanasius was not interested at all in the human sufferings of Christ: what was important to him is that these sufferings are borne by the Word of God and thus overcome. Theopaschism is the logical outcome of Athanasius' position. Christ's victory is celebrated in the liturgy, in a space oriented towards the direction whence the incarnate Word will come again in glory, a space increasingly marked out and given a structured symbolic significance, in which the church incorporate in Christ, the church as the body of Christ, celebrates the mysteries of redemption. The body of Christ confers a redeemed significance on the cosmos and marks out a sacred space in which this redemption is celebrated and effected. From the eleventh or twelfth century onwards in the West devotion to Christ becomes devotion to his human suffering: the body of Christ presents itself as a sacred humanity, rather than opening up a sacred space. The sufferings of that sacred humanity become a focus for meditation and devotion. The outward signs of the Passion point to an inward love in the soul of the Saviour, to which humans seek to respond. For Abelard, for instance, the central purpose of the Incarnation is the revealing of this love.[27] But it was Bernard, the persecutor of Abelard, who was in the forefront of this growing devotion to the sacred humanity of Christ.[28] So, for example, in his twentieth sermon on the Song of Songs he says:

Above all things, it is the cup that you did drink, O Good Jesus, the work of our redemption, that makes you lovely to me. It is this above all that easily draws to itself all the love I have to offer. This it is, I say, that attracts our devotion most sweetly, which exacts it most justly, and retains it most closely, and affects it most

---

[25] See Gross 1963.
[26] See Athanasius, *de Incarnatione* 44.
[27] See Weingart 1970, 121ff.
[28] See Prestige 1940, 180–207 (chapter called: 'Eros: or, Devotion to the Sacred Humanity').

vehemently. The Saviour laboured greatly in this, nor in the creating of the world did he take on a work of such effort . . . Behold how much he loves![29]

Et afficit vehementius! Afficere, affectus: these words take on a special meaning for Bernard. They refer to inward feeling: not, certainly, superficial emotion, but something deeper, beyond the reach of the intellect. So, for instance, when Bernard contrasts the superiority of love as a motive for serving God, in contrast to fear and hope of reward (a traditional contrast), he explains this superiority thus (and not at all traditionally): 'neither fear nor the hope of reward can convert the soul; they may change one's manner, or even one's behaviour, but they can never touch one's feeling (*affectum*)'.[30] Bernard is following through Augustine's logic of inwardness (though in detaching inwardness from the movement of the intellect he strikes out on a path foreign to Augustine): the sufferings of the sacred humanity witness to a love for us that fires in us a love for Him. *Cor ad cor loquitur:* and that speech is facilitated by an imaginative participation in what Christ endured for us. The body discloses a *presence*, and makes possible (in a fractured and imperfect way) communication between souls inward to themselves. (In passing it is worth noting that the Dionysian notion of hierarchy, originally coined to analyse the structure of the cosmos, is used in the twelfth and thirteenth centuries to explore the depths of the soul's *inwardness*).[31] This deep attachment between souls (and between the soul and Christ) is frequently expressed in highly erotic imagery (or so it appears to us): Bernard is fond of expanding on the kisses that are so frequently mentioned in the Song of Songs, though often in contexts that are not at all erotic (for example, the kiss expressing the union of the two natures of Christ,[32] or between the Holy Spirit and the church[33]).[34]

It is perhaps not then surprising that the twelfth century sees a striking shift in the valency of the term *corpus Christi*. As Henri de Lubac long ago demonstrated, before the middle of the twelfth century, the expression *corpus Christi* referred either to the historical body of Christ or to the church, while the Eucharistic body of Christ was designated *corpus Christi mysticum*. But from that time onwards, the traditional language shifted and *corpus Christi mysticum* came to designate the church, while the Eucharist came to be called *corpus Christi*, or *corpus verum*.[35] A number of

---

[29] Bernard, *Sermones super Cantica Canticorum* xx.2.
[30] Bernard, *de Diligendo Deo* xII.34.
[31] See, for example, Bonaventure, *Itinerarium mentis in Deum* iv.4.
[32] Bernard, *Sermones super Cantica Canticorum* II.3.   [33] Ibid., vIII.
[34] The use of (to us) strongly erotic language in relation to friendship can be traced back to Anselm. See, most recently, R. W. Southern's discussion of this in Southern 1991, 138–65.
[35] See Lubac 1949.

Plate 3 'Ave verum corpus': the body of Christ viewed by the faithful (rather than incorporating them). Anonymous master, 'The Mass of St. Giles', *circa* 1500.

important changes are implicit in this verbal shift. First of all, the direction of signification is reversed. Whereas traditionally the celebration of the Eucharist had disclosed (or pointed to) the realization of the church (the celebrating community) as the Body of Christ, so that the

church is the hidden meaning of the Eucharist, with this change the
Eucharist, the consecrated host, becomes the hidden meaning of the
church, and becomes an object of devotion, or adoration, in itself. One
can see in this the collapse of the notion of sacred space: the Eucharist
shrinks from a sacred action, involving movement, taking place in space,
to a consecrated host, occupying a (relatively small) volume of space.[36]
The *nature* of the eucharistic presence becomes a much more critical
problem: and the doctrine of transubstantiation emerges as the answer
explaining how the historical body of Christ is present in some 'literal'
way. Henri de Lubac remarks, 'as attention is concentrated on eucharistic realism, and the problem of presence is substituted for the problem of
sacred action, the very foundation of the distinction once maintained
between *corpus quod pependit ligno* [the body that hung on the cross] and
corpus quod in mysterio immolatur [the body that is offered in the sacrament]
disappeared for the most part.'[37] De Lubac's understanding of the shift in
signification between the church and the Eucharist – between body and
body – has been further analysed by the great authority on seventeenth-
century French mysticism, Michel de Certeau.[38] On the one hand, the
fading of the distinction between the historical body and the eucharistic
body of Christ enhanced the power of the hierarchical priestly ministry
of the church, for the priesthood has control over the miracle of
transubstantiation that makes the body of Christ accessible in the
present. But, on the other hand, as de Certeau puts it, 'the "mystery", the
sacramental body, is recaptured under the philosophical formality of the
sign, that is to say, of a visible "thing" which designates an invisible
something else: the visibility of this object is substituted for the common
celebration, the communal operation; it points to the proliferation of
secret effects (of grace, of salvation) of which the real life of the church is
composed.'[39] The sacramental body is a signal for invisible manifestations of grace in the church, which is its real life, its 'mystical' reality. For
de Certeau, this is part of the reason for the emergence of 'mysticism', as
both phenomenon and theology, in the post-Tridentine church. But
more immediately it sheds a great deal of light on the late medieval
church, with its combination of greatly enhanced sacerdotal authority
and a proliferation of 'physical phenomena of mysticism' (as they have
been called):[40] a combination that is sometimes manifest as a sharp
tension (as when those favoured with such physical mystical phenomena

[36] Cf. de Lubac's comment: 'un mystère, au sens ancien du mot, est plûtot une action qu'une chose':
Lubac 1949, 60.
[37] Ibid., 185.   [38] See Certeau 1982 and 1964.   [39] Certeau 1982, 113.
[40] By Herbert Thurston, see Thurston 1952.

claim the right to criticize the sacerdotal hierarchy: Catherine of Siena is the most famous example of this), and sometimes as a kind of collusion (when mystical phenomena are used to underwrite sacerdotal authority: something facilitated by the fact that canonization in the West was, from the thirteenth century onwards, firmly controlled by the papacy).

This tension/collusion between formal hierarchy and a potentially uncontrolled and physically manifest mysticism can be seen in the cult of *Corpus Christi*. On the one hand, the body of Christ is abstracted from its communal celebration (and from its cosmic context) and becomes a miraculous (but, in principle, formally reproducible) production of the priesthood; but, on the other hand, devotion to the body of Christ present in the host takes on a whole variety of unofficial forms, that are abundant in physical effects (trances, cases of miraculous sustenance by the Eucharistic host alone), and even bypasses the official priestly control of the Eucharist altogether (as when the Eucharist is received in a vision by those denied the Eucharist by a priest).[41]

Such freeing of the Eucharist from its traditional liturgical and symbolic context, combined with the way, already mentioned, in which Augustine's logic of inwardness made of the body an index of inwardness and a means of communication, perhaps lies behind the enormous importance of the bodily in *female* mysticism in the Middle Ages, something that has been explored above all by Caroline Bynum.[42] This is manifest in a variety of ways: from physical effects (for example, virtually all those who have experienced the *stigmata* – replicas of the wounds of Christ – have been women: there seem to have been no male instances between the most famous stigmatist of all, Francis of Assisi, and the twentieth-century Padre Pio, and it is only in the case of women that these wounds have periodically bled, on Fridays or on Good Friday), through asceticism (extremes of asceticism are much commoner among women saints than among men) and the prominence of metaphors of feeding and nourishment in their writings (doubtless related *à rebours* to fasting), to the rich physicality of their imagery (food is a central image with such mystics as Hadewijch, Beatrice, and the two Catherines – of Genoa and Siena).[43]

Various interpretations have been offered for the prominence of these bodily strategies in late medieval female spirituality: a popular interpretation (which ignores, however, the positive significance often invested in the bodily) sees this as a way in which women internalized the dominant

---

[41] See the examples cited by Caroline Walker Bynum in Bynum 1987a, 230.
[42] See Bynum 1987a, and her articles collected in Bynum 1991b.
[43] See Bynum 1987a, *passim*.

misogyny of male-dominated medieval Christianity as self-hatred. A more comprehensive, and comprehensible, interpretation has been suggested by Caroline Bynum who sees the utilization of bodily symbolism and symbolic practices as a way in which women made a bid for taking control of their lives and gaining access to power in a society where men were increasing their already considerable monopoly of power. The assertion of *sacerdotium* over *imperium* as a result of the Papal Reform Movement, the migration of learning from monasteries (which included monasteries for women and made possible such learned women as Hildegard of Bingen or Hrosvita of Gandersheim) to the universities (from which women were excluded: it has been remarked that Heloise was perhaps the last traditionally educated woman until the Renaissance), even the decline of feudalism with the growth of the medieval town: all these made the position of women still more marginal. But food and the body were women's concerns: the body had always been regarded as feminine in contrast with the masculine intellect – physicality was woman's problem; food is prepared by women (for men to eat). And so strategies that focused on the body and food offered women access to power. Through their bodies they could make manifest their oneness with Christ who in His body suffered for the salvation of humankind. Assimilation to Christ, physically manifest in stigmata and miraculous periodical bleeding, gave access to a power and authority, not of office, but of experience: an authority, not hierarchical but 'charismatic'. But the stigmata were not only signs of assimilation to Christ, they *bled*: exuded blood which was redemptive (in an everyday, as well as religious, way: bleeding was a widely prescribed medical remedy), and nutritive (for milk was but blood transformed). Bynum points out that in medieval art wounds and breasts can be interchangeable as symbols.[44] What has happened, perhaps, is that the body has been freed from space and time – in the ways suggested above – so that it functions primarily as an index, an expression, of inward feeling. And it does this through traditional ideas of the bodily that can be traced back to Plato's *Timaeus* and beyond: the body nourishes and is nourished, it is vulnerable, it suffers. So the body on the Cross is no longer the clothed, priestly/victorious figure of earlier Christian art, but a suffering body: in its suffering manifesting the love of God for humankind in the Incarnate One. The body in the Eucharist is less the bread of heaven than the body broken.[45] And the individual human body receives redemption and

---

[44] See Bynum 1987a, 102–8, which discusses medieval iconographic evidence.
[45] See Bynum 1987a, 48–69.

becomes itself a source of redemption by assimilation to this body (in both its historical and sacramental forms). One is tempted here to speak of individualism, but perhaps it is better to speak of the seeds of an individualism that will develop later. For, as Augustine's concern with inwardness released a concern for community made possible by that humility which alone discloses our inward reality, so these late medieval manifestations of inward piety led not to isolated individualism (even the late medieval enthusiasm for the eremitical ideal is probably wrongly thus construed), but to concern for community. *Corpus Christi* devotion is fostered by and fosters guilds;[46] and much female spirituality was fostered by and fostered communities such as *béguinages*. These are not, perhaps, communities in a traditional sense: they are fostered, not natural, societies rather than communities; and *béguinages* differed from traditional religious communities by the absence of formal vows. But their existence calls in question any notion of individualism *tout court*.[47]

Another index of the significance of the body in the late Middle Ages can be found in theological arguments about the nature of the resurrection body and in the striking change in the last quarter of the twelfth century in the medieval attitude to leprosy. Leprosy (*lepra*) is a vague term in medieval Latin covering eczema, psoriasis, skin cancers, as well as what we know as leprosy. Until the middle of the twelfth century leprosy is rarely heard of, and when it is mentioned it is a disease of the rich and powerful. In an important article, Pegg suggests that an explanation for this can be found in the confused state of society in the early Middle Ages – a confusion reflected in a corresponding fragility in legal recourse for righting abuses of power, so that a charge of leprosy cut through the jungle of legal competence and allowed a simple solution. A leper was excluded from the traditional ranks of society and robbed of any claim to authority: he lived as an outcast, but was not regarded as contagious.[48] In the last quarter of the twelfth century there is a marked change: leprosy seems to become common, and it afflicts the poor, beggars, vagabonds, and heretics. They are now not just excluded from society – in fact the classes now afflicted with leprosy were already outcasts from society – but they are regarded as contagious and made to live in special institutions, *leprosoria*. In Italy, they are called *lazzaroni*, after Lazarus, the brother of Mary and Martha whom Jesus raised from the dead (see John 11). Pegg sees this change as a result of the dramatic

---

[46] See Rubin 1991 and 1986.
[47] See Caroline Walker Bynum's criticism of Colin Morris's idea of the 'discovery of the individual' (in especially, Morris 1972) in Bynum 1982, 83–109.   [48] See Pegg 1990, especially 271.

centralization of society in twelfth-century Europe. This created a large group of poor who had no foothold in this society: their being scapegoated as lepers, non-persons, made the match between theory and reality more tidy. But this was conceptualized by an assertion about their *bodies*: the decay and fragmentation manifest in the body of the leper recalled the decay and fragmentation of society to which the central-ization of power in twelfth-century Europe was a response. A similar anxiety about decay and fragmentation is seen by Bynum in debates about the resurrection of the body and the related question of the veneration of relics.[49] Guibert of Nogent in his *de Pignoribus sanctorum* objects to the breaking up of relics, and their 'privatization' as personal amulets, essentially, Bynum argues, because the relics of the saints are pledges of the resurrection, in which decay and dissolution will be overcome. The breaking-up and the distribution of relics is a symbol contradictory of their significance. Similarly, in the debates about the resurrection of the body, Bynum argues, 'the fundamental religious and cultural problem is decay':[50] resurrection is important as counteracting decay. 'If corruption or fragmentation or division of the body (the transition from whole to part) is the central threat, resurrection (the reassemblage of parts into whole) is the central victory.'[51] In all these cases the body is made to bear the weight of anxiety about decay and corruption: anxiety about the integrity of the resurrection body mirrors anxiety about the neatly unified body politic of medieval Christendom. Again it is possible to see how similar anxieties translate in different ways in the world of Christian origins and the world of the high Middle Ages. 'Decay and death' seem a constant: but, whereas concern about this is reflected in anxiety about the individual body in the high Middle Ages, in the classical patristic theology of Athanasius it is seen rather as a cosmic threat, translated for the most part in mythological and metaphysical terms.[52] Relics, too, are a constant in Christian devotion (at least so far as patristic and medieval Christianity is concerned), but the way in which they serve to mark out a sacred space in late antiquity and the early Middle Ages[53] seems to be lost sight of by the high Middle Ages.

In conclusion, it hardly seems necessary to say that to speak of the body in Western Catholic Christianity, even if one confines oneself to the

---

[49] See Bynum 1991a, and her 'Material Continuity, Personal Survival and the Resurrection of the Body: A Scholastic Discussion in its Medieval and Modern Contexts', in Bynum 1991b, 239–97, and now 1995.
[50] Bynum 1991a, 77.   [51] Ibid.   [52] See, especially, Athanasius, *de Incarnatione*.
[53] See Markus 1991, 142–50.

pre-Reformation period, is not to speak of one thing. Western Catholic Christianity covers a period of profound changes and the place of the body reflects these changes. I have argued that these changes can be placed on an axis, moving from seeing the body as microcosm reflecting in itself a cosmic story, to seeing the body as interpreter of human inwardness. That certainly oversimplifies, but it will have served its purpose if it brings out something of the nature of the changes in the understanding and experience of the body in Western Catholic Christianity before the Reformation.

BIBLIOGRAPHY

Ariès, P. and Béjin, A. (1985), *Western Sexuality*, Oxford.
Behr, J. (1993), 'Shifting Sands: Foucault, Brown and the Framework of Christian Asceticism', *Heythrop Journal* 34, 1–21.
Brown, P. (1988), *The Body and Society. Men, Women and sexual renunciation in early Christianity*, New York.
  (1986), 'The Notion of Virginity in the Early Church', in ed. B. McGinn and J. Meyendorff, *Christian Spirituality*, I, London: 427–43.
Bianchi, U. (ed.) (1985), *La Tradizione dell'Enkrateia. Motivatione ontologiche e protologiche*. Atti del Colloquio Internazionale, Milan, 20–23 April 1982, Rome.
Bynum, C. W. (1982), *Jesus as Mother. Studies in the Spirituality of the High Middle Ages*, Berkeley–Los Angeles–London.
  (1987a), *Holy Feast and Holy Fast. The Religious Significance of Food to Medieval Women*, Berkeley–Los Angeles–London.
  (1987b), 'Religious Women in the Later Middle ages', in ed. Jill Raitt, *Christian Spirituality*, II, London: 121–39.
  (1991a), 'Bodily Miracles and the Resurrection of the Body in the High Middle Ages', in ed. T. Kselman, *Belief in History. Innovative Approaches to European and American Religion*, Notre Dame–London: 68–106.
  (1991b), *Fragmentation and Redemption. Essays on Gender and the Human Body in Medieval Religion*, New York.
  (1995), *The Resurrection of the Body in Western Christianity, 200–1336*, New York.
Camporesi, P. (1988), *The Incorruptible Flesh*, Cambridge.
Certeau, M. de (1964), ' "Mystique" au XVIIe siècle. Le problème du langage "mystique" ', in *L'Homme devant Dieu. Mélanges offerts au père Henri de Lubac*, vol. 2 (Théologie, 57), 267–91.
  (1982), *La fable mystique. XVIe–XVIIe siècle*, Paris.
Doob, Penelope Reed (1990), *The Idea of the Labyrinth from Classical Antiquity through the Middle Ages*, Ithaca–London.
Foucault, M. (1990), 'The Battle for Chastity' in ed. L. D. Kritzman, *Michel Foucault; Politics, Philosophy, Culture*, London: 228–41.

(1988), 'Technologies of the Self', in eds. L. H. Martin, H. Gutman, and P. H. Hutton, *Technologies of the Self: A Seminar with Michel Foucault*, London: 16–50.

Gross, J. (1963), *Entwicklungsgeschichte des Erbsündendogmas*, vol. 2, Munich–Basle.

Laeuchli, S. (1972), *Power and Sexuality. The Emergence of Canon Law at the Synod of Elvira*, Philadelphia.

Lawless, G. (1987), *Augustine and his Monastic Rule*, Oxford.

Lubac, H. de (1949), *Corpus Mysticum. L'Eucharistie et l'Église au moyen âge*, 2nd edn., Paris.

Morris, C. (1972), *The Discovery of the Individual 1050–1200*, London.

Nebenzahl, K. (1986), *Maps of the Bible Lands*, London.

Markus, R. A. (1991), *The End of Ancient Christianity*, Cambridge.

Moreton, M. J. (1982), 'Εἰς ἀνατολὰς βλέψατε: Orientation as a Liturgical Principle', *Studia Patristica* 17, 575–90.

Pagels, E. (1988), *Adam, Eve and the Serpent*, London.

Pegg, M. G. (1990), 'Le corps et l'autorité: la lèpre de Baudouin IV', in *Annales, économies, sociétés, civilisations* 45/2, 265–87.

Prestige, G. L. (1940), 'Eros: or, Devotion to the Sacred Humanity', in *Fathers and Heretics*, London: 180–207.

Rousselle, A. (1983), *Porneia; de la maîtrise du corps à la privation sensorielle*, Paris (English trans., Oxford, 1988).

Rubin, M. (1986), 'Corpus Christi Fraternities and late Medieval Piety', *Studies in Church History*, 23, 97–109.

(1991), *Corpus Christi*, Cambridge.

Southern, R. W. (1991), *Saint Anselm. A Portrait in a Landscape*, Cambridge.

Thurston, H. (1952), *The Physical Phenomena of Mysticism*, London.

Weingart, R. E. (1970), *The Logic of Divine Love. A Critical Analysis of the Soteriology of Peter Abailard*, Oxford.

White, C. (1992), *Christian Friendship in the Fourth Century*, Cambridge.

CHAPTER 8

The image of the body in the formative phases of the Protestant Reformation

David Tripp

Recent discussions of the image of the body have raised the question whether some forms of Christianity, especially Protestantism, inculcate a contempt for the human body, and whether this alleged low esteem for corporeity is associated both with a hostile attitude to any acceptance of the real presence in the Eucharist and also with an individualistic approach to society, an unwillingness to see society in terms of corporate cohesion. Part of the concern of this chapter is to begin to investigate this question, an issue which has not received much attention from interpreters of the Reformation, whether historians or theologians. The approach must be tentative; but to find out whether the questions involved are worth asking, we must try to answer them.

The Reformation is not a simple phenomenon, nor one that can tidily be subsumed under one manageable concept.[1] There were explicitly theological and spiritual reformations, Catholic and Protestant and more radical, reformations committed to the repristination of religious life. There were also reformations of civic life on a moralizing basis[2] very different from the Lutheran or Reformed understanding of grace. (For an example of a local, moralizing, reformation which imposed new and perhaps additional limits on the status of women, see Roper 1989). In addition, there were political reformations involving major reallocations of power. Our concern here is with the explicitly theological concerns of some Protestant reformers, taking little account of the subsequent changes of the 'Enlightenment' and since. In recent decades, the sixteenth-century figures have come back into the centre of attention, and their writings are exerting a new and direct influence; our choice of focus is therefore not solely antiquarian.

It is unwise, though tempting, to assume that the Protestant Reforma-

---

[1] cf. Rupp 1966, 1969. Purely for reasons of space, the 'radical Reformation' is left unnoticed here.
[2] Blickle 1985 has begun to show that, at town and parish (*Gemeinde*) level, the process of reformation took on a character very different from that envisaged by the theologians.

tion dissolved an over-arching unity prevailing throughout Christendom. From the fourteenth century at least, English celebrants saying the *Te igitur* of the Roman canon, the prayer which formed the mind of every priest of the Latin rite, defined the Christian unity of worship as not only *una cum famulo tuo Papa nostro N, et antistite nostro N*, but also *et rege nostro N* – not only must Christians be one through communion with the pope and the local bishop, but also with the monarch. Christian identity is subtly redefined in national rather than global terms. Beside this misleadingly small-seeming sign of the dissolution of the *corpus Christianorum* may be set another, the equally silent revolution of the abandonment of the traditional Christian ban on usury.[3] The old prohibition, however little it was honoured in practice, had preserved for Christians the Jewish principle set out in Deuteronomy 23:19–20: usury denies the mutual acceptance that belongs within the kinship of a *plebs sancta*. The collapse of this ban represents not only an enormous institutional rejection of the church's moral tradition, but also a far-reaching threat to neighbourly and fraternal unity. In so far as Protestantism tolerated usury (see Tawney 1926, 79–132; and see Viner 1978, for cautionary remarks on the whole Weber thesis), it was perpetuating a paradigm shift which had taken place in the European '*corpus Christianum*' long since (cf. Tawney 1926, 14–81). These developments in practice were matched by a growing national sense, at the expense of an assumption of Christian solidarity, evidenced in ecclesiastical administration and in scholastic discussion of the nature of the church, from the high Middle Ages onward (Shaw 1959).

It is against this background of a dissolving ecclesial body that both 'Protestant' and 'Catholic' reformations reaffirmed the claim of God upon the whole body – of the individual, of the church, of society at large. This principle was not at all in dispute between Catholic and Protestant reformers. What was, and still is, at issue is the nature of that divine claim, and the essence of proper human response to it. Much that is indispensable in Protestant doctrine is shared with the pre-Reformation church, and it is bad history to assume that Catholic convictions which survive in Protestant Christianity are marginal features or detritus spared by oversight. What is essential to understanding Protestant Christianity is to see it as centred upon a doctrine concerning God: that the Triune God is gracious and freely forgiving, and, normatively through the Incarnation, confers on trusting creatures a gift of love

[3] See Divine 1959.

which cannot be earned or deserved. Every other issue, whether agreed among the protagonists of the Reform or disputed, is secondary to this.

This central theme of Protestant Christianity was to be illuminatingly expressed[4] by Marguérite of Navarre (1547, 1873 edn., 134):

O Redeemer, shall I fear to draw near to your goodness, seeing that you have deigned to take upon yourself the very flesh that we bear? As God, nothing could touch you, nothing could bring you down to earth from high heaven, if you had not been well pleased in love to come down. You have united divinity with our dust. Why? Who can understand it? It was a work that cost you dear. The heart must indeed be iron or rock which cannot be split or melted by love; for without seeming to compromise (*facher*) yourself, you allowed your whole body to be pierced, to accept death on a cross, your holy blood to be shed in streams, in order to mark our foreheads with the sign of Tau [sc., the Cross, but cf. also Revelation 22:4]. Any that does not love you in return deserves rebuke, and to be deprived of all your benefits.

A doctrine so concerned with God made flesh must be concerned with the body in every sense.[5]

We shall look at three determinative figures of the sixteenth-century theological Reformation – Luther, Zwingli, and Calvin – and consider in summary terms, and, so far as is practicable, with special reference to their most influential publications, their appreciations of the body, their uses of the image of the body in relation to society, and their respective proposals for eucharistic worship,[6] considered in the light of their attitudes to the body. A simple index of their attitudes to the body in a not specifically religious context is needed; as that index, we shall seek out their judgement on dancing.[7] In conclusion, we shall look at Richard Baxter, one of the few post-Reformation figures who, caught in a historical vortex, had to attempt some sort of synthesis of the conflicting inheritances of the Reformers, and put the same questions to him.

[4] Marguérite of Navarre is symptomatic of central Reformed spirituality even though she did not formally change denominations. She was able to combine both Catholic and reforming spirituality without forfeiting her integrity; she thus typifies the spiritual continuity between the reform and the pre-Reformation church.

[5] This translation, and all others, unless otherwise indicated, are my own. I have tried to retain the sentence-forms and rhythms of the originals, especially where the originals are uneven and difficult, and so reflect the tentative and exploratory state of the writer.

[6] The liturgical texts chosen are those which reflect the latest and most maturely considered judgement of the liturgical authors, so far as that is ascertainable.

[7] Other possible indicators include: attitudes to sleep, food, art, marriage, etc. I choose dancing because the topic was frequently the subject of explicit controversy (see, for example, Phillips 1977). In the English setting, where dancing was allowed by the 'Book of Sports', attack on the act was also attack on the Establishment. In itself, dance combines sexuality, sense, pleasure, and the use of time; attitudes to it seem therefore to be indicative of an entire evaluation of corporeity.

MARTIN LUTHER

'Every Christian [in his Latin version, "a human being"] is of a two-fold nature, spiritual and bodily. As to the soul, he is called a spiritual, new, inward person, as to the flesh he is called a bodily, old and external person.' Not only does this place Christians in an odd situation – as bodily beings, they are slaves to everything, everyone's inferiors; while as spiritual beings, they are free, with dominion over all things, and inferior to none – but it also determines what can and cannot bring them real benefit: 'We take the one who is an inward, spiritual person, and note what belongs to this state – that such an one is and is called a devoted, free Christian person. It is obvious then that no outward thing, whatever it is called, can make them free or devoted, for neither their devotedness and liberty nor yet their wickedness and bondage are bodily or outward things. What does it help the soul if the body is unfettered and fresh and healthy, and eats and drinks and lives as it pleases? And on the other hand, what harm does it do the soul if the body is fettered, sick, and weary, is hungry and thirsty and suffers as it does not wish to?' (Luther 1520, edn 1953, 39).

Here, indeed, Luther distinguished levels of essential humanness, and, in a sense, the body comes a poor third to the mental and the spiritual. Comparing the human make-up with Israel's desert tabernacle (Luther 1526a, *CH* IV, 426–7), he comments that 'the spirit is the *sanctum sanctorum*, God's dwelling in dark faith, without light, for he or she believes what they neither see nor feel, nor conceive: their soul is the *sanctum*, where there are seven lampstands, that is, understanding in all its forms, the power to distinguish, knowledge and awareness of bodily, visible things. Their body is the *atrium*, which is open to everyone to see what they are doing and how they live.'

But incomparably more important for Luther than this conventional hierarchical reckoning of the elements of humanity is the biblical distinction between the carnal and the spiritual. The carnal, which affects all areas of human functioning, is the self *curvatus in se*, making itself its own norm, doing its own thing, ignoring God and God's will. To describe sin as carnality is not, for Luther, the same as identifying sin with fleshly desire; as is now clear (Braun 1908; Wald 1993, 33–44), Luther unambiguously places the core of sin in the will. The spiritual is the whole self, body and all, ideally, open to God and trusting and rejoicing in God by means of God made flesh: 'In order . . . that we may become truly holy, it is necessary that God preserve, first, our spirit, and then our soul and body, not only from outward sins but much more from false and apparent good works' (preface to the *Letter to the Romans*, Luther trans. Jacobs 1932, 449, adapted; see comments in Miles 1984). Just as creation itself is grace, so the hallowing of the body, of the totality of the person, is God's loving purpose: 'for Luther' (according to Althaus 1959, 18), 'the *iustificatio impii* is the most majestic particular instance of creation out of nothing'.

In an important early work (Luther 1519, in *CL* 1, 197: 16–23), we read his comment on one aspect of the meaning of the Mass, combining affirmation of the real presence with vigorous body images for church and also for society at large (see commentary of Stock 1982, especially 336–47):

Communicare – in Latin, it is 'taking a share (*gemeynschaft*)' . . . while in German we call it 'going to sacrament', though it also means that Christ is one body with all the saints, just as the people of a city are one community (*gemeyn*) and body, each single citizen is a limb of the next, and of the whole city. Just so, all the saints are limbs of Christ and the Church, which is a spiritual, eternal City of God, and whoever is accepted into this same city must be described as being accepted into the community of the saints and incorporated with Christ's spiritual Body and made a limb of his –

and here, since the metaphor is still clearly a live one, we render '*glid*' as 'limb', and not merely as 'member'.

The life of faith is a life for the entire person, in Luther's interpretation. In his 1535 'A Simple Way to Pray' (*WA* 38, 364), he wrote: 'Anything that needs to be done well, needs to possess the whole person, with all their senses and members.' Physical actions concomitant to prayer, though they are not essential, have Christ's approval; and are in the sphere of Christian liberty (see Damerau 1977, 32–4); further, 'external gestures explain and commend themselves from themselves, for it is the Spirit who impels them' (*EA* 9, 263).

Luther's comments on dancing interestingly reflect his affirmation of corporeity. In a letter to his little son Hans (*WBr* Nr 1595, English translation from Atkinson 1968, 249), he pictured heaven as a place of happy dancing. Addressing directly the question of the rightness of dancing, in a sermon for Epiphany II (*EA* 11, 39–50), Luther said:

because it is the custom of the country, just like inviting guests, dressing up, eating, drinking, and making merry, I can't bring myself to condemn it, unless it gets out of hand, and so causes immoralities or excess. And even though sin has taken place in this way, it's not the fault of dancing alone. Provided they don't jump on the tables or dance in church . . . But so long as it's done decently, I respect the rights and customs of weddings – and *I* dance, anyway!

In Luther's 'German Mass' of 1526, we meet an insistence on the totality of Christ, God made flesh, present to give himself to his people, linked with a summons to trust God's grace totally, and in that trust to serve God and neighbour with soul and body:

Dear friends of Christ, since we are gathered here in the Name of the Lord, to receive his Holy Testament, I exhort you, firstly, to lift up your hearts to God, to pray with me the Our Father, as Christ our Lord has taught us and comfortably promised us a hearing . . .

[prayer is to be for God's mercy; for the hallowing of his Name; for purity of doctrine];

And also that his reign may come and be increased, to bring all sinners, those blinded and trapped by the devil in his kingdom, to the knowledge of right faith in Jesus Christ his Son, and to complete the number of Christians. That we may also be strengthened by his Spirit, to do and to suffer his will, both in living and dying, in good and ill, and at all times to break, offer up, and slay our will;

That he would also give us our daily bread, keep us from lust and anxiety of the belly, but yet let us be provided with everything good, enough for its need;

That he would also forgive us our guilt, as we forgive those guilty against us, that our heart may have a sure and joyful conscience before him, and that we may never have fear or terror of any sin;

That he would not lead us into temptation, but help us through his Spirit to compel the flesh, to despise the world with its nonsense, and to overcome the devil, for all his tricks;

And lastly that he would free us from all ill, both bodily and spiritual, in time and in eternity . . .

[After the Our Father:]

And secondly I exhort you to receive the Testament of Christ with right faith, and above all the Word in which Christ bestows on us his Body and Blood for forgiveness; hold fast in your heart that you are commemorating and giving thanks for the unfathomable love which he has shown to us, in that by his Blood he has freed us from God's wrath, sin, death, and hell; and therefore take to yourselves outwardly the bread and wine, that is, his Body and Blood, for outward assurance and pledge. (*CL* III, 304–5; also in Pahl 1983, *CD* 36–9)

The present tense, 'Christ bestows', in the above paragraph, is not a rhetorical flourish. The 'word' is for Luther more than a lesson, but an act of real presence (Roth 1952), here-and-now real presence; Christ, objectively present in his church, makes his body and blood (which are ubiquitous, sharing this property with his deity in *communicatio idiomatum*) objectively available by his utterance.

ZWINGLI

At a very sensitive point in Zwingli's reforming programme as it developed, the ideals of Christian education, Zwingli's 1523/1526 'Little Book of Instruction on how Lads should be Christianly taught and brought up' (Zwingli 1523b, 14) insisted that a young Christian, because Christ died for all, cannot but aspire to be of service to all:

In this, in common with all his neighbours, he will not lose sight of the fact that a family or household is a single body, in which all the members experience happiness and grief together, and help one another, to such an extent that whatever happens to one happens to them all.

Zwingli extended this principle to the conclusion, amongst others, that, to provide the Canton's body politic with stout defenders, the right-minded boy will put his back into vigorous exercise – 'running, jumping, stone-throwing, boxing, wrestling', in fact, anything but swimming: the body politic of Zurich does not need human fish!

His entire little treatise (see Locher 1979, 126–7) is nominally addressed to a child, Gerold, 'when just now you came forth again from the warm bath [an allusion either to the washing of a neonate, or to some custom of puberty], and everyone greeted you with joy, and busied themselves with showering gifts on you, some with this kind, others with that kind'. Zwingli's warm and affectionate tone of gusto for the human body is maintained through his didactic gift for the boy. Even restraint, the youngster is assured, is a means to pleasure (Zwingli 1523b, A.iii; 1523 version only): 'it usually works out that when you pour only a little into the glass, you drink with more enjoyment'. Zwingli's cardinal lesson (Zwingli 1523b, 5: from both versions) is consistent with this: that God is known through the created world, 'that the divine friendship foresees, arranges and bestows not only the things needed by the soul, but also the things needed by the body'.

It is clear that Zwingli vigorously affirms the value of the individual body and the body-image as a paradigm of society. His eucharistic theology (Zwingli 1526, 1527a), with its insistence, apparently theologically naive, that the elements cannot be identified with Christ's body and blood on the grounds that his resurrected body and blood have gone up into heaven and therefore cannot be present here on earth as well (see Courvoisier 1963; and McGrath 1990, who is more nuanced, but lacking a sufficiently wide context), cannot be interpreted as implying a low evaluation of corporal existence. Like Luther, he was concerned not to present a view of Christ as something that any manipulative theological or ecclesiastical system could use as a means of domination. He may also perhaps have sensed a need in himself to counterbalance a tendency to Docetism, for he can describe Christ *en passant* (Zwingli 1523b, 8) as 'ein ewiger Gott und ein ewiger Geist', with no mention at all of the Incarnation. Further investigation is needed into Zwingli's emphasis on Christ's heavenly mediation, and the implications of this for his interpretation of the Ascension in relation to the Eucharist; also into the implications of his use of the terms *lyb* (living body) and *lychnam* (body, but chiefly 'corpse'); but even more investigation is needed into his vivid assertion of Christ's divine person present in the entire eucharistic act, and into his resultant emphasis, greater than anywhere else in sixteenth-century Christendom, on the church as Christ's, or God's, Body.

Thus, in Zwingli's 1525 'Action, or Use of the [Lord's] Supper' (Pahl 1983, *CD* 194–5), we read:

[in the exhortation before the Our Father:] . . . let each one therefore recall, according to Paul's word, what consolation, faith, and confidence he or she has in that same our Lord Jesus Christ, so that none may profess to be a believer who in fact is not one, and so become guilty of the Lord's death. Nor let anyone sin against the whole Christian community, which is one single Body of Christ.

[from the prayer between the Our Father and the Narrative:] O Lord, almighty God, who have made us by your Spirit in the unity of faith to be your one Body, which Body you have bidden to utter praise and thanks to you for the goodness and generosity in which you gave up your only-begotten Son, our Lord Jesus Christ, to death for our sin, grant that we may witness to the same so loyally that we may never dishonour this the unfeigned truth by hypocrisy or falsehood. Grant us also to live in that innocence which befits your Body, your kindred and children, so that those who have no faith may learn to acknowledge your name and glory. Lord, protect us, so that your name and glory may in no wise be blasphemed because of us; increase for us in every way our faith, that is, trust in you, that live and reign, God into eternity! Amen!

CALVIN

For Calvin, the body, though marginal within the essence of humanity, is none the less integral to the divine image (*Inst.* I.xv.3; cf. Battles 1961, vol. I, 188):

Seeing that the soul is not the totality of human nature, are we not obliged to find it absurd that, in view of this, humanity should be called God's image? Nonetheless . . . the image of God extends to . . . all the complex whole with which Adam was endowed when he enjoyed a right mind, had his affections well regulated, his senses well tempered, and everything in him well ordered to represent by such adornments the glory of his Creator. And though the primary seat of the divine image was set up in the mind and heart, or in the soul and its faculties, yet there was no part of human nature, even including the body itself, in which some sparks did not glow.

Beside Luther and Zwingli, Calvin seems lukewarm in this appreciation of bodily reality. In the tone and rhythm of many of his remarks, rather than his direct utterances, a cautious attitude to the flesh seems to meet us. If this impression is not merely subjective, Calvin's difference from Luther and Zwingli may be a matter simply of individual disposition, the result of a greater experience of exile and rejection, or perhaps even a linguistic phenomenon. Luther and Zwingli, German speakers, different though their eucharistic theologies are, share a humorous enjoyment of the life of the body. However absurd the suggestion may be, it must be asked whether the Francophone Calvin could readily express, and therefore feel, what Luther and Zwingli felt. The whole issue of how language may determine what we *can* appreciate about the body (cf. Grün and Reepen 1988; Huxley 1977, 20), is raised at this point, though it cannot be considered here. As well as being, allegedly, a disease of thought, language may also be a lobotomy of feeling.

Calvin's judgement on dancing is simply summed up (Wallace 1959, 174–5; Höpfl 1982, 202). It is to be classed among the *mala in se*. It is a preamble to fornication, 'a shameful display of impudence', tending 'to besot profane men' (see *Harmony* 1854, vol. II, 225; *Jeremiah* 1854, 60). This must not however be taken as symptomatic of a denigration of corporeity; Calvin's vituperation is based on the conviction that the relationship between the sexes, properly ordered by being consciously ordered to God as its giver, is a most precious gift, the misuse of which is a tragedy of the first order (cf. Biéler 1963, 39). As designed by the Creator, that relationship is meant to be '*une douce mélodie*'. But it is a melody which all too easily loses its pitch.

In God's patient design the body has an indispensable role in directing the wayward and sluggish soul. Calvin's words in *Institution* III.xx.16 (Battles 1961, vol. II, 873, adapted) have many parallels elsewhere in his passages of spiritual counsel, and are the rationale of a great quantity of

consistent devotional advice and practice (Karay Tripp 1990, 1991;
Woods 1992; Prieur 1994), which can be traced at least as far as the
eighteenth century:

God has by nature planted in the minds of humankind the principle that their
prayers are lawful only when their minds are uplifted. Hence the rite of the
lifting-up of the hands . . . one common to all ages, and still in force.

Even though Calvin carefully subordinates the body to the spirit, lest
the body think too highly of itself, his concern is essentially with the
wholeness, the moral integrity, of the entire person; and we find that his
advice on the use of the body looks beyond the individual to the
corporate life of the church and of society in general. His 'Sermons upon
the Booke of Iob' (ET from Golding 1574, 226) include this:

the lifting up of our hands unto heaven is nothing, unless our heart go before it,
so as the hands may be a true record of that which is in the man, and of that
which God himself knoweth to be there . . . although it behove us to withdraw
when we pray unto God: it is still not meant that in the common prayers we
should not stir up one another by example . . . But God will have us pray
together in common, and as it were with one mouth, to the end there may be
one solemn confession of our faith, and every man may be edified by his
neighbour.

Calvin could envisage (see Biéler 1959) a new and glorious body politic
growing up in a life springing from baptism and fed by the Eucharist; but
for the present every Christian must endure the tension of belonging to
two bodies. In his exposition of 1 Corinthians 12 (see Bohatec 1937,
628–9), he notes that every human society is a body, within which
reconciliation of conflicting interests is naturally and rightly sought; but
that Christian believers form also 'a spiritual and secret (*arcanum*) Body of
Christ'.

Of the Eucharist in particular (*Institution* iv. xvii. 18; ed. Benoit, vol.
iv, 396; ed. Tholuck, vol. ii, 412 my emphasis), Calvin reflects: 'if we
direct our view and our thought to heaven, and are thither borne to seek
Christ there in the glory of his kingdom, just as the signs guide us *to come
to him in his wholeness* (*a venir a luy tout entier, ad eum integrum*), in this way we
shall be distinctly fed with his flesh under the sign of bread, nourished
with his blood under the sign of wine, so as *to have enjoyment of him in his
wholeness* (*pur avoir jouyssance entierement de luy, ut demum toto ipso perfruamur*)'.
In these words (where for the original we look firstly to the French,
which Calvin seems to have intended to be the most available, and in a

sense the normative, text), a struggle with Docetism has been traced (see Fischer 1987, 435 and n.). I urge rather the view that here we see Calvin's key to the unity of the spiritual and of the this-worldly, both in worship and in citizenship, both in private and corporate spirituality and ethics: the unity of deity and humanity, flesh included, in the person of Christ, to whom all things move within the plan of God.

For this reason, we ought not to draw too negative conclusions from Cavlin's reticence on questions of the body, individual or corporate, in the eucharistic rite of his 'Forme de prières ecclésiastiques' of 1542 (see Pahl 1983, 359–60). Of the individual body, he says only that adulterers, rogues, thieves, rapists, topers and gluttons, and such like, are in danger of receiving at the Lord's Table, not Christ's body and blood, but damnation; a similar peril attends those who approach while out of charity with their neighbours. (Derivative passages in the English Prayer Books of 1552 and 1661 will at once occur to English readers).

Calvin insists that Christ wishes to give his entire very self to communicants; but this happens, even at this very moment, essentially in heaven, while the earthly celebration is as it were a mystical shadow of that supernal reality:

let us believe in his promise, which Jesus Christ, who is the infallible truth, has uttered with his mouth: namely, that he wishes to make us truly partakers of his body and his blood, so that we may possess him entirely, in such wise that he may live in us and we in him . . . To do this, let us lift up our spirits and our hearts on high, where Jesus Christ is in the glory of his Father, and from whence we await him in [the day of] our Redemption. And let us not be preoccupied (*ne nous amusons point*) with these earthly and corruptible elements that we see with the eye and touch with the hand, in order to seek him there, as if he were enclosed in the bread or the wine. For then will our souls be disposed to be nourished and enlivened by his substance, when they are thus lifted up, above all earthly things, to come even into heaven, and to enter into God's kingdom, where he dwells.

THE 'ABENDMAHLSSTREIT' AND SOME OTHER ISSUES

The Protestant reformers' eucharistic controversy has been generously studied (for example, Bizer 1940; Gerrish 1988); but the place within it of body-imagery with its wider associations does not seem to have attracted attention. When that aspect is drawn in, the conventional line-up (of Luther vs. all comers; Protestants *contra mundum*) looks questionable. Both Luther and Zwingli share a vigorous appreciation of the physical and the communal body, but their views on the body present in the eucharistic action differ sharply: for Luther, the bread *is* Christ's Body, while for Zwingli the bread *means* that Body (while the church, not the elements, *is* Christ's Body). For Zwingli and Calvin, Christ's individual body must be away in heaven: only for Calvin, however (see Miles 1981), is the true locus of worship and the entire Christian life not on earth at all but in heaven.

We have observed that the *corpus Christianum* had been showing increasing signs of rupture long before the Reformation. Further investigation is needed into the degree to which eucharistic belief, whatever the official formulae claimed, had likewise been losing its cohesion in the Western church in the same centuries. As with the growth of political thought through these same centuries (see Skinner 1978, especially vol. I, xi–xii), we cannot assume that monolithic-looking public manifestos reflect the dominant and effective opinions.

The use of body-imagery for general society, though present and significant in the Reformers' political thought, cannot be said to be central to the problems of authority which most troubled them. (It may or may not be significant that the image of the ruler's body, *pace* Kantorowitz 1957, does not seem to have seized their attention). Certainly Calvin was more confident in the possible co-existence of sacred and secular dimensions in national life (Höpfl 1991, vii–xxiii); but Luther is innocent (see Watson 1946) of so separating the two as to bequeath a rationale for Nazism. Fascism was not (is not) a peculiarity of nominally Protestant nations – and the Lutheran 'scholastic' theologian Hutter speaks for all Protestant traditions when he writes (Hutter 1610, xxvii.4, 125): 'Of a necessity, all Christians have a duty to obey their magistrates and laws: except when these command people to sin – and then it is God who must be obeyed rather than humankind.' Nor is Protestantism in general responsible for the post-Cartesian retreat of spirituality into the privacy of the hidden soul (Mauss 1950, 360–1), still less for the nineteenth-century Anglo-Saxon table-manners (Fordyce 1987, 141) and other codes 'designed to set careful limits upon the possibilities of social interaction and communion, to reinforce and justify existing social relationships rather than to change them'.

It remains true, however, that the Protestant Reformation left its heirs no settled comprehensive system, only with many unresolved questions of principle and usage, not least in decisions relating to the body.

EMBODYING THE REFORMATION VISION WITHIN A RIVEN
BODY POLITIC: THE CASE OF RICHARD BAXTER (1615–1691)

In the third generation of reformers, the Anglican Richard Hooker
(Hooker 1843 edn, vol. II, 384–9 and vol. I, 386), could describe the
community at large as 'a collective body'; but he reserved the full
force of the term for 'that mystical body which the eye of man is not
able to discern' (i.e., the essentially invisible church universal), with a
secondary application to 'Christian churches . . . in number many,
and every one of them a perfect body by itself, Christ being head and
Lord over all'. He still found it possible to insist, even in the face of the
evidence of his own time, that 'there is not any man of the Church of
England but the same man is also a member of the commonwealth,
nor any member of the commonwealth which is not also of the
Church of England' – yet even Hooker could not simply identify the
bodies politic and ecclesiastical.

The English Reformation's eucharistic stance was (is!) not entirely
clear. The 'Black Rubric', even in its toned-down 1661 wording, committed Anglicans to a Zwinglian account of the presence. The Articles
favour rather a Calvinist approach. The structure of Cramer's rite
(Ratcliff 1980, 12–19) conveys a nuanced Zwinglian understanding; but
(see Ratcliff 1976, 203–21), by placing the Dominical 'words of institution' at the climactic end of the 'Prayer of Consecration', it still contrives
somehow to leave room for a Lutheran, or even more conservative,
interpretation. The Elizabethan Settlement proved to be of limited
durability. Official reformation had not gone far enough for many,
especially for advocates of thoroughgoing reordering of church, state,
and morals on Calvinist principles.

The Calvinist (Puritan) challenge to England's halting between two
opinions was most sharply expressed in reference to social customs,
particularly dancing. The Puritan Philip Stubs, in his *Anatomie of Abuses*
(Stubs 1585, ff. 99–99v), thus rebukes moderate Anglicans:

And whereas they conclude, that [dancing] is a wholesome exercise for the
body, the contrary is most true, for I have known divers, that by the immoderate
use thereof, have in short time become decrepit and lame, so remaining to their
dying day. Some have broke their legs with skipping and vaulting, and some
have come by one hurt, some by another, but never any came from thence
without some part of his mind broken and lame, such an unwholesome exercise
it is. But say they, it induceth love; so I say also, but what love? Truly a lustful
love, a venerous love, a concupiscensious, bawdy and bestial love, such as

procedeth from the stinking pump and loathsome sink of carnal affection and fleshly appetite, and not such as distilleth from the bowels of the heart, ingenerated by the Spirit of God.

In Stubs we hear a man obsessed by carnality, a man in love with wrath. A very different spirit is breathed by a Puritan of the next generation, Richard Baxter, 'a mere Catholick', whose ministry co-incided with most of the social and ecclesiastical upheavals of the seventeenth century, and whose constant labour was for reconciliation in church and state in the midst of those upheavals – a labour which failed.

On the particular matter of dancing, Baxter's judgement in his 'Christian Directory' (Baxter 1707, *PW* I, 369), following Calvin, and his successors such as Stubs, is negative and severe, but without Stubs' venom. Dancing must be classed among 'sinful sports', it is not 'becoming a noble soul', it 'bewitcheth and befooleth'; it wastes precious hours; it obscures the just sense of spiritual need; it is under God's judgement; it is a preparation for destruction. But, though the body has its role in the temptations which lead to sin, the real seat of sin is 'an excess of complacency', an illegitimate act of the will (I, 77). To be carnal is therefore not a matter of being in the life of the senses, but of worshipping one's will (I, 210–18). The Christian calling, Baxter insists (I, 548), is of the whole person:

Look also to your tongues and the deportment of your bodies that the whole man may worship God in holiness, as he requireth. Pretend not your good meanings, nor the spirituality of your worship, to excuse you from worshipping with your *Bodies*. Your *Hearts* must be *first* look'd to; but your *Words* and *Bodies* must be next look'd to: And if you regard not *these*, it is hardly credible that you regard your *Hearts*.

Properly ordered, Baxter can even say (I, 212), the pleasure of the senses is a pointer and an invitation to delight in God:

As a musician that toucheth but the keys of his Harpsical or organ, causeth that sweet harmonious sound, which we hear from the strings that are touched therein; so God ordained the order, beauty, sweetness, &c., of the creature, as should suddenly touch the inward sense with an answerable delight in God, who is the giver of the life of every creature. But where is that Christian that doth thus eat, drink and thus take pleasure in all his mercies?

It must be remembered that this advice comes from a man constantly oppressed by a sense of ill health, by a body described ('Dying Thoughts', Baxter 1824, 564) as 'a shoe that pinched me'.

Parishioners and readers troubled in conscience as to the proper posture at communion summed up for Baxter the national and ecclesiastical confusion of the England in which he grew up and served. He reveals (Baxter 1707, *PW* 1, 676, also Baxter 1679, 150–1) more appreciation than most British theologians then or since of the varied traditions of the church universal. Kneeling, with Luther and the English Prayer Book (as well as with the Roman rite, though that is an acknowledged similarity with no implications of doctrinal agreement), he could tolerate. Standing, with Zwingli, he knew to be the ancient norm, but did not have the confidence to insist on. Sitting, with Calvin and the Reformed majority and with Independents, both Congregational and Baptist, was Baxter's preference. In this matter as in so many others, Baxter was a quiet man in a noisy age. His gentle concluding advice, with a quaint hint at compromise, reads:

it is to be noted that the Church of England requireth only to receive it kneeling; but not to eat or drink it kneeling when they have received it . . . it is utterly unmeet to be too rigorous in urging a Uniformity of Gesture, or for any to be censorious of other men for a Gesture.

For Baxter, the ideal of the Christian body is an international *corpus Christianorum*, held together and protected (Baxter 1707, *PW* 1, 727) by a 'Catholick Prince'. But none such can as yet be found. National churches must therefore be tolerated. Within each, within the general community, although exacting moral standards should be enforced, much of the traditional morality could not be preserved without compromise. As to usury, for example (Baxter 1707, *PW* 1, 814–17), unlike Luther (Luther 1524), but with Zwingli and Calvin, Baxter found it permissible to take moderate interest on loans.

Baxter's 'Savoy Liturgy', an attempted eirenical substitute for both Prayer Book and Westminster Directory (Ratcliff 1976, 222–43), includes prayers (Pahl 1983, *CD* 490–3) explicitly for the sanctification of the elements, 'that they may be sacramentally the body and blood of [the Father's] Son Jesus Christ', and that the Spirit, working within the Body which has Christ for its Head, might 'fill us with thankfulness and holy joy, and with love to one another'. The rite was as unsuccessful as an instrument of *rapprochement* as the famous attempt of the Worcester regiment to cement the *Entente Cordiale* by adopting a French march (see Mauss 1950, 367–8). Interestingly, however, Baxter's eirenic stance and sense of oneness with older tradition was, three centuries later, to find a sympathetic hearing with Anglo-Catholic liturgical reformers (see Dix 1945, 608–12).

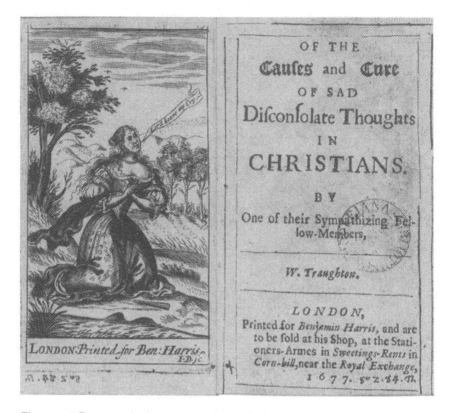

Plate 4   A Protestant body at prayer; from a Reformed work of spiritual direction,
William Traughton's *Of the Causes and Cure of Sad Disconsolate Thoughts in Christians*
(1677), title-page.

Baxter's counsel to all Christian communicants (Baxter 1707, *PW* I,
611) sums up his ecclesiology, with the all-pervading sense of the church
as gracious body, however seldom the image itself is explicitly used:

Perform all your worship to God, as in Heart-Communion with all Christ's
Churches upon Earth; even with those that are *faulty*, though not *with their
faults*. Though you *can be present* but with one, yet *consent as present in spirit* with
all, and separate not in Heart, from any one; any further than they separate
from Christ.

A TENUOUS TRADITION?

The early exponents of Protestant Christianity reflect a discovery, however inconsistent and uneven, of a sense of body in the person, in the general community, in the church, in the Eucharist. It was the permutations on the theme that were novel (and diverse) rather than any initial denigration. Yet the average Protestant of recent generations is hardly at all the conscious heir of any such tradition. The popular rediscovery of Protestant roots may combine with our present new emphasis on corporeity to revive the Reformers' affirmation of body as gift and sacrament, rather than as burden and threat, in Protestant theory and practice. Even in the period when Protestantism was becoming most rationalistic and body-fearing, it was possible for something of the Reformers' insistence of the wholeness of humanity in encounter with God to be maintained, and applied in new techniques of education, by Pestalozzi (1749–1827; see Silber 1973, especially 74–6, 175–225), and that at a time when he was disturbingly aware of losing his Protestant roots.

What kept the Reformation themes, this included, available to all, not only for outstanding geniuses like Pestalozzi or for the learned, was above all the ritual texts, chiefly hymns (see Runze 1898), which remained in use or have found their way back into use. Even when they speak of giving up the body, the body is sung of as a treasure:

> Nehmen sie den Leib,
> Gut, Ehr', Kind und Weib –
> Lass fahren's dahin:
> Sie haben kein Gewinn –
> Das Reich muss uns doch bleiben.

BIBLIOGRAPHY

Althaus, P. (1959), *Der Schöpfungsgedanke bei Luther* = Sitzungsberichte der Bayerischen Akademie der Wissenschaften, philologisch-historische Klasse, Munich: Jg 1959, Heft 7.
Atkinson, J. (1968), *Martin Luther and the Birth of Protestantism*, Harmondsworth: Pelican.
Barclay, A. (1927), *The Protestant Doctrine of the Lord's Supper in the Eucharistic Teaching of Luther, Zwingli and Calvin*, Edinburgh: Oliver & Boyd.
Baxter, R. (1679), *The Nonconformist's Plea for Peace*, London: George Bell.
  (1707), *Practical Works* [=*PW*], London: Thomas Parkhurst.
  (1824), *The Saints' Everlasting Rest*, London: Thomas Kelly.

(1928), *Breviate of the Life of Margaret Baxter*, ed. J. T. Wilkinson as 'Richard Baxter and Margaret Charlton. A Puritan Love Story', London: George Allen & Unwin.

Biéler, A. (1959), *La pensée économique et sociale de Calvin* (=Publications économiques et sociales de l'Université de Genève XIII), Geneva: Librairie de l'Université.

(1963), *L'homme et la femme dans la morale calviniste. La doctrine reformée sur l'amour, le mariage, le celibat, le divorce, l'adultère et la prostitution considerée dans son cadre historique*, Geneva: Labor et Fides.

Bizer, E. (1940), *Studien zur Geschichte des Abendmahlsstreits im 16. Jahrhundert*, Gütersloh: Mohn.

Blickle, P. (1985), *Gemeindereformation. Die Menschen des 16. Jahrhunderts auf dem Wege zum Heil*, Munich: R. Oldenbourg, ET as *Communal Reformation*, Atlantic Highlands, NJ, and London: Humanities Press, 1992.

Bohatec, J. (1937), *Calvins Lehre von Staat und Kirche mit besonderer Berücksichtigung des Organismusgedankens* (=Untersuchungen zur Deutschen Staats- und Rechtsgeschichte, 147. Heft), Breslau: M. & H. Marcus.

Bouwsma, W. J. (1988), *John Calvin: a Sixteenth Century Portrait*, New York and Oxford: Oxford University Press.

Braun, W. (1908), *Die Bedeutung der Conkupiscenz in Luthers Leben und Lehre*, Berlin: Trowitzsch.

Calvin, J. (1542), 'Petit Traicte de la saincte Cene de nostre Seigneur Jesus Christ' (1542), in ed. F. M. Higman, *Jean Calvin – Three French Treatises*, London: Athlone Press, 1970, 101–30.

(1542), *Forme des Prières Ecclésiastiques*; see Pahl (1983), *CD*, 347–67.

(1550), *Les Scandales*, ed. O. Fatio, C. Rapin, Geneva: Droz.

(1845), *Harmony=Harmonia ex tribus Evangelistis composita* (1555), ET by W. Pringle as *Commentary on a Harmony of the Evangelists, etc.* vols. 2 and 3, Edinburgh: Calvin Translation Society, 1845, 1846.

(1854), *Jeremiah=J.* Owen, trans., *Commentary on the Book of the Prophet Jeremiah and Lamentations*, IV, Edinburgh: Calvin Translation Society.

(1559), *Institutio Christianae religionis*, ed. A. Tholuck, Berolini, G. Thome, 1846.

(1560), *Institution de la religion chrétienne*, ed. J.-D. Benoit, Paris: Librairie philosophique J. Vrin 1957–1963.

Institutes of the Christian Religion, ET by F. L. Battles in *Library of Christian Classics*, xx, xxi, London, SCM 1961.

Inst.=any of the three preceding titles.

(Sermons on Job, 1563)=A. Golding (1574), translation.

Courvoisier, J. (1963), *Zwingli. A Reformed Theologian*, London: Epworth.

Damerau, R. (1977), *Luthers Gebetslehre 1515–1546, Zweiter Teil* (=Studien zu den Grundlagen der Reformation Bd 14), Marburg: Damerau.

Divine, T. F. (1959), *Interest*, Milwaukee: Marquette University Press.

Dix, G. (1945²), *The Shape of the Liturgy*, Westminster: Dacre Press.

Fischer, D. (1987), 'L'Eucharistie chez Calvin, en rapport avec la doctrine du

Ministère', *Freiburger Zeitschrift für Philosophie und Theologie* 34/3, 415–35.

Fordyce, E. T. (1987), 'Cookbooks of the 1800's', in ed. K. Grover, *Dining in America 1850–1900*, Amherst MA: University of Massachusetts Press, and Rochester, NY: Margaret Woodbury Strong Museum, 85–113.

Gerrish, B. A. (1988), 'Discerning the Body: Sign and Reality in Luther's Controversy with the Swiss'. *Journal of Religion* 68/3, 377–95.

Golding, A. (1574), *Sermons of Master John Calvin, vpon the Booke of Iob*, trans. by A. Golding, London: Lvcvs Harison, George Byshop.

Graham, W. F. (1987), *The Constructive Revolutionary. John Calvin and his Socio-Economic Impact*, Richmond, VA: John Knox Press.

Grün, A. and Reepen, M. (1988), *Gebetsgebärden*(=Munsterschwarzacher Kleinschriften 46), Munsterschwarzach: Vier-Turme-Verlag.

Hieron, S. (1608), *A Dispute upon the question of kneeling, in the acte of receiuing the sacramentall bread and wine* . . ., London: n.p.

Hooker, R. (1843), *Works*, Oxford: Tegg.

Höpfl, H. (1982), *The Christian Polity of John Calvin*, Cambridge University Press.

  (1991), ed. and trans., *Luther and Calvin on Secular Authority*, Cambridge University Press.

Hütter, L. (1610), *Compendium locorum theologicorum*, ed. W. Trillhaas (=Kleine Texte 183), Berlin, de Gruyter 1961.

Huxley, A. (1977), *The Doors of Perception*, London: Granada.

Kantorowitz, E. H. (1957), *The King's Two Bodies. A Study in Medieval Political Theology*, Princeton, NJ.

Karay Tripp, D. (1990), 'The Reformed Tradition of Embodied Prayer: Glorifying God in the Body'. *Liturgy* 8/4, 91–7.

  (1991), 'Daily Prayer in the Reformed Tradition', *Studia Liturgica* 21/1, 76–107, and 21/2, 190–209.

Kohler, E. (1959), *Martin Luther und der Festbrauch* (=Mitteldeutsche Forschungen 17), Köln und Graz, Bohlau.

Locher, G. W. (1979), *Die Zwinglische Reformation im Rahmen der europäischen Kirchengeschichte*, Göttingen und Zurich; Vandenhoeck und Ruprecht.

Loescher, J. R. (1981), *The Divine Community. Trinity, Church and Ethics in Reformation Theologies*, Kirksville, MO: 16th-Century Journal Publishers.

Luther, M. (1519), 'Ein Sermon von dem Hochwirdigen Sacrament', in *CL* I, 196–212.

  'Von den guten Wercken', in *CL* I, 227–98.

  (1520), *Von der Freyheyt eyniss Christenmenschen (de libertate christiana)*, ed. L. E. Schmitt, *Von der Freiheit eines Christenmenschen*, Halle/Saale: VEB Max Niemeyer Verlag,[2] 1953.

  (1524), 'Von Kaufshandlung und Wucher', in *CL* III, 1–46.

  (1526a), 'Dass diese Worte Christi: "Das ist mein Leib" noch feststehen' (1526), in *CH* IV (1890), 335–480.

  (1526b), 'Deutsche Messe und ordnung Gottis diensts', in *CL* III, 294–309; cf. Pahl 1983, *CD* 25–48.

  (1535) 'Ein einfeltige Weise zu Beten', in *WA* 38, 351–73.

CH = *Luthers Werke für das christliche Haus*, Braunschweig: Schwetzke, 1889–1893.
CL = *Luthers Werke in Auswahl*, eds. O. Clemen and A. Leitzmann, Berlin: de Gruyter 1933 (vol. 1),1959⁵ (vol. 3).
EA = *Dr Martin Luthers sämtliche Werke*, Erlangen 1826–52.
WA = *Dr Martin Luthers Werke*. Kritische Gesamtausgabe, Weimar 1883– .
WBr = *Dr Martin Luthers Werke = Briefe*.
Works, trans. C. M. Jacobs, Philadelphia, PA: Muhlenberg 1932.
Works, American edn, ed. H. C. Oswald, St Louis, MO: Concordia 1955– .
McGrath, A. (1990), 'The Eucharist: Reassessing Zwingli', *Theology* 93/751, 13–19.
McGuire, M. B. (1990), 'Religion and the Body. Rematerializing the Human Body in the Social Sciences of Religion', *Journal for the Scientific Study of Religion* 29/3, 282–96.
Marguérite (de Valois, reine) de Navarre (1547), *Les Marguérites de la Marguérite des Princesses*, ed. P. Funk, Paris: Librairie des Bibliophiles 1873.
Mauss, M. (1950), *Sociologie et anthropologie*, Paris: Presses Universitaires de France.
Miles, M. (1981), 'Theology, Anthropology and the Human Body in Calvin's *Institutes of the Christian religion*', *Harvard Theological Review* 74/3, 303–23.
 (1984), '"The Rope Breaks When it is Tightest:" Luther on the Body, Consciousness, and the Word', *Harvard Theological Review* 77/3–4, 239–58.
Moltmann, J. (1993), 'Covenant oder Leviathan? Zur politischen Theologie der Neuzeit', *Zeitschrift für Theologie und Kirche* 90/3, 299–317.
Pahl, I. (ed.) (1983), *Cena Domini I: Die Abendmahlsliturgie der Reformations-kirchen im 16./17. Jahrhundert* (=Spicilegium Friburgense 29), Freiburg Schweiz, Universitätsverlag (cited as *CD*).
Phillips, J. H. (1977), 'Les chrétiens et la danse. Une controverse publique à la Rochelle en 1639', *Bulletin de la Société de l'Histoire du Protestantisme Français*, 123, 362–80.
Prieur, J. M. (1994), 'La place du corps dans le culte réformé', *Etudes théologiques et religieuses* 69/1, 29–38.
Ratcliff, E. C. (1976), *Liturgical Studies*, eds. A. H. Couratin and D. H. Tripp, London: SPCK.
 (1980), *Reflections on Liturgical Revision* (ed. D. H. Tripp, as *Grove Liturgical Study No. 22*), Bramcote: Grove Books.
Roper, L. (1989), *The Holy Household: Women and Morals in Reformation Augsburg*, Oxford: Clarendon Press.
Roth, E. (1952), *Sakrament nach Luther*, Berlin: Töpelmann.
Royannez, M. (1979), 'L'eucharistie chez les évangeliques et les premiers réformés français (1522–1546)', *Bulletin de la Société de l'Histoire du Protestantisme Français* 125, 548–76.
Runze, G. (1898), 'Zur Interpretation des Lutherliedes "Ein' feste Burg",' *Zeitschrift für wissenschaftliche Theologie* 41, 412–52.
Rupp, E. G. (1952), *The Righteousness of God*, London: Hodder & Stoughton.

(1966) 'Patterns of salvation in the First Age of the Protestant Reformation', *Archiv für Reformationsgeschichte* 57/1–2, 52–66.

(1969), *Patterns of Reformation*, London: Epworth.

(1985), 'Prayer and devotion; the New Emphasis of the Protestant Reformation,' *His Dominion* 11/4, 2–11.

Sabatier, A. (1904), *Les religions de l'authorité et la religion de l'esprit*, Paris: Fischbacher.

Shaw, I.P. (1959), *Nationality and the Western Church Before the Reformation*, London: SPCK.

Silber, K. (1973³), *Pestalozzi. The Man and His Work* (author's English version), London: Routledge & Kegan Paul.

Skinner, Q. (1978), *The Foundations of Modern Political Thought*, 2 vols., Cambridge University Press.

Stock, U. (1982), *Die Bedeutung der Sakramente in Luthers Sermonen von 1519* (=Studies in the History of Christian Thought 27), Leiden: Brill.

Stubs (or Stubbes), P. (1585), *The Anatomie of Abuses*, London: pr., R. Iones, ³.

Synott, A. (1993), *The Body Social. Symbolism, Self and Society*, London and New York: Routledge.

Tawney, R. H. (1926), *Religion and the Rise of Capitalism.* (Holland Memorial Lectures, 1922), New York: Harcourt Brace.

Turner, C. E. A. (1949), 'Puritan Origins in Science', *Journal of the Transactions of the Victoria Institute* 81, 85–105.

Viner, J. (1978), *Religious Thought and Economic Society. Four Chapters of an Unfinished Work*, Durham, NC: Duke University Press.

Wald, B. (1993), *Person und Handlung bei Martin Luther* (=Schriftenreihe der Gustav-Siewerth-Akademie 9), Weilheim-Bierbronnen, Gustav-Siewerth-Akademie.

Wallace, R. S. (1953), *Calvin's Doctrine of Word and Sacrament*, Edinburgh: Oliver & Boyd.

(1959), *Calvin's Doctrine of the Christian Life*, Edinburgh: Oliver & Boyd.

(1988), *Calvin, Geneva and the Reformation*, Edinburgh: Scottish Academic Press.

Watson, P. S. (1946), *The State as Servant of God*, London: Epworth.

Woods, S. (1992), 'The Body Penitent. A 1560 Calvinist Sonnet Sequence', *American Notes and Queries* 5/1, 137–40.

Zimmerman, G. (1993), 'Gottesbund und Zwei-Reiche-Lehre bei Calvin und in den "Vindiciae contra tyrannos"', *Zeitschrift für Kirchengeschichte* 104/1, 28–48.

Zwingli, H. (1523a), 'Von Götlicher und menschlicher grechtigheit', in *sW* II, 471–525.

(1523b) 'Herr Ulrich Zwinglis leerbiechlein wie man die Knaben Christlich vunterweysen vnd erziehen soll / mit kurtzer anzaye aynes gantzen Christlichen lebens', ed. (with text also of 1526 edn) A. Israel in *Sammlung selten gewordener pädagogischer Schriften des 16. und 17. Jahrhunderts*, 4, Zschopau, Raschke 1879.

(1524), 'Action oder Bruch des Nachtmals' in Pahl 1983, *CD* 182–98.

(1526), 'Ein klar underichting vom nachtmal Christi' in *sW* iv, 773–862.

(1527a), 'Das diss wort Jesu Christi, Das ist min lychnam der für uch hinggeben wirt, ewiglich den alten eynigen sinn haben werdend', in *sW*, v, 795–977.

sW = *Huldrych Zwinglis sämtliche Werke*, ed. E. Egli, in Corpus Reformatorum 88, Braunschweig 1904, Leipzig 1905.

PART III

Beyond the West: Eastern religious traditions and the body

CHAPTER 9

Zoroastrianism and the body

Alan Williams

Zoroastrianism is one of the world's most ancient and influential religions, yet nowadays it is practised in one of the world's smallest religious communities. Its influence upon the doctrines and rituals of Judaism and Christianity is well known, as are the similarities with Brahmanic Hinduism. Yet it is neither gnostic nor semitic in its religious conceptions, nor does it conform to the terms of reference familiar to students of Indian religions. Its understanding of the body is strangely familiar to Western readers. Its supreme values are truth, order, and justice; the virtues which it cultivates above all are wisdom, fortitude, the will to be victorious, and the striving to fulfilment and prosperity of individual and community. All of these are reflected in a distinctive understanding of the body.

In Zoroastrianism the body is not something which is to be mortified or even disadvantaged unduly in favour of non-corporeal existence. Indeed asceticism, celibacy, and self-mortification are frowned upon in the religious texts as demonic tendencies.[1] There is an apposition of terms such as body and soul, matter and spirit in Zoroastrianism, but it is not a hard-edged dualism such as we find in some other religions. From the most ancient scripture, the *Gāthās* of the prophet Zarathuštra, the body is seen as part of man's ultimate nature, not merely as a means to attaining a more complete, incorporeal nature. Like the rest of Ahura Mazdā's physical creation, the body is to be treated with respect. Indeed the body here and now is seen as reflecting the inner nature, and it has been rightly observed that bodily sickness denotes sickness of soul;[2] conversely, bodily health, maturity and fecundity are regarded as

---

[1] This point has sometimes been exaggerated by over-enthusiastic writers on this religion, to the extent that Zoroastrianism is depicted as hedonistic and even blockheaded. As often, R. C. Zaehner found the *bon mot*: 'Zoroastrianism is neither this-worldly nor other-worldly: it is both-worldly. But always the primacy is given to the other world, the world of unseen spirit, out of which this world of visible matter is born' (Zaehner 1961, 278).

[2] Ibid., 277.

reflecting spiritual wholeness. The very goal of the religion, eschatologically, is the attainment of bodily perfection and fullness in a state of spiritual harmony and freedom from evil in the resurrected 'Future Body' (Pahlavi *tan ī pasēn*) at the end of time when the spiritual world is finally able to coalesce with a renovated material world, once the demonic forces of Angra Mainyu (=Pahlavi Ahriman), the 'Hostile Spirit', have been expelled from the world. In the present state of the physical world, however, which has been attacked by evil, the human body, though intrinsically pure and a source of intelligent life and good action must be carefully protected, just as the boundaries of all the good creation must be maintained, against demonic insurgence. Indeed the body is a symbol of the integrity of the world order of Ahura Mazdā against the chaos of Angra Mainyu which threatens from without.

The body is to be kept in a sufficiently pure condition for normal living; for sacred rituals this state must be heightened. An array of practices and prohibitions establishes a rigorous regime of purity for Zoroastrians. However, it cannot be stressed enough that the underlying concept of purity is not one of a sterile, fixed condition, but rather of a state free from evil which is at the same time highly receptive to the creative forces of holiness and goodness. Perhaps strangely for Western understanding, purity is felt to be an intensely fecund state: the higher the state of purity, the more intense may be the impregnation by the creative forces of the divine beings (Avestan *yazata* and *am ∂šasp ∂nta*) of Ahura Mazdā. Bodily purity, therefore, is directly linked to bodily vitality and creativity. The sacred liturgy of Zoroastrianism, the *Yasna* (literally 'sacrifice') gives formal expression to the connection between purity and creativity.[3]

According to the Pahlavi texts of the ninth century AD, which most fully articulate the theology and anthropology of Zoroastrianism, the cosmos itself proceeded from the body of Ahura Mazdā in 'Endless Light'. In some texts the living world emerges from the macrocosmic body of a primal man, Gayōmard, 'Mortal Life'.[4] Ahura Mazdā created the present world in a perfect state, but it was afflicted by the alien Angra Mainyu, the 'Hostile Spirit'. In this 'corrupted' (rather than 'fallen') state

---

[3] In several Pahlavi texts God celebrates the *Yasna* liturgy himself as the very act of creation, and for the creation of the primal man, Gayōmard, for Zarathuštra's birth and revelation (see Williams 1990, vol. 2, 31). The future saviour, Saošyant, similarly performs the *Yasna* to waken the dead (see ibid., vol. 2, 83). The only scholar to have discussed this subject at length was M. Molé, in his monumental *Culte* . . . (1963, 86–147), but see also Lincoln 1988.

[4] See further Williams 1985.

of the world, Man is the supreme creature.[5] Man's cultivation of spiritual power through goodness and wisdom is fertilized by regular enactment of liturgical and devotional rites, requiring physical, as well as spiritual and mental, purification. A rigorous process of reward and punishment is consequent on all action. It is fully a religion of accountability, and therein lies a threat or, better, burden of responsibility which enforces the religious and, consequently, social laws. Much of this accruing of reward and punishment devolves on the physical body. In the first place actions, wherein the body is fully engaged, weigh more heavily in the process of judgement of the soul. Second, although reward and punishment are meted out in the spiritual *mēnōg* realm of incorporeal existence, in fact the language of corporeality persists even in the narratives of the afterlife, presumably because bodily experience is all that can be grasped by mortal, incarnate minds. An example of this is the Pahlavi text *Ardā Wīrāz Nāmag*, 'Book of the Righteous Wīrāz'.[6] Wīrāz, whilst still a living mortal, ascends to heaven and descends to hell to witness the rewards and punishments enjoyed by the righteous and the wicked. The pleasures of heaven are expressed in terms of fragrances, splendid costumes, luxurious food, golden couches, and creature comforts. The majority of the book, however, is taken up by lurid descriptions of the torments of hell, which catalogue a grisly routine of butchery in the repeated skewering, cutting off, gouging out, and stuffing with filth, of different parts of the physical body. The loosely related correspondences between the original offence and the hellish punishment presumably indicated a lesson for the faithful. Mercifully, there will be a time of resurrection of all mankind and, after a divine judgement, each human being will live in the 'Future Body', incorruptible, eternal, and blissful. Meanwhile, and until that time, Ahriman and his broods of demons are all too eager to attack and destroy Mazdā's creation of this world. Man has to stop them.

A passage from an important Pahlavi text on purity rules displays certain fundamental doctrines and explains the intimate connection between the spiritual and physical worlds. It is said that Zarathuštra sat before Ahura Mazdā in the spiritual world 'learning His word by heart'. Ahura Mazdā is visible with 'head, hands, feet *etc.*, and clothes as men

---

[5] 'By the fact of the creation of the creator, Man is a composite, as regards nature and power, of all the *mēnōg* and *gētīg* creations, constituted in fullness of strength over the other creatures of the *gētīg* of which he is the chief for the governing of the whole and for triumphing completely over the demons with the strength of all the creatures' *DkM*. 245.3ff., trans. de Menasce 1973, 233.

[6] Most recently translated by Gignoux 1984, and Vahman 1986.

have', and the prophet asks if he might take hold of God's hand. He is told 'I am intangible spirit.' How, then, may he worship Ahura Mazdā and the Immortals when he departs their company and returns to the physical world? Ahura Mazdā's reply is:

each one of us has given to the material world a foster-mother of his own, whereby he makes effective in the material world, through that body, that proper activity which he performs in the spiritual world.[7]

There are seven principal 'foster-mothers' (Pahlavi *dāyag*), also called 'bodies' (*tan*) and 'counterparts' (*hangōsīdag*), namely the seven Blessed Immortals (Pahlavi *amahraspand*, Avestan *am ∂šasp ∂nta*) and their physical counterparts in the world.

The text continues:

Whoever teaches care for all these seven [creations] does well and pleases [the Immortals], then his soul will never arrive at kinship with Ahriman and the demons. When he has cared for them [*i.e.* the creations], then the care of these seven Immortals is for him, and he must teach [this] to all mankind in the material world.

For the righteous Zoroastrian, care for these seven physical creations, sky, earth, water, plant, beneficient animal, man, fire, coalesces with the religious duty to please and worship the seven *am ∂šasp ∂ntas* of the divine presence. Man should not pollute any of these elements, for by doing so the *am ∂šasp ∂ntas* would be harmed. The perishable body (Pahlavi *tan ī sazōmand*) is a worldly state of righteousness. Evil is seen always to come from *outside* the boundaries of the body. The body is one of the outer walls of defence against the enemy:

Being on one's watch is this, one who makes his body like a fortress, and who places watch over it, keeping the gods inside and not letting the demons enter.[8]

One's body (*tan ī xwēš*) is the gateway to one's moral and spiritual nature:

one . . . does battle against the non-material demons (*druz ī mēnōg*) . . . in particular does not let these fierce demons into one's body: Greed, Envy, Lust, Wrath and Shame.[9]

The body, like the rest of the divine creation, is vulnerable to the attacks of evil, for the evil spirit, Ahriman, is without a body of his own and is parasitic upon all life – his very 'existence' is the denial of existence:

[7] *Šāyist Nē-Šāyist* ('What is allowed and not allowed'), ch. 15.4; text and translation with slight modification, Kotwal 1969, 56f.
[8] *Dēnkard*, ed. Madan 1911 = DkM., 583.5–7, trans. Shaked 1979, 203, E 34a.
[9] DkM. 477.18, Shaked 1979, 11, §23.

It is possible to put Ahriman out of the world in this manner, namely, every person, for his own part, chases him out of his body, for the dwelling of Ahriman in the world is in the body of men. When he will have no dwelling in the bodies of men, he will be annihilated from the whole world; for as long as there is in this world a dwelling even in a single person for a small demon, Ahriman is in the world.[10]

The bodies of sorcerers, witches, murderers, and whores, for example, are possessed by evil forces so much that these are thought of as being evil persons, but the body of the righteous person is not evil, which contrasts with the Manichean attitude to the body. A Zoroastrian text explains:

against that which the [Zoroastrian] restorer of righteousness Ādurbād taught: to drive the demons from one's body, the demon-inspired Mānī said that the human body is a demon.[11]

For the Manichean particles of light were trapped in the prison of the flesh; for the Zoroastrian it was a religious duty to make the gods an abode in the body:

Make the gods abide in your own body, and if you make them abide in your own body, then you will have made them abide in the whole world.[12]

The condition of their abiding is a state of purity (*abēzagīh, pākīh*) or health (*drustīh*). High states of ritual purity must be attained by priests before they may perform sacred ceremonies for they must reproduce within the precincts of the ritual, as far as possible, the pristine state in which God created the world. Priests must be in a high state of purity to resemble the state of Ahura Mazdā himself.[13]

Until this century Zoroastrians were traditionally scrupulous in maintaining their numerous rules and observances of purity. These served to protect a strong group identity even in an environment of oppression by Muslims in Iran. Moreover, in caste-conscious India the Parsi Zoroastrians kept their social and religious identity by using rules of purity whereby outsiders were excluded. Purification of the body may seem to the modern reader to be the most private of these rules, affecting only the individual; in fact the rules and rites were emphatically of *public* concern, and infringement of them resulted in nothing less than social ostracization and public ignominy. Purification, moreover, is symbolic

---

[10] *DkM.* 530.20–531.3, Shaked 1979, 103, section 264.
[11] *DkM.* 218.6–8, see de Menasce 1973, 210.
[12] *DkM.* 216.15–17, de Menasce 1973, 209.
[13] Molé has made this point well: 'le sacrifice est une répétition de l'acte par lequel le monde fut créé. Le vrai sacrificateur n'est pas le prêtre qui officie; ce n'est même pas Sošāns, c'est Ohrmazd, le dieu Créateur' (1963, 125, and see further 126–32).

of the purification of the soul, but nevertheless the impurity suffered by
the individual was viewed as being altogether real and, if allowed to
persist, was thought to result in serious physical, moral and spiritual
injury, both for the individual and the community at large.

The main purification rites of Zoroastrianism are described under four
headings, in order of increasing complexity and sacred power: *Pādyāb-
kustī*; *Nāhn*; *Rīman*; *Barašnom-ī nō šab*. These rites are performed variously
according to the severity of the pollution which must be removed and the
state of purity which must be attained.

(1) *Pādyāb-kustī*, the simplest in form, performed like a private ablution
several times a day by the practising Zoroastrian, is one of the minimum
requirements of the faith. It is performed alone by priest or layperson
upon rising from sleep, after urinating or defecating, before meals and
before daily prayers (recited properly five times daily). The procedure is
as follows:
(i)   First a short prayer formula invokes the name of Ahura Mazdā, then
      the holiest prayer of righteousness, Aš∂m Vohū is recited;
(ii) the exposed parts of the body, e.g. face, hands and feet, are washed
      in ordinary water;
(iii) only then is the *kustī*, the sacred thread worn around the waist over
      the *sudra*, sacred undershirt, untied and ritually retied whilst a short
      prayer formula is recited.
Thus, following the pattern of the more complex rites of purification, the
actual washing of the body is enclosed before and after by prayer
formulae.

(2) *Nāhn*, Parsi Gujarati for 'bath', is more elaborate and is administered
by a priest, usually in the home. *Nāhn* is given on four main occasions: to
a child before it undergoes the initiatory ceremony of putting on the *sudra*
and *kustī* for the first time; to a bride and groom before their marriage
ceremony; to a woman forty days after giving birth; to any adult
Zoroastrian during the *Frawardīgān* holy days at the end of the year.
There are three main stages of the *Nāhn*: purification of the soul, mind,
and body; these are enclosed by an initial *Pādyāb-kustī* and a concluding
ritual retying of the *kustī*:
(i) *Pādyāb-kustī* is performed;
(ii) the candidate recites a *bāj*, i.e. an initial enclosing prayer; he or she
     then chews a pomegranate leaf (regarded as a token of fecundity),

and sips a little *nīrangdīn* (ritually consecrated bull's urine) mixed with a pinch of *bhasam* (ash taken from a temple fire); consumption of these two most holy substances effects an internal purification of the soul;

(iii) a prayer of repentance, *patēt*, is said by the candidate, by which the mind is purified;

(iv) a ritual bath is taken, preceded and followed by recitation of the enclosing *bāj* prayers; this is administered by a priest, who passes the purifying agents to the candidate on a long handled ladle from outside the bathing area. First the candidate rubs a little consecrated bull's urine over his or her body three times, then the same is done with some sand, then with some consecrated water. Consecrated water is also sprinkled upon the new clothes to be worn by the candidate. Then the candidate washes his or her body with water from a vessel into which a few drops of consecrated water have been added, thus purifying all the water.

(v) The candidate dresses and reties the *kustī* over the *sudra* whilst reciting the accompanying prayer formula.

(3) *Rīman*, the name of the rite 'unclean', refers to the person to whom this rite should be administered, i.e. someone who has come into contact with carrion or bodily refuse; it is known also as the *sī-šūy* 'thirty washings',[14] and again it is administered by a priest, but more than in the previous rite, which takes place on auspicious occasions, in this rite the priest takes the greatest care to avoid even symbolic contact of indirect touch via an implement or by a glance of the eyes with the *rīman*;[15]

(i) The *rīman* enters an area enclosed by a *kaš*, 'furrow';[16]

(ii) the *rīman* takes sips of consecrated bull's urine whilst the priest pours into the *rīman*'s hands, from a long-handled ladle, the three agents used for cleansing the physical body, one after the other: *gōmēz* (unconsecrated bull's urine), sand, and water; with these the *rīman* washes his or her own body;

(iii) stage ii is repeated 9 times (totalling 27 washings);

(iv) pure water is then poured over the body of the *rīman* three times from the head down, thus making a total of 30 washings in all.

---

[14] According to Boyce (1975, 313) it was still undergone in some of the orthodox Yazdī villages in Iran in the early 1960s, although she notes that 'In Kerman . . . it was regarded then as a rite solely for women.' Among the Parsis the rite was replaced by a simpler purificatory act and *Rīman* is not even mentioned by the authoritative Parsi work on Parsi religious ceremonies (Modi 1922).

[15] This, in summary, is the rite according to Yazdī custom described by Boyce (1975, 312f.).

[16] i.e. like the *kaš* drawn around the corpse in the death rites.

Although this latter is relatively elaborate, it does not suffice to remove the most serious pollutions.[17]

4. *Barašnom-ī nō šab*: here only a brief account can be given of this complex rite, but it has been amply described elsewhere.[18] The name means 'purification of the nine [days and] nights', and it is the longest and most elaborate of the purification rites, intended to drive the corpse demoness from those who have suffered grievous pollution by contact with a corpse, or from similarly polluting bodily events such as a miscarriage. As has been observed,[19] it may also be undertaken not so much for the removal of a particular impurity, but rather for the increase of existing purity for some special purpose. Priests would frequently have to undergo the *barašnom* for this reason in order to purify themselves for the performance of the most sacred rites of the religion. It is a prolonged rite, imposing nine days and nights of seclusion on the candidate within the *barašnomgāh*, 'place of the *barašnom*', an enclosed, roofless place remote from human habitation, where nothing living grows. Within this walled area the ritual precincts are drawn out on a north–south axis within a series of nine *kaš* 'furrows', within which there is a series of nine stones.

(i) The polluted person, whom we may again call the *rīman*, first drinks some consecrated bull's urine, *nīrang*, as in the *rīman* ritual.

(ii) Then, naked, he or she enters the enclosure within the *kaš* from the north, the direction of hell, moves south, towards heaven, and squats upon the first stone.

(iii) Here he or she is purified with *gōmēz*, sand and water, in much the same way as in the *rīman* or *sī-šūy*, i.e. the cleansing agent is poured from a ladle, held at a distance by a priest, over the head of the *rīman*. In a strict, set order the *rīman* rubs the *gōmēz* etc. over all parts of the body from the head down to the toes, conscious that the corpse demoness is being chased down the body.

(iv) After the three washings on the first stone, prayers are said by the *rīman*.

---

[17] 'If anyone becomes *rīman* by coming into contact with *nasā* (carrion) and although it is made known that he has undergone the *sī-šūy* bath, even then he should keep himself aloof [from others], and until the time *Barašnom* is administered he should not go near fire or water . . . [or else] it is a great sin' (Unvala 1922, 135, trans. Dhabhar 1932, 152).

[18] See Modi 1922, 102–153; Boyce 1975, 313–19. Choksy 1989, 23–52 describes ancient, medieval and modern versions of the ritual process.

[19] Boyce 1975, 317.

(v) The process iii–iv is repeated on the remaining eight stones. (Two priests are in attendance throughout, one of whom tethers a dog, whose gaze is purifying to the *nīman* and inimical to the corpse demoness.)

(vi) On a tenth stone the candidate washes in water which is poured from above.

(vii) The candidate then dresses in white garments, ties the *kustī* and withdraws to a secluded place to pass the time in prayer.

(viii) Subsequent ablutions are performed on the fourth, seventh, and tenth mornings, after which the individual rejoins his or her family free from the pollution.

Throughout the *barašnom* the candidate should avoid contact with the bare earth as far as possible in order to avoid harming it and the Amahraspand Spandarmad. Physical contact with other persons is prohibited, but the candidate is assisted by one *parestār* 'attendant', who provides meals and who keeps the candidate company.

By giving this brief description of the purity rites I intend to show something of the pattern of Zoroastrian attitudes to the body. Unfortunately, concentration on these alone may give a misleading impression of austerity and outlandishness. Purification rites, by their very nature, are rigorous and astringent. They must be seen in the wider context of Zoroastrian life, which can only be alluded to in this essay. However, we note that these purification rites were intended for all, young and old, male and female, priest and layperson. They are not exclusive, nor are they seen as punishments, but rather as means of attaining merit and freedom from sin.

Man exists in both the *mēnōg* 'spiritual' and *gētīg* 'material' worlds: the body (*tan*) and vital soul (*gyān*) exist in the *gētīg* during this mortal life, as does the soul (*ruwān*). At death, after the separation of the vital soul from the body, the *ruwān* passes through a judgment and to the *mēnōg* world, to heaven or hell. According to a traditional account man has two other parts to his nature, a 'form' (*ēwēnag*) and a 'spirit' (*frawahr*) both of which never leave the state in which they were created in the *mēnōg*. The realm of 'unmixed evil' is, like that of 'unmixed good', a spiritual state, *mēnōg*, and the demons are the root of all evil, and constantly they prey upon the physical world. The demons have no access, however, to the Ahuric realm of unmixed good in the *mēnōg* world of heaven.

The Zoroastrian understanding of the individual living body is not comparable to modern scientific or western secular notions of the body

Plate 5   Zoroastrian priest in a state of ritual purity, reciting prayers for the dead before a fire during a service in the funerary precincts of the Zoroastrian community of Hong Kong.

as a merely material thing. It is understood strictly in the terms of the purity rules which govern, and indeed *define*, the Zoroastrian's body. Thus the frontier between man's spiritual and physical nature is an open one, regularly crossed in both directions as the purity rules regulate man's communication with the divine world. Within the physical and social body processes of transformation are necessary for life to continue; for example, eating and defecation are necessary for perpetuation of the individual body; sexual behaviour and childbirth are necessary for perpetuation of the social body: all four processes necessitate breaches in the boundaries of the system and are thus hedged around with strict rules. The boundary is crossed when, as a result of the above mentioned processes of change, matter is perceived as dead and is regarded as dangerous exuviae,[20] for such matter is prey to the demonic forces. Nail parings, extracted teeth, cut hair, blood, semen, and waste products of the physical body must be correctly disposed of in order that the pollution which they attract may be minimized. Ritual washing and prayer must be performed in order to reseal symbolically the boundary which has been ruptured by matter leaving the system (i.e. body). Indeed, some pollutions are so potent that the person in contact with them, not just the polluted matter, must be excluded from the body of the community either temporarily (in the case of the menstruating woman) or permanently (in the case of the corpse-bearer).

The body is thus a primary focus of meaning which is taken over into many other contexts of bounded systems in Zoroastrian society. For Zoroastrianism the body was indeed a symbol of Zoroastrian society. Mary Douglas' idea that 'the powers and dangers credited to social structure [are] reproduced in small on the human body'[21] seems to be borne out by the example of this religion.[22] This is understandable when it is understood that from the prophet Zarathuštra onwards the religion preaches a philosophy of growth, evolution and triumph over ill: for this nothing could be closer to hand as an illustration than the human body itself. In the words of R. C. Zaehner:

Zoroastrianism is the religion of growth, increase, fulfilment, and prosperity, the religion of creative evolution. The growth in virtue of the individual is seen as part of the growth of the whole community: it is part of the *patvandishn i ō Frashkart*, 'the continuous evolution towards the making excellent', a continuous growth of the whole of humanity into the plenitude of perfection planned for it by God. The consummation of [all] things is increase – from one thing, many things.[23]

---

[20] See further Williams 1989.
[21] Douglas 1970, 115.
[22] For a more detailed analysis of this see Williams 1989.
[23] Zaehner 1961, 268.

BIBLIOGRAPHY

Boyce, M. (1975), *A History of Zoroastrianism*, vol. 1, Leiden.
  (1977), *A Persian Stronghold of Zoroastrianism*, Oxford. repr. Universities of America Press, 1989.
  (1979), *Zoroastrians, their Religious Beliefs and Practices*, London, 3rd revised repr. 1988.
Choksy, J.K. (1989), *Purity and Pollution in Zoroastrianism*, Austin.
Dhabhar, B. N. (1932), *The Persian Rivayats of Hormazyar Framarz*, Bombay.
Douglas, M. (1970), *Purity and Danger: An Analysis of Concepts of Pollution and Taboo*, Harmondsworth: Penguin.
Gignoux, P. (1984), *Le livre d'Ardā Vīrāz*, Paris.
Kotwal, F. M. P. (1969), *The Supplementary Texts to the Šāyest nē-šāyest*, Copenhagen.
Lincoln, B. (1988), 'Physiological Speculation and Social Patterning in a Pahlavi Text', *Journal of the American Oriental Society* 108, 135–40.
Madan, D. M. (ed.) (1911), *The Complete Text of the Pahlavi Dinkard*, Bombay.
Menasce, J. de (1973), *Le troisième livre du Dēnkart*, Paris.
Modi, J. J. (1922), *The Religious Ceremonies and Customs of the Parsis*, Bombay: repr. Garland, 1979.
Molé, M. (1963), *Culte, mythe et cosmologie dans l'Iran ancient*, Paris.
Shaked, S. (1979), *The Wisdom of the Sasanian Sages (Dēnkart VI)*, Boulder.
Unvala, M. R. (1922), *Dārāb Hormazyār's Rivāyat*, Bombay.
Vahman, F. (1986), *Ardā Wirāz Nāmag*, London and Malmo.
Williams, A. V. (1985), 'A Strange Account of the World's Origin, *PRDd. XLVI*', *Acta Iranica* II.x.25, *Papers in Honour of Professor Mary Boyce*, Leiden, 683–97.
  (1989), 'The Body and the Boundaries of Zoroastrian Spirituality', *Religion* 19, 227–39.
  (1990), *The Pahlavi Rivāyat Accompanying the Dādestāt ī Dēnīg*, 2 vols. Copenhagen.
Zaehner, R. C. (1961), *The Dawn and Twilight of Zoroastrianism*, London.

CHAPTER 10

Medical and mythical constructions of the body in Hindu texts

Wendy Doniger

INTRODUCTION[1]

Those of us who are engaged in the wild-goose chase of the search for universals once hoped to find support for our quest in the universal human problems posed by the universal structure of the human body. Since the body is the experience that furnishes the symbolic materials with which different cultures express the equally basic human experience of history, we hoped to ground even religious history in the study of the body. But, just as history is inevitably mediated by historiography, so the body is always mediated by symbolic expression of the culture. The deconstructionists argue that the body is not given, but constructed, and that each culture constructs it differently. Yet one could argue that the body of a contemporary American and the body of an ancient Hindu are both the same (two eyes, two hands . . .) and different (because of what each of the embodied people think about eyes and hands). The body is both given and constructed.

I have therefore found it appropriate to approach the Hindu attitude to the body from two angles. First, I will present the evidence for the uniquely Hindu construction of the body through reference to a group of seminal texts about embryology – how the human body is literally constructed – from various Hindu disciplines, asking the Passover question: Why is this paradigm different from all other paradigms? But then I will go on to treat the Hindu variants of certain rather highly inflected mythological somatic themes that occur in religions throughout the world: the head, the eyes, the tongue, the genitals, the breast, and the foot. The peculiarly Hindu inflection of these quasi-universal themes will

---

[1] Since this essay was first drafted, two further pieces on Indian bodies have appeared in ed. Kasulis 1993: Frits Staal, 'Indian Bodies' (59–102), and Gerald James Larson, 'The Concept of Body in *Āyurveda* and the Hindu Philosophical Systems' (103–21). Both of these essays are excellent supplements to the present sketch.

give us a different sort of view of Hindu cognitive assumptions about the body.

BASIC HINDU TEXTS ON EMBRYOLOGY

One could, of course, make a study of the Hindu approach to the body through an analysis of every major text, starting with the *Ṛg Veda* (which celebrates the body exuberantly) and the Upaniṣads (which warn of its treachery), through Sanskrit love poetry (predictably pro-body and libertine) and the Yogic texts (also pro-body, though in a rather different key, and certainly not libertine), and so forth. I have confined this chapter to a few ancient Indian disciplines that have made relatively explicit the assumptions that most Hindus share about the construction of the human body (bearing in mind the universalist agenda), while at the same time noting the significant differences between them.

Medical texts

A basic assumption of Hindu medical texts (and one with interesting European parallels) is the doctrine of the three humours, closely related to the Hindu belief that all matter, including the human body, is composed of the three elements of lucidity (*sattva*), energy (*rajas*), and torpor (*tamas*): 'Wind, bile, and phlegm are said to be the group of humours, the sources of disease, in the body; and energy and darkness are said to be the source of disease in the mind. Pathological changes that are regarded as curable are counteracted by medicines possessing qualities opposite [to the humours of the changes], applied with proper regard for place, dose, and time. But no cure is prescribed for diseases that are incurable' (*Carakasaṃhitā* 1.1.1.54–62a. O'Flaherty 1988, 93–4.) This remains the prevailing view of Ayurvedic practitioners today.

But the medical texts themselves acknowledge the existence of multiple theories about the body even within their own system:

Once a group of sages were summoned by the king to debate this question: The person is a mass of soul, senses, mind, and sense objects. But is the origin of the person also thought to be the origin of diseases, or not? The sages offered various answers. One said, 'The individual person is born from the Soul, and so the diseases are also born from the Soul.' Another: 'No. When the mind that is conscious of lucidity is overwhelmed by energy and torpor, then it causes the origin both of the body itself and of pathological changes in the body.' Another: 'No. All creatures are born from *rasa* [the fluid essence of digested food], and so the various diseases are also born from *rasa*.' Another: 'No. The individual person is born of the six elements of matter [earth, water, fire, wind, space, and mind or soul], and so diseases are also born from the six elements.'

Then another sage replied: 'No. How could someone be born out of the six elements, without a mother and a father? A person is born from a person; a cow from a cow, and a horse from a horse. Diseases such as urinary disorders are known to be hereditary. So the two parents are the cause.' 'No', said another, 'for a blind person is not born from a blind person. But a creature is known to be born of his karma, and so diseases are also born from karma.' 'No', said another. 'An agent must always precede an action [karma]. And no person can be the result of an action that has not been done; this is clear enough. No, nature is the cause, one's own nature, the cause of both diseases and the person, just as it is the nature of earth to be rough, water to be fluid, wind to move, and fire to be hot.' 'No', said another. 'The Creator had an unlimited imagination, and it was he who created the happiness and unhappiness of this universe, sentient and insentient.' 'No', said another. 'The individual person is born of time, and diseases are born of time.'

Now, as the sages were arguing in this way, Punarvasu said, 'Don't talk like this. It is hard to get to the truth when people take sides. People who utter arguments and counter-arguments as if they were established facts never get to the end of their own side, as if they were going round and round on an oil press. Not until you shake off the torpor of factionalism from what you want to know will true knowledge emerge. The use of good food is one cause of the growth of a person, and the use of bad food is a cause of diseases.' To which one of the sages replied, 'Physicians have an abundance of different opinions. Not all of them will understand this sort of teaching.' (*Carakasaṃhitā* 1.1.15.3–34. O'Flaherty 1988, 92–3)

Despite the acknowledgement of the complex metaphysical factors that influence the birth and development of the body, the final view stated, which Hindu texts always present as the favoured view, did in fact prevail in Hindu medical science: food is presented as the primary cause of the body, bad food as the primary cause of disease, and good food as the primary cause of healing. This is one reason for the great emphasis on the right and wrong food in the legal texts, to which we will now turn.

'The Laws of Manu'

The Laws of Manu, the paradigmatic text of Hindu religious law, composed in the early centuries of the present era, expresses several different attitudes to the body. First, in keeping with the general, rather grudging lip-service that he pays to the philosophy of renunciation, Manu offers a chilling image of the body: '[A man] should abandon this foul-smelling, tormented, impermanent dwelling-place of living beings, filled with urine and excrement, pervaded by old age and sorrow, infested by illness, and polluted by passion, with bones for beams, sinews for cords, flesh and blood for plaster, and skin for the roof' (*Manu* 6.76–7). Here, as elsewhere in Indian civilization, this attitude to the body is coupled with a virulent misogyny.

Manu also expresses a basic uneasiness about the body, especially about the openings through which fluids may escape or enter. Thus the obsessional concern for the control of what enters the body (food) is balanced by an equally obsessional concern for the regulating of excretions (including sexual excretions) and the cleansing of the openings of the body. This physical model, of danger flowing in and out of the body at all times, is echoed in the social model of karmic transactions, where social dangers flow in and out of the body through contact with other people – primarily through the exchange of food or sex. The extreme degree of Manu's fear of pollution through such contact found few parallels in the West other than, perhaps, the attitude to lepers, until the present day, when the paranoiac public attitude to people with AIDS provides, I think, a sad parallel to Manu's attitude to people with social diseases (which is to say any diseases at all, since diseases are punishments for sins against society) or social disabilities (such as birth into a low caste).

But women, and the body, also have their uses for Manu: as vessels for the procreation of male heirs. There are two different, conflicting models of paternity in Manu, expressed through a single agricultural metaphor: The sower of the seed is the biological father, who may or may not be the legal husband; the woman is the field, and the owner of the field is the legal husband. The son born in the field (the wife) by a man other than her legal husband is known as the *kṣetraja*, literally 'born in the (husband's) field', the wife's natural son (*Manu* 9.167). But there are two ways of looking at this metaphor:

(a) The man who owns the field (i.e. the wife) owns whatever crop is sown in the field. Manu assumes that the field is entirely neutral, and that the crop (son) sown in it will always resemble the seed (the father). Therefore you should never waste your seed by shedding it in another man's 'field' or wife, but you are not harmed if another man sheds his seed in your wife (in that you own the son resulting from that act). Manu thus forbids a man to commit adultery in another man's wife, but encourages him to let a brother produce a Levirate heir in his own wife, through the Indian practice of *niyoga*, in which the widow of a man who has produced no male heirs is appointed to have a son by that man's younger brother. This argument – that the man owns the woman – prevails in India.

But, on the other hand, it might also be argued that (b) the man who owns the seed, and who in any case determines the characteristics of the crop, owns the crop. This supplies a reason why a man might want to shed his seed in someone else's field, but it now also argues that a man should make sure that only his own seed is sown in his own field. This argument – that the man owns his own seed – takes a secondary place, as it would both encourage adultery (you would produce legitimate sons in all sorts of women) and make Levirate marriage meaningless (since the son that your brother produced in your wife would be his son, not yours).

They say that a son belongs to the husband, but the revealed canon is divided in two about who the 'husband' is: some say that he is the begetter, others that he is the one who owns the field. The woman is traditionally said to be the field, and the man is traditionally said to be the seed; all creatures with bodies are born from the union of the field and the seed. Sometimes the seed prevails, and sometimes the woman's womb; but the offspring are regarded as best when both are equal. Of the seed and the womb, the seed is said to be more important, for the offspring of all living beings are marked by the mark of the seed. Whatever sort of seed is sown in a field prepared at the right season, precisely that sort of seed grows in it, manifesting its own particular qualities. For this earth is said to be the eternal womb of creatures, but the seed develops none of the qualities of the womb in the things it grows. For here on earth when farmers at the right season sow seeds of various forms in the earth, even in one single field, they grow up each according to its own nature. Rice, red rice, mung beans, sesame, pulse beans, and barley grow up according to their seed, and so do leeks and sugar-cane. It never happens that 'One seed is sown and another grown'; for whatever seed is sown, that is precisely the one that grows. (*Manu* 9.31–42)

The basic argument seems sensible enough; Manu acknowledges that the quality of the field does influence the quality of the crop (crops grow better in a well ploughed or 'good' field), but argues, correctly, that the basic characteristics of the field do not influence the basic characteristics of the crop (barley, rather than mung beans, grows in any field in which it is planted). But Manu also discusses the question of the ownership of the crop (the son) in terms of a pastoral image, the point of which is not quite so obvious:

Just as the stud is not the one who owns the progeny born in cows, mares, female camels, and slave girls, in buffalo-cows, she-goats, and ewes, so it is too (with progeny born) in other men's wives. If [one man's] bull were to beget a hundred calves in other men's cows, those calves would belong to the owners of the cows, and the bull's seed would be shed in vain. This is the law for the offspring of cows and mares, slave girls, female camels, and she-goats, and birds and female buffalo. (*Manu* 9.48, 50, and 55)

These pastoral verses appear in Manu interspersed with the agricultural metaphor of seed and field, and are used in support of the prevailing argument, that the one who owns the female, rather than the one who owns the seed, owns the offspring. But Manu himself elsewhere acknowledges the equal contribution of the mother and the father to the nature of the child when he discusses mixed marriages, again in terms of the mixed agricultural-pastoral metaphor. And he concludes: 'Some wise men value the seed, others the field, and still others both the seed and the field; but this is the final decision on this subject: seed sown in the wrong field perishes right inside it; and a field by itself with no seed also remains barren. And since sages have been born in [female] animals by the power of the seed, and were honored and valued, therefore the seed is valued' (*Manu* 10.70–72).

Thus Manu moves into increasingly complex areas of speculation. Even the relatively simple agricultural image proved ambiguous; the pastoral image introduces further complications, especially when, as Manu admits in the last line of the passage cited, humans mate with animals; and, when it comes to human beings, a third factor is introduced: the behaviour of the child, which must be regarded as a factor separate from the genetic contribution of either of his parents (let alone the genetic contribution of the 'owner of the field' in the case of an adulterous connection).

It may well be that it is because men have given most of our texts their final form that those texts speak primarily of a man as the active knower of the passive woman-as-field (of knowledge, and of progeneration), just as they speak of the soul as the knower of the body-as-field, *kṣetrajña* (which forms a natural pun with *kṣetraja*; but which is the source and which the echo?). But elsewhere, particularly in chapter nine, Manu acknowledges the creative role of the woman as body/field, when he assumes that a Brahmin with wives of various classes produces children whose status is in part determined by their mothers' status. And, finally, the human genetic pool is entirely transformed by culture, by the ritual transformations of the *saṃskāras*, so that a child obtains what McKim Marriott calls his 'coded substance' – his somatic as well as social essence – not only from his parents, but from his teachers and priests, as Manu also argues (*Manu* 2.169–71).

In later Indian thinking about the woman's contribution to the child, it was often argued that the woman had seed, too, like the man; her seed, physically incarnate in her menstrual blood, contributed the soft parts of a child (the flesh and blood), while the man contributed the hard parts (bone and sinew) (O'Flaherty 1980, 21, 35–9, 50–1). Manu does not take account of this tradition, but it may well be that it underlies many Hindu folk beliefs, and folk stories, about human sexuality. The agricultural model remains a referent to this day in India, but it is not always accepted. Lina Fruzzetti and Ákos Östör have demonstrated the variants that Bengali villagers ring on the basic theme (Fruzzetti and Östör 1976), and E. Valentine Daniel has recorded a wonderful conversation in which Tamil villagers cynically reject the whole concept of the seed and the field in favour of the concept of female seed (Daniel 1984, 163–70).

Purāṇas

The Purāṇas treat of many subjects also treated by Manu and the medical textbooks, and they offer several explanations of conception and birth, which differ both from one another and from the ones that we have seen in Manu and the medical texts. The *Mārkaṇḍeya Purāṇa* assumes that the menstrual blood (*rajas*, also the term for the quality of energy) is the woman's seed; hence the seed of which the child is born is regarded as twofold, male and female:

The impregnation of human women is the emitting of the seed in the menstrual blood. As soon as [the soul] is released from hell, or from heaven, it arrives (in the womb). Overpowered by that [soul], the two-fold seed becomes solid. It becomes a speck of life, and then a bubble, and then flesh. And just as a shoot of a plant is born from a seed, so from the flesh the five limbs (two arms, two legs, and the head) are born, with all their parts. The subsidiary limbs, too – fingers, eyes, nose, mouth, and ears – grow out of the (five) limbs; and out of the subsidiary limbs, in the same way, grow the nails and so forth. The hair on the body grows in the skin, and the hair of the head grows after that.

The birth-sheath grows larger as it takes on flesh. Just as a coconut grows big along with its shell, so the sheath of the embryo, that opens out on the bottom, grows bigger. The embryo grows up in the bottom of the womb, placing its two hands beside its knees, with its two thumbs on top of its knees, the fingers in front; behind the two knees are the two eyes, and in between the knees is the nose; the buttocks rest on the two heels, and the arms and shanks are outside. In this way, the living (human) creature gradually grows up inside the woman's womb; other living creatures position themselves in the stomach according to their shapes.

The fire inside the stomach makes the embryo hard, and it lives on what is eaten and drunk [by the mother]. The sojourn of the living creature inside the stomach is meritorious and is made of retained merit. A channel called the 'Strengthener and Nourisher' is attached to the inside of the embryo's navel and to the channel from the woman's entrails, and the embryo stays alive by that means. For what the woman eats and drinks goes into the embryo's womb, and the living creature's body is strengthened and nourished by that so that it grows.

Then it begins to remember its many previous existences in the wheel of rebirth, and that depresses it, and it tosses from side to side, thinking, 'I won't ever do *that* again, as soon as I get out of this womb. I will do everything I can, so that I won't become an embryo again.' It thinks in this way as it remembers the hundreds of miseries of birth that it experienced before, in the power of fate.

Then, as time goes by, the embryo turns around, head down, and in the ninth or tenth month it is born. As it comes out, it is hurt by the wind of procreation; it comes out crying, because it is pained by the misery in its heart. When it has come out of the womb, it falls into an unbearable swoon, but it regains consciousness when it is touched by the air. Then Viṣṇu's deluding power of illusion assails him, and when his soul has been deluded by it, he loses his knowledge. As soon as the living creature has lost his knowledge, he becomes a baby.

After that he becomes a young boy, then an adolescent, and then an old man. And then he dies and then he is born again as a human. Thus he wanders on the wheel of rebirth like the bucket on the wheel of a well. (*Mārkaṇḍeya Purāṇa* 10.1–7, 11.1–21)

The predominance of the father in the making of the body, that Manu insists upon, is here undercut not only by the role of the mother in contributing to the physical substance of the body, but also by the role of the embryo itself, whose previous lives, unrelated to the lives of its father or mother, are recalled at the very start (when the soul is 'released from hell or heaven') and during gestation (when he is overwhelmed by remorse and regret), and remain relevant even when they are forgotten at the moment of birth.

MYTHOLOGICAL PATTERNS IN HINDU TEXTS

Let us turn now to Hindu variants of mythological somatic themes that occur in religions throughout the world, keeping one eye on the images that these stories add to our basic Hindu construction of the body and the other on the implications of the fact that similar stories are also told in other cultures.

The head

Let us begin, appropriately, with the head. There is a corpus of Hindu myths in which a man splits a high-caste woman into a head and a body, each endowed with life, which then join with the supplementary part of her Untouchable shadow 'double' to form two other women, each consisting of two vividly contrasting halves. Pierre Sonnerat, in the eighteenth century, recorded a version of an oral Tamil tale:

Māriatale, the wife of the ascetic Jamadagni and mother of Paraśurāma, ruled over the elements, but she could only keep this empire as long as her heart remained pure. One day she was fetching water from a pool, and, following her usual custom, was rolling it up in a ball to carry it home. She happened to see on the surface of the water several male demigods [Gandharvas], who were sporting gymnastically right under her head. She was taken by their charms, and desire entered her heart. The water that she had already collected immediately turned to liquid and mingled back with the water of the pool. She could no longer carry it home without the help of a bowl. This impotence revealed to Jamadagni that his wife had ceased to be pure, and in the excess of his anger, he commanded his son to drag her off to the place set aside for executions, and to cut off her head. This order was executed; but Paraśurāma was so afflicted by the loss of his mother that Jamadagni told him to go and get her body, to join to it the head that he had cut off, and to whisper in its ear a prayer that he taught him, that would immediately revive her. The son ran in haste, but by a singular oversight, he joined the head of his mother to the body of a Pariah woman who had been executed for her crimes – a monstrous assemblage, which gave to this woman the virtues of a goddess and the vices of an unfortunate wretch. The goddess, having become impure through this mix, was chased out of her house and committed all sorts of cruelties; the gods, seeing the ravages that she was making, appeased her, by giving her the power to cure smallpox and promising her that she would be supplicated for this disease . . . Only her head was placed in the inner sanctuary of the temple, to be worshipped by Indians of good caste; while her [Pariah] body was placed at the door of the temple, to be worshipped by Pariahs . . . Māriatale, having become impure through the mixing of her head with the body of a Pariah, and fearing that she would no longer be adored by her son Paraśurāma, begged the gods to grant her another child. They gave her Kārtavīrya; the Pariahs divide their worship between his mother and him. This is the only one of all the gods to whom are offered cooked meats, salted fish, tobacco, and so forth, because he came from the body of a Pariah. (Sonnerat 1782, 245–7)

The mixed woman, created by the fusion of Māriatale's head and the body of the Untouchable woman, is a monster, impure and destructive, disease incarnate – ambivalent disease, whose Untouchable, human, body brings the fever that is cooled by the grace of the divine head. This is the most basic of all theological doubles: she is the goddess who both brings disease and removes disease, the lord who giveth and taketh away, the *mysterium fascinans et tremendum* that Rudolf Otto describes as the essence of the sacred – in this case, a creature with a head that is *fascinans* and a body that is *tremendum*. The tension within her is so great that she does not remain integrated in ritual; she is split up once again, the divine head at last purified by being divorced from its polluting body, and the Pariah body put literally on to the doorstep, liminal, forever marking the pale of the Hindu society that sees woman as a divine-headed and Untouchable-bodied monster.

How is the mixture of classes in Māriatale's head and body related to her sexual ambivalence? The opposition between the chaste and the erotic woman is expressed through a series of oppositions between the head and the body in the myth, but it is not entirely clear what is symbolized by this opposition. The *structure* of this theme seems to remain constant throughout a large corpus of myths about beheadings: the head is severed from the body; *something* is cut away from something else. But what is that something? It might appear that the head is rational and chaste, the body emotional and lustful. But, in India, particularly but not only Tantric India, the head is where semen is stored. It may well be, therefore, that by removing Māriatale's (sexual) head, the *body* becomes purified. On the other hand, beheading means that you can not *think* (straight) any more, that your sexuality has destroyed your rationality. The Tamil text seems to be saying that the head is pure, the body polluted. The head is the source of Māriatale's sexual identity and her legal status: if she has a divine head, she is a pure goddess. Her impure half, the half that lusts for the demigod, is the *real* woman, the denied woman, the passionate woman, as polluting and despised as the Untouchable. This half becomes the body of the finally integrated Mriatale, who is identified with the divine head but functions with an Untouchable body. Lower-class women, here as elsewhere, represent the more erotic side of a woman.

Māriatale's divine half reflects the unreasonable image of the entirely pure wife, symbolized by the impossible ability to roll water up, solid and dry, with nothing to sustain it. This is itself an image that cannot be sustained; the woman's natural emotion is expressed in the vision of the water that melts back into its natural liquidity and mingles again with the waters of the pool from which it was frozen. The image of the rolled-up water leaking back into the river is the image of a pure woman who feels passion, an ice maiden who is melted by lust; and such a woman can exist in India only when she is physically split.

The eyes

Among the many, many things that eyes symbolize in Hindu mythology, is the sexual role that somewhat substantiates Freud's hypothesis of upward displacement. A stunning example of this is the story of Indra, Ahalyā, and Gautama, a much-told tale of which this is one fairly late variant:

Once upon a time, there was a great sage named Gautama who knew the past, present, and future. His wife, Ahalyā, surpassed the celestial nymphs in her beauty. One day, Indra, lusting for her beauty, secretly propositioned her, and she, the idiot, bulling, gave in to Indra. But the sage Gautama, realizing what had happened because of his special powers, came there and cursed Indra, saying, 'You will be branded with a thousand of the sexual organs of a woman that you lust for, but when the All-Maker makes a heavenly woman named Tilottamā and you see her, the marks will become a thousand eyes.' When Gautama had given the curses he desired, he returned to his asceticism. Ahalyā became terribly transformed, into a stone, and Indra was covered all over his body with the sexual organs of a woman. (*Kathāsaritsāgara* 17.137–48)

Indra is called 'Thousand-eyed' in many myths, as are several other Vedic gods; the thousands of eyes were sometimes identified with the stars in the sky and sometimes personified as the god's spies. In this version of the story, however, Indra becomes thousand-eyed only at the end of the story (while Gautama has, from the start, the magic eye of knowledge – of the past, present, and future – which he uses to trap the lovers). Indra is branded, like Cain, with the mark of his sin, a common punishment in *The Laws of Manu*, for Manu recommends that an adulterer be branded – with a vagina if the woman in question is his guru's wife (*Manu* 8.352 and 9.237), and Gautama is very like a guru. Indra's curse is ended when the Creator makes a celestial whore, Tilottamā; appropriately, for Indra is elsewhere said to have sprouted his thousand eyes in the first place in order to see Tilottamā as she danced to seduce a group of demons (*Mahābhārata* 1.203.15–26). Here, Indra is freed when he wants to see Tilottamā so much that the female sexual organs become eyes.

Indra's curse of a thousand vaginas on his body literally emasculates him, or at least enfeminizes him, and may therefore be roughly equivalent to a castration. And the modification of this curse to merely having a thousand eyes on his body is a stunning example of upward displacement. In terms of the history of the story, however, we can see that the myth that changes Indra's vaginas into eyes is reversing the course of time; his ancient feature of a thousand eyes was the source of a myth that gave him (through downward displacement?) thousands of vaginas that were later turned back into eyes.

The tongue

Continuing with the theme of upward displacement, there is a corpus of myths about the tongue, that views it, too, as a sexual organ:

Long-tongue was a demoness who used to lick up the oblations with her long tongue. Indra sent Sumitra to seduce her. But Long-tongue turned him down, pointing out, 'You have just one penis, but I have "mice" on every limb, on this limb and on that limb. This won't work.' When Indra gave Sumitra penises on every limb, he succeeded in seducing the demoness. They lay together. As soon as he had his way with her, he remained firmly stuck in her. He summoned Indra, who ran against her and struck her down with his thunderbolt and killed her. (*Jaiminīya Brāhmaṇa* 1.16–63; O'Flaherty 1985, 102–3)

The demoness has, in addition to her multiple genitalia (matching the multiple genitalia of her arch-enemy, Indra), the organ of speech. The long tongue with which she licks up the oblation is the organ of sacrificial as well as sexual aggression. Her name, and some of her functions, are derived from the bitch named Long-tongue who threatens the oblations elsewhere in the Veda. (*Ṛg Veda* 9.101.1; *Maitrāyaṇī Saṃhitā* 3.10.6; *Aitareya Brāhmaṇa* 2.22.10). And her long tongue sets the precedent both for the long tongue of Kālī (who is thus depicted in many icons) and for the demon Raktabīja ('Blood-seed'), from every drop of whose blood a new demon appears; to conquer him, the goddess emits multiforms of herself who extend their tongues to lick up each drop of blood before it can fall to the ground (*Vāmana Purāṇa* 30.27).

Throughout this corpus, the tongue seems to function as a female source of sexual and martial power, rather than cultural power. In this it differs from the tongue in many other mythologies, where, for example, women who are raped often have their tongues cut out to keep them from speaking. The tongue of the demoness in Hindu mythology is mute.

The genitals

The genitals, by comparison (or compensation) have voices. It seems almost superfluous to devote a separate section to the genitals, which we have already encountered thinly disguised as eyes and tongues. But Hindu mythology also calls a spade a spade, and there are a number of myths where the genitals are detached from the body and take on a life of their own (as, in fact, they do in the French *fabliaux*). Indeed, one encounters the *liṅgam*, or phallus, of the god Śiva, more often detached

Plate 6   Śiva Manifesting within the Liṅga of Flames, worshipped by Brahmā and
Viṣṇu. Jodhpur school, Rajastan, *circa* 1850. Opaque watercolour on paper.

from his body than attached to it. At the time of creation, the flame *liṅgam*
arose out of the waters of chaos, stretching up to the sky and down to the
bottom of hell, infinite in both directions (*Kūrma Purāṇa* 1.25). Then Śiva
himself tore it off his body when he was disillusioned with human
creation (O'Flaherty 1973, 130–6; 1975, 137–41). And, finally, the sages in
the Pine Forest castrated Śiva and caused his *liṅgam* to fall to the ground
when he had seduced their wives (O'Flaherty 1973, 172–209; 1975,
141–9). On each of these occasions, a voice, issuing either from the *liṅgam*

itself or from a 'disembodied voice' (*aśarīra vāc*) accompanying the *liṅgam*, instructed the onlookers that Śiva was angry, and told them that they could appease his wrath if gods and humans would promise to worship his *liṅgam* forever after, which, in India, they still do.

The sexual organ of the goddess is also detached from her body, but in this case it happens after she has committed suicide. Then Śiva carries her body on his back until Viṣnu takes his discus and cuts it apart; where each organ falls, a shrine arises, and the most sacred shrine of all is the place where her sexual organ fell, in Assam (O'Flaherty 1975, 249–51). In both cases, male and female, the genitals pose great dangers as long as they are attached to the human (or divine) body; only when they are detached are they safe, indeed the object of worship. Only when they are detached do they find their voices. Here we may recall that, when the head and body expressed other unbearable tensions in Hindu attitudes to the body, they, too, found resolution only when they were detached from one another.

The breast

Breasts, too, frequently become detached from the human body in Hindu mythology, but breasts, like eyes and mouths, are more often anti-sexual organs than sexual organs. In Orissa, for instance, it was believed that men had a single source of sexual fluids: from blood, semen was made. Women, however, had a solid lump at the base of the brain, that, when melted by the heat of desire, became transformed into female semen, the fluid that flowed down into the genitals, lubricated the woman for intercourse, and constituted half of the genetic substance that produced a child (the other half being the man's seed); after the child was conceived, this female seed went back up into the woman's brain, formed a solid lump again, and then, after the birth of the child, was heated by maternal love and transformed into milk, that flowed down into the breasts. It was thus physiologically impossible for the woman to be simultaneously erotic and maternal (see Marglin 1985; O'Flaherty 1980, 17–64).

Unlike genitals, breasts tend to become more rather than less destructive when detached from the female body. This is certainly the case with Kaṇṇaki, long-suffering heroine of the great Tamil Epic, the *Śilappaddikāram*, who, to avenge her husband's death, tears off her left breast, which bursts into flame and burns down the city. Another famous destructive breast is that of Pūtanā:

The horrible Pūtanā ['stinking'] a devourer of children, was sent by Kaṁsa to kill his nephew, Kṛṣṇa. She wandered through cities, villages, and pastures, killing infants . . . One day Pūtanā came to Kṛṣṇa's village, and she saw there on the bed the infant Kṛṣṇa. She took the infinite one onto her lap, as one might pick up a sleeping deadly viper, mistaking it for a rope. Taking him on her lap, she gave the baby her breast, which had been smeared with a virulent poison. But the lord, pressing her breast hard with his hands, angrily drank out her life's breath with the milk. (*Bhāgavata Purāṇa* 10.6.1–20, 30–44; O'Flaherty 1975, 214–15).

Again, the intolerable tension between two images of the body, here the breast as emblem of the mother and the breast as emblem of the seductive female, bursts only when the symbol itself, the breast, is burst.

The foot

The foot is a complex symbol of mortality in Hindu mythology, and it, too, becomes detached from the body. The sun god is called Mārtāṇḍa ('dead in the egg') because he is born deformed (*Śatapatha Brāhmaṇa* 3.1.3–5); in later mythology, Aruṇa, the charioteer of the dawn, has no legs; his mutilation may indicate that his legs do not develop in the egg. Later mythology also speaks both of the mutilation of the sun and, more specifically, of the mutilation of the foot of his son:

Saṃjñā married Vivasvan [the sun] and bore him a son, Manu, the lord of creatures; then she bore him twins, Yama, the king of the dead, and his sister, Yamī [or Yamunā]. But she was repulsed by the heat of the sun and afraid of his semen/energy. She looked at her own shadow [Chāya] and said, 'I am going away to my father's house. Please stay here and be kind to my three children, and do not speak of this to my lord.' The shadow said, 'Even if I am dragged by the hair, even if I am cursed, I will never speak of your intention, O goddess. Go where you wish.' Vivasvan, thinking that the shadow was Saṃjñā, begat in her two sons and a daughter. But the shadow did not behave as affectionately to the first-born children as Saṃjñā had behaved to them, who were her own children. Manu put up with this in her, but Yama could not bear it. He threatened the shadow Saṃjñā with his foot, and she cursed him: 'Since you threaten with your foot the wife of your father, your foot will fall off.' Then Yama and Manu went to their father and Yama said, 'Mother shuns us, the older sons, and favors the two young ones. I lifted my foot toward her, but I did not touch her body with it, and she cursed me. I do not think she can be my mother, for a mother does not behave badly even toward badly behaved sons.' His father said, 'It is impossible to make the words of the wife of your father fail to come true, but I will do you a favor, because of my affection toward you. Worms will take flesh from your foot and go to the surface of the earth. Thus her words will come true, and you will be saved.'

Then Vivasvan realized that the shadow was not the true mother. He went to Samjñā's father, Tvaṣṭṛ, the blacksmith of the gods, who trimmed away his excessive energy, and then he took the form of a stallion and approached his wife, who had taken the form of a mare, engendering in her the equine twin gods called the Aśvins. (*Mārkaṇḍeya Purāṇa* 103–105; *Bhāgavata Purāṇa* 6.6.38; O'Flaherty 1975, 66–70)

The mutilated foot is a synecdoche for the mortality of the body as a whole. The foot here takes on a voice, too, for the Sanskrit text actually conceals a pun: 'foot' (*pāda*) also means a measure of poetry (as it does in English), and the trick of the poem is what saves Yama's foot. A similar pun on *pāda* meaning both a foot and a fourth part occurs in Manu 1.81–2: 'In the Winning Age, religion is entire, standing on all four feet, and so is truth; and men do not acquire any gain through irreligion. But in the other [Ages], through [such wrong] gains, religion is brought down foot by foot; and because of theft, lying, and deceit, religion goes away foot by foot.' Here, as elsewhere, the foot is associated with loss, particularly the loss of immortality (for the creatures in the Winning Age live a very long time, and lifespans diminish gradually from then on). Thus, one of the signs that distinguish a mortal from an immortal is that a mortal's feet touch the ground, while an immortal hovers ever so slightly above the ground. And the incarnate god Kṛṣṇa is killed when a hunter named, surely significantly, 'Old-age', mistakes him for an animal and shoots him in the foot (*Mahābhārata* 16).

The mortality of the foot in India has close parallels in the mythologies of Greece (think of Achilles' heel, Oedipus' swollen foot, and the riddle of the sphinx), and of ancient Judaism (recall the serpent that is to bruise the heel of man once he is expelled from Eden). But in India, the foot has other, perhaps more culturally specific connotations. It is also a symbol of political oppression: the Śūdra, the servant, the lowest of the four classes of society, is born from the foot of the primeval man (*Ṛg Veda* 10;90; *Manu* 1.31), and this is often cited in justification of the fact that Śūdras are outside the social system (only the other three classes are 'twice-born', admitted to the transformative rituals), and condemned to the service of the other classes. The gesture of the añjali, cupping the hands and touching them to the head, is an abbreviation of a large gesture (also carried out on important occasions) by which one stoops down and gathers the dust from a respected person's feet and places it upon one's own head.

CONCLUSION

Here, too, however, we may recall the Christian image of the woman who dried the feet of Jesus with her hair. Once again, it proves difficult to draw the line between the particularly Hindu images and the more widely shared images of the human body. But the Hindu development of these images enhances our understanding of the various ways in which different cultures have constructed the same body. Moreover, the specific human details of the myth might make it possible to generalize about shared human assumptions about the human body in greater detail than is allowed by more general comparisons of paradigms of embryology and anatomy. It might make it possible, for instance, to speculate about shared ideas concerning amputation and mutilation, organ transplants and sex-changes, and invisible links between apparently disparate parts of the body.

So, having moved from the head to the foot (the traditional way of describing a Hindu woman, in contrast with a goddess, who is described from foot to head), we are free to detach ourselves both from individual parts of the Hindu body (an act that is, as we have seen, a very Hindu thing to do) and from the Hindu body as a whole (an act that is the goal of most Hindu philosophical systems).

BIBLIOGRAPHY

Sanskrit texts

Aitareya Brāhmaṇa (Calcutta, 1896).
Bhāgavata Purāṇa (Bombay, 1832).
Bṛhaddevatā of Śaunaka. (Cambridge, Mass., 1904).
Carakasaṃhitā (two volumes, Delhi, 1963).
Jaiminīya Brāhmaṇa (Nagpur, 1954).
Kathāsaritsāgara (Bombay, 1930).
Kūrma Purāṇa (Varanasi, 1972).
Mahābhārata (Poona, 1933–69).
Maitrāyaṇī Saṃhitā (Wiesbaden, 1970).
Manu (The Laws of Manu). Trans. by W. Doniger, with B. K. Smith (Harmondsworth: Penguin Books, 1991).
Mārkaṇḍeya Purāṇa (Bombay, 1890).
Ṛg Veda, with the commentary of Sayana (London, 1890–92).
Vāmana Purāṇa (Varanasi, 1968).

Secondary Sources

Daniel, E. V. (1984), *Fluid Signs: Being a Person the Tamil Way*, Berkeley: University of California Press.

Fruzzetti, L. and Östör, Á. (1976), 'Seed and Earth: a Cultural Analysis of Kinship in a Bengali Town', *Contributions to Indian Sociology* N.S., 10/1, 97–132.

Kakar, S. (1990), *Intimate Relations: Exploring Indian Sexuality*, University of Chicago Press.

Kasulis, T. P. (ed.), with R. T. Ames and W. Dissanayake (1993), *Self as Body in Asian Theory and Practice*, Albany, NY: SUNY Press.

Marglin, F. A. (1985), 'Wives of the God-King: The Rituals of Hindu Temple Courtesans', Paper presented at the conference on The Erotic Theme in the Cultural Traditions of India, Minneapolis, 10–12 May 1985.

O'Flaherty, Wendy Doniger (1973), *Asceticism and Eroticism in the Mythology of Śiva*, Oxford University Press.

(1975), *Hindu Myths*, Harmondsworth: Penguin Books.

(1976), *The Origins of Evil in Hindu Mythology*, Berkeley: University of California Press.

(1980), *Women, Androgynes, and Other Mythical Beasts*, University of Chicago Press.

(1985), *Tales of Sex and Violence: Folkore, Sacrifice, and Danger in the Jaiminīya Brāhmaṇa*, University of Chicago Press.

(1988), *Other People's Myths: The Cave of Echoes*, New York: Macmillan.

(ed. and trans.) (1990), *Textual Sources for the Study of Hinduism*, University of Chicago Press.

Sonnerat, P. (1782), *Voyages aux Indes Orientales*, Sonnerat. Paris, n.p.

Sullivan, B. M. (1990), *Kṛṣṇa Dvaipāyana Vyāsa and the Mahābhārata: A New Interpretation*, Leiden: E. J. Brill.

The body in Theravāda Buddhist monasticism[1]

Steven Collins

I

I begin with a remarkable passage from the *Vinaya*, the canonical texts concerning monastic discipline. A monk has had sexual intercourse with his former wife, and thus caused the Buddha to promulgate the monastic rule forbidding sex: the Buddha says

It would be better, foolish man, to put your male organ into the mouth of a terrible and poisonous snake than into a woman ... It would be better, foolish man, to put it into a blazing, burning, red-hot charcoal pit than into a woman. Why? On account of *that*, foolish man, you might die, or suffer deathly agony, but that would not cause you to pass, at the breaking up of the body after death, to a lower rebirth, a bad destiny, to ruin, to hell. But on account of *this*, foolish man, [you may]. (*Vin* III 19[2])

Buddhist monastic training, like many other forms of Indian spiritual practice, notably those of *yoga*, seeks to control and finally eliminate many bodily drives and affects.[3] Sexual desire is perhaps the most common target, but there are others: according to another passage of the *Vinaya*, when the Buddha had taken his son Rāhula into the monkhood without the family's permission (Rāhula's opinion is not recorded) the Buddha's own father Suddhodhana complained, declaring that 'love for a son cuts into the skin, [goes right through the body and] lodges in the

---

[1] [Note added March 1994] This chapter was written in its original form in 1987, and slightly revised in 1990. I have not been able to take into account anything published since that time. If I were writing the piece now, it would be different in style but not in substance. In the interim I have written another article (Collins 1994), which might usefully be read in association with this one.

[2] References to Pali texts are to Pali Text Society editions; abbreviations are those used in the *Critical Pali Dictionary*.

[3] It is important to stress at the outset that this chapter concerns only certain aspects of the meditative life of monasticism, and of its social location. The Theravāda tradition, and still more Buddhism as a whole, contains many other and different attitudes to the body: temple paintings and sculptures, and much Buddhist poetry, for example, show a very fine aesthetic appreciation of physical beauty.

Plate 7   In the meditation room of a forest monastery in Mitirigala, Sri Lanka. Written on the saffron wall-hanging is a Sinhalese translation of *Dhammapada* 371, which urges monks to meditate.

marrow of one's bones' (*Vin* I 82–3). But even this love (or affection, *pema*), we read elsewhere (*S* III 7; cf. *A* II 213ff.), is to be rooted out from the body, as are the impulses of lust, desire, or 'thirst' (*taṇhā*, Sanskrit *tṛṣṇā*).

It is, I think, both uncontroversial and unoriginal to suggest that behind much – though by no means all – of the religions of mankind lie the aspirations to avoid death and to impose control and order on life. The human body, subject to the wayward imperatives of sexuality and doomed to decay and death, is implicated in both. Obviously different attitudes on these matters are possible: think, for example, of the common suggestion that some form of immortality, perhaps the only form available to individuals, comes precisely from the perpetuation of our biological inheritance in children and future generations. Moreover, physical self-reproduction is obviously a necessary collective task for any human society; as also is the organization of sexual life and relations to this end. But, although sexual activity is necessary to social existence, at the same time it presents problems: it seems reasonable to assume that the drives of sexuality contain in themselves no limitation of range, and so to infer that *any* ordered social and cultural life must demand in this respect, as in others, a minimum degree of asceticism and self-restraint. This is an issue which concerned two of the founding fathers of the sociological study of religion. Durkheim, as is well known, held that a general function of religious ascetics is to demonstrate, symbolically and in exemplary fashion, the self-control and self-denial necessarily incumbent on all members of society.[4] The need to control sexuality is part of a wider need to avoid chaos and give order to human life: and this comes into conflict with what Max Weber described, in a marvellous phrase, as 'the peculiar irrationality of the sexual act, which is ultimately and uniquely unsusceptible to rational organisation'.[5] I find it helpful to see Buddhist doctrine and monastic practice in terms of two of the senses in which Weber used the concept of rationality: it refers both to 'the kind of rationalization the systematic thinker performs on the image of the world: an increasing theoretical mastery of reality by means of increasingly precise and abstract concepts'; and also to 'the methodical attainment of a definitely given and practical end by means of an increasingly precise calculation of adequate means'. On the individual level, the ideal-typical Buddhist monk or nun lives a religious life in which the body, sex, and death are perceived to be immediately and inextricably related: they constitute the realm of desire, suffering, and

---

[4] Durkheim 1915, 299–325; cf. Lukes 1973, 434–5.
[5] Weber 1963, 238. The following two citations are from Weber 1948, 293.

rebirth from which release, *nirvāṇa*, is sought. But both in theory and in practice this self-perception can occur, as can the wider monastic life in which it is possible, only within the wider context provided by the continuing generations of lay society.

In what follows I shall outline certain forms of self-perception or 'body-image' as prescribed in texts of Buddhist meditation theory, which are intended to apply to any monastic practitioner, male or female. I shall then contrast them with forms of social behaviour and perception as prescribed in texts and revealed in modern ethnography: there is some complexity in detail here, since the Theravāda order of nuns died out in medieval times, and has not been revived. But there are women in modern Theravāda countries who do follow what from the outside we can call a monastic life, and whom I shall call, for brevity, 'nuns': describing and defining their social status is a more complex issue than I have space to address here, but it is not one which affects my argument.[6]

II

Conceptually, Buddhism is dualistic: the body comes to an end at death, whereas consciousness continues. This consciousness, constantly changing after death as during life, can be reborn (or 'stationed') in immaterial heavens: and in final *nirvāṇa* there is no physical existence at all.[7] (I leave aside the vexed question of whether or not this state involves consciousness in some form.) On the one hand, the dualism of Buddhist thought can and does lead to the kind of extreme attitude to the body for which we have the familiar label 'Manichaean': the body and its desires are rejected, and escape from it is the final religious goal. On the other hand, such an attitude clearly cannot provide a direct vehicle of religious motivation and aspiration for the members of a continuing, self-reproducing human society. In fact, the austerely transcendentalist and immaterialist conception of *nirvāṇa* is carried into ordinary material life in various ways: by texts, relics and statues, and – as I shall try to show – by the bodies of monks and nuns. In a much more than merely symbolic sense, these things embody in time and matter the eternal and immaterial Truth – they actualize, we might say, the ideology. Consider,

---

[6] In Buddhist monastic law, and in the civil law of their societies, they are counted as laywomen; where ordinary laymen and women take 5 Precepts, the third of which is to refrain from adultery, they – like certain older men – take eight or ten Precepts permanently, which turns the third into a vow of celibacy.

[7] See Collins 1982, chs 7 and 8.

for example, the idea of the Buddha's two bodies. (In Mahāyāna traditions, we find three and sometimes more.) He has a *dhammakāya*, a 'Body of Truth', which is the truth of his (and all other Buddhas') Teachings, and the texts which contain them; and a *rūpakāya*, a 'Body of Form', which is both the physical human organism known as Siddhattha Gotama, and which came to an end at some time in the fifth or fourth centuries BC, and also the relics of that body (and of those of former Buddhas) preserved and enshrined in stupas, temples, and sometimes in statues of the Buddha. These latter, sometimes called *Buddharūpā*, 'Buddha-forms' or 'Buddha-bodies', like the relics of his historical body, immediately and vividly convey the presence of the Buddha and his saving Truth, and are – like the scriptural texts which embody 'the Body of Truth' – the objects of extensive ritual and other activity. These ideas of the various 'bodies' of the Buddha concern the first and second of what are called the 'Three Jewels': that is, the Buddha and his Teaching (*Dhamma*). It will be my aim here to show how it has also been embodied in the experience and action of actual Buddhists, those who constitute the third Jewel, the Monastic Community (*Saṃgha*).

III

The external life of the Buddhist Monastic Community is regulated by the Monastic Rule, the *Vinaya*. The prohibitions on sexual behaviour in the Rules are an intriguing subject of study in themselves (and not only because the things prohibited are described in very great detail!). The third of the five basic Buddhist moral precepts is to refrain from *kāmesu micchācāra*, literally 'wrong behaviour in regard to (sense-) desires'. For laypeople, 'wrong behaviour' means adultery: for monks and nuns, it means a graded hierarchy of prohibitions, prescribing various punishments for various offences, the worst being permanent expulsion from the monastic community for any form of sexual intercourse. These publications relate, of course, to the external behaviour of the individual: many of the rules regarding actual or potential sexual misconduct, as so frequently throughout the *Vinaya*, are said to have been promulgated because of the effect caused by the offending behaviour on society, and on the reputation of the monkhood within it. But Buddhist jurisprudence (in this respect unlike much of Hinduism and Jainism) also recognizes that responsibility cannot be ascribed for unintentional infringements of its laws. In a more general sense, the standard Buddhist analysis of *karma*, action and its results, always explains it as involving, and sometimes simply as consisting in, intention. Moreover, this emphasis on intention reminds one that at the highest level of Buddhist spiritual training, where adherence to external prohibitions can be taken for granted, it is the inner existence of desire in any mental form which is the focus of attention. Thus although sexual activity in dreams, for example, being unintentional, does not breach any article of monastic discipline (*Vin* III 39, 112, 116), it is seen as evidence of residual desire, and thus as involving a karmic result (*Sp* 521, *Mp* III 317–18, *Vbh-a* 408). The enlightened saint, the *Arhat*, is specifically said to be so completely beyond passion and desire as no longer to be subject to wet dreams (*Vin* I 295, *Kv* 163ff., 617–18 with *Kv-a ad loc.*).

In moving thus from the prohibitions on external behaviour to the eradication of all inner manifestations of desire, we move from the realm of the monastic rules to that of spiritual training and meditation. Most forms of meditation take place in the simple sitting posture familiar to all of us in the West nowadays; certain forms of 'mindfulness' training can also take place while walking methodically to and fro, often on a specially constructed meditation walkway (*cankama*). Advanced practitioners are said to remain mindful and aware, and in that sense to meditate, in all the 'four postures', standing, sitting, lying, and moving, both awake and asleep. Attitudes to the body can be traced both in general evaluations and comparisons applied to it, and in specific forms of meditation.

First, on the general level, the following two stories from the canonical collection of poems by nuns may suffice to give the idea. When the parents of the future nun Sumedhā tried to persuade her to accept marriage to 'handsome (*abhirūpo*) King Anīkaratta', part of her reply was:

Why should I cling to this foul body, impure, smelling of urine, a frightful water-bag of corpses, always flowing, full of impure things? . . . A body is repulsive, smeared with flesh and blood, food for worms, vultures and [other] birds . . . The body is soon carried out to the cemetery, devoid of consciousness; it is thrown away like a log by disgusted relatives. Having thrown it away in the cemetery as food for others, one's own mother and father wash themselves, disgusted; how much more do common people? (*Thī* 466–9[8])

The second and even more drastic episode concerns the nun Subhā (the name means 'beautiful' or 'pure', and its opposite, *asubha*, is used as a technical term in meditation for the meditations on the 'foul' or 'repulsive' parts of the body and corpses to which I will turn presently). She is pursued in a wood by a young man, who attempts to seduce her;

[8] The translation is from Norman 1971, 46.

he is particularly struck by the beauty of her eyes, which he compares to blue lotuses and to those of a celestial goddess. She explains to him that 'An eye is like a little ball set in a hollow, with a bubble in the middle and full of tears; eye-secretions occur in it; an eye consists in various [different] parts rolled together in a ball'; she then wrenches one of her eyes out and gives it to him. Not surprisingly, the text tells us that 'straightaway his passion ceased, and he begged her pardon'. She goes to the Buddha and he restores her sight (*Thī* 366–99).[9]

In one famous text (*S* II 94–5), the Buddha says that if one is looking for something permanent and lasting, one would do better to try the body, which lasts up to a hundred years, than the mind, which changes every moment. None the less, perception of the body's impermanence is one side of the overwhelmingly negative evaluation of it in meditative reflexion, the other being its impurity. The body is compared, amongst many other things, to an abscess (*S* IV 83), an anthill (*M* I 144), a ball of foam (which is quickly rubbed away) (*S* III 142), a pot (which as standardly in all Indian thought represents that which is created and necessarily destroyed sooner or later) (*Dhp* 40), a hospital (in which consciousness lies like an invalid) (*Vism* 478), and a prison (*Vism* 479). In the great compendium of doctrine and meditation compiled by Buddhaghosa in the fifth century AD, the *Path of Purification* (*Visuddhimagga* 500) it is quite straightforwardly proposed as an argument for the undesirability of rebirth, that to be born again will involve spending nine months in a womb, itself disgusting and 'malodorous' as all parts of the body, situated next to the intestines, bowel, bladder, etc.; and then, even worse, birth itself involves passing through the vaginal passage, covered in blood and other horrific substances. How could anyone possibly want *that*?!

Such reflections on the impermanence and impurity of the body are said to apply equally to monks and nuns. If there is any real difference between the genders in this matter, it is that monks are frequently said to regard the female body as dangerously desirable; this sentiment is part of the outright misogyny which, unfortunately, is to be found in a certain range of Buddhist literature. Nuns, on the contrary, are not said to have reflected, at least overtly, on the corresponding attractiveness of men;[10] but in one place, at least, the Buddha says that for women as for men

---

[9] For a complete translation see Norman 1971, 38–46.

[10] See Lang 1986, who makes this point in a comparison of the *Thera-* and *Therīgāthā*. In my opinion, the argument in Lang's paper is very much overstated, since only this difference between the genders is to be found; and unfortunate though it may be, the difference is hardly one confined to Buddhist texts.

nothing can take hold of one's mind (or 'obsess the heart') as the bodily appearance, voice, scent, taste, and touch of the opposite sex (*A* I I–2). In the detailed prescriptions for meditation on loving-kindness, compassion, and sympathetic joy, monks and nuns are both recommended not to begin by taking a member of the opposite sex as their object, for obvious reasons (*Vism* 296, 314, 316; cp. 184).

To turn to the second and more specific area of meditation: those kinds concerned with the body, particularly the more extravagantly described impurities, are not thought to be topics suitable for everyone, but are best for those of greedy and/or intelligent temperaments. Only mindfulness of death and the development of loving-kindness are thought to be 'generally useful'. But it is indicative of the ambiguous status of the more directly ascetic attitudes in Buddhism (an ambiguity to which I shall return) that Buddhaghosa does record a varying opinion: 'some say perception of foulness [in corpses], too [is suitable for everyone]' (*Vism* 97). Indeed, one canonical passage extolling the virtues of 'mindfulness of the body' goes so far as to say that 'those who do not practise [it] do not enjoy the deathless' (*A* I 45). There are a number of different ways in which the meditations on the body are collected; the following list is synthesized from a number of canonical and commentarial texts.[11]

Meditations on the body

1. Mindfulness of in- and out-breathing.
2. Mindfulness of the four modes of deportment (standing, sitting, lying, moving).
3. Mindfulness consisting in full awareness (of where attention is directed, of physical position and movement, eating, washing, dressing, etc.).
4. Reflection on the four material elements: earth/solidity, water/fluidity, fire/heat, air/movement.
5. Reflection on the repulsiveness of food.
6. Reflection on the repulsiveness of the body, in its 31 parts: head-hairs, body-hairs, nails, teeth, skin, flesh, sinews, bones, bone-marrow, kidney, heart, liver, midriff, spleen, lights, bowels, entrails, gorge, dung, bile, phlegm, pus, blood, sweat, fat, tears, grease, spittle, snot,

---

[11] These are: the *Kāyagatāsati Sutta* (M III 88ff.), *Satipaṭṭhāna Sutta* (M I 55ff.), *Mahāsatipaṭṭhāna Sutta* (D II 290ff.) (with their commentaries), *Khuddakapāṭha* III with *Paramatthajotikā* I 37–75, *Visuddhimagga* chs. 6, 8, 11.

oil-of-the-joints, and brain-in-the-head.

7. Perception of foulness/Cemetery Meditations:

Series 1 – gradual decomposition of a corpse, in nine stages:
swollen and festering, a few days old
pecked at by crows, vultures, dogs and worms
a skeleton, with pieces of flesh and blood, held in by tendons
a blood-smeared skeleton without flesh, held in by tendons
a skeleton without flesh or blood, held in by tendons
bones scattered in all directions
bones coloured white like a conch
bones more than a year old, heaped together
bones gone rotten and reduced to dust

Series 2 – ten varieties of dead body:
corpses bloated, livid, festering, cut-up, gnawed, scattered, hacked and scattered, bleeding, worm-infested, and a skeleton.

In nos. 1–3, the mindfulness of breathing, of the modes of deportment and full awareness, attention is constantly given to how the body 'is of a nature to arise and pass away'; in no. 4, the reflection on the four material elements, the mediator is to compare himself to a butcher, cutting up the carcase of a cow and dividing it into portions; in no. 5, the perception of the repulsiveness of food (there are four types of 'food', only one of which is physical, to which I refer here), elaborate attention is paid to the precise details of the transformations of food in the processes of eating, digestion, and excretion, and the food thus eaten and transformed is to be regarded merely as a necessary evil for the maintenance of the body during the monk's 'crossing over suffering': it is to be viewed with as much distaste, one reads, as that with which parents, lost in a wilderness, would regard eating the flesh of their only child, as a necessary evil which allows them to survive and escape (*S* ii 98–9, cited *Vism* 347).

In no. 6, the perception of the repulsiveness of the body, extended accounts are given for each of the thirty-two parts, full of lingering attention to detail, stressing in each case the 'malodorousness' of the phenomena, and using some striking similies. I will allow myself to mention only a few. Uneven teeth are like a row of old chairs in a waiting room; the heart, in someone of speculative temperament, is the colour of lentil soup; snot is an 'impurity that trickles out from the brain'; the stomach is home for thirty-two families of worms, for whom it provides at once 'maternity home, toilet, hospital and burial ground', and it is like a bowl in which food lies like dog's vomit; and the brain is like a lump of dough in an old gourd rind, the colour of milk turned sour but not yet become curds. In all of these cases, apart from reflecting on the inherent repulsiveness of it all, the meditator is to use the comparisons to reflect that just as, for example, dough in a gourd rind is not conscious of itself as being there, but simply exists in physical juxtaposition, so too the brain is not conscious of being in the skull. In the cemetery meditations, no. 7, the meditator is to reflect in the case of each corpse or skeleton 'this [my own] body is of the same nature as that, will become like that, cannot avoid [becoming like] that'.

IV

No doubt much of this could be paralleled from *memento mori* writings from many other traditions, particularly from the Christian Middle Ages. Such sentiments in Buddhism are to be seen against the background of the pan-Indian concern with purity and pollution, where both the permanent social status and the temporary condition of the individual are threatened by what anthropologists often describe as *irruptions biologiques*. These biological assaults on the refuge of civilized life include birth, menstruation, excretion, sexual fluids, death, and a variety of aspects of the cooking and eating of food. The whole Indian social system of caste, as is well known, revolves around rules of marriage and commensality based on purity and impurity of this nature.[12] While the Buddha denied that caste had any bearing on religious matters (he did not, as is sometimes claimed, reject caste completely), it seems obvious that this cultural pattern is preserved in the Buddhist attitudes to the body so far described. In other forms of Indian religion, both Hindu and Jain, the connection between the body, desire, and death can lead to extreme forms of physical asceticism: in Buddhist texts such practices always appear as extreme and fruitless forms of self-mortification, of the kind which the Buddha tried out to its limits before discovering his 'Middle Way'.

The story will be familiar to most people: the Buddha's early life was spent in an extravagant luxury unusual even for the royal family into which he was born. At the age of 29, after seeing a sick man, an old man, a corpse, and an holy man (who, unlike the young prince, seemed to have

---

[12] The classic account is Dumont 1980.

understood the meaning of the other three 'sights'), he embarked on a life of asceticism. His self-mortification was so fierce that he became extremely thin, with his ribs showing through his skin (an image frequently represented in iconography). Finding, however, that this brought no answer to the riddles of life, suffering, and death, he began to eat again in moderation, and subsequently became enlightened. His First Sermon presents the Truth he awakened to, and begins by setting out the two extremes between which his Path was the 'Middle Way': there is 'devotion to indulgence of pleasure in the objects of sense' (i.e. the ordinary life of family and household) which is 'inferior, low, vulgar, ignoble and leads to no good'; and there is 'devotion to self-torment' (i.e. the life of self-mortificatory asceticism) which is 'painful, ignoble, and leads to no good' (*Vin* I 10). There are many places in the canonical texts where this 'self-torment' is criticized; one evocative example of the ideal Buddhist attitude is provided by the monastic rule against murder and suicide. The story goes that some monks had practised the Cemetery Meditations and had become disgusted with their own bodies; they were ashamed of them, we are told, in the same way that young persons proud of their appearance might be ashamed of a dead dog hanging round their neck. They then either committed suicide or got others to kill them. The Buddha condemned their actions, promulgated the rule, and went on to include under it any form of inciting or assisting another person to commit suicide (as an offence punishable by permanent expulsion from the monastic Order) (*Vin* III 68–71).[13]

This emphasis on moderation leads away from what might seem the excesses of the meditations on the body. From this point of view, food is to be taken in moderate amounts, to maintain the body in a condition appropriate for comfortable practice of meditation. Standard comparisons used here compare a monk's eating to a chariot-driver maintaining his vehicle (e.g. *M* I 10), or to a bird taking its two wings with it as it flies (the monk's wings being his robes and food-in-moderation; e.g. *D* I 71). Indeed, in many contexts the comfort and ease of the monastic life are stressed. A good example is the Discourse on the Advantages of the Monastic Life (*Sāmaññaphala-sutta*). Progress through the stages of meditation brings states of increasingly refined 'joy and ease born of detachment, concentration, and purification'; the meditator then 'pervades, drenches, permeates and suffuses his body with [three states], and there is nowhere at all throughout his entire body which is not suffused

---

[13] Suicide is not forbidden, however, to enlightened saints under certain specific circumstances; see Wiltshire 1983.

with them'. This bodily joy, ease, and purification is compared to a ball of lather saturated with perfumed soap powder, a deep pool suffused with the cooling waters of an underground spring, lotus flowers growing in water permeated by its moisture, and a person dressed in clean white clothes (*D* 1 73–6).

In a similar vein, and in contrast with the emphasis on the 'malodorousness' of the body described earlier, in the *Path of Purification* Buddhaghosa writes that 'the bodily perfume of virtuous monks' brings pleasure to the gods. If this is so, he asks 'what of the perfume of his virtue? [This] is more perfect by far than all the other perfumes in the world, because the perfume virtue gives is borne unchecked in all directions' (*Vism* 58). As we shall see, this metaphor has a social dimension; here I adduce it to parallel the physical pleasure very frequently celebrated as a product of Buddhist meditation (at least for those who have advanced some way with it). This pleasure is referred to as *diṭṭhadhamma-sukhavihāra*, 'dwelling happily in this life', and *phāsuvihāra*, 'comfortable living'. Those with the profoundest experience of meditation may be called 'body-witnesses' (e.g. *D* III 105), who have 'touched with the body' not only various immaterial realms of the cosmos, but also 'the deathless' – that is, *nirvāṇa* (e.g. *M* I 477, *A* II 87, III 356, *It* 46, 62, *Pp* 11, 14).[14] Those who are not so far advanced, but who can look forward to rebirth in one of the heavens will find there just this kind of bliss; indeed, different meditative levels are explicitly correlated with various heavens, and dying in such a state allows the physical happiness of meditative attainment to continue celestially.[15] The meditations called 'Divine Abidings' (loving-kindness, compassion, sympathetic joy, and equanimity) are meant literally to produce such heavenly happiness. Among the results of successful practice of them are that the practitioner 'sleeps happily, wakes happily, and dreams no evil dreams . . . is not affected by fire and poison and weapons . . . the expression on his face is serene, he dies unconfused and . . . is reborn in the Brahma-world [one of the heavens]' (e.g. *A* v 352). Certainly anyone who has seen Buddhist monks, particularly in a Buddhist country, can confirm the striking appearance of good health and contentment which they very frequently display. (Whether they are reborn in heaven is not open to such empirical confirmation.)

A famous Buddhist text from around the beginning of the modern era,

---

[14] It is perhaps worth remarking that the commentaries to these and other such passages usually gloss *kāya* not in its normal sense of '(physical) body', but as *nāma-kāya*, 'mental body'.
[15] See, for example, the table given in Collins 1982, 217.

the *Questions of King Milinda*, which purports to record a debate between a
Bactrian-Greek king and an Indian Buddhist monk, here as so often
crystallizes the issue: the king asks 'is the body dear to those who have
gone forth [to the monastic Order]?' The monk Nāgasena replies that it
is not. 'Then why,' replies the king 'do you treasure it and foster it?' The
monk answers by likening the body to a wound received in battle, which
is anointed and bandaged, so that it might heal. Similarly, although the
body is 'not dear' to monks, he says, they protect it as a means of
promoting the holy life. He then cites some verses comparing the body to
an abscess with nine holes, in the style sketched earlier (*Mil* 73–4). Later I
shall try to produce an account, from the point of view of an outside
interpreter, which will parallel exactly the structure of this Buddhist
explanation. That is, I shall try to show that the positive nurturing of the
body is complementary rather than opposed to the negative attitudes of
the body-meditations. None the less, it is fairly obvious that the two
approaches stand in potential conflict. One place where this conflict can
be seen to emerge within Buddhism is in connection with a set of ascetic
practices called the *dhutaṅgas*.[16] One of these, no. 13, is clearly a form of
physical self-mortification familiar from other Indian traditions; another, no. 11, is presumably a prerequisite of the 'Perception of Foulness'
meditations sketched earlier. But, although they receive a whole chapter
in the *Path of Purification* (as does the Perception of Foulness), and
although the first, wearing rag robes seems to have become the name of a
monastic faction in ancient and medieval Ceylon, it also seems clear that
they have had an ambiguous history in Buddhism, one which continues
today. The list of thirteen is not found in the canonical texts, and the
more extravagant practices are certainly marginal and unemphasized.
There are passages where the list seems to be condemned.[17] In modern
Sri Lanka and Thailand, as Michael Carrithers and Jane Bunnag have
recorded, although the idea (and practice) of such heroic supererogatory
asceticism is often accorded great popular acclaim, in the longer term
the cleanliness and decorum expected of monks becomes the greater
demand. As Bunnag says,[18] such '*dhutaṅga* monks [who in Thailand are
most noted for their wandering life style] are frequently regarded as
being on a par with tramps, beggars and other kinds of social derelicts'. A

[16] These are: 1. wearing rag robes; 2. using only three robes; 3. begging alms; 4. not omitting any
house when begging; 5. eating once a day; 6. eating only from the bowl; 7. not taking second
helpings; 8. living in the forest; 9. living at the foot of a tree; 10. living in the open air; 11. living in a
cemetery; 12. being satisfied with whatever dwelling one receives; 13. sleeping in a sitting position
and never lying down.

[17] See Carrithers 1983, 62–2, etc.   [18] 1973, 54.

similar picture can be seen in regard to the movements of women in modern Buddhist countries who lead, to varying degrees, an ascetic or meditative life style. There seem for a long time to have been poor women living near temples and holy places, dressed in white and living on charity: but they have not been accorded high status, and so the new movements of 'nuns' have taken specific care to differentiate themselves from such 'beggars'. Correct physical decorum is a recognized requirement of their public life.[19]

Thus, although the inner meditative reflection of a monk or nun emphasizes the body's impurity and impermanence, their social position also requires what one might call 'a spotless performance'. The metaphor of 'the perfume of virtue' referred to earlier is a term used both in canonical and later texts (A I 225–6, Dhp 54, Dhp-a I 422), and in modern Sinhalese usage[20] for the social reputation of the well-behaved monk or nun, a reputation gained and maintained through carefully composed deportment, and through social interaction where they are treated as revered superiors. The good monk is depicted thus: 'having entered a house, or gone into the street, he goes with downcast eyes, looking forward the length of a plough yoke, restrained, not looking [at anything around him]' (Nidd I 474, Vism 19).[21]

This emphasis on decorum and social presentation carries over into the texts dealing with monastic virtue. Of the 227 Vinaya rules for monks, and 311 for nuns, 75 are 'Training Rules', solely concerned with matters of dress, deportment, and etiquette; and in the rest of the list 'rules on [clothing] are much more numerous than rules about lodgings or food'.[22] In Buddhaghosa's theoretical treatment of morality (sīla) these concerns are equally prominent.[23] A pervasive image in his discussion has it that a monk should keep his sīla unstained and untorn; as Gombrich puts it, 'sīla is envisaged as a kind of protective cloak in which the monk is to remain wrapped, a cloak of decorum'. Gombrich shows how the theoretical emphasis on intention in the Buddhist understanding of karma is, in practice, subject to 'an overwhelming demand for empirical evidence of a monk's internal state'.[24] I mentioned earlier the Buddhist emphasis on intention, and the fact that Buddhist jurisprudence requires that an act be committed consciously for it to be judged as

---

[19] See Nissan 1984, 37–8, Bloss 1987, 22.

[20] M. B. Carrithers, personal communication. Compare the medieval *Saddhamma-sangaha* (72), which tells us that the breath of monks who preach, and of those who assent to sermons in the words 'sādhu, sādhu' is sweet-smelling.

[21] See Carrithers 1983, 56–8 for a fine description and discussion of this 'good conduct'.

[22] Wijayaratna 1990.   [23] See Keown 1983.   [24] 1984, citations from 93, 100.

an offence; but it would be absurd, on the other hand, to hold that an intention to commit murder, for example, is as bad as an actual murder. Accordingly, Buddhist jurisprudence (as opposed to psychological analysis) requires the external act (*As* 97; *cf. Sp* 439, *Kkh* 30).

In the texts, good and bad conduct, purity and impurity, etc., are regularly said to occur through body, speech, and mind; the rules of morality (*sīla*) and the Monastic Code (*vinaya*) are said to govern body and speech only: obviously, mental life cannot be directly disciplined by external rules (*Sp* 18–9). But, in fact, almost always when texts use this tripartite division, virtue and vice are said to operate in the three places together. Thus the usual assumption is that the internal mental condition of a monk or nun can be inferred from his or her physical and verbal behaviour, since it is the latter which express the former – to themselves as much as to anyone else. The empirical evidence for the state of virtue is well described in the following definition of 'proper conduct' (*ācāra*) in the *Path of Purification* (*Vism* 19): the monk is

respectful, deferential, possessed of conscience and shame, wears his inner robe properly, wears his upper robe properly, his manner inspires confidence whether in moving forwards or backwards, looking ahead or aside, bending or stretching, his eyes are downcast, he has a [good] deportment, he guards the doors of his sense-faculties, knows the right measure in eating, is devoted to wakefulness, possesses mindfulness and full-wareness, wants little, is contented, is strenuous, is a careful observer of good behaviour, and treats the teachers with respect.

Much of this phraseology is the same as that used in elucidating the second and third sections of the meditations on the body discussed earlier: from the present perspective, I suggest that such meditation is a form of private self-control and self-supervision required by the expected public body-image.

v

In the preceding two sections of this chapter I have tried to juxtapose the *deconstruction* and rejection of the body in meditative analysis with the *construction* of it in social behaviour as a unified and valued public object. In concluding, I shall now try to show that these two emphases are not mutually contradictory, but complementary. This can be described on both the individual (psychological) and communal (economic) levels. My argument here will be comparative: I shall quote from three scholars writing on the early and medieval periods of Christian monasticism, and try to show that what they say can be applied, *mutatis mutandis*, to the Buddhist case.[25]

First, then, on the individual level: earlier, in discussing sexual prohibitions, I moved from the external rules prohibiting forms of behaviour to the internal conquest of desire, manifested in the absence of wet dreams. In a study of some texts by the fourth century Latin writer John Cassian, Michel Foucault remarks similarly how the discussion of the 'deadly sin' of fornication is hardly at all concerned with external actions, either with others or alone. Rather, the focus of interest is the internal 'battle for chastity' in the mind, in both waking and sleeping states. This battle is waged gradually, requiring a constant vigilance over thought, imagination, and impulse, until the final stage is reached, where (as a blessing of grace and not an attainment of effort) even 'involuntary nocturnal pollutions' cease. This process, Foucault asserts, is best described *not* as 'the internalization of a whole list of forbidden things, merely substituting the prohibition of the intention for that of the act itself'; rather, it is 'the opening up of an area', 'a process of "subjectivization"' which is quite different from, and much more than, a simple 'sexual ethic based on physical self-control'.[26] In a Buddhist canonical text, the elderly monk Bakkula, who has been in the robes for 80 years, is asked by a non-Buddhist ascetic how many times during that time he has had sexual intercourse. Bakkula tells him that this is an inappropriate question; better to ask how many times have ideas or images of desire (*kāma-saññā*) arisen in his mind; when the ascetic asks this question, he replies that he is not aware of this ever having happened (*M* III 125). An enlightened monk called Dabba Mallaputta was wrongly accused of having had sexual intercourse on a number of occasions; on being asked by the Buddha whether it was true, he replied each time that he was not aware of having had intercourse in a dream, leave alone while awake (*Vin* II 78, etc.). The Buddha elsewhere characterizes the 'highest brahmin' of old as having nothing to do with sex 'even in dreams' (*Sn* 293).

I suggest that the *Vinaya* rules, the meditations on the body, and the effort to eradicate desire for material and sexual existence, serve to create in the body of the Buddhist monastic practitioner the space for an

---

[25] In what follows I shall be speaking at a level of considerable abstractive generality, which would certainly need extensive ethnographic correction and elaboration if it were taken to be a descriptive as well as an analytic account. For example, only a small minority of monks or nuns ever meditate to any significant level, so my remarks can only be taken as referring to ideal types: but then, much of the social and psychological perception I shall be sketching *itself* makes use of ideal types.

[26] Foucault 1985, 24–5.

individualized or 'subjectivized' analysis. In so far as salvation is conceived as a spiritual state manifested in both mind and body, the attempt wholly to inhibit (or perhaps, exorcise) all sexual drives and thoughts, and not merely to prevent overt sexual activity, necessarily induces psychic conflict, a conflict which opens up the interior terrain for which texts and doctrines provide the map. In this private zone of operations the de-sexualized, and thus in one sense de-socialized individual can embody in imagination the immateriality posited in the doctrines of Buddhism, and in this way 'touch the deathless with the body'.

This kind of socio-religious theatre (a term, I stress, which I do *not* mean to be either pejorative or reductivist) is necessarily more than a soliloquy, even if the leading players are in one sense radically individualized. For the existence of monks and nuns 'outside society', as that wholly misleading phrase has it, is made possible only by the support, material and behavioural, of the laity (the chorus, perhaps). This leads me to the second comparative quotation, and to begin to move from the individual to communal levels. Peter Brown, writing recently about the same texts of John Cassian as was Foucault, but in relation to the Desert Fathers whose wisdom Cassian is retelling, discusses the 'perfect "purity of heart"' granted by God to a few saints:

They had been freed from sexual fantasies in dreams associated with nocturnal emissions . . . The sexuality of the emission created a disjunction between [the monk's] public, daylight self and a last oasis of incommunicable, privatized experience. When such dreams ceased, the last fissure between the private person and his fellows could be assumed to have closed . . . The total expropriation associated with the life of the desert had begun, as in the case of Antony, with the surrender of private wealth. It ended with the surrender of the last traces of sexual fantasy. This was a sure symptom, in Cassian's mind, and in that of his Egyptian informants, that the dispersal of the last, most hidden treasures of the private will had taken place . . . In the desert tradition, the body had been allowed to become the discreet mentor of the proud soul . . . The rhythms of the body itself, and, with the body, his concrete social relations determined the life of the monk: his continued economic dependence on the settled world for food, the hard school of day-to-day collaboration with his fellow ascetics in shared rhythms of labor and mutual exhortations in the monasteries slowly changed his personality. The material conditions of the monk's life were held capable of altering the consciousness itself.[27]

[27] Brown 1988, 231–2, 237.

In the Buddhist case, the concrete social relations of importance to 'the rhythms of the body' are those I have outlined which make the monk or nun a visibly clean, pure, and decorous object. It is only in an ideological sense that they can be said to 'leave society'. From the interpretative point of view, a monastic life exchanges one social position for another: that is, belonging not to a natural family but to 'the lineage of the Buddha'. From this social position monastics can be construed, by themselves and others, in both attitude and behaviour, as independent and autonomous agents; the orientation towards a purely personal and immaterial goal both differentiates them from the laity, bound up in networks of material concern, and creates the actual behavioural space in which the 'subjectivized' interiority inculcated by meditative practices can take place.

But the communal dimension of the monastic's 'de-socialized' body is not restricted to the provision of a stage on which the individual drama of salvation is played out. Here we come to my third and last comparative quotation, and to a topic almost always underrated in the study of religions: money, or, in a pre-monetary economy, the ownership of property. Jack Goody, writing of the medieval Christian Church, has claimed that

the maintenance of the church as an organisation, the church as a corporation with its specialised priesthood, the church of literate societies rather than the less substantial church of Durkheimian sociology, such an organisation requires its own property. To maintain a complex hierarchy of priests requires a large endowment . . . [T]he major means by which church property in Europe became as substantial as it did was probably by gift and by inheritance.[28]

In Buddhist history, property has not usually been inherited from lay owners, but resources and land have regularly been donated by laity: kings, for example, frequently gave whole villages to monasteries and to eminent monks (though not equally often, perhaps, to nuns). Equally, I would not wish to follow Goody in attempting to derive the rules of marriage and family organization in Buddhist countries from the needs and directives of the church, as he has done for the history of Europe.[29] But the general point is simple and clear: any social institution such as the Buddhist monkhood, which cannot reproduce itself from within, must have not only a regular influx of new members from the circumambient society, but also a real and continuing existence 'outside society' – guaranteed by economic independence – if it is not to become

---

[28] Goody 1976, 46.   [29] See Goody 1983.

simply an aspect or phase of the productive and reproductive cycles of ordinary life. (In practice throughout South and Southeast Asia there have always been factors tending towards just this.) Monks and nuns as 'sons and daughters of the Buddha' may be, as the texts say, the heirs to his spiritual wealth, but they also need a material inheritance if there is to be independent continuity in such a non-reproductive 'family'. In this perspective, the ascetic celibacy of monasticism, inculcated and underlined by meditations on the body, is one attempt to guarantee that it will not be drawn back into just those kinship-based social and property relations against whose interrelated and repetitive patterns the goal of liberation is defined. Correspondingly, the composed, pure, and autonomous body of the monk or nun presented in social life instantiates for lay supporters the immediate existence of that sacred, immaterial, and undying Truth which their own bodily concerns make impossibly distant from them, and with which they can thus be connected by their material support of its human embodiments.

Thus the body in Theravāda Buddhism may be seen, both individually and socially, as one central part of the basis in lived experience from which the metaphors of rebirth (*saṃsāra*) and immaterial release (*nirvāṇa*) take flight. Or, as a canonical text has it (*S* 1 62): 'in this fathom-long carcase, with its perception and reflection, there is the world, the arising and cessation of the world, and the way leading to the cessation of the world'.

BIBLIOGRAPHY

Bloss, L. (1987), 'The Female Renunciants of Sri Lanka: the *Dasasilmattawa*', *Journal of the International Association of Buddhist Studies*, 10/1, 1–31.
Brown, P. (1988), *The Body and Society: Men, Women and Sexual Renunciation in Early Christianity*, New York: Columbia University Press.
Bunnag, J. (1973), *Buddhist Monk, Buddhist Layman*, Cambridge University Press.
Carrithers, M. (1983), *The Forest Monks of Sri Lanka: An Anthropological and Historical Study*, Delhi: Oxford University Press.
Collins, S. (1982), *Selfless Persons: Imagery and Thought in Theravāda Buddhism*, Cambridge University Press.
(1994), 'What are Buddhists *doing* when they deny the self?', in ed. F. Reynolds and D. Tracy *Religion and Practical Reason* (Towards a Comparative Philosophy of Religions series), Albany, NY: SUNY Press, 59–86.
Dumont, L. (1980), *Homo Hierarchicus*, (rev. edn, University of Chicago Press).
Durkheim, E. (1915), *The Elementary Forms of the Religious Life*, London: George Allen and Unwin.

Foucault, M. (1985), 'The Battle for Chastity', in eds. P. Ariès and A. Béjin, *Western Sexuality*, Oxford: Basil Blackwell.

Gombrich, R. F. (1984), 'Notes on the Brahmanical background to Buddhist Ethics', in eds. G. Dhammapala, R. Gombrich, and K. R. Norman, *Buddhist Studies in honour of Hammalava Saddhātissa*, Nugegoda, Buddhist Research Library Trust, Sri Lanka, 91–102.

Goody, J. (1976), *Production and Reproduction*, Cambridge University Press.

(1983), *The Development of the Family and Marriage in Europe*, Cambridge University Press.

Keown, D. (1983), 'Morality in the *Visuddhimagga*', *Journal of the International Association of Buddhist Studies* 6/1, 61–75.

Lang, K. C. (1986), 'Lord Death's Snare: Gender-Related Imagery in the Thera- and Therīgāthā', *Journal of Feminist Studies in Religion*, 2/2, 63–79.

Lukes, S. (1973), *Émile Durkheim*, London: Pelican.

Nissan, E. (1984), 'Recovering Practice: Buddhist Nuns in Sri Lanka', *South Asia Research*, 4/1, 32–49.

Norman, K.R. (1971), *Elders' Verses II*, London: Pali Text Society.

Weber, M. (1948), *From Max Weber: Essays in Sociology*, London: Routledge and Kegan Paul.

(1963), *The Sociology of Religion*, London: Methuen.

Wiltshire, M. (1983), 'The "Suicide" Problem in the Pali Canon', *Journal of the International Association of Buddhist Studies*, 6/2, 124–40.

Wijayaratna, M. (1990) *Buddhist Monastic Life*, Cambridge University Press.

CHAPTER 12

Some Mahāyāna Buddhist perspectives on the body

Paul Williams

It would be wrong to see Mahāyāna Buddhism as a school or sect of Buddhism the members of which might be said to have an exclusive perspective on the body capable of placing alongside that of Theravāda. To be a Theravāda Buddhist is a matter of monastic rule; as Richard Gombrich has pointed out, a Theravādin is a monk or nun who adheres to the version of the *pātimokkha* (Skt: *prātimokṣa*), the basic monastic rule, contained in the Pali canon (Gombrich 1988, 112). Being a follower of Mahāyāna is as such nothing to do with holding a particular monastic rule. Rather, it is a matter of motivation for the spiritual life. To be a follower of Mahāyāna, the Tibetan systematizer Tsong kha pa states, writing in the late fourteenth century, is dependent upon the extent to which one has the *bodhicitta*, the altruistic mind which seeks perfect Buddhahood for the benefit of all sentient beings (1990, 285). Thus a person is a Mahāyānist if one has (or genuinely aspires to have) this motivation which in Mahāyāna writings is seen as being the highest of all motivations. To have such a motivation is to be a *bodhisattva* – an 'enlightenment-being' – and is not thought to be in rivalry or contradiction with ordination into a particular monastic tradition, holding a particular *pātimokkha* rule. Thus, from this point of view, the perspective of Mahāyāna's own self-understanding, there could in theory be a Theravāda follower of Mahāyāna (see also Williams 1989, ch. 1).

The great Tibetan scholar Tsong kha pa's (1357–1419) tradition of the *lam rim*, the stages of the path, provides us with a useful framework for understanding what is going on in assessing Mahāyāna perspectives on the body. Tsong kha pa follows Atiśa (982–1054) in dividing Buddhist practitioners by motivation into three 'scopes' – the lesser, the middling, and the superior. Those of lesser scope act for the pleasures of *saṃsāra* – the recurrent round of unenlightenment – in this or in future lives, while those of middling scope, disgusted with *saṃsāra*, are dominated by renunciation and seek for their own personal liberation, *nirvāṇa*. Both of these scopes are clearly not those of Mahāyāna practitioners, who adopt the superior scope of wishing to bring an end to all the sufferings of all beings – that is, they generate the *bodhicitta* (Atiśa 1983; Tsong kha pa 1990, *passim*; Williams 1989: 197 ff.). It is crucial to Tsong kha pa's understanding of those three scopes that in the last analysis they represent as such not three different types of practitioners, but rather three stages in the spiritual growth of every practitioner. Therefore from a Mahāyāna perspective, and within the same text identifiable as Mahāyāna inasmuch as it teaches the Mahāyāna motivation as the highest spiritual aspiration, may be found teachings appropriate to the other two scopes as stages on a path to the Mahāyāna and eventual Buddhahood. Thus an attitude to the body found strongly stated in non-Mahāyāna writings and ably treated by Steven Collins in his paper on Theravāda Buddhist monasticism may also be found in Mahāyāna sources even if, as we shall see, a different attitude may be advocated as Mahāyāna *qua* Mahāyāna elsewhere, perhaps within the same source. How we assess doctrinal perspectives for Atiśa and Tibetan writers like Tsong kha pa depends on the position of those perspectives in a scheme of practice which is, when taken as a whole, one of Mahāyāna, in that its final goal, and therefore overall rationale, is envisaged in Mahāyāna terms.

A TERMINOLOGICAL INTERLUDE

The body (*kāya*), the *Dharmasaṃgīti Sūtra* tells us – introducing an instruction for meditation – 'is just a collection of feet and toes, legs, chest, loins, belly, navel, backbone, heart, ribs and flanks, hands, forearms, upper-arms, shoulders, neck, jaw, forehead, head, skull, accumulated by the action that causes existence, the abode of sundry passions, ideas and fancies' (Bendall and Rouse 1971, 216; Śāntideva 1961, 124). The scripture (*sūtra*) continues in a fashion familiar also from Theravāda sources to enumerate some of the disgusting internal constituents of the body. It is called by various names, such as *kāya*, *deha*, *āśraya*, *śarīra* and others, but no matter what the name the body which we all know and most of us love is impure, putrid and smelly, full of diseases and fundamentally impermanent (Bendall and Rouse 1971, 216–7).

The word *kāya* is perhaps the most common word for 'body' used in Pali and Sanskrit, and it is particularly important in the context of Buddhalogical speculations concerning the two, three, four, or five *kāyas* of the Buddha. '*Kāya*' bears some of the flexible ambiguity of the English 'body' in that it can be used for the physical body, a collection (as in 'a body of people') and it appears also as the essence or main part (as in 'the body of the text'). The connection between the first and second meanings here is played on by Vasubandhu (*c.* fourth century CE) when he refers in his *Karmasiddhiprakaraṇa* to the physical body (*kāya*/Tib: *lus*) as 'a special collection of great material elements and events derived from the great material elements, a corporeal mass associated with sense faculties' (Anacker 1984, 118). The body in Buddhist eyes is not an independent entity set against others, 'me' contrasted with and in opposition to 'you', but is just the coming together in a patterned heap of a collective of material elements, a coming together which, in conjunction with the mind, is capable of sensing. That coming together and patterning is due to previous karmic volitions going back into infinite time. The idea of *kāya* as essence or main part may be behind the gloss of *kāya* with reference to the *dharmakāya*, the highest *kāya* of the Buddha, in Paramārtha's (sixth century CE) extended Chinese translation of the *Mahāyānasaṃgrahabhāṣya* as 'reality' (Chin: *shih*), essence or nature (on the *kāyas* of the Buddha see Williams 1989, ch. 8). This also ties in with *āśraya*, support, as a word for the body, another term favoured by Paramārtha, who wished to portray the *dharmakāya* of the Buddha as the true ultimate reality and support (Griffiths et al. 1989, 64).

Śarīra is a term used both for the physical body (that which is treated by doctors: see Conze 1973, 117) and also relics preserved in *stūpas*. Tibetan also has two principal words for the body, *sku* and *lus*, although whereas the terms *kāya* and *śarīra* might be said to have a 'horizontal' relationship of close and overlapping meaning (both can refer in the same way to the ordinary physical body), *lus* and *sku* could be said to bear a 'vertical' relationship inasmuch as *lus* is the nonhonorific and *sku* the honorific term for the same thing – the body. Thus the Tibetan uses whichever honorific or nonhonorific word is appropriate to translate both *kāya* and *śarīra* (and any other Sanskrit word which refers to the body) when these terms are used to mean the physical body. Sanskrit lacks the extensive system of honorifics possessed by Tibetan and some other Oriental languages; Tibetan lacks the vast Sanskrit vocabulary of equivalents or near equivalents. Tibetan has to use other terms for the same Sanskrit word when the Sanskrit term is used with its 'divergent' meanings. Thus Tibetan can use *sku* to distinguish the use of *kāya* with reference to the Buddha in order to contrast it with *kāya* used of ordinary human beings, for which it will use *lus*. This honorific/nonhonorific distinction is one which Buddhist Sanskrit does not make. But Tibetan has to use other words for the Sanskrit *kāya* when used to designate a heap or collection, or *śarīra* when referring to relics: *tshogs* for a collection, *sku gdung* for relics. For all these reasons Tibetan can sometimes clarify a reading of the Sanskrit – but lose some of the poetic ambiguity and alternative interpretations of the Sanskrit original.

THE BODY AS DISGUSTING AND REPULSIVE

The *Samādhirāja Sūtra* echoes the entire Buddhist tradition, Mahāyāna and non-Mahāyāna, when it states that one who wishes to attain enlightenment quickly should not cling to body and life (Régamey 1990 reprint, 49–5, 83–4). Those who cling to body and life become involved in unskilful actions. Fools cling to this foul body; such fools after death go to hell realms as a result of the unskilful actions which they have committed. Vimalakīrti, in the *Vimalakīrtinirdeśa Sūtra*, portrays the body as impermanent, fragile, weak, suffering, the receptacle of numerous illnesses (Lamotte 1962, 132), a view repeated in Tibetan medicine, which sees bodily health as the result of a fragile balance between the humours, and illness the natural state of sentient beings (Donden 1986, 17).

Enlightenment in Buddhism lies in seeing things the way they really are. Although this is usually held to involve understanding the final nature of things – in Mahāyāna thought, emptiness of inherent existence, or mind-only as the case may be – such an understanding only partially encompasses what is meant by seeing things the way they really are. From the beginning Buddhism had spoken of four cardinal mis-perceptions – seeing permanence where there is impermanence, happi-ness where there is only suffering, Self where there is no Self, and purity where there is impurity. Probably the most important aim of meditation in Buddhism is to close the gap between our habitual misperceptions and what is actually the case. To see happiness where there is only suffering, and purity where there is impurity, is in Buddhism quintessentially a bodily matter. This is made clear by Āryadeva (third century CE) who devotes two chapters of his *Catuḥśataka* to analytic meditations resulting in the dissolution of these misperceptions. Both chapters concern the body which, Āryadeva says, is to be perceived as an enemy (Lang 1983: *CS* 2/1. See also Śāntideva's (eighth century CE) *Bodhicaryāvatāra* 8:121 in Batchelor 1979). The body is the source of suffering, and there is more suffering in life than pleasure, as well as more unhappy people. Pleasure gives way to unhappiness. Even if one lacks physical suffering, one still has mental suffering. The Buddhist is ever mindful of the suffering of impermanence and death, which comes to all. As one gets older, so sufferings increase, and all embodied beings are tormented by hunger, cold, and numerous other torments (such as the 84,000 worms). Āryadeva concludes his pessimistic meditation on the body: 'The impermanent certainly harms. Where there exists harm there is no happiness. Therefore all that is impermanent is called "suffering".'

Yet is it pessimistic? In the modern Western world of preventive medicine and incubators we are apt to forget the conditions under which people in the past lived, and probably the majority of the world still does. With justification the Buddhist sees Āryadeva as being realistic, viewing things the way they really are. The body, embodiment, genuinely *is* and has been a source of great suffering for many people throughout history. Attachment to a body which lives in harsh conditions squalid by modern standards, which is often ill, and when not ill is still infested with parasites, the life span of which is not great, is not particularly wise. Even where life is comfortable, the ever present possibility and eventual certainty of death makes embodiment – physical life itself – a source of what existentialists call *Angst*. The body is your enemy, for the body can make you constantly miserable and finally kills you.

Desire for the body of the opposite sex is, in Buddhism, simply a particularly time-consuming and destructively absurd version of the general desire for a body. Not only is a body suffering by nature, Āryadeva states, it is also by nature impure. In the Indian context most of Āryadeva's readers, those to whom these meditations were offered, would have accepted the broad direction of this point. As Steven Collins has pointed out, Buddhists in India were heirs to a tradition which identified corpses, entrails, and bodily fluids with sources of pollution which, if not neutralized, purified, could entail social consequences of a catastrophic kind. Caste position and role was and is intimately related to matters of relative purity and pollution. The very fact of embodiment means constant pollution, and the constant need for purification. In having a body it is indeed true, according to the traditional Brāhmanic world-view, that one carries round a bag of impurity, a constant threat which cannot be controlled, only neutralised after its occurrence. It is noticeable that in village Hinduism to the present day all the forms of involuntary pollution – sweating, excretion, death, and so on – are bodily in nature (Mathur 1964; 119–20). Richard Lannoy, in his book *The Speaking Tree*, has pointed out the close association in traditional Indian

thought between the state of the body and mental or spiritual vitality
(1971, 95). Bodily secretions, particularly those which come from below
the waist, are not only polluting, but can also represent a physical,
mental and spiritual weakening (ibid., 153).[1] Buddhist writers, although
ostensibly removed from the Brāhmanical world-view, were in fact in
these matters heirs to it. Most of the greatest Mahāyāna thinkers, such as
Nāgārjuna (second century CE), are said in class terms to have come from
Brahmin or Kṣatriya families. No wonder Āryadeva and Śāntideva,
apparently sons of kings, both describe the body as an enemy.

The common strategy of Nāgārjuna, Āryadeva, and Śāntideva, here,
as in philosophy, is to take the presuppositions of their opponents and
show their contradictory nature. The body is not like a bag containing
faeces, urine, and so on. It *is* that bag, or, as Nāgārjuna puts it, 'an
ornamented pot of filth' (Hopkins, 1975, v. 151. See also v. 162). Even the
normal Brāhmanic methods of purification cannot purify its inner parts
(Lang 1983, 3:21). It is only because containing urine is common to
everyone that we do not avoid such polluting people, as we do lepers (v.
22). Śāntideva asks why it is we are attached to sexual intercourse, which
involves the polluting lower parts of bodies, if we will not admit to being
addicted to impurity (Batchelor 1979, 8:52, cf. v. 59). The fact is that I
contain pollution; why do I desire other bags of pollution (v. 53, cf. v. 61)?
If we spit out nice things like food, that too becomes polluting. Thus the
very presence of something within the body renders it polluting (v. 62). If
we cannot see this, then perhaps we should go to one of the most
polluting places of all from a Brāhmanic point of view – the cemetery.
There we can see what is inside the body. We all agree *that* is polluting.
Even when living the body emits a foul smell. Otherwise why do we wear
perfumes and so on (vv. 65–6). In fact in its natural state, prior to our
absurd adornments, the body is disgusting. To adorn it is to adorn
something which is disgusting and which is a constant source of harm –
'this entire world is disturbed with insanity' (vv. 68–9). Nāgārjuna states:

> He who lies on the filthy mass
> Covered by skin moistened with
> Those fluids, merely lies
> On top of a woman's bladder. (Hopkins 1975, v. 157)

---

[1] For classical sources on the particularly polluting nature of the body below the navel see Meyer
1930, 248–9, n. 5. This is said to be why at death the soul of a virtuous person leaves the body from
one of the upper openings of the body, while the soul of a wicked man literally goes downwards.
We are not far from the suggestion that frequent sexual activity could habituate the mind to a
downward flow, to 'base sensations' which could lead to hell. On the association of sex with a loss
of spiritual power in Theravāda Buddhism see Spiro 1982, 297.

But Nāgārjuna makes it quite clear that this is not a version of misogyny. He is writing to a king, but he adds that 'your own body is as filthy as a woman's' (v. 165).

Disgust for the body engenders renunciation of the body and eventually also renunciation of sexual activity. In terms of Atiśa and Tsong kha pa's three scopes this is the stage of the second scope, renunciation of *saṃsāra* which leads to enlightenment. For Tsong kha pa, teaching the foulness of the body is not appropriate for those of lowly scope who are concerned with developing that righteous perspective which leads to favourable rebirths. It is not, in other words, for the much maligned 'man-in-the-street'. Since the foulness meditation is introduced before the third Mahāyāna scope, it is not surprising to find that on this topic Mahāyāna writings share a common ground with non-Mahāyāna. On the other hand a proper understanding of the body, and attendant renunciation, is for Tsong kha pa presupposed in material – including material on the body – which could be called characteristically Mahāyāna.

SUICIDE

Renunciation of the body is a renunciation of attachment, that burning craving which would fuel the process of rebirth. Buddhist writers do not conclude that renunciation of the body should entail suicide. This is absurd, for, while the body is a cause of suffering, it is not the root cause, which is craving motivated by a fundamental misperception of things, ignorance. Generally suicide, which is usually said to lead to a very much less favourable re-embodiment, has been strongly condemned by the Buddhist tradition. However, there are exceptions, most notably in the mythical but highly influential context of the *Lotus*, the *Saddharmapuṇḍarīka Sūtra*. There we are told of the *bodhisattva* Bhaiṣajyarāja who in a previous life is said to have made the most perfect offering to the Buddhas by setting fire to his body. This offering is enthusiastically praised by the *sūtra*, as is the burning of a finger or toe with a similar motivation (Hurvitz 1976, 295 ff. See also Williams 1989, 154–5). It is not specifically stated in the *sūtra* that the offering is the result of a disgust with the body, but, as we shall see, such self-sacrifice is thought in the Mahāyāna context to be made possible because of a detachment from the body which flows from the meditations we have already examined.

Religious suicide, often through burning the body, or burning limbs of the body in order to show devotion and generate merit, is a feature of

Plate 8　Mahāyāna Buddhists stress that the body is a useless object of attachment unless it can be used for the benefit of others. In this painting the Vietnamese monk Ven. Thich Quang-Duc burns himself to death in 1963 in protest at the Vietnamese government's persecution of Buddhism. Such a suicide is thought to spring from non-attachment in one of great mental strength and stability motivated by compassion for those who suffer.

East Asian Buddhism no doubt inspired by the example of the *Lotus Sūtra*. In Chinese Buddhism to the present day it is normal to burn a number of places on the head with moxa as part of the ordination ceremony, and burning-off whole fingers as a sacrifice and offering generating merit is by no means uncommon (Welch 1967; 298–300, 324 ff.). Holmes Welch mentions several cases of complete burning in the nineteenth century. In seventh-century China a certain monk named Fa-k'uang committed suicide through cutting his throat, having lamented 'Only because of birth and death [i.e. embodiment] am I involved in the endless wheel of transmigration.' Two nuns who were sisters came to dislike their bodies after reading the Bhaiṣajyarāja chapter of the *Lotus Sūtra*, and following that model burnt themselves to death (See Jan Yun-hua 1964, 247 and 250–1. See also Ku 1984, 88–9). Chinese pilgrims to India describe cases of religious suicide there also, but note that this was understood in India to be a definite misunderstanding of the teaching. As I-ching states 'It is not in our power to imitate a Bodhisattva' (Jan Yun-hua 1964, 257), that is, the stories found in *sūtras* are exhortatory hyperbole, and not intended to be followed literally by all and sundry. In China, while it was recognized that religious suicide contravenes the Buddhist precepts, there was nevertheless elsewhere a certain admiration for the renunci-ation and courage involved. In giving up something as precious as the body, these people had been able to renounce that for which almost all people blindly grasp, thus setting us all a great example (ibid., 260–3). Tsan-ning, writing in the tenth century, offers a strong defence of religious suicide. In giving up that which it is difficult to part with, one has finally obtained some use for 'this impure and sinful body'. It causes 'immense benefit'. This can be done by *bodhisattvas*, who do it for a positive purpose and are not afraid of rebirth (263–5). Here we begin to see glimpses of what might be called a characteristically Mahāyāna perspective on the body, *qua* Mahāyāna.

THE BODY AS MEDIUM FOR FULFILLING THE BODHISATTVA VOW

Melford Spiro, writing on Burmese Theravāda Buddhism, has com-mented that the Buddhist attitude to the body 'comes close to being phobic' (1982, 296). This is perhaps misleading inasmuch as it universal-izes a particular meditation which has a set role in terms of a spiritual path and the place of practitioners on that path. Meditation on the foulness of the body is, as we have seen, appropriate to the second of Atiśa and Tsong kha pa's three scopes. Those who are at the levels of the lesser and superior scopes meditate on the preciousness of the body – notably the human body – but in different ways and with different results. In Tsong kha pa's tradition of the *lam rim* those of the lesser scope, beginners, are exhorted first to appreciate the rarity and value of a human rebirth. Compared with the number of sentient beings, those born as humans are very rare indeed. To be a human with what is called the 'precious human rebirth' – to follow the Teaching and not to be too stupid to understand it, to have the material requisites, chance and leisure to practise – is held to be much, much rarer still. The human body is said to be more valuable than a wish-fulfilling gem, but only if it is used in a positive way. Otherwise it is just a foul body. In other words, the human body not used for noble ends is disgusting. It gains value precisely through the ways in which it can be used. The meditator subsequently meditates on the impermanence of the body, how easily it can be lost before it has been used in a positive way, and future rebirths which are likely to be unpleasant. The result of all this is to generate enthusiasm and a strong motivation for following the Dharma, the Teaching, right away.

Thus, far from always treating the body in a negative way, we will often find Mahāyāna works which speak of the immense value of the (human) body. In the same verse as he refers to the body as an enemy, Āryadeva adds that even so the body should be protected, since a 'virtuous person who lives for a long time produces much merit from it' (Lang 1983, 183/561). According to the *Ratnacūḍa Sūtra*, quoted by Śāntideva in his *Śikṣāsamuccaya*, one who is aware of the impermanence of the body, far from seeking death or being phobically enfeebled, gains vigour in acting virtuously as a *bodhisattva* for the benefit of others (Bendall and Rouse 1971, 217). His compassion for others, whose bodies are like his own, increases. We are clearly here at the level of the superior Mahāyāna scope. For the genuine follower of Mahāyāna the body is valuable precisely inasmuch as it can be used to advance on the path to Buddhahood for the benefit of all sentient beings, and to benefit others in more direct and immediate ways. In the *Akṣayamati Sūtra* the *bodhisattva* is exhorted to recognize that the body entails various sufferings, but not to be distressed by this, since the body can be used for his or her great purpose (ibid., 24).

There are many stories popular in Mahāyāna countries in which the Buddha in a previous life as a *bodhisattva*, or some other *bodhisattva*, gives his body or various limbs for the benefit of others and in order to advance on the path to Buddhahood. The *bodhisattva* gives his tongue (*Vajradhvaja*

Sūtra, ibid., 25–6); he gives his body to a starving tigress (*Suvarṇabhāsottama Sūtra*, ch. 18 in Emmerick 1970). In the *Aṣṭāsāhasrikā Prajñāpāramitā Sūtra* Sadāprarudita offers his body – his 'heart, blood and marrow' – in order to raise money to honour the Dharma-preacher Dharmodgata (Conze 1973, 285). From a Mahāyāna perspective this is the other and complementary side to the meditations on the foulness of the body, and its reality presupposes such meditations while at the same time going beyond them. The meditations on foulness entail renunciation, but renunciation for the *bodhisattva* is not in order to abandon the world by entering some transcendent *nirvāṇa*. It is rather to benefit the world. When a Vietnamese monk burns himself to death in order to draw attention to the suppression of Buddhism it is seen in Mahāyāna as being a noble act. He is able to do it, perhaps, because of his meditations on the undesirability of the body, but it is not done *because* the body is undesirable. Rather something usually accepted as intimately precious is sacrificed for the benefit of others. Meditation on impurity provides the means, not the motive. In this respect the beneficent suicide of the true *bodhisattva* is very different from the suicides condemned by I-ching. Śāntideva in his *Bodhicaryāvatāra* meditates and resolves that having renounced this foul body it has now been given to others. Since it is no longer his own, he has no wish for it, they are free to kill, abuse, or beat it as they please (Batchelor 1979, 3:13 ff).[2]

A particularly striking case of a *bodhisattva* using the body as skilful means for teaching others detachment can be found in the *Gaṇḍavyūha Sūtra*. The beautiful Vasumitrā appears to all to be a woman of ill-repute, but in reality she is an advanced *bodhisattva* teaching detachment from lust in whatever way is appropriate. Some, it seems, require kissing and embracing in order to enter the enlightening absorptions which free them from this passion (Cleary 1987, 148). In another *sūtra* a female *bodhisattva* declares that 'If a living being is bound by his lust, I shall let him enjoy his lust first and then show him [the suffering of] departure' (Ku 1984, 237). This called 'enjoyable skill-in-means'. Loving and leaving gains cosmic significance! The *Tathāgatācintyaguhyanirdeśa Sūtra* has the female *bodhisattva* also showing her lover her body as a corpse in order to release him from his lust (ibid., 140–1).

---

[2] The fact that Śāntideva adds in v. 15 that he will let them do anything with his body which does not harm themselves, shows that this is a meditation to be mediated through wisdom into actual practice. If a sadist wishes to kill him it would be unwise to let the sadist have his fun simply because the body has been given away. For a sadist to kill will have extremely unpleasant karmic results for the sadist, and may also prevent the *bodhisattva* from doing even more virtuous deeds (at least in this life).

Thus the *bodhisattva* embraces embodiment in order to release others from their addiction to the flesh. The body becomes the crucial means for fulfilling the *bodhisattva*'s vows, that is, for the attainment of Buddhahood. The *bodhisattva* does not fear rebirth, the taking up of further bodies. As Śāntideva puts it, in a favourite quotation of the Dalai Lama:

> For as long as space endures
> And for as long as living beings remain,
> Until then may I too abide
> To dispel the misery of the world.
> (*Bodhicaryāvatāra* 10:55, trans. Batchelor)

The single coin with two sides – the foul, disgusting nature of the body combined with its great value to the *bodhisattva* in fulfilling his or her spiritual path and benefitting others – represents a doctrinal awareness in Mahāyāna which structurally parallels the Theravāda actuality uncovered by Steven Collins. Collins contrasts the deconstruction and rejection of the body in Theravāda meditation with its construction in social behaviour as a unified and valued public object, two dimensions which he shows are not contradictory in Theravāda, but complementary. The characteristically Mahāyāna aspect lies in an elaborate extension and formalization of the valued public dimension, the linking of this dimension with what is now seen as the actual final goal of Buddhism as Buddhism – the temporal and supreme benefit of all sentient beings – so that the social dimension becomes part of the very definition of what final enlightenment, Buddhahood, involves. This dimension and linking becomes doctrinally explicit. It is no longer a question of deconstruction in meditation and reconstruction in social behaviour, but rather two types of meditation linked to different stages on the spiritual path and therefore different doctrinal categories. The ideal then is that the use of the body realized and appreciated through meditation on the *bodhicitta*, and the beneficial ways in which one can help others, should be expressed in actuality through the *bodhisattva*'s social involvement and engagement.

ALTERNATIVE BODIES AND DIFFERENT WORLDS

As we have seen, the purpose of contemplating the disgusting nature of the body is renunciation. But there is another reason for these meditations mentioned in Mahāyāna sources, although in its most general aspect it need not be thought of as uniquely Mahāyāna. The

Vimalakīrtinirdeśa Sūtra, after a discourse on the repulsiveness of the human body, exhorts the practitioner, full of disgust for a body of *that* type to turn towards the contrasting body of the Buddha (Lamotte 1962, 133–8). *Buddhānusmṛti* – the recollection of the Buddha, particularly his wonderful body – is common to all Buddhist traditions, and indicates the possibility of a body which is not that of ordinary humanity (Williams 1989, 217ff.). There is some evidence from literary sources of a fervent desire which must have been widespread to see this wondrous body. What little evidence we have suggests that this desire may have been felt particularly acutely in Central Asian Buddhism during the formative years of Mahāyāna, and it has been argued that Kashmir and Central Asia were major influences on the development of devotional cults based on visualizing 'celestial' *bodhisattvas* or Buddhas, centered on their glorified bodies more often than not dwelling in Pure Lands, those realms – frequently portrayed affectively in heaven-like terms – where a Buddha dwells in glorified form teaching the Mahāyāna to all who come near, and emanating infinite forms to help those others who are unable to do so.

I have discussed elsewhere the lengthy and complex issue of the different 'bodies' of the Buddha (ibid., ch. 8). It is clear from our previous treatment of the word *kāya* that this term covers a range of meanings not all of which are equatable with our usual use of 'body' as a material organism. These other meanings (support, collection, etc.) are all relevant to understanding the *dharmakāya* as it is presented in the different Buddhist traditions – the Buddha's true nature, the lesson of which he embodies. I do want to say some words here, however, about the Buddha's glorified body, what in the developed three-body schema is usually classed as the Enjoyment Body, for this body is said to be some sort of physical organism, which possesses the 112 marks of a superior being and dwells in a Pure Land teaching only – in the developed theory – Mahāyāna to those *bodhisattvas* who are advanced enough to reach that level.

In Mahāyāna the Buddha's glorified body is pure, and its dwelling place is pure. Thus the Buddhist condemnation of the putrid and disgusting body does not extend to all bodies. Vasubandhu makes this last point explicit in his *Karmasiddhiprakaraṇa*, for if all bodies were defiled there could be no bodies for gods (Anacker 1984, 118). In the Brāhmanic world view gods are said to have pure bodies; the same applies in Buddhism. The discovery of sweat on the body, a polluting bodily fluid, is precisely one of the signs that a god is going to die. To be polluted is to cease to be a god. In the light of our discussion of pollution and the human body we might imagine a culture which simply does not see urine, faeces, etc. as polluting. Animals, after all, do not see these things this way. From the general position of Indian culture those beings are simply wrong; such things are polluting whether we know it or not. But, in terms of Buddhist practice, not to see these things as polluting would be unfortunate for the very pragmatic reason that it would neutralize a particularly powerful meditation. Detachment from the body is necessary to enlightenment. Without an appreciation of impurity, therefore, enlightenment is that much harder to attain, which may be one reason why gods in Buddhism are often thought of as gods to be incapable of enlightenment. In general it is usually (although by no means invariably) said in Buddhism that enlightenment requires a human body.

Pollution in Brāhmanic culture is intimately related to issues of food. Food can very easily become polluted, through contact with the ground, the bodily fluids of another, or an outcaste and so on (Lannoy 1971, 151–4). Polluted food pollutes the eater. One's own bodily fluids are the body's discards, again polluting to oneself and others. In the *Udayanavat-sarājaparivarta Sūtra* it is said that the nine holes of the body ooze due to pollutions from various foods (Paul 1979, 43). Thus glorified beings with pure bodies are frequently thought in India not to eat, and not to emit bodily fluids of any type. There is a myth well known in all Buddhist circles which relates to what happens at the beginning of a cosmic cycle (see, for example, Ling 1981, 102ff). The myth looks to the Buddhist equivalent of the Golden Age, and traces moral and cosmic decadence. In the (relative) beginnings beings were 'mind-made' and born into a World of Radiance, without sun, moon etc., or sex distinctions. This birth is not sexual. It is called 'self-produced' or 'spontaneous'. These beings were happy, blissful, 'self-luminous, traversing the air, continuing in glory'. They did not need to eat gross material food. As time passed a scum formed on the surface of the earth. Some beings tasted it. It was delicious. Others joined in. With the eating of food, the beings lost their radiance and bliss, and the sun, moon, and other luminous heavenly bodies appeared. As further time passed, the bodies of beings became coarse, concepts of beauty and arrogance appeared. Other foods developed, bodies became coarser, and eventually sex distinctions also appeared. With sex distinctions came sex acts, after sex acts stealing, violence, and other immoralities.

Thus food causes cosmic decadence. Coarse food eventually brings about coarse polluting bodies, with the sexual intercourse and womb-birth which involves polluting bodily fluids. The strong connection between Buddhist doctrinal thought and ideas usually considered part of the Brāhmanic social nexus (purity, pollution, with their implications for social position and conduct) is worth underlining. Nevertheless commentators do not condemn all food. According to Asaṅga some beings to the present day, such as gods (of the lower god realms) and hell beings, live on a very subtle kind of food which involves no nasty pollutants such as faeces or urine.

A linkage of the primal radiant beings' bodies with the Brāhmanic conception of gods on the one hand, and Buddhas on the other, is made quite clear by Tsong kha pa who states explicitly that the radiant beings' bodies are akin to those of the gods and also, rather strangely, possess the 112 marks of a superior being which are also possessed (although not exclusively) by Buddhas (Wayman 1974, 26–7). It is only to be expected that beings in Pure Lands such as Buddhas, and others who, according to general Pure Land devotional theory are only one stage removed from Buddhahood, would have bodies at least as good as those radiant beings at the beginning of the cosmic cycle prior to moral and physical collapse. Indeed, in one major sense, not having coarse material bodies which result from gross food and produce bodily fluids is precisely one constituent of what it means to live in a *Pure* Land, and thus to be close to a glorified Buddha. Even outside Mahāyāna thought, within a tradition which some consider had a major influence on the rise of Mahāyāna, it had already been taught that the Buddha in our gross world only appears to have a body of the same coarse nature as the rest of us. Really his body is self-born and mind-made, just like the pure bodies of the radiant beings. It is not surprising, therefore, that the Buddha in this tradition is said to have a body free from dirt, a mouth essentially clean, never to be really ill, and not to need to eat. His appearing to do all these things is simply in order to conform to the ways of the world (Harrison 1982). In Mahāyāna, too, we find *sūtras* stating that the Buddha has no polluting elements such as faeces and urine, and has no feeling of hunger or thirst, which presumably means that he does not need to eat. Because the Buddha's body is the result of immeasurable merit it could not be an ordinary polluted and polluting body (Ku 1984, 231–2). In the Pure Lands as well as we find that there are no faeces, no urine, no tears, and no bodily ailments (Dantinne 1983, 191, 221). If there is food in the Pure Land, it is miraculous food which does not need to be farmed but just appears when wanted (ibid., 193, 222). The *Akṣobhyavyūha Sūtra* points out that this is just like one of the god realms. Birth in the Pure Land is generally said to be self-born or spontaneous (see the *Sukhāvatīvyūha* para. 41, 249), and would appear to entail a mind-made body.

In non-Mahāyāna Buddhism, too, human beings living in a polluted world full of suffering seek rebirth elsewhere in bodies which are not subject to pollution. There are the god realms, although from those ordinary people cannot normally become enlightened. Or there is rebirth with the forthcoming Buddha, Maitreya, in the god realm where he awaits his last birth. The aspirant could then return to this earth with Maitreya and attain enlightenment at his feet (Conze 1959, 238–42). In Mahāyāna, on the other hand, there are infinite Buddhas and *bodhisattvas* all indicating the supremacy of their way by the very purity of their being, dwelling at this very moment in Pure Lands where they can help the aspirant immediately on the path to enlightenment. According to the *Sukhāvatīvyūha Sūtra* it is not difficult, through the compassion of a particular Buddha known as Amitābha, to attain his Pure Land. In most cases one simply needs to call his name with faith as few as ten times and rebirth is assured. In this life we can meditate visualizing that Pure Land and look forward to a flight from this body towards purity and no oozing apertures.[3] There, in those auspicious surroundings, we can attain perfect Buddhahood for the benefit of all sentient beings. Given the premises, this is a sensible form of religion. Little wonder, then, that for the benefit of sentient beings some Pure Land practitioners in China – including, according to one tradition, the great master Shan-tao – committed suicide in order to hasten their rebirth into the Pure Land (Williams 1989, 260).

SUBTLE BODIES, ILLUSORY BODIES AND RAINBOW BODIES –
ENTER THE VAJRAYĀNA

Buddhist Tantricism (Vajrayāna) springs from obscure sources undoubtedly in some sense under the influence from outside the Buddhist tradition as it is usually understood. It may well have remained for a number of centuries outside the mainstream tradition of monastically and doctrinally based Buddhist orthodoxy. But crystallized into a complete system by those who employ the most extensive development

---

[3] In Amitābha's Pure Land it is said there are only men, i.e. all beings have what the Buddhist tradition has almost universally considered to be the best sort of body for spiritual development, although given that the possession of even male sexual organs is linked with a fairly coarse bodily (and nutritional) development it is not clear what this might mean. The Buddha, as is well known, is supposed to have as one of his marks a male organ which is withdrawn into a sheath, a presence yet absence of maleness.

of Tantric techniques and theories – the Tibetans – Vajrayāna Buddhism has become integrated in a more or less comfortable way into wider Mahāyāna framework. Thus Mahāyāna is seen to have two wings: Sūtrayāna, the doctrines and practices based on non-Tantric materials, and Vajrayāna. According to Tsong kha pa and his tradition, there is no difference between these two in eventual goal – full Buddhahood for the benefit of all sentient beings. The difference lies solely in technique, which entails in the case of the highest class of Tantra, Anuttarayoga, a difference in speed of attainment, the attainment of complete enlightenment from beginning to end in one lifetime (Hopkins 1977, especially 139ff). Thus Buddhist Tantricism is thought to be a branch of Mahāyāna, and as such is animated through and through by the *bodhicitta*, the altruistic aspiration to highest enlightenment.

As a set of techniques for attaining Buddhahood and benefiting others there is a sense in which the body, its strata and potential, forms the principal theme of Vajrayāna thought and practice. According to the *Hevajra Tantra* 'with the non existence of the body, whence could there be bliss' (Snellgrove 1959, 2:2:35). 'Great gnosis dwells in the body . . . yet though it dwells in the body it is not born from the body' (ibid., 1:1:12). The saying of the Tantric *yogin* Saraha (tenth century CE?) is well known: 'I have not seen a place of pilgrimage and an abode of bliss like my body.' Within this very body is the Buddha himself hidden (Dasgupta 1946, cited in Eliade 1969, 228). Kāṇha (date roughly similar to Saraha?), 'the naked yogin, the skullbearer' 'wanders alone in the city of his body' (Beyer 1974, 259). The modern Tibetan Lama Yeshe, in his valuable elementary *Introduction to Tantra*, states that, while in the Sūtrayāna the physical body is largely a negative factor, indeed the truth of Suffering incarnate, in Vajrayāna the material human body itself is supremely valuable because such a body contains within it the very constituents whereby highest enlightenment can be attained in one lifetime (1987, 116–17). Nevertheless, as we have seen, in the Mahāyāna variety of Sūtrayāna the body is not seen as entirely a negative factor; it has considerable value in that through the body the *bodhisattva* path can be expressed. The strong contrast in treatment of the body between Sūtra and Vajrayāna is exaggerated. Yet there is something in that contrast, for in Vajrayāna the value of the body lies in the very *structure* of the physical body itself. The human body is valuable not only because of what can be done with it, but also because of what it actually *is*. In Vajrayāna terminology as it pertains to the highest systems (generally known as Anuttarayoga) which alone are relevant here, the human body is the basis of enlightenment because it bears the channels, winds, and drops.

According to Tantric theory (owing something to older pan-Indian doctrines reflected, for example, in classical Indian and Tibetan medical theory) the human being has three bodies – coarse, subtle, and very subtle. The coarse body is what we normally call the physical body, consisting of the four great elements (earth, water, fire, and wind) and their derivatives. The subtle body is made up of 72,000 channels, rather like veins, which pervade the coarse body. In these channels flow 'subtle winds' – vital energies – and it is these vital energies which are responsible for all bodily movement. Winds are also essential to the motility of consciousness, for consciousness is said to 'ride' on the winds 'as a horseman rides his mount'. Generally in Tantric theory this is always the case – consciousness, even the Buddha's consciousness, always has a physical correlate in a wind, although there are different levels of wind corresponding to coarse, subtle, and very subtle consciousnesses. Thus there is a direct link made in Tantric theory between consciousness and the physical. The quality of the wind can affect that of consciousness (and vice versa). A very mobile wind can generate a frantic coarse consciousness. Since winds as physical can be affected by physical means, physical means come to play a role in affecting consciousness, and actions relating directly to the body become intimately related to the issue of bringing about enlightenment. Moreover consciousness can also affect through the winds the gross physical body (this becomes important in Tibetan medical theory. See Donden 1986, 63–4). Thus the winds are said to be the root of *saṃsāra* and *nirvāṇa* (Dhargyey 1985, 120). From the point of view of Vajrayāna meditation the most important wind is the life-supporting wind. In Tantric theory it is held to be the very subtle life-supporting wind, bearing its very subtle consciousness, which travels out of the body at death, and into a new body. In a living body this very subtle wind and consciousness is said to be centered in a very small hole in the central channel of the heart wheel (*cakra*: see K. Gyatso 1982, 27). It is this very subtle wind and consciousness which is the very subtle body, and in normal human life it is contained within a small sphere the size of a large mustard seed or small pea composed of red and white drops, white above and red below. This sphere lasts until death, and is known as the indestructible drop.

In the body there are three main channels. The central channel runs in a straight line from the tip of the sexual organ to the crown of the head, and then arches down to a spot between the eyebrows. It is said to be pale blue. Generally, immediately to either side are the left and right channels, white and red respectively. At four places the left and right channels coil round the central channel, and these coils form knots which are the channel wheels (*cakras*). These are at the navel, the heart, the throat and the crown of the head. There are also two other *cakras*, at the 'secret place' at the base of the spine and the opening or tip of the sex organ.[4]

The white and red drops are said to be the pure essence of the seminal fluid and blood respectively. Subtle drops are contained in the central channel hole at the heart wheel; gross or coarse drops flow through the other channels. The head forms the main centre for the white drops, while the red drops are centered in the navel. The melting and flowing of these drops generates bliss. The seed for blood comes from the mother; that for seminal fluid from the father. Thus it is in general only a human body, a result of womb-birth requiring male and female parents, which has the white and red drops. Since the possession of these drops and the bliss which they can generate, which implies also channels, winds, and a coarse womb-born body, is a *sine qua non* of generating Buddhahood in Tantric thought, it follows that in general only a human body provides the facilities for attaining perfect enlightenment (K. Gyatso 1982, 28. Cf. 217ff.).

Normally the winds are said to move in channels other than the central channel, and are thus accompanied by coarse everyday consciousness. There are exceptions, notably at death where the winds dissolve involuntarily into the central channel, and then into the very subtle life-supporting wind at the heart, which eventually leaves the body. Since the purpose of Tantric meditation is also to cause the winds to enter and dissolve into the central channel, some of the experiences of consciousness which accompany these death processes are similar to those of the enlightenment process. Thus death may be used by a *yogin* in order to help his attainment of enlightenment (see Hopkins and Rinbochay 1979).

The path to enlightenment in Tantric meditation using the body-structure delineated above involves two stages: the Generation Stage and the Completion Stage. In the Generation Stage the meditator visualizes that he or she is already a 'deity', a Tantric Buddha. In

---

[4] My account of these aspects of Tantric subtle physiology is brief and compressed in the extreme, intended to give a rough impressionistic account only. For details see the books by Cozort 1986, 42ff; Dhargyey 1985, 114ff., and in particular K. Gyatso, 1982, 17ff. Some systems, for example, have further *cakras*.

Anuttarayoga Tantra this would be a Buddha in wrathful symbolic form, such as Vajrabhairava, Hevajra, or Cakrasaṃvara, thus integrating the darker side of the psyche into the process of enlightenment. This 'deity' is surrounded by his universe, the *maṇḍala*.[5]

The process of meditation in Generation Stage *yoga* is broadly to visualize the deity in front and then absorb it into the meditator's mind. The mind is strongly visualized to take on the aspect of clear-light bliss radiance, as the mind of the deity. With this mind the *yogin* meditates on emptiness. This visualization brings about an integration of the bliss mind and emptiness. From this bliss and emptiness (which is said to be like the *dharmakāya* and also the clear-light experience of death) out of a vibration of compassion arises one's own mind as a seed-syllable (like the Enjoyment Body of the Buddha, and also the intermediate state between death and rebirth). The seed-syllable which is one's own mind then becomes that mind in the form of, say, Vajrabhairava. The visualization must be perfect; the world around the meditator must be seen to be Vajrabhairava's pure *maṇḍala* realm, and all sound his sacred formulae or *mantras*. This is akin to the process of rebirth, and the generation of the Transformation Body of the Buddha, the third of the Buddha's bodies in Sūtra Mahāyāna. Thus in meditation the whole death process is transmuted into the path, and the body of the meditator is in this very life seen to be the pure body of a Buddha. All is already the Buddha's Pure Land; there is in reality no impurity, no pollution. One's own mind is a Buddha's mind of clear-light bliss and emptiness. This is done in deep meditation, but it continues even outside the meditation session. Gradually it becomes more real, but the *yogin* is still only using a relatively gross consciousness. He cannot use really subtle consciousnesses until the winds can be made in this life and under control to genuinely dissolve into the central channel (as they do at death).

In the Completion Stage this process actually occurs. Through the power of deep and strong meditation the winds are gathered together and caused to enter the central channel, causing various drops to melt, generating various blisses and wisdoms (for elaborate details see Cozort

---

[5] An important part of Anuttarayoga Tantra practice is the body *maṇḍala*, whereby the meditator visualizes that he or she generates each of the parts of his or her body, or visualizes each of the parts of the lama's body, as a deity. For an example, see Gyatso 1988, 73ff. Thus, both within and outside meditation, the practitioner is expected to see his or her body full of Buddhas and *bodhisattvas*, and, of course, totally pure, a Pure Land itself. Indeed it is common in Tantric practice to see the body as a microcosm, containing the universes and all the deities, with the spinal column as Mt. Meru, the central cosmic axis. See here the now rather dated works by S. B. Dasgupta 1974 reprint, 146–7; and Tucci 1969, 108–9.

1986 and K. Gyatso 1982). Eventually the winds are caused to dissolve partly and then completely into the indestructible drop at the heart. By the time this happens in meditation the coarse and even the subtle bodies of the *yogin* are as if dead, cataleptic. He is in a completely internalized, very subtle, and spiritual world. The psychological accompaniment to the dissolution into the indestructible drop is the dawning in meditation of the very subtle mind of what is called 'metaphorical' (*dpe*) clear-light. While dwelling in this state, the winds are said to eventually vibrate slightly, and from this vibration one genuinely appears in the form of the Tantric deity, as what is called an 'illusory body'. While remaining in this body the meditator experiences a reversal of consciousness back to ordinary everyday consciousness. The illusory body is said to shimmer, like a mirage, to pass through things. It is made of the very subtle wind, and visible only to oneself and others who have the illusory body. It appears to be some sort of 'astral' body, but it is held to be in a sense more real than the ordinary gross body. It has all the 112 marks of a superior being (Cozort 1986, 95). One is reminded here of the primal radiant beings in the old Buddhist myth, and Tsong kha pa specifically equates them, although, since the primal beings had not attained their bodies through controlled meditation, they fell from their state (Wayman 1974, 26–7). The illusory body is said to be capable of separating from the coarse body and travelling wherever it pleases. It is the meditator in the body of a Tantric deity generated while still involved with an ordinary coarse human body – indeed it is in general only possible because the meditator possesses an ordinary coarse human body.

At the end of meditation the illusory body has to return to the coarse body. For this reason among others it is said to be an impure illusory body. So long as one is chained in this way to a coarse physical body it is held to be impossible to attain full Buddhahood, although even when one attains the pure illusory body and can rapidly reach Buddhahood it remains possible to use one's coarse physical body if that would be of benefit to sentient beings (Cozort 1986, 99). When the innate blissful mind of clear-light is used to meditate on emptiness[6] a state of what is called 'actual' clear-light occurs, and from that, by a similar process to the one outlined earlier, there occurs the pure illusory body. In the state of the pure illusory body one has the possibility of extraordinary

---

[6] Absence of inherent existence in the object under analysis, and therefore in all things. For emptiness as understood in Madhyamaka, which is presupposed in the largely dGe lugs (pronounced: Geluk) account of Anuttarayoga Tantra followed here, see Williams 1989; 60–3. Not all Tibetan traditions would accept the nature or role of emptiness here. Cf. ibid., 107–8.

miraculous achievements, emanating endless other forms, all of which can study, visit Buddhas to receive teachings, and help sentient beings.[7] Meditating on emptiness and performing various deeds for the benefit of sentient beings in this state, the factors of immense wisdom and merit necessary for Buddhahood, which are said in the Sutrayana traditions to take incalculable aeons to complete, are rapidly completed, and full Buddhahood is reached when the clear-light mind becomes the mind of the Buddha, and the pure illusory body becomes the Buddha's actual body (Cozort 1986, 112). The generation of Buddhahood is thereby a generation out of the very subtle body. Thus, in this account of Anuttarayoga Tantric meditation based on materials from Tsong kha pa's dGe lugs (pronounced: Geluk) tradition, the Tantric physiology and yogic techniques are integrated into the path to Buddhahood for the benefit of all sentient beings as it is portrayed in Sūtra Mahāyāna.

We have seen that in both Sūtra and Vajrayānas an enlightened Buddha can and does manifest infinite bodies for the benefit of sentient beings. It is important to appreciate this point. In spite of the generally disparaging attitude towards the body in Buddhism, for Mahāyāna Buddhism enlightenment is thought of in essentially embodied terms. There are two constituents of perfect Buddhahood – wisdom and compassion. As Nāgārjuna points out, wisdom generated during the *bodhisattva* path eventually produces the Buddha's *dharmakāya*. Merit, through compassion, brings about the form bodies of the Buddha, which is to say, in the three-body schema (not known by Nāgārjuna), the glorified Enjoyment Body and the numerous transformation bodies (Hopkins 1975, v. 212). Thus something like what we normally call

---

[7] For many accounts of the wonderful deeds said to be done by advanced *bodhisattvas* in numerous bodies, the myriads of emanations which are held to appear from every pore of their bodies, the miraculous abilities by which they manifest 'unobstructed, all-pervasive' bodies filling the universe with sun and moon appearing within, see the *Gaṇḍavyūha Sūtra* (Cleary 1987, *passim*). The Tantric account is thought by its adherents to explain how these wonderful experiences are possible, and can be brought about. The extraordinary descriptions of the *Gaṇḍavyūha Sūtra*, which presumably to some extent describe the actual experiences of meditators, whereby the body is felt paradoxically to expand to encompass the entire universe, while still remaining the meditator's body, may be one of the influences behind the great Japanese Zen Master Dōgen's (1200–53) view that 'The entire world of the ten directions is nothing but the true human body' (Dōgen 1985, 91). Moreover for the *Gaṇḍavyūha Sūtra* the Buddha him-(her- or it-)self is ultimately the entire universe – all things (see Williams 1989, ch. 6). Dōgen's concern in this, as all issues, was to completely transcend all forms of dualism. The body and mind are one; furthermore 'All things and all phenomena are just one mind – nothing is excluded or unrelated' (ibid., 154). Thus truly the body is all things. For descriptions of Zen *satori* in which this form of expansion seems to occur, see Dumoulin 1963, 273ff. Crucial to Dōgen's perspective is his non-dualistic vision of the Buddha-nature whereby all things in their very nature (cherry blossom *qua* cherry blossom), are the Buddha-nature.

embodiment is an essential constituent of Buddhahood, but an embodiment which is manifested solely for the benefit of others. This ties the embodiment of Buddhahood with the compassionate, pragmatic attitude to the body manifested in the *bodhisattva* path. We have also seen that, from the Anuttarayoga Tantric perspective, the actual material cause of the embodiments of the Buddha is the very subtle wind. As a wind is always necessary to consciousness, wherever there is consciousness there is also embodiment in the minimal sense of accompanying form as wind. For a Buddha, this form expresses itself through infinite compassion as the Buddha's form bodies.

The rainbow body referred to in the rDzogs chen (pronounced: Dzokchen) traditions in Tibet is however slightly different from the illusory body which we have looked at so far. We are dealing here with a different meditation system and different practices, felt by followers of rDzogs chen to be superior to those of Anuttarayoga. The contemporary Tibetan teacher Namkhai Norbu, who is himself a practitioner of rDzogs chen, explains that the rainbow body of this tradition is unlike the illusory bodies of other teachings in that the rainbow body has no dependence on very subtle wind. Inasmuch as wind (which is after all form) is thought to be a relative dimension, it is held to be not involved in the very highest attainment (Norbu 1986, 124). Those masters in rDzogs chen who are thought to attain the rainbow body, at death are said to dissolve the very elements of their bodies into light, which is held to be the pure essence of the elements.[8] Namkhai Norbu mentions a number of cases known to him. Often stories of rDzogs chen masters concern simple folk, unlearned, unpretentious, frequently married lay people, but quietly advanced in *yoga*. A *mantra*-carver, as recently as 1952, gave instructions that he should be closed up in a tent for seven days. After that time it is said that all that was found in the tent were his nails and hair. Many are said to have seen this, including Chinese Communist officials (1989, 39). Hair and nails are always left behind when a rDzogs chen practitioner attains the rainbow body, as they are thought to be the body's impurities, too impure to purify into light. Thus the rainbow body is held to be the result of purifying into light the actual body of the meditator, which continues to exist in its subtle light aspect (ibid., 39–40). According to Namkhai Norbu the practitioner is therefore thought not really to have 'died'. He or she remains active in a rainbow body, helping sentient beings, and can be seen by those who are sufficiently advanced.

---

[8] The clear light into which the elements of the body are dissolved is their essential nature. It is an aspect of their absolute dimension as undefiled mind-energy unlike, as such, wind.

He adds that great *yogins* like Padmasambhava (eighth century) however do not need to wait until death in order to manifest the rainbow body. They participate in the Great Transfer, whereby such practitioners transform into a rainbow body while still alive. Their bodies are said to gradually become invisible to one with normal perception (Norbu 1986, 128–9).[9]

There are here differences in detail between the rDzogs chen and the Anuttarayoga Tantra systems. Nevertheless, in broad attitude to the body they are similar, and in harmony with the wider Mahāyāna context. Compassion requires some sort of active embodiment; embodiment is an expression of spiritual attainment, the spontaneous overflow of enlightenment which necessarily flows for the benefit of all sentient beings precisely because it *is* enlightenment. For both Buddha and *bodhisattva* in their different ways the body is the expression of their spiritual being. Their body is their Being-for-others (to use a Sartrean term, a concept Sartre himself never came to terms with). But that Being-for-others is thought in Mahāyāna to be only possible because of a letting-go of the body which comes in general from meditations on repulsiveness. Thus Mahāyāna, as is right and proper, is linked with the wider Buddhist framework. The third scope presupposes progression through the two previous scopes. As His Holiness the Dalai Lama has said somewhere, 'In Buddhism there are no absolutes. But if there were one it would be compassion.' If there were one it follows that it would be, for the Buddhas and *bodhisattvas*, their active embodiment.

BIBLIOGRAPHY

Anacker, S. (1984), *Seven Works of Vasubandhu*, Delhi: Motilal Banarsidass.
Atiśa (1983), *Bodhipathapradīpa* in *A Lamp for the Path and Commentary*, trans. Richard Sherburne, SJ, London: George Allen and Unwin.
Batchelor, S. (1979), *A Guide to the Bodhisattva's Way of Life*, Dharamsala: Library of Tibetan Works and Archives.
Bendall, C. and Rouse, W. H. D. (1971 reprint), *Śikṣā Samuccaya*, Delhi: Motilal Banarsidass.

---

[9] Namkhai Norbu specifically states that the rainbow body and the attainment of the Great Transfer are the same, one just comes earlier than the other (1986, 129). According to Tulku Thondup, and possibly the great rNying ma scholar kLong chen rab byams pa (1308–63), however, they are different (Thondup 1989, 82–6; see also 138–9), and for the Great Transfer we have a 'light body'. Perhaps there is a difference here within the rDzogs chen tradition. Cf. the *Kālacakra Tantra* tradition which is in many relevant respects unlike other Anuttarayoga Tantra traditions (Cozort 1986, 118ff., and Dhargyey 1985).

Beyer, S. (1974), *The Buddhist Experience: Sources and Interpretations*, Encino and Belmont, CA: Dickenson.

Cleary, T. (1987), *The Flower Ornament Scripture*, vol. 2, Boulder, Colo.: Shambhala.

Conze, E. (1959), *Buddhist Scriptures*, London: Penguin.

(1973), *The Perfection of Wisdom in Eight Thousand Lines and its Verse Summary*, Bolinas: Four Seasons Foundation.

Cozort, D. (1986), *Highest Yoga Tantra*, New York: Snow Lion.

Dantinne, J. (1983), *La Splendeur de l'Inébranlable (Akṣobhyavyūha)*, I, Louvain-la-Neuve: Institut Orientaliste.

Dasgupta, S. B. (1946), *Obscure Religious Cults*, University of Calcutta.

(1974 reprint), *An Introduction to Tantric Buddhism*, Berkeley and London: Shambhala.

Dhargyey, Geshe Ngawang (1985), *Kālacakra Tantra*, trans. by Allan Wallace and Ivanka Vana Jakic, Dharamsala: Library of Tibetan Works and Archives.

Dōgen (1985), *Moon in a Dewdrop: Writings of Zen Master Dōgen*, trans. various, ed. Kazuaki Tanahashi, San Francisco: North Point Press.

Donden, Y. (1986), *Healing Through Balance: An Introduction to Tibetan Medicine*, ed. and trans. by J. Hopkins, New York: Snow Lion.

Dumoulin, H. (1963), *A History of Zen Buddhism*, trans. Paul Peachey, Boston: Beacon.

Eliade, M. (1969), *Yoga: Immortality and Freedom*, trans. by Willard Trask, 2nd edn, London: Routledge and Kegan Paul.

Emmerick, R. (1970), *The Sūtra of Golden Light*, London: Luzac.

Gombrich, R. (1988), *Theravāda Buddhism: A Social History from Ancient Benares to Modern Columbo*, London: Routledge.

Griffiths, Paul J., Hakamaya, Noriaki, Keenan, John P., Swanson, and Paul, L. (1989), *The Realm of Awakening: Chapter 10 of Asaṅga's Mahāyānasaṃgraha*, New York and Oxford: Oxford University Press.

Gyatso, Geshe Kelsang (1982), *Clear Light of Bliss: Mahāmudrā in Vajrāyana Buddhism*, trans. by Tenzin Norbu, London: Wisdom.

Gyatso Tenzin, H. H. the Dalai Lama (1988), *The Union of Bliss and Emptiness*, trans. by Thupten Jinpa, New York: Snow Lion.

Harrison, P. M. (1982), 'Sanskrit fragments of a Lokottaravādin tradition' in eds. L. A. Hercus, F. B. J. Kuiper, T. Rajapatirana, and E. R. Skrzypczak *Indological and Buddhist Studies*, Canberra: Australian National University, Faculty of Asian Studies, 211–34.

Hopkins, J. (1977), *Tantra in Tibet: The Great Exposition of Secret Mantra*, London: George Allen and Unwin.

Hopkins, J., with L. Rimpoche and Klein, A. (1975), *The Precious Garland and The Song of the Four Mindfulnesses*, by Nāgārjuna and the Seventh Dalai Lama, London: George Allen and Unwin.

Hopkins, J., with Rinbochay, L. (1979), *Death, Intermediate State and Rebirth in Tibetan Buddhism*, London: Rider.

Hurvitz, L. (1976), *Scripture of the Lotus Blossom of the Fine Dharma*, New York: Columbia University Press.

Jan Yun-hua (1964), 'Buddhist self-immolation in Medieval China', *History of Religions* 4, 243–65.

Ku, Cheng-mei (1984), 'The Mahāyānic View of Women: A Doctrinal Study', unpublished Ph.D. thesis, University of Wisconsin-Madison.

Lamotte, E. (1962), 'L'Enseignement de Vimalakīrti (Vimalakīrtinirdeśa)', Louvain: University of Louvain.

Lang, K. (1983), 'Āryadeva on the Bodhisattva's Cultivation of Merit and Knowledge', unpublished Ph.D. thesis, University of Washington.

Lannoy, R. (1971), *The Speaking Tree*, Oxford University Press.

Ling, T. (1981), *The Buddha's Philosophy of Man: Early Indian Buddhist Dialogues*, London: Dent Everyman.

Mathur, K. S. (1964), *Caste and Ritual in a Malwa Village*, London: Asia Publishing House.

Meyer, J. J. (1930), *Sexual Life in Ancient India*, vol. 1, London: George Routledge and Sons.

Norbu, Namkhai (1986), *The Crystal and the Way of Light*, New York and London: Routledge and Kegan Paul.

——— (1989), *Dzogchen: The Self-Perfected State*, trans. by J. Shane, London: Arkana.

Paul, D. Y. (1979), *Women in Buddhism*, Berkeley, CA: Asian Humanities Press.

Régamey, K. (1990 reprint), *Philosophy in the Samādhirājasūtra: Three Chapters from the Samādhirājasūtra*, Delhi: Motilal Banarsidass.

Śāntideva (1961), *Śikṣāsamuccaya*, ed. P. L. Vaidya, Darbhanga: Mithila Institute.

Snellgrove, D. (1959), *The Hevajra Tantra: A Critical Study*, 2 vols., London: Oxford University Press.

Spiro, M. (1982), *Buddhism and Society: A Great Tradition and its Burmese Vicissitudes*, Berkeley, CA: University of California Press.

Sukhāvatīvyūha Sūtra, in P. L. Vaidya (ed.) (1961), *Mahāyānasūtrasaṃgraha*, part I, Darbhanga: Mithila Institute.

Thondup Rinpoche, Tulku (1989), *Buddha Mind: An Anthology of Longchen Rabjam's Writings on Dzogpa Chenpo*, ed. H. Talbott, New York: Snow Lion.

Tsong kha pa (1990), *mNyam med Tsong kha pa chen pos mdzad pa'i Byang chub lam rim che ba*, Delhi: Sherab Gyaltsen. Reprint of the Beijing edition.

Tucci, G. (1969), *The Theory and Practice of the Maṇḍala*, trans. by A. H. Brodrick, London: Rider.

Wayman, A. (1974), *The Buddhist Tantras: Light on Indo-Tibetan Esotericism*, London: Routledge and Kegan Paul.

Welch, H. (1967), *The Practice of Chinese Buddhism, 1900–1950*, Cambridge, MA: Harvard University Press.

Williams, P. (1989), *Mahāyāna Buddhism: The Doctrinal Foundations*, London: Routledge.

Yeshe, Lama (1987), *Introduction to Tantra: A Vision of Totality*, London: Wisdom.

The Taoist body and cosmic prayer

Michael Saso

The use of the entire human body, mind, heart, and belly, as a single unit in meditation is a unique phenomenon found in Taoist and Tantric Buddhist practice. Though using different terms to describe the process, Taoist ritual contemplation and Buddhist Tantric practice define prayer as the simultaneous use of mind, mouth, and body for encountering the absolute (*wu-wei chih tao*) or the other-shore Anuttara-samyak-saṁbodhi. In this meditative process, the mind is used to contemplate the sacred image, the mouth is used to chant sacred phrases that make the image one with the meditator, and the body is used to seal the union through physical dance steps or hand dance, called mudra (*shou-yin*, hand seal).

These three locations in the Taoist and the Tantric Buddhist body are focus points for a kind of prayer that visualizes the human body and the outer cosmos to be related, that is, to be analogously one in their meditative and orderly physical cycle of activity. To put it more succinctly, the human body in both systems relates to the cosmos in the manner shown in the following structural model:

body	(inner cosmos)		cosmos	Tantric	time	Buddha as:	Tao as:
head	*ch'i* (energy/breath)	mind	heaven	mandala	past	dharma	gestator
heart	*shen* (spirit)	will	earth	mantra	future	lotus	mediator
belly	*ching* (intuition)	intuition	underworld	mudra	present	vajra	indweller

In this chart the inner body is seen to be related to the external world both spatially and temporally. That is, the head with its powers of mind is related to the heavens, the heart to the earth, and the belly to the water or the fiery underworld. The head houses the intellect, the power to form images and concepts, judge, and regulate *ch'i* (the flow and concentration of breath). Thus one of the main points of focus during meditation is the mind and its regulation. The chest, residence of the will, focused in the heart and pericardial region, is linked with the earth and its physical

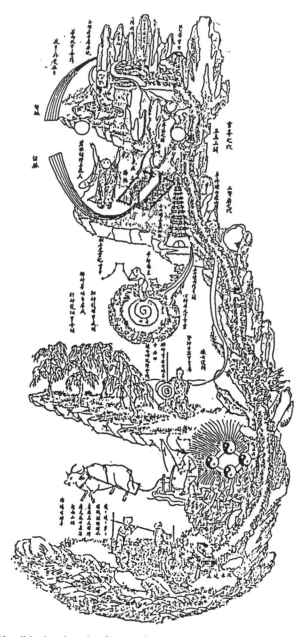

Plate 9   Woodblock print, the Cosmic Body, nineteenth-century, Baiyun Temple,
Beijing. The head corresponds to the heavens, the chest to earth, and the lower
abdomen to the water and river delta areas close to the underworld.

changes. The belly, residence of the intuitive powers and feelings, relates directly to the lower parts of nature, the watery and fiery underworlds. It is to be noted that for both Taoist and Buddhist meditation (specifically Zen and Tantric meditation) the belly is the focal point for meditative concentration, as will be explained below.

It is the aim of this study to focus on the ways in which Taoist ritual and meditation integrate the body with the workings of the outer cosmos. I have treated of Tantric Buddhist meditation in other places.[1] Its similarity with Taoist forms of ritual and meditation is striking, and the parallels many.[2] While pointing out some of these analogies, I shall for the most part explain the textual origins and the practice of the Taoist form of inner and outer cosmic prayer, that is, the way in which the body and the outer nature are envisioned as part of a natural process.

TAOISM

By way of definition it must be pointed out to the reader unfamiliar with the special terminology of the Taoist meditative system that Taoism (pronounced 'Daoism') is a religious philosophy born and nurtured in China, as distinct from Buddhism which was brought to China from India. For the Chinese, religion is a matter of practices and festivals, rather than a belief-oriented system; and Chinese culture is influenced by three different teaching systems, Confucian, Buddhist, and Taoist, a state of affairs aptly expressed in the Chinese phrase *San-chiao kuei-i*, 'three teachings, one culture'. Thus the teachings of Confucius are guidelines for social behaviour, Buddhism for the afterlife, and Taoism for relations between the human body and nature. There is no contradiction, in the Chinese mind, in practising all three of these systems at once. Thus one can practise Taoist or Zen meditation and still maintain one's own belief system (such as Christian, Islamic, or agnostic). Taoism is, in this system, a way of keeping one's life in harmony with nature's temporal and spatial changes. We shall now examine these relationships, in their literary origins, practice, and analogies with other systems.

The classical meditative and liturgical texts used by Taoists as means

---

[1] For which see Saso 1990c.
[2] See Saso, *Mystic, Shaman, Oracle, Priest* (forthcoming), an extended study of the differences in the mystic way of 'apophasis', or 'kenotic' emptying of mind and heart, in comparison with the Mongol and Korean shaman, the Tibetan oracle, and the Bon, Naxi Dongba, and redhead Taoist rituals.

to, or as background preparation for, liturgical prayer and meditation are the following:

1. The *I-ching* (Book of Changes). This ancient book, also included with the Confucian classics, is used as a meditative rather than a divining manual. The structural basis of the *I-ching*, the eight trigrams, is also the design for the meditative and liturgical mandala used by Taoists for liturgy and meditation.[3]

2. The *Tao-te-ching* (Scripture of the Tao and the Virtue, associated with the ancient philosopher Lao-tzu), and the *Chuang-tzu* (Writings of Chuang-tzu, the second Taoist philosopher, died 290 BC), are required reading for Taoists of the various major schools. These are: the Cheng-i (Orthodox Unity) Taoists, today centred on Dragon-Tiger Mountain (Lung-hu-shan), also known as the T'ien-shih (Celestial Master) sect, that was founded by Chang Tao-ling in AD 142;[4] the Shang-ch'ing (Highest Clarity) Taoists of Mount Mao (Mao-shan) near Nanking who go back to revelations in AD 364–370; and the Ch'üan-chen (Complete Perfection) school located in the White Cloud Monastery (Pai-yün-kuan) in Peking, that was first developed by Wang Ch'ung-yang in 1167.

3. The *yin-yang wu-hsing* cosmology, translated as 'yin-yang five phases', or 'five movers' by various Western scholars. Texts explaining yin-yang cosmology as it relates to Taoist liturgy and meditation are mainly found in the *Tao-tsang*.[5]

4. The *Tao-tsang* (Taoist canon, edited in AD 1445), and its various supplements (AD 1607, 1920), contain the texts for both liturgy and meditation.[6]

5. Private teachings and hand-written manuscripts which Taoist masters keep for their own disciples, many of which texts are not found in

---

[3] For a further explanation of the use of the eight trigrams in liturgy, see Saso 1990a, 81, and Saso 1990b, 10.

[4] The Cheng-i school, known as 'The Tao of the Celestial Master', is attributed to Chang Tao-ling at the end of the Han dynasty (second century AD). His grandson, Chang Lu, was the theocratic head of the school in 'Han-chung' (Sze-ch'uan and Shensi) at the beginning of the Three Kingdoms period (third century AD). Ts'ao Ts'ao, ruler of one of these kingdoms, granted the movement official status. Their registers (*lu*; lists of rituals, spirits and their summons, meditations and powers granted to the Taoists of this school) are found in *TT* 878 (see n. 9, below). The association of Cheng-i Taoism with Dragon-Tiger Mountain (Lung-hu-shan) in Kiangsi province can perhaps be dated to the Sung dynasty (960–1280), though legend says that Chang Tao-ling moved there during his lifetime.

[5] For studies of liturgical Taoism in western languages, see Schipper 1982, 1985, and Lagerwey 1987; for Taoist meditation, see Robinet 1979.

[6] The *Tao-tsang* has recently been published in reduced editions in Taiwan (1961) and PR China (1988).

the published canon. These manuscripts are an important source for studying the Taoist tradition. Lengthy field experience with personal practice of meditation is required to receive accurate and valid explanations of meditative practices.[7]

The meaning of the term Taoist (*tao-shih*) in the Chinese usage is defined by the use of the above texts, rituals, and meditations within a prescribed limit and range of teachings, according to designated rules of transmission. A true Taoist is licensed to perform in accord with schools and teaching approved by government authority.[8] The schools and their methods of ritual-meditation include:

1. the Cheng-i meng-wei registers (*TT* 878),[9]
2. the Ling-pao (Numinous Treasure) scriptures,[10]
3. the Shang-ch'ing scriptures,[11]
4. the Pole Star registers,[12]
5. the Ch'ing-wei (Clear Tenuity) thunder registers,[13]
6. the Ch'üan-chen school.[14]

Besides these six major schools, there are other sects, including the Shen-hsiao (Divine Empyrean), the Lü-shan (Mount Lü), and other provincial Taoists, whose manner of performing rituals does not necessarily include the use of written materials or the practice of meditation. This kind of Taoist is called 'redhead' (*hung-t'ou*) in many parts of southeast China.[15] The rituals of the redhead Taoists are similar

[7] See Saso 1975 and 1978 for examples of hand-written manuals used by Taoist masters and not found in the extant canon. Three more copies of the Sung-dynasty canon have been recently found in PR China, but unfortunately have not yet been opened for scholarly study. Even with more complete copies of the canon, oral explanation of meditative and liturgical practice is always required to understand their applied meaning.

[8] This rule, which has been in use since the Six Dynasties (AD 260–560), and into the Sui-T'ang era (589–906), is continued in the PRC today. See Saso 1987, 1–7.

[9] References to the *Tao-tsang* (*TT*) use the Harvard-Yenching Index.

[10] The Ling-pao school was founded on the basis of Shang-ch'ing teachings and yin-yang cosmology in the late fourth century. The *Tung-hsüan* (Mystery Cavern) section of the Taoist canon traditionally holds its scriptures, but, in fact, fascicles with Ling-pao headings are found throughout the canon. The basic texts of the Ling-pao tradition are the *Ling-pao chen-wen* (True Writs of Numinous Treasure), for which see Saso 1977.

[11] Robinet 1979 and 1984 give an exposition of the Shang-ch'ing scriptures and the major meditative text of the school, the *Huang-t'ing-ching*.

[12] Robinet 1979, 159–273.

[13] See Boltz 1987, 39–41, 68–70.

[14] See Kubo 1967 for an extended study of the Ch'üan-chen school.

[15] See Saso and Chappell 1977, ch. 4, which includes the description by John Keupers of redhead ritual as found in northern Taiwan. The use of the word 'redhead' is not standard throughout southeast China and Taiwan. In northern Taiwan it usually refers to Taoists who specialize in rituals for the living, but do not use the 'heart-fasting, sitting in forgetfulness' meditations of the

in many ways to the Dongba rites of the Naxi and the Bonpo rituals of Tibet. The people of the villages where redhead priests work call them *fa-shih* (magician-priests) rather than *tao-shih* (Taoists). Thus the distinction between meditating ritual experts who are called Taoists and village healers called *fa-shih* is observed at the village level, if not always by scholars working from canonical texts.

There are other practices which do not follow the standard Chinese definition of *tao-shih* that are nevertheless (mistakenly, in my view) called 'Taoist' in the popular Western paperback press. Amongst these are the 'Tao of sex' which promotes the notion that long life can be attained by repressing the flow of semen, and secret societies such as the I-kuan-tao (Way of Unity) which have the word 'Tao' in their title. The former practice, called *fang-chung* (arts of the bedchamber) in Chinese, is forbidden to Taoists of the six major schools above.[16]

For the purpose of this study, the term *tao-shih* as used by the Taoists of the six major schools above refers only to men and women who have received a *lu* or register, which licenses him (or her) to perform public ritual and practise meditation within the canonical tradition. It is important to make this distinction when teaching the practice of Taoist meditation, because of the use of a special formula for emptying the body (i.e., the head, heart, and belly) of all spiritual energies and images and achieving union with the gestating principle of the cosmos.[17] The meditative process, which follows the forty-second chapter of the *Tao-te-ching*, is explained below. Thus, by definition, the term *tao-shih* and the meditations used by him or her in ritual and self-perfection practice are based on a self-emptying process which can perhaps best be described in Western terms as kenosis, i.e., the prayer of emptying. That is to say, meditation for the Taoists of the six major orders listed above today consists in emptying the images, spiritual powers, and impurities out of the macrocosm, and subsequently achieving union with the Gestating Tao.

six schools. In many parts of southern Taiwan the word 'redhead' refers only to *fa-shih* (exorcist-healers), as described in Keupers' article.

16　See Saso 1990b, 33. Repressing semen was supposed to bring longevity to the person who practised the arts of the bedchamber. The figure of the God of Longevity shows a white-bearded ancient holding a peach in one hand, and a gnarled staff in the other, with a huge extended forehead where the 'saved semen' is stored. *The Secret of the Golden Flower*, which has been translated several times into English (see Wilhelm 1962, Cleary 1992), is an example of a sexual hygiene manual wrongly interpreted by the translators to be a manual of meditation. The Taoists of the six schools today forbid the practice.

17　The term *wu-wei chih tao* is interpreted to be the Tao of Lao-tzu's forty-second chapter, 'The Tao gave birth to the One . . .' in the Taoist meditation tradition. The fourth chapter of the *Chuang-tzu* is cited in this regard by the Taoist meditation masters: namely, 'fasting in the heart, sitting in forgetfulness . . . united as One with the Tao'. See Saso 1990a, 115–17.

Ch'i, Shen, Ching

The earliest form of this meditation, called *fa-lu*, is attributed to the Celestial Master school.[18] Taoists still use this formula today to begin meditation.[19]

The early *fa-lu* developed from the notion that the human body is divided into three sections, corresponding to the heaven, earth, and watery underworld. Just as Tao gives birth to *ch'i*, yang and yin in the macrocosm, so also it gives birth to *ch'i*, *shen* (spirit; yang) and *ching* (intuition; yin) within the microcosm of the body. This correspondence incorporates all of the spirits of the outer cosmos within the human body. The correlation of micro- and macrocosm is illustrated in the following chart, as a gloss on the forty-second chapter of the *Tao-te-ching*.

The Tao (*wu-chi*) gives birth to:						
one	tai-chi	*ch'i*	heaven	head-mind	gestating	all star and heaven spirits
two	yang	*shen*	earth	heart-will	mediating	all earth, mountain spirits
three	yin	*ching*	water	belly-intuition	indwelling	all water spirits

The above chart is a structural rather than a conceptual model; that is, the slots rather than the words are important. Thus any triadic relationship may be fitted into the triple world model of the Taoist cosmos. When explaining the system, the Taoist master may write in place of 'head-heart-belly' the alchemical-meditation terms 'upper, middle, lower cinnabar fields'. Instead of 'heaven-earth-water' the words 'heaven, earth, underworld' or 'heaven, earth, man' are sometimes found. Three icons, symbols of the Tao as gestating, mediating, and indwelling, are displayed in the village temple when the Taoist master performs rites of cosmic renewal.[20] The Tao as gestating, 'Yuan-shih t'ien-tsun' (Heavenly Worthy of Primordial Beginning), the Tao as mediating, 'Ling-pao t'ien-tsun' (Heavenly Worthy of Numinous Treasure), and the Tao as indwelling, 'Tao-te t'ien-tsun' (Heavenly Worthy of the Tao and the Virtue), are summoned forth from the microcosm within the Taoist's body, the upper, middle, and lower

---

[18] See *TT* 193, *Teng-chen yin-chüeh* (Secret Instruction for the Ascent to Perfection), 3.6b. Here T'ao Hung-ching, ninth master of Mao-shan, attributes the *fa-lu* ritual meditation to the Han-chung region at the end of the Han period.

[19] See Saso 1978, ch. 5, for a detailed explanation of the *fa-lu*. The lengthy study of Ōfuchi (1983) gives a different version of the rite as practised in Taiwan.

[20] See Saso 1990a for a description of the rite of renewal (*chiao*) performed in village temples and Taoist monasteries throughout China.

cinnabar fields respectively, and visualized to be present. Their images
are suspended from the north wall of the village temple, the place of
honour reserved for the tutelary deity of the temple.[21]

Thus the mind energy (*ch'i*), soul-spirit in the heart (*shen*), and intuitive
powers of the belly (*ching*) are intimately related to the work of the Tao
gestating, mediating, and indwelling in nature. That which occurs in the
mind, heart, and belly of humans influences the entire outer cosmos.
The human mind controls *ch'i* (breath, energy). *Ch'i* is visualized to be
circulating through the body during meditations which the Taoists call
'internal alchemy', just as the Tao-gestated *ch'i* of nature brings about
the orderly changes of the seasons. The depths of the person, the fiery or
watery underworld, is a place from which souls in the underworld and
worries held in the belly are released by ritual acts and meditation. The
notion of soul (*shen*, or spirit), the immortal part of the person that
continues to exist in the invisible world after death, is at the core and base
of the Taoist system.

The burial robe of the marchioness of Tai found at Ma-wang-tui (and
dating from the second century BC), shows a triple-layered cosmos in
which the lady appears three times: in the centre of the robe on earth, at
the foot of the robe in the underworld, and at the top of the robe in the
heavens. A banquet is laid out between the underworld and the realm of
the living, with the image of a pig, mediator between the human world
and the afterlife, supporting the banquet. Two dragons, representing the
circulation of *ch'i* energy encircle the centre (earth) and top (heaven)
pastiche, while two large fish are entwined around the vision of hell. The
offering of the food-banquet for the dead, and the presence of the freed
soul of the marchioness in the heavens, are connected by intertwining
layers of *ch'i*. The lady depicted in the heavens sits within the top central
position of tai-chi or primordial breath, with the moon, symbol of yin,
and the sun, symbol of yang, to her left and right. The transcendent Tao
of *wu-wei* from which the scenes are gestated is not pictured on the
surface of the robe. A copy of the *Tao-te-ching* is found by the side of the
princess, suggesting the use of the manual from an early time.[22]

[21] Note that the statues and images ordinarily displayed in the village temple are covered by
embroidered cloth during Taoist ritual. The pantheon of Taoist spirits is displayed in the form of
scrolls suspended around the temple, a mandala or geometrically patterned representation of the
Taoist cosmos, and the Taoist's body. The Taoist priest meditates and offers ritual from the
centre of the mandala, harmonizing the village and each of its members with the workings of Tao
in nature.

[22] See Saso 1990b, 61, for an illustration of the Ma-wang-tui robe. The illustrations on the robe give
solid archaeological evidence of the correspondence of head, chest, and belly with the heavens,
earth, and underworld.

The notion that the soul leaves the body at death, and descends into a fiery or watery underworld to be alchemically purified before being released into the heavens is found throughout Asia until the modern day. In the healing rites of the Mongolian and Korean shaman much effort is given to finding the soul, and releasing it from the sufferings of the underworld as a means to heal illness or rectify the misfortunes of the living.[23] The Taoists also consider the soul to be an essential part of the inner body's wholeness and healing. The soul leaves the body and death occurs when the *ch'i* (life energy) and the *ching* (physical powers) are exhausted. *Ch'i* and *ching* are used whenever the mind makes judgements and the will pursues selfish or evil goals. When *ch'i* (mind energy), *shen* (soul), and *ching* (intuition) are in harmony, on the other hand, the body is healthy, lives to a ripe old age and works in concert with nature. These three powers are perfected by the meditations of internal alchemy.

The Taoist notion of *shen* (soul/spirit) makes the heart or 'middle cinnabar field' the residence of the soul in the body; the will and the power to love and hate are functions of the soul. Next the *ch'i*, centred in the upper cinnabar field, in the centre of the head, governs the powers of intellect, imagination (visualization), and the projection or circulation of *ch'i* energy during meditation. The lower cinnabar field in the abdomen, third, governs the emotions and the intuitive powers. The process of emptying the mind of images and the heart of desires awakens the ability of the intuitive powers of the belly to realize oneness with the Tao's presence, working in nature. This process is also used meditatively in Cheng-i style ritual, as is explained below.

PLANTING THE REALIZED WRIT

The Cheng-i (Celestial Master) school also developed a meditative system in which the five phases of the outer cosmos with all their colours and temporal and spatial relationships stored in the five organs of the body are summoned forth and displayed in the temple during ritual meditation. This meditation is performed in conjunction with the three-cinnabar-field ritual meditation.

The meditation in which the five phases are visualized as spiritual

---

[23] The differences between the Altaic shaman (Koren, Mongol, Oweke, and others), and the Tibetan oracle, the Chinese possessed medium, Tibetan Bon, and the Naxi Dongba rites are significant. In the opinion of the author, these practices should not be linked together with the generic term 'shaman', as happens so frequently in western publications. See my forthcoming work *Mystic, Shaman, Oracle, Priest* (research in progress).

energies, brought forth from within the microcosm of the Taoist's body and 'planted' in the five directions of the village temple is called *an-chen-wen* ('planting the realized writ') in Taoist ritual terminology.[24] The five phases are summoned forth from the Taoist's body and planted in the village temple as a part of the cyclical renewal of the cosmos. Only after the body is emptied of all images and energies can union with the Tao be realized. The relationship between the body and the outer cosmos is represented as follows in the orally transmitted teachings of the Taoist master:

space	colour	time	organ	symbol	phase	goal
east	green	spring	liver	dragon	wood	plant
south	red	summer	heart	phoenix	fire	ripen
west	white	autumn	lungs	tiger	metal	reap
north	purple	winter	kidneys	turtle	water	rest
centre	yellow	centre[a]	spleen	crucible[a]	earth	union

[a] the body's centre is seen to be an alchemical furnace

A contract between the human body's microcosm and the macrocosm is made by 'planting' a talisman in five containers of rice, each placed in the east, south, west, north, and centre of the Taoist altar. This ritual, called *su-ch'i*, is found in structural form in Ch'üan-chen Taoist ritual of the Sung dynasty, and among minority ethnic groups of southwest China.[25] There is a significant difference in the popular trance medium, shaman, and Ch'üan-chen use of the five colours for healing *vis-à-vis* the classical Taoist use of the five auras: the classical Taoist rite 'empties' (through means of apophasis) the colours from the body, while the popular medium, shaman and Ch'üan-chen Taoist ritual 'fills' (by

[24] This meditation is found in a liturgy called *su-ch'i* used in rites of renewal. *Su-ch'i* means 'night announcement', and is usually, but not always, performed late at night, symbolizing that moment when yin (night, darkness) gestates yang (light, day), in the daily process of yin's and yang's cycle. The 'planting of the (five) true or Tao-realized writs' is structurally similar to the imperial court ritual called 'monthly commands' and 'bright temple'. These were rites offered seasonally for the emperor's and nation's well-being. Taoists were called upon to perform especially the latter, and were even appointed to the Board of Rites during the Ming dynasty. See Liu 1976. The earliest accounts of Chang Tao-ling recorded in the dynastic histories relate that the founder of the Celestial Master school used the 'monthly commands' chapter of the *Li-chi* (Book of Rites) as a model for liturgy.

[25] The structural use of five colours, directions, images, and five talismanic contracts is found among Yao and other minority groups in Yün-nan, Kui-chou, Kuangsi, and Laos. A *su-ch'i* ritual manual found on the Laotian–Chinese border in a Yao collection is in the author's possession. Taoism among the Yao and other minorities has been studied by Professor Jacques Lemoine of Paris (see Lemoine 1982).

kataphasis) the consciousness and the body with the colour and image. This distinction marks a crucial difference in the medium-shaman experience on the one hand and the mystic 'kenotic' experience on the other.

In the classical Taoist meditation, based on the emptying philosophy of Lao-tzu and the *Chuang-tzu*, the meditator systematically summons the five colours out from the body's internal organs, and 'plants' them in the five directions, around the sacred area in which the meditative ritual takes place. He or she uses the eidetic (creative) imagination to construct a mandala-like representation of the five colours, visualized as five spirits, to the east, south, west, north, and directly in front of the meditator. These spirit images connect the human body to specific stars and constellations in the heavens. Thus the human body becomes one with the stars in the heavens (head), the seasons and spatial directions of earth (chest), and the frightening images of demons that control the underworld (belly):

space	colour	spirit	start	daemon	valour[26]
east	green	Fu-hsi	dragon	Chu-mang	3
south	red	Shen-nung	scorpio	Chu-jung	2
centre	yellow	Huang-ti	N. Pole Star	Hou-t'u	5
west	white	Shao-hao	Big Dipper	Ju-shou	4
north	purple	Chuan-hsü	Wu-ti[27]	Hsüan-hsü	1

To establish this relationship between the body and the outer cosmos, the Taoist inserts a coloured talisman into a bushel of rice placed in the east, south, centre, west, and north of the ritual area,

[26] The numbers in the last column (titled 'valour') refer to the *Ho-t'u* (Sacred River Chart) used in Taoist meditation for visualization processes, which bring about kenotic emptying before union with the transcendent Tao. The stars, on the other hand, represent the constellations that surround the North Pole Star or centre of the northern heavens. Just as the heavens revolve around the North Pole Star, so the Taoist must always be aware of Tao's presence in the lower cinnabar field within the body. The stars that surround the North Pole Star and the five organs that are their counterparts in the body, must 'have audience with the Tao', as Taoist terminology has it.

[27] The *Wu-ti-tso* is a Chinese constellation of the northern heavens consisting of five stars, representing the five thrones of the kings of the five phases. The numbers 1, 3, 5, 7, and 9 represent the North Pole Star, the Three Pure Ones (south), the Five Thrones (north), the Seven Stars of the Big Dipper (west), and the Nine Stars of Dragon (east). This numerical arrangement is used only for the constellations surrounding the North Pole Star. The numbers of the *Ho-t'u* chart of the Prior Heavens in the last line, 1, 2, 3, 4, and 5, stand for the 'raw' or newly born powers of the five phases. The numbers 6, 7, 8, 9, and 10 represent the 'cooked' or the ripened phases. See Saso 1990a, ch. 1, for an explanation of the *Ho-t'u* 'Prior Heavens' symbol.

respectively. The talisman is sometimes drawn on a coloured piece of cloth, according to the direction, i.e., green in the east, red in the south, and so forth. At other times the talisman is drawn in the air so that scholars and bystanders may not see it. To draw the talisman is itself a sacred act, taught only to the disciples of the Taoist master.[28] The countenances of the various spirits and daemons envisioned during the meditation are taught orally to the disciple. Scrolls are hung around the sacred meditation area only during village ritual, depicting for the laity the images and location of the Taoist spirits in the sacred ritual area.[29]

THE TAO OF TRANSCENDENT BIRTHING

Once the body has been emptied of all spirits and images, the process of the Tao-gestating nature is reversed in order to attain union with the Tao of gestation. Just as the Tao gave birth to the one, two, three, and the myriad creatures in an outward procession, so now the Taoist master walks back over the way of the gestating Tao to reach the Tao of transcendent birthing. To do this meditation of inner alchemy, the five colours are refined by a meditative process into three base colours: purple, gold-yellow, and white. The three base colours, symbols of impediments to union with the Tao, are burned to ashes with fire from the heart, and washed with water from the kidneys 'until nothing remains'. The process is as follows:[30]

(1) The green wood of east and the red fire of south are combined in the 'lower cinnabar field' (lower belly) of the meditator until a bright purple aura is envisioned, emanating from the entire belly. This bright purple colour symbolizes primordial ch'i, the energy gestated when 'Tao gave birth to the one'. The bright purple ch'i is stored in the pineal gland

---

[28] The Taoists of the lower Yangtze river area, including Mao-shan, Su-chou, Wu-hsi, and Shanghai, draw the talismans in the air by moving the eyes, or more specifically the 'wisdom eye' located in the centre of the forehead. The talisman is kept a secret from lay people and scholars because the procedure for learning the meditation requires practising the way of the *Tao-te-ching* and the *Chuang-tzu*, and taking the vows of a Taoist practitioner, which include the promise not to use Taoist meditation to earn money or gain fame and reputation, and to preserve the sacredness of the meditative system from secular or commercial use. The meditation must be learned from a Taoist master, as a part of an oral rather than a written tradition.

[29] Buddhist temples also make use of the four heavenly kings to guard their gates, just as Taoists use protective spirits and daemons around the sacred area where the meditation ritual takes place. Tantric Buddhist temples in Japan and Tibet make special use of these figures as a part of permanent temple iconography. The Taoist spirits are used in the village temple only during ritual meditation, then rolled up and hidden in the Taoist's private library collection.

[30] See also Saso 1990a, ch. 2, for a description of this process.

in the head, the upper cinnabar field, the seat of thought and judgement.

(2) The energies of yellow earth in the centre of the cosmos are refined into a bright gold colour, in the lower cinnabar field furnace, a process visualized to take place in the belly of the meditator. The bright gold aura represents the human will, the power of love and compassion. This energy is stored in the middle cinnabar field, the heart.

(3) The energies of west's metal and north's water are brought into the fires of the lower cinnabar field in the body, and refined until they turn a bright white. This bright white energy represents the intuitive powers of wisdom.

These three powers are called *ch'i*, the source of intellect, *shen*, the soul or source of the human will, and *ching*, the emotional and intuitive powers of the belly. It is important to note that, in the Taoist and Buddhist prayer systems, intellect and judgement are lodged in the head, will or love in the heart, and intuition and mystic union with the transcendent in the belly. Thus prayer which touches the ultimate or transcendent must take place in the belly, not in the head. The intellect is limited in its knowledge to data that come through the senses, while the intuitive powers of the belly are aware of the absolute directly. This awareness can only take place when the intellect and will are 'empty', i.e., in the state of kenosis, a 'dark night' of the intellect and senses.

In the final act of inner alchemical meditation, the three colours purple, yellow, and white are circulated through the body and brought to rest in the lower cinnabar field, the 'centering' point of the meditator. Fire is brought from the pericardial region, to burn all images of the sacred and secular. Water is visualized as gushing upward from the kidneys to wash away and extinguish all desires from the heart. When all colours, images, and desires are burned away, the Tao's presence is felt in the empty centre of the microcosm.[31]

The goal of the meditation, described in the Inner Chapters (1–7) of the *Chuang-tzu* is to bring about a great peace and detachment in the meditator, allowing him or her to be always at one with the workings of the Tao in greater nature. Such a person's very presence can bring great blessing to the village community. The people bring their petitions to the Taoist at this point of village ritual, to have them presented before the transcendent Tao. The Taoist dances the ancient 'Steps of Yü' at this point, used to stop the floods and restore nature's blessing in China's

---

[31] The meditation of union is attributed to the fourth-century woman mystic Wei Hua-ts'un of the Shang-ch'ing school. See Saso 1995.

mythical past.[32] The names of each person in the village are written on the grand memorial sent to the heavens by fire after the rite has ended. The Taoist then dances a second dance, called 'Intoxicated with Heaven's Peace', during which the five talismans planted in the village community are harvested and stored in the five organs of the Taoist and the villager participants. The cycle of gestation, planting, harvesting, and contemplating the Tao present in the cosmos complete the ritual meditation.

The four mantic words of the *I-ching* are used by the traditional Taoist masters as a means to explain the Tao's workings in nature. *Yüan* stands for Tao's primordial planting, *heng* for offering ritual, *li* for harvesting, and *chen* for contemplating and resting in Tao's presence. The tradition of ritual meditation practised in this manner can be found in the major Taoist centres of China, including Dragon-Tiger mountain in Kiangsi province, Mao-shan near Nanking in Kiangsu Province, Wu-tang-shan in Hupei, Hsin-chu city in Taiwan, and other Taoism centres throughout China.

OTHER RITUAL MEDITATIONS

Besides the traditional rites of the major Taoist schools, there are many other kinds of meditation and ritual practice used by the Taoists of modern China. The Ch'üan-chen Taoists, approved by the government of the People's Republic as the official custodians of many Taoist shrines open to the public, separate meditation from the rituals used to fulfil the liturgical and festival needs of the people. Pai-yün-kuan (White Cloud Temple) in Peking held a grand Chiao Ritual (Lo-ch'eng-chiao) in September, 1993, to dedicate the repairing and reopening of the temple after the destruction of the Cultural Revolution. Eight rituals of reversal (*chiao*) were performed simultaneously, by Taoists from all over China. For most of the Taoists at this public event the rites followed the external form of chanting canonical texts, sending off memorials and petitions to the heavens, and praying for blessing. True to the style of Ch'üan-chen Taoism, the meditations of emptying were done in private quite separately from the performance of public ritual.[33] Even though the

---

[32] For the liturgical dance called 'Steps of Yü', see Saso 1990a, 74.

[33] Min Chi-t'ing, the Ch'üan-chen Taoist master and teacher of liturgy at the Pai-yün-kuan, can perform the liturgies and knows the meditations of Cheng-i, Mao-shan, and Wu-tang-shan Taoism. On the occasion of the 1993 grand dedicatory rite of renewal, he pointed out to me and my students from the Academy of Social Sciences that reform Taoists perform the meditations of emptying separately from public ritual. The laity are just as aware of Tao's presence through prayer of petition, as are meditators in the state of kenosis, he said.

external ritual style is similar for traditional and reformed Taoists, the visualization techniques are different for each master.[34]

Taoist practitioners of martial arts (*wu-shu*) also make use of the methods for emptying the heart-mind and centering on the lower cinnabar field before exercise and competition in combat. The Pole Star School of martial arts, of Wu-tang-shan in Hu-pei province, as well as the Hsin-i and Shan-ta styles of boxing, use meditation as a basis for movements meant to defend the weak from harm and expel evil from the village community. Like the meditations of traditional Taoist kenosis, Wu-tang-shan style martial arts must be learned from a master. The meditation, which has been cursorily described in Western sources, is based upon an eidetic visualization in which the meditator sees him- or herself joined bodily with the Big Dipper in the heavens. One of the ways of centering on the Big Dipper's heavenly motion is as follows:

The meditation must be performed on a clear night when the Dipper is visible in the northern heavens. The meditator implants the four stars of the Dipper's pan on the left and right foot, right and left knee respectively. The three stars of the handle are then envisioned to be in the navel, the heart, and the tip of the tongue. The stars are implanted one-by-one while using a mudra or *shou-yin* hand symbol called the 'Pole Star Mudra'. The fourth and fifth fingers of both hands are pressed down over the thumb, while the index and middle finger are extended straight upward. The left hand is the scabbard and the right hand the sword of Hsüan-t'ien shang-ti (Highest Lord of the Dark Heaven), the spirit protector of the Wu-tang-shan martial arts. The sword mudra of the right hand is inserted into the scabbard of the left, then withdrawn and pointed towards the Big Dipper in the heavens. The meditator now looks at the Big Dipper, to determine in which direction the seventh star or tail of the Dipper is pointing. It is from this direction, at precisely this moment, that the transcendent Tao gestates primordial *ch'i* energy into the cosmos. The meditator notices how the pan of the Dipper always points to the centre of the northern heavens, just as he or she must always be centered on the Tao of transcendent action. The primordial *ch'i* of the Tao is seen to descend directly from the North Pole Star, through the tail of the Big Dipper and the sword mudra of the meditator into the lower

---

[34] Field researchers are often not aware of the variations found amongst the masters themselves, who pass on their meditative techniques to their disciples in an oral rather than a written tradition. Thus, a text from the Taoist canon can be interpreted in a variety of ways by the traditional and Ch'üan-chen masters. Saso 1978, ch. 5 gives many examples of how a modern Taoist interprets various texts quite differently from standard dictionary definitions. Scholars who rely on textual interpretation alone miss the meditative abundance of the Taoist tradition.

cinnabar field of the meditator.[35] Thus centered on the Tao, the circulation and storage of *ch'i* energy for the performance of martial arts is begun.

There are other forms of popular ritual found throughout southeast and southwest China that resemble or make use of Taoist texts and visualization, but are not truly Taoist; i.e., they are not kenotic or emptying in character, but rather kataphatic or filling with lesser spirits and local phenomena of nature. Though scholars and official Chinese sources often catalogue these practices as 'Taoist', because they use Taoist texts, symbols, and icons, in fact they are called by different names and have disparate effects on the body. Such practice can (but does not always) include what is called 'redhead' or 'red hat' (*hung-t'ou*) Taoism, the rituals of the Yao, Miao, Na-hsi, Moso, and Bon Tibetan practices, and the Ngapa or Ngawa rites of Tibetan conjurers in parts of Amdo (North East Tibet, Ch'ing-hai, Kansu, and parts of Kham East Tibet). Though the mantra incantations and mudra hand symbols used by Taoist and popular religious experts are often similar if not identical, the goal and physical effect on the body are different. The Taoist sense of emptying kenosis and peace distinguish the traditional meditative system from the popular rites that summon violent spirits, exorcise evil demons, and attempt to control the elements such as wind, rain, hail, snow, and other forces of nature. Apophasis or 'emptying' distinguishes the truly Taoist practice from the kataphatic or 'filling' rites of the medium, shaman, oracle and popular priest.

BIBLIOGRAPHY

Ames, R. (1992), 'The Meaning of Body in Classical Chinese Philosophy', in ed. T. P. Kasulis, with R. Ames and W. Dissanayake, *Self as Body in Asian Theory and Practice*, Albany, NY: SUNY Press, 157–78.
Ames, R. (ed.) (1994), with W. Dissanayake and T. P. Kasulis, *Self as Person in Asian Theory and Practice*, Albany, NY: SUNY Press.
Bokenkamp, S. (1983), 'Sources of the Ling-pao Scriptures', in ed. M. Strickmann, *Tantric and Taoist Studies in Honor of R. A. Stein*, Brussels: Institut belge des hautes études, 434–86.
Boltz, J. (1987), *A Survey of Taoist Literature*, Berkeley, CA: University of California Press.
Cleary, T. (trans.) (1992), *The Secret of the Golden Flower*, San Francisco: Harper.
Hay, J. (1929), 'The Body as Microcosmic Source of Macrocosmic Values in

---

[35] The registers containing the names and appearances of the spirits who are summoned for this meditation are contained in Saso 1979, ch. 3.

Calligraphy', in ed. T. P. Kasulis, with R. Ames and W. Dissanayake, *Self as Body in Asian Theory and Practice*, Albany, NY: SUNY Press, 179–212.

Kasulis, T. P. (ed. with R. Ames and W. Dissanayake) (1992), *Self as Body in Asian Theory and Practice*, Albany, NY: SUNY Press.

Keupers, J. (1977), 'A Description of the Fa-ch'ang ritual as practiced by the Lü Shan Taoists of North Taiwan,' in ed. M. Saso and D. W. Chappell, *Buddhist and Taoist Studies* I, Honolulu: University of Hawaii Press, ch. 4.

Kohn, L. (1991), 'Taoist Visions of the Body', *Journal of Chinese Philosophy* 18, 227–52.

Kubo, N. (1967[1], 1988), *Chūgoku no Shūklō Kaikaku, Zenshin Kyō no Seiritsu*, Kyōto: Hōzōkan.

Lagerwey, J. (1987), *Taoist Ritual in Chinese Society and History*, New York: Macmillan.

Lemoine, J. (1982), *Yao Ceremonial Paintings*, Bangkok: White Lotus.

Liu, T. Y. (1976), *Selected Papers from the Hall of Harmonious Wind*, Leiden: Brill.
(1983), *New Excursions into the Hall of Harmonious Wind*, Leiden: Brill.

Needham, J., et al. (1983), *Science and Civilization in China*, vol. 5, part 5, *Spagyrical Discovery and Invention – Physiological Alchemy*, Cambridge University Press.

Ōfuchi, N. (1983), *Chūgokujin no Shūkyō Girei*, Tokyo: Fukutake Shoten.

Robinet, I. (1979), *Meditation taoiste*, Paris: Dervy livres; ET, *Taoist Meditation*, trans. by N. Girardot and J. Pas, Albany, NY: SUNY Press, 1993.
(1984), *La révelation du Shangquing dans l'histoire du taoisme*, Paris: École Française d'Éxtreme Orient.

Saso, M. (ed.) (1975), *Chuang-lin Hsü Tao-tsang*, 25 vols. Tapei: Ch'eng-wen Press.
(1977), 'On the Ling-pao Chen-wen', *Tōhōshūkyō* 50, 1–22.
(1978), *The Teachings of Taoist Master Chuang*, New Haven: Yale University Press.
(1979), *Dōkyō Hiketsu Shōsei*, Tokyo: Ryūkei Shosha.
(1987), 'Religion in the People's Republic', *China News Analysis*, Hong Kong, 15 December, 1–7.
(1972[1], 1990a), *Taoism and the Rite of Cosmic Renewal*, Pullman: Washington State University Press.
(1990b), *Blue Dragon White Tiger: Taoist Rites of Passage*, Washington DC: The Taoist Center.
(1990c), *Tantric Art and Meditation*, Honolulu: University of Hawaii Press.
(1995), *The Gold Pavilion: Taoist Ways to Peace, Healing and Long Life*, Boston: Tuttle Press.

Saso, M. and Chappell, D. W. (eds.) (1977), *Buddhist and Taoist Studies*, I, Honolulu: University of Hawaii Press.

Schipper, R. (1978), 'The Taoist Body', *History of Religions* 17, 355–87.
(1982), *Le corps taoiste: Corps physique et corps social*, Paris: Libraire Artheme Fayard.
(1985), 'Vernacular and Classical Ritual in Taoism', *Journal of Asian Studies*, 45, 21–51.

Wilhelm, R. (tr.) (1929[1], 1962), *The Secret of the Golden Flower*, New York: Harcourt, Brace and World.

CHAPTER 14

Perceptions of the body in Japanese religion

Michael Pye

BODIES, BATHS, AND FESTIVALS

Perceptions of the body in Japanese religious situations cover a subtle range which corresponds to the spectrum of Japanese religions themselves. Yet these, for all their great variety, have much in common with each other. The same may be said of Japanese society and culture in general. That is, there is immense variety, and yet in general it is easy to discern common themes and common values which have a wide currency. Consider the train system. Although trains are run by various companies with competing styles and colour schemes, they all run on time except when earthquakes and typhoons intervene.[1] The importance of recognizing both variety and coherence in Japanese religion, in particular for the theme of 'body', will shortly be pursued further. Before turning to the dimension specifically provided by religion however, it is as well to notice the salient features concerning the body which are widely recognizable in ordinary Japanese life.

Physical touch is almost entirely avoided except in private. There is an almost total lack of openly demonstrative physical contact between family members or close friends. Kissing in public is practically unknown. Even greetings after considerable absence do not usually involve an embrace before the eyes of others. Far less is it acceptable for the bodies of unconnected persons to touch each other either casually or communicatively.

This is not related to shame, however, for others' bodies may be freely seen in gender-segregated public baths, except for tokenist and only semi-efficient concealment of the genitals when stepping in and out of

---

[1] This should not be construed in Britain as a statement in favour of the privatization of the railways, which is most unlikely to lead to the fine national service which is taken for granted in Japan. The *shinkansen* network, resulting from priority being given to a national strategy, is an example to the whole world.

the water itself. Rather, there is an invisible social wall around each body, which seems to emphasize physical individuality.

It may be contended, contrary to popular stereotypes about Japan, that this well-isolated, individual, physical body is assumed to be the locus of existential meaning, whether in terms of hedonistic enjoyment, personal well-being, some kind of self-transcending realization, or even suicide as an honourable solution to the insoluble. So it is therefore that sophisticated films may include an aesthetic exploration of pure sensuality without positing any profound relationship between persons. So it is that the forty-seven samurai ritually disembowelled themselves after avenging the stain on their master's reputation, and are honoured for it to this day, partly in *kabuki* performances and partly at their tombs at the Zen temple Sengakuji. So too is 'attaining buddhahood in this very body' (*sokushin jōbutsu*) the goal and promise of Shingon Buddhism, one of the major traditions of Japan and still a fountainhead of inspiration for many today. On this more will be said below.

Let us return however to the immediate social reality. As most residents in Japan would no doubt agree, the serried ranks of workers hurrying from underground station to office every morning hardly awaken a sense of 'buddhahood in this very body'. Nor do the millions returning each evening in various degrees of exhaustion, and in some cases of post-professional inebriation. Such vast numbers of bodies coming into involuntary close contact are less reminiscent of Buddhism than of the throngs who crush into the great Shinto shrines at their major festivals, or even the heaving, swaying mass of near naked young men transporting their divinity (*kami*) on a sacred journey or returning it to its usual home thereafter.

This near nakedness (never total[2]) is an intended contradiction to the normal clothing worn in daily life, as nowadays in the transport system and the office. The enforced proximity of bodies in train or bus is not supposed to create ecstasy. The squashed public tries to pretend that it is not squashed. In other words people try to pretend that there is no bodily contact between them even when it is inevitable. But in the near-nakedness of the 'naked' festival the situation is different. There is no question of physical contact between specific individuals. In this regard normal life rules are maintained. However the theoretically naked young

---

[2] Nakedness is not total on such occasions in spite of the term *hadaka-matsuri*, meaning 'naked festival', which is often used to refer to them. A loin-cloth is usual. Note that the majority of Shinto festivals do not even involve this near-nakedness. In a great many cases period costume is used, for a variety of historical reasons.

men represent one living organism. Their individuality is taken up ecstatically (with the assistance of *sake*, i.e. rice-wine) in the totality of the group. Together they surge forward, seeking the right destination, symbolizing in some cases what is nothing less than a social orgasm as rival groups seek to put on the finest display of frenzied activity or compete to be the first to insert their totems at a common shrine.[3]

VARIETY AND COHERENCE IN JAPANESE RELIGION

Various attempts have been made to identify the unifying themes of Japanese religion (singular), one of the best being that by H. Byron Earhart in his book *Japanese Religion, Unity and Diversity* (1982). However one major point has never been clearly stated and understood, namely that the original 'primal' religion, Shinto, has been radically displaced in modern times by an even more widely based primal religion now borne along by the people in general. Japan's new primal religion is one which has the fundamental features of any other, namely geographic and social particularism, a strong concern with genealogy and ancestors, careful attention to the passing of the year (which may be called 'calendricity') and a care for economic security and other forms of welfare. It is in this primal religion that Shinto and other specific religions of Japan in various ways participate, by means of a widely understood set of symbols and other features which together may be regarded as the common language of Japanese religion. This cannot be set out in full here.

Of course the various Buddhist traditions – denominations, sects, schools, movements – have their specific teachings and activities. The same is true for the many new religions, which incorporate features of very diverse origin, both foreign and indigenous. In particular however this also holds good for Shinto itself. Though still in principle, or perhaps in retrospect, a primal religion, Shinto has so adapted itself to the needs of the centuries, especially the modern centuries, that it has an extremely well-organized and to some extent centralized superstructure, just like any other specific religion in the same field. Thus, in principle, there is a high degree of specificity as between various religions in Japan, which should not be overlooked even when attention is drawn to the common features.

One of the general features of Japanese religions which is frequently noted by observers is that they share a great sense of practicality, and a

---

[3] A fine example of this may be seen in the *bonten-matsuri* (*matsuri* means festival) at Yokote in Akita Prefecture, which follows on the more well-known *kamakura* (i.e. igloo) festival in early February.

relative lack of interest in metaphysics. People often have a simplified view of the spiritual beings (*kami*) who are presumed to reside at the Shinto shrines. More intellectual concepts of 'God' are usually accompanied by some idea such as 'I could believe in God if I wanted to' or 'I believe in God but I do not believe in his existence.' The buddhas and *bodhisattvas* of Mahāyāna Buddhism for their part are generally felt to belong to a large family of celestial helpers who are competent each for some specific human need, such as good eyesight in the case of Yakushi Nyorai.[4] By contrast with the vagueness of metaphysics, the practicality of Japanese religion means real practice (*jissen*), ritualized with greater or less precision. For this reason alone the location, direction, and processes of the body are generally regarded, in a more or less relaxed way, as a matter of considerable importance.

BODY THEMES IN JAPANESE BUDDHISM

This practicality might be regarded as the common denominator of some of the best known Buddhist comments on the body. As anticipated above, 'attaining buddhahood in this very body' (*sokushin jōbutsu*) is the goal and the promise of Shingon Buddhism. In the *zazen* of the Sōtō Zen school the same equation is made in principle, for it is through *zazen*, meaning 'seated zen' in the very position of a meditating buddha, that one experiences one's own essential buddha-nature. Note in the same vein the less well-known formula 'mind and body (or form) are not two' (*shiki-shin funi*). Buddhahood itself is not an abstract metaphysical concept, but the fundamental quality of a living being. Admittedly the living being him- or herself is ordinarily not aware of this, thanks to the common condition of 'ignorance'[5] and therefore is provisionally in need of Buddhist instruction and Buddhist practice.[6] Accordingly much Japanese Buddhism is devoted to the ways and means of immediately seizing this reality in the here and now, common practice bearing the

[4] Cf. Pye 1983.
[5] On one reading of Buddhism 'ignorance' (Sanskrit *avidya,* Japanese *mumyō*) is the key feature of the human condition, being the first link in the sequence of dependent origination (*pratitya-samutpāda*), and that with which Buddhist understanding, or enlightenment, is contrasted. The enlightenment of the Buddha consisted in a penetrative understanding of his own karmic constitution (expressed as knowledge of former existences) and present state, while his body was poised in a state of perfect mindfulness under the tree in the forest. On a complementary reading, taking the four noble truths as a framework, the common condition of humankind is suffering.
[6] The *provisional* quality of *all* Buddhist instruction and practice is well understood by all thoughtful Buddhists and may be generally understood in terms of 'skilful means'. On this see the present writer's *Skilful Means, A Concept in Mahayana Buddhism* (Pye 1978).

promise of 'attaining' Buddhahood in this very body, even while, theoretically, there is nothing to attain which is not already given.

In passing it may be noted that this is related to the theme running through Y. Yuasa's fascinating work *The Body, Toward an Eastern Mind-Body Theory* (1987), for he emphasizes the process of attaining unity between the mind and the body first understood to be complementary and distinct from each other. As his translator T. P. Kasulis puts it: 'In the Japanese tradition, however, the mind–body theories generally focus on how a disciplined practice allows one to attain body–mind unity' (Yuasa 1987, 4). However Yuasa's work is not followed here as such, for it is based on a strongly oppositional view of 'eastern' and 'western' thought, which is not shared by all. Moreover 'eastern', 'Buddhist', and 'Japanese' seem to be largely conflated, while, in fact, the materials drawn upon are largely Buddhist. Note also that in the end his conclusions seem to be more about the mind or the psyche than about the body (ibid., 233–40).[7]

It is evident that this view of the body, this very body, as the locus of nothing less than enlightenment, that is, Buddhahood, has a complex background in Indian Mahāyāna Buddhism, transmitted via China and Korea to Japan. It was set out in a brief but influential work by Kūkai (774–835), who himself visited China directly and then established 'esoteric' Buddhism (i.e. *mikkyō* in the form of Shingon Buddhism) in Japan. This brief work has been translated two or three times, notably by Professor Hisao Inagaki under the title *Kūkai's Principle of Attaining Buddhahood with the Present Body*.[8] Though this work is brief it is packed with concepts and allusions which would need detailed elucidation. Indeed it pertains to the character of Shingon Buddhism that it is full of such details whose meaning is not immediately evident and into which it is necessary to be led. This is what is meant by 'esoteric teaching' in this case. It is not really a question of teachings which are kept secret. Rather it may be regarded as a style of teaching in which the meaning is gradually disbursed, a style which was also widespread in the dominant Tendai school at the time of Kūkai. It is therefore at the risk of giving an impression of undue clarity that we may focus briefly on the idea of the six elements as the constituent factors of the body, the six being earth, water, fire, wind, space, and consciousness. According to Kūkai these

---

[7] This is not the place for the detailed review which would have become necessary had the conception of this article followed Yuasa's lead. In fact the article was almost completed before the book came into my hands.

[8] Ryukoku Translation Pamphlet Series No. 4 (Inagaki 1975).

elements are related to each other in a state of mutual penetration and harmony, or, to adopt another expression, they are 'mutually unhindered'.[9] Viewed thus they are nothing less than the realm of ultimate reality, or the realm of Dharma. As to practice, Kūkai emphasized 'three mystic practices', namely of body, speech, and mind. The body practice takes the form of esoteric hand signs known as *mūdra*, the speech practice refers to the recitation of mantras, and the practice of mind or consciousness is concentration (i.e., in Sanskrit, *samādhi*). If these three practices are correlated, the practitioner will be able to identify with Mahāvairocana Buddha, a cosmic buddha understood to be identical with the whole universe, but in this very body.

A detailed exposition of this would lead into many features which are particularly characteristic of Shingon Buddhist teaching.[10] However it should be noted that the use of the mantra in various forms is also of great importance in other traditions of Japanese Buddhism. If the various doctrinal interpretations are temporarily disregarded, it may be argued that the *nenbutsu*, the mantra used in Pure Land and in True Pure Land Buddhism, which calls upon Amida Buddha with the simple words Namu Amida Butsu, is an intensely individual practice which identifies the believer, in absolute dependence, with Amida Buddha. The doctrinal structure is faith-oriented, and the believer's hope is in rebirth in the Pure Land as a kind of staging-post for the eventual attainment of nirvana. And yet the abandonment of self through the utterance of the *nenbutsu* leads to a flooding of this life with the light of the great Buddha of the western Pure Land, and thus to a mystical anticipation of buddhahood itself. There is a remarkable, and justly famous statue of the great *nenbutsu* teacher and practitioner Ippen, which shows a string of buddhas proceeding from his mouth, one for every utterance of the mantra. Thus buddhas are not merely projected from the consciousness, as in all Mahāyāna Buddhism, but produced from the body in visible form, indeed produced from the throat.

The mystical equation with buddhahood is no less evident in the case of Nichiren and his followers. Nichiren taught 'three great mysteries', one of them being, similarly, the recitation of the name of the *Lotus Sutra* as a mantra, running in full Namu Myōhō Renge Kyō (Hail to the Sutra of the Exquisite Dharma of the Lotus). Thereby the believer is identified, through a symbolic act, a practice, with the very quintessence of the Dharma, believed to be summed up in the *Lotus Sutra*. This equation may

[9] Ibid., 23.
[10] For a more complex discussion see Yuasa 1987, ch. 7. For more information see Kiyota 1978.

also be found in the very short *Heart Sutra*. This concludes with a mantra which is meaningful in Sanskrit but not in Japanese (i.e. in the Chinese transliteration of the Sanskrit which is pronounced in Japanese fashion). Indeed the *Heart Sutra* may be understood altogether as a mantra in that, as some say, it can be recited with one breath. The common feature of all of these practices is immediacy, physical immediacy, and this they share with the practice of *zazen*, in Zen Buddhism, for all the doctrinal differences.

The above traditions and practices have been carried down to the present day and may be easily observed. No longer observable is one of the most dramatic methods of equating the body with the ultimate sanctity of nirvana, namely self-mummification (while still alive, inducing death), which is known in both Japanese and Chinese Buddhist history. This theme has been pursued most recently in Massimo Raveri's latest work *Il Corpo e il Paradiso* (1992). It may be argued however that this extreme form, being limited to the practice of a few individuals who were consequently revered, leads away from the more widely assumed religious perceptions of the body which are otherwise being considered here. For the present purpose it will be better to return to the wider, and more generally accessible world of popular Japanese religion.

THE WATERFALL

Some austerities practised in order to attain supernormal powers and special religious authority are much easier for the ordinary person to identify with. Interestingly, they do not even have to be tied formally to any specific Buddhist organization. With this in mind there now follows a brief description of a scene (observed in 1980) which links Buddhist activities with the more complex religious practices known as Shugendō, also deriving from the Japanese middle ages.[11]

A group of about thirty practitioners dressed in white are chanting sutras in a Shingon temple while an officiant carries out a fire ceremony (*goma*). This is a straightforward Buddhist ceremony which is common all over Japan. The officiant and other richly robed priests then emerge and return to their quarters. The other participants however, of both genders and various ages, turn towards a small mountain path to the side of the temple and begin to climb. They are led by a woman aged forty, as indicated in conversation after the event, carrying a staff. Their progress

---

[11] For a fascinating, wider account of this subject with valuable reports from the field see Blacker 1975.

is accompanied by loud throaty blasts on a couple of huge conches with attached mouthpieces, carried by attendants. The conch is a common accessory for Shugendō practitioners, but at the same time evokes the Buddhist expression 'blowing the conch of Dharma', i.e. proclaiming Dharma, the teaching of the Buddha.

After a walk of several hundred metres, the temple below lost from view, the small crowd arrives at a shallow pool encircled by steep rocks, into which a waterfall tumbles from a height of some ten metres. The volume of water is not great, but the fall has a concentrated force. Nearby is a wooden hut which turns out to be a dressing room. The open side of the pool, opposite the waterfall, is marked by a Shinto-style symbolic entrance consisting of two thin, slightly curving bamboo poles with a demarcatory rope (*shimenawa*) slung between them. Inside the pool area, to one side, is a small shrine with a second *shimenawa* before it. This is nothing more than a small open altar for offerings to the *kami* (god) of the place. In the context of Japanese religion a 'shrine' is any place where a *kami* resides, or can be located, and can receive offerings. In this case offerings are presented by two male attendants before the main practice begins. Looking up to the very top of the waterfall, another small *shimenawa* is stretched across its mouth, less than a metre wide, declaring it a sacred spot. Nearby, high up, stands a stone statue of Fudō Bosatsu, the Bodhisattva Immovable (Acala), bearing his symbolic sword with which the passions may be severed.

After the preliminary offerings have been presented from a position within the shallow water of the pool, the central woman practitioner advances towards the waterfall itself, her hands folded, takes the edge of the fierce jet on one shoulder, and then the other. Gradually she eases herself fully under the stream of water and continues a series of recitations with occasional changes of bodily position. The recitations consist of the *Heart Sutra* and the mantra of Fudō Bosatsu, namely *nomaka samanda bazara dan kan*. The changes of bodily position are partly to dramatize the effect of her appearance, but demonstrate also the totality of her immersion under the pressure of the water. When she has finished, after about twenty minutes, she retires to the dressing hut. It is then the turn of her followers to step carefully under the water. They are guided and held steady by the male attendants, but even so they do not dare to go fully beneath the powerful stream. They only let themselves be touched lightly by it, reciting the *Heart Sutra* as they go.

The above description illustrates the easy juxtaposition of themes

Plate 10   The waterfall ritual: recitationist changing position under the waterfall, with *shimenawa* in foreground and Fudō Bosatsu above.

from various quarters, Buddhist and Shinto, which continues to be typical of much Japanese religion, in spite of the serious attempt to pull them apart in the nineteenth century. In fact what we see here, and this is, if anything, more significant than the historical perspective, is Japanese religion once again in the making. It is not exactly a new religion which is being invented. The events described are however left on one side by the Buddhist clergy of the temple down below, in spite of the relatively easy tendency of Shingon Buddhism to syncretize. Nor is the Shinto world, in its clear, organized form,[12] involved in any way. The woman performer is a freelance religious personage. The other people present are drawn by faith in her special abilities, and for this reason go on beyond the temple below, up the mountain. They have made a rather long journey from various parts of the Kantō plain (surrounding greater Tokyo), the woman herself coming from Niiza City in Saitama Prefecture, just north of the metropolis. It is a pilgrimage to a special site, followed by an act of austerity. As far as the subject under consideration is concerned the point is that it focusses on the body, which at one level is thereby to be maintained in health, but which at another level is to be the basis for its own transcendence.

THE PILGRIM

A similar point may be made with reference to Japanese Buddhist pilgrimage, which also enjoys a mediatory position between organized Buddhism temple systems and the general religious public. The phrase 'Buddhist temple systems' is used here to avoid the terminology of denomination and sect, though this is not so far off the target as is sometimes supposed. The classic forms of Japanese Buddhist pilgrimage are circulatory in the sense that they link a long series of temples, each of which is to be visited.[13] There are two main types, the Shikoku pilgrimage which links eighty-eight temples with a special hall dedicated to Kūkai (774–835), known religiously as Kōbō Daishi or affectionately and religiously as Daishi-sama, the suffix '-sama' being common for any venerated *kami*, buddha, or *bodhisattva*. The other main type is devoted to Kannon-sama (=Avalokiteśvara); however we are concerned here specifically with the first type. In both types the *Heart Sutra*, mentioned above, is a frequently recited text.

The eighty-eight temples spread around the island of Shikoku (Japan's fourth largest island) represent in the Japanese mind one of the ideal types of pilgrimage. It is known that its traversal is a relatively arduous and also expensive task. Traditionally the route is divided into 4 parts corresponding to the 4 traditional provinces of Shikoku, but also to 4 stages of spiritual development. Thus the temples in the province of Awa

---

[12] By this I mean Shinto as organized in the Association of Shinto Shrines which links together those shrines which are clear-cut organizational entities at the present time, no longer having any serious links with Buddhism.

[13] The main features are set out in a detailed catalogue of texts and artefacts by the present writer entitled *O-Meguri, Pilgerfahrt in Japan* (Pye 1987).

are designated *hosshin*. This means decision, in the sense of giving rise to the thought of enlightenment as a *bodhisattva* does at the outset of the spiritual path. The second province is Tosa, whose temples are designated *shugyō*, meaning discipline in the sense of religious practice. The third is Iyo, identified with the achievement of enlightenment (*bodai*), and the fourth province, Sanuki, is identified with nirvana (*nehan*). The importance of this staging in the minds of pilgrims who traverse the route today is admittedly not very great. It suffers from the fact that this very long pilgrimage is sometimes completed in sections determined by practical travel arrangements which do not coincide with the four stages. In guide books the four stages tend to appear as a rather marginal extra to the important business of acquiring the full collection of seals from the various temples, showing that the pilgrimage has been completed. In so far as the idea continues to have some currency, however, it illustrates the spatial articulation of the journey which is physically carried out. Of this even the modern pilgrim is most certainly aware. The body still has to be moved round the pilgrimage route, even when recourse is made to motorized transport. At the same time the pilgrim either is aware, or has time to *become* aware, of the relativity of spatial extension in terms of Buddhist perceptions. Hence the traditional pilgrim's straw hat (and this continues to be seen often enough) bears the ancient lines:

> Through ignorance the three worlds are a prison
> Through enlightenment the ten directions are empty
> Originally there is neither east nor west
> Where then shall be south and north?

Thus the pilgrim carries on his or her head a perpetual question-mark over the current activity of his or her body. Even while going round a circuit of temples which are geographically defined, the pilgrim carries his or her own reminder that the ten directions, like other aspects of experience, are, in the Buddhist sense, empty. The pilgrim's moving body is the locus of latent enlightenment.

CONCLUDING REFLECTIONS

It should perhaps be made clear that these examples attempt to characterize a complex state of affairs in brief, drawing both on well-known threads in traditional knowledge and on field observations. A detailed discussion of the relevant Japanese *terminology*, since it is less than neat, might produce a less coherent and yet not necessarily more reliable view.

For example, the Buddhist phrase 'attaining buddhahood in this very body', used above, includes the Chinese character pronounced *shin* (in Japanese) meaning body; this also occurs in the expression *shūshin* meaning self-cultivation or self-discipline, which was the term for moral education in modern, pre-1945 Japan. This definitely goes beyond the idea of a purely physical body, such as might be assumed in a typical Western discussion about the relationship between body and mind. Indeed the native Japanese reading assigned to this Chinese character, namely *mi*, has the meaning of self as an identifiable social factor, something like 'one's where one is,' and thus designates a locus of social and existential meaning. By contrast the daily word for body, *karada*, used in any conversation about washing, hurting, or health, has a stronger sense of physical embodiment. The Chinese-derived reading for the character which is nowadays used to write *karada*,[14] namely *tai*, which in Japanese only occurs in compounds, carries forward this sense of embodiment into less physical contexts. Thus one speaks of the *shintai*, the physical symbol of a Shinto *kami*, the *kami*-body (*shin* in this case being written with a different character, which is used also for *kami*). Somewhat analogously, the ideologically important concept of *kokutai*, current particularly in the 1930s and 1940s, meant the body of the nation, providing a national corporeal counterpart to the destiny and function of individual Japanese subjects in the Imperial system as then understood. Because of these cross-overs, the terminology picture is not tidy, and etymological considerations, popular though they are in Japan itself, may easily lead to undue emphasis on some particular religious doctrine or other, rather than to a reliable general characterization.[15]

In the field of observation the theme could also be pursued further in many directions. The more it is pursued, the more the variety of diverse religions will appear. Central to the independent religion Tenrikyō, for example, which is neither Buddhist nor Shintoist, is its dance, known as *o-tsutome* (service). This graceful corporate discipline with prescribed foot and fan movements may be regarded as a counterpart to the community

---

[14] The character read *shin* and *mi* has also had the reading *karada* associated with it in the past.

[15] A further complication arises out of the phrase *shikishin funi*, 'mind and body are not two', also mentioned earlier. Here the word for body is *shiki*, being the reading for the Chinese character used to translate the Buddhist Sanskrit term *rūpa*, form. This is well known to Japanese Buddhists from the equation, in the *Heart Sutra*, of form and emptiness. The *shin* of *shikishin* is here not body, but mind, that is mind in the sense of *citta* or *vijñāna*. The implication of this expression is therefore that 'mind' includes or comprehends embodiment.

service, also physical, which is also expected of all believers. These are organized developments from what began in the nineteenth century as a healing movement. It seems appropriate that the body continues to play a central role in this religion, albeit a ritualized one. Rather different is the ecstatic dance of the 'Dancing Religion' (Tenshō Kōtai Jingū Kyō), which is loosely linked with Buddhist themes such as the idea of non-self, or rather the *experience* of non-self, for the self is lost in the movement of the body. This highly physical concept cannot be unrelated to the foundress' experience of receiving revelations, as she herself said, through her belly. Yet another variety is found in Konkōkyō, a religion known for the universal guidance offered by its leader. The availability of this guidance is symbolized by the fact that he sits visibly in personal meditation in the religion's central hall, all day, every day. Thus the constant, reliable availability of religious guidance is focussed in a single body.

Different though they are, these examples show that awareness of the body, of its strength or weakness, of its location and direction, continue to play an important role in Japanese religious consciousness. If we regard religious behaviour itself, therefore, rather than approaching the matter mainly through a string of concepts, a view at once more plastic and more coherent seems to emerge. It has been seen that the variety of practices focussed on the body across the whole spectrum of Japanese religions is quite enormous. However these practices do share the widespread assumption that the individual, physical body is not something to be neglected or avoided, but rather is itself the very locus of existential meaning. In a very vivid way the body is commonly regarded as the focus of its own transcendence, whether this be through some kind of revelation, through spiritual growth, or through unexpected transformation.

BIBLIOGRAPHY

Blacker, C. (1975), *The Catalpa Bow, A Study of Shamanistic Practices in Japan*, London.
Earhart, B. H. (1982), *Japanese Religion, Unity and Diversity*, 3rd edn., Belmont, CA.
Inagaki, H. (1975), *Kūkai's Principle of Attaining Buddhahood with the Present Body* (Ryūkoku Translation Pamphlet Series 4), Kyōto.
Kiyota, M. (1978), *Shingon Buddhism*, San Francisco.
Pye, M. (1978), *Skilful Means, A Concept in Mahayana Buddhism*, London.
    (1983), 'Suffering and Health in Mahayana Buddhism', in ed. D. Goodacre, *World Religions and Medicine*, vol. 4, Oxford, 25–31.

(1987), *O-meguri, Pilgerfahrt in Japan* (Schriften der Universitätsbibliothek Marburg 31), Marburg.

Raveri, M. (1992), *Il Corpo e il Paradiso, Esperienze ascetiche in Asia Orientale*, Venice.

Yuasa, Y. (1987), *The Body, Toward an Eastern Mind-body Theory*, Albany, NY.

CHAPTER 15

'I take off the dress of the body': Eros in Sufi literature and life

Annemarie Schimmel

When I was a very young scholar, I incurred the wrath of one of my professors, incidentally a lady, because I had translated the famous Bektashi novel *Nūr Bābā* by Yakup Kadri (written in 1922) into German.[1] She found that the blending of religious fervour and earthly love and the story of a Sufi shaikh slowly seducing a lady from Istanbul society were altogether repellent and irreligious, although the language itself of the book was chaste, beautiful, and inoffensive. Her judgement reflected in a certain way the criticism of many adversaries of the Bektashi order in Turkey who used to attack the members of this order because of their allegedly illicit and immoral practices, that is, because they admitted women into their communal meals and rituals. It was also too easy to accuse them of promiscuity, not to mention the use of wine and other evils condemned by the *sharī'a*.[2]

Such criticism of Sufi orders, or of single Sufi saints, by outsiders, nay even by the members of more sober fraternities, goes back to the Middle Ages. The pious Ibn Khafīf of Shiraz, one of the sternest ascetics of the tenth century, was accused of improper practices[3] by Ibn al-Jauzī (himself a member of the Qādiriyya[4]), and so was his spiritual successor, Kāzarūnī (d. 1035), who emulated him in his strictly lawbound attitude; yet, it was rumoured that in his *khānqāh* 'keeping company with the unbearded' was common.[5] The veil of secrecy which surrounds many practices in Sufism could easily lead to such accusations, and even in modern Turkish or Arabic literature one finds statements similar to that of Ibn 'Aqīl: 'When a shaikh is alone with a foreign woman, they say "His daughter who is just being invested with the patched frock!"'[6]

---

[1] German trans., *Flamme und Falter*; see Kadri 1948.
[2] See Birge 1965; further, Trimingham 1971.
[3] Ibn al-Jauzī 1921–2, 396. About Ibn Khafīf: see Dailamī, 1955.
[4] See Makdisi 1974.   [5] Ed. Meier 1948, 502.
[6] Meier 1976, 350. A typical example is the Turkish novel by R. H. Karay, *Kadınlar Tekkesi*, originally published *ca.* 1952 (see Karay 1964²).

In later times it was indeed not unusual for female family members of faithful followers to be offered to the shaikh or Pir for temporary use.[7] Furthermore, some practices during the annual festivities at certain saints' shrines have justly led to criticism from more orthodox circles. Noted in this report is the *'urs*, in Tanta, Aḥmad al-Badawī's last resting place. *'Urs*, literally 'wedding', is the term for the anniversary of a saint's death, so called because his soul has reached the final union with the divine beloved. Aḥmad al-Badawī (d. 1278) was the founder of a rural order with deep reminiscences of pre-Islamic, Egyptian customs, including the celebration of his *'urs* according to the solar calendar, which may well have its root in age-old fertility rites.[8] This aspect is alluded to in the oft-quoted story that Aḥmad's most famous follower in later centuries, the pious author ash-Sha'rānī (d. 1565), was inspired by a hidden voice to consummate his marriage in the saint's burial place. The free mixture of sexes during the *maulid* in Tanta was often criticized, so much so that some Mamluk sultans even forbade the Mamluks to attend the fair in Tanta.[9] The followers of the saint, then, could easily remind their critics of the fact that, during the *ṭawāf* around the Ka'ba in Mecca, men and women were celebrating jointly. Besides, in their opinion, whosoever visits the place and sins yet gains God's mercy.[10] The strong tensions in Tanta and the atmosphere have been recently described in an Arabic psychological novel, 'Abdul Hakīm Qāsim's *Ayyām al-insān as-sab'a*, which deserves a detailed analysis.[11]

Perhaps even more notorious than the *maulid* of Aḥmad al-Badawī was the fair in Sehwan in the Indus Valley, an old Shiva sanctuary (Siwistan), which became the seat of a most fascinating Sufi saint in the thirteenth century. Although this La'l Shahbāz Qalandar is described as a stern ascetic, his followers belong to the group of qalanders who claim not to be bound to the law, and his asceticism manifests the *jalāl*-side of religion as do the strange acts of worship at his tomb.[12] The existence of a remnant of Shiva cult, a stone *lingam*, in the sanctuary explains much of the happenings there, as they have been described by some travellers.[13] Recently the celebrations have been purged, as have the festivities in

[7] See Lambrick 1960, a book that deals with the mystico-social movement of the Ḥurr in Sind during the 1930s and 1940s.

[8] Trimingham 1971, s.v. 'Badawiyya'; and the article 'Ahmad al-Badawī', in eds. Gibb *et al.*, 1960, *Encyclopaedia of Islam, New Edition*, I, 280; Kriss and Kriss-Heinrich 1960, 69f.; Littmann 1951.

[9] See Schimmel in ed. Gräf 1968, 277.

[10] Meier 1976, 482f.   [11] See Naguib 1972.

[12] About him see Subhan 1960, 258f.; Sadarangani 1956, 6ff.; Gramlich 1966, 71, 78.

[13] For a satirical but largely correct account about Sehwan and other places in the Indus Valley see Mayne 1956; further, Burton 1973.

another saint's tomb within the city limits of Islamabad, which was a favourite gathering place for prostitutes. In events of this kind, examples of which could certainly be multiplied, enemies of the movement and puritanic reformers could easily find a key to the alleged sexual libertinism of the Sufis in general.

A study of early Sufism reveals, however, the picture of a predominantly ascetic movement with strong control of body and spirit. Utter avoidance of anything unlawful, even doubtful, was a condition of the Path; the discipline was extremely strict. And yet we find shockingly obscene words and tales in the works of some of the greatest masters, who otherwise certainly cannot be accused of licentious conduct. Fritz Meier remarks[14] that even the sternest ascetic sometimes needed a kind of relaxation with dirty jokes, and we have here a case of the well-known polarity between ritually unbridled behaviour (*Zügellosigkeit*) and renunciation, as defined by G. van der Leeuw who says: 'The enormous spiritual power which is pressed together in the course of the ascetic training and practice is set loose for some moments and squandered lest the pressure become too strong.'[15] That explains, to a certain extent, the introduction of dirty stories in the books of wisdom such as Sanā'ī's *Ḥadīqat al-ḥaqīqa*. When Rūmī, taking over a statement of Sanā'ī, claims that:

My dirty jokes are not dirty jokes, but instruction,[16]

he probably alludes to this secret of compression and setting loose. The verse occurs in Book V of the *Mathnawī*, famous for the great number of more or less obscene stories that, beginning at the end of Book IV, fill many pages of this volume, a single one being left to the very end of Book VI. In all of them, however, the poet suddenly plunges into a hymnical praise of true, divine, love.

This literary aspect is always slightly embarrassing for the lover and translator of medieval Sufi poetry. But we have to admit that, in the case of many Sufis of the lower order, the constant complaint of the critics was justified, that is, that their *qibla* consisted of *shikam*, *shamʿ* and *shāhid*: stomach, candles (in festivities), and a beautiful boy.

[14] Meier 1976, 205.   [15] Van der Leeuw 1956, 257.

[16] Rūmī 1925–40, v, 2496, with Commentary, viii, 275, where the reader is referred to Sanā'ī, *Ḥadīqat al-ḥaqīqa* ix, fol. 229a. In the printed edition of the *Ḥadīqa* (ed. M. Razawī; see Sanā'ī 1329/1950) this verse is lacking, although chapter 9 contains enough 'dirty jokes'. The *Mathnawī* (so cited hereafter) is noted for the following stories which Nicholson preferred to translate into Latin instead of English: The Evil Woman and the Tree (iv, 2544ff.); The Maid and the Donkey (v, 1338ff.); The Catamite and the Sodomite (v, 2497ff.); Jūḥā dressed as Woman in the Mosque (v, 3325ff.); The Slave-girl and the Impotent Caliph (v, 3942ff.); The Adventure in a *ʿazabkhāna* (vi, 3843ff.).

This, of course, contradicts the traditional attitude of the moderate Sufi masters as expressed by Sulamī, the best interpreter of the normal ethical behaviour. According to him one of the most important aspects of Sufism is to preserve one's *ḥayā'* (sexual modesty; also: sense of decency, or shame) in every state, for 'ḥayā' is part of faith'.[17] Rūmī, however, bursting out in frenzied passion, turns the *ḥadīth* over: 'Shame hinders you from true faith.'[18] Shame, for him, became a catchword for man's unwillingness to sacrifice reputation and worldly interests in the way of God, in the intoxicated dance toward the Beloved.

But let us turn back to the foundations of classical Sufi conduct. The traditional Sufi leaders recognized seven gates to hell: pride, cupidity, lust, anger, envy, avarice, and hatred,[19] and the story of the two fallen angels, Hārūt and Mārūt, as told in the Koran (Sura 2:96f.), could well illustrate the danger of following one's own sensual desires. (The old image of the whore of Babylon can easily be detected in the Babylonian well where the two angels are incarcerated.) There was no mercy for those who did not follow the path of asceticism and in early Sufism that meant largely sexual restriction. Hujwīrī makes the most outspoken statement in this respect: 'Sufism is founded on celibacy . . . There is no flame of lust that cannot be extinguished by strenuous effort because whatever vice proceeds from your self, you possess the instrument that will remove it.'[20] Shiblī (d. 945) explains Sura 24:30: 'O Muḥammad, tell the believers to refrain their bodily eyes from what is unlawful, and to refrain their spiritual eyes from everything except God', a saying that Hujwīrī elaborates by stating: 'In truth, until God clears the desire of lust in a man's heart the bodily eye is not safe from its hidden dangers.'[21] But it is hoped that finally true, that is, spiritual, love will extend its empire over the different parts of the body and divest all the senses of their sensual qualities.[22] Man should tread on passion, *hawā*, in order to fly in the air, *hawā*, as the early Sufis said with a pun. But they discovered this lust everywhere: the lust of the eye is sight; of the ear, hearing; of the nose, smelling; of the tongue, speech; of the mind, thought. There is no dearth of dramatic descriptions of this lust under the image of rapacious animals, such as the wolf or the disobedient dog.[23] Satan, or rather one of

---

[17] Kister 1954, 31.   [18] *Mathnawī*, ii, 1368, and Commentary, vii, 289.
[19] So R. A. Nicholson in *Mathnawī*, Commentary, vii, 68.
[20] Hujwīrī, trans. Nicholson 1959, 364 (hereafter Hujwīrī/Nicholson 1959).
[21] Ibid., 156.   [22] Ibid., 364.
[23] Kāzarunī compared it to a wolf, and so did Maulānā Rūmī, see Rūmī 1336/1957–67, *Dīwān*, no. 2862 (hereafter *Dīwān*). In *Mathnawī*, v, 43ff., one finds the comparison with the rooster. For more comparisons see Schimmel 1978, Part II, chap. 4, 'Imagery Inspired by Animals'.

Plate 11 'Heavenly and Earthly Drunkenness'. Three stages of intoxication: the worldly level of carousing, the intermediate Sufi level of 'intoxication' with the divine Beloved, and, at the highest level, the dance of the angels. Sulṭān Muḥammad, *circa* 1527, opaque watercolour and gold on paper, illustration for *The Dīwān of Ḥāfiz*.

the satanic manifestations, was, according to Sayyid 'Alī Hamadhānī (d. 1385), contained in the *dhakar*,[24] and Hujwīrī tells the story of a Sufi from Merw who in the bath wanted 'to amputate the member which is the source of all lusts and keeps you afflicted with so much evil . . . But God revealed to him: "If you do this I swear by My glory that I will put a hundredfold lust and passion in every hair in that place!" '[25]

The lower instincts, the 'flesh', were made to undergo a strict education in which hunger played a dominant role.[26] That is why we find extended periods of fasting in the course of the *via purgativa*, whereas on the higher levels fasting was often seen as a state of grace, comparable with that of the angels who feed on Divine Light.

One should not assume that for these early ascetics their renunciation was a goal in itself; it was rather the ladder that was to lead them to a higher goal, and, as such, it can be seen as a sacrifice for the sake of something infinitely more precious, namely, for God's love; for asceticism is, typologically, another, less bloodstained, form of sacrifice. The Sindhi pun that the loving woman soul by becoming a *qurbānī*, a sacrifice, will become a *qarībānī*, a near one, points to this idea.[27] The Sufis felt that sex disturbs the pure surrender of the soul (*Störungsmotiv*).[28] And since their aim was to be with God alone, without the world and its distractions, one can very well understand their aversion to everything worldly; they were disgusted by the world (*Weltekel*) and had therefore also to hate women, since through woman this world is renewed and continued. This hatred for the world was a central aspect of Buddhism, and we may accept the influence of this attitude on the Khorassanian ascetics, headed by Ibn Adham from Balkh, the old capital of Buddhist Bactria. Similar views of Mediterranean Christian ascetics may have influenced early Muslim ascetics in Syria and the Iraq.[29] After all, they were befriended in their dreams by the houris of paradise, if they refrained from earthly desires; and it is stated that such dreams enhanced their piety.[30] Rūmī points to this combination when he likens the spiritual perfection enjoyed by the elect to the virgin brides of paradise.[31]

The fear of the demonic power of sex and its dangers are well known

---

[24] Teufel 1962, 85.   [25] Hujwīrī/Nicholson 1959, 209.

[26] One may also think of the fact that sexual intercourse is prohibited in daytime during Ramadan.

[27] Shāh 1958, Sur Kōhyāri, IV, 9.

[28] Schubart 1941, 177. The book gives an excellent introduction to the various aspects of eros and religion, although it presents a mere caricature of Islam.

[29] For these relations, see Andrae 1947.   [30] Meier 1976, 205f.

[31] *Mathnawī*, V, 3292, and Commentary, VIII, 290, where the 'spiritual experiences', *dhauq-i jān*, are described as *qāṣirāt aṭ-ṭarfī*, 'with chaste looks', as the Koran describes the houris (Sura 37:47; 38:52, 55:56).

in Sufism. The very fact that the sexual act requires a ritual bath of the whole body indicates the danger of this act, in which demonic powers might easily interfere as they were thought to do in older religions in childbirth, marriage, and death.[32] Out of fear of the uncontrollable, dangerous, and yet fascinating power of sex logically develops the tendency to see all the dreaded (hence hated) aspects of life in woman: the concept of the *nafs*, the lower self, luckily feminine in Arabic, offered the early ascetics innumerable possibilities for voicing their hatred for the principle of lust and, as its corollary, the continuation of this world which seemed to be a veil before the pure, eternal Beauty of God. The ascetics' equation of the world with an old ugly crone, a rotten prostitute who entices man and then leaves him in misery, belongs to the same order of thought and goes parallel with similar expressions in Buddhism and medieval monastic Christian tradition.[33] 'The animal qualities prevail in woman', thus says even Rūmī,[34] who has described in the story of Kharaqānī's hideous wife and the saint's appearance riding on a lion the supremacy man gains over the world once he has subdued this female *nafs*.[35] It was Rūmī who time and again repeated stories about, and allusions to, the feminine *nafs* and the masculine spirit, a spirit who expresses man's deep sorrow in the world by exclaiming:

First and last my fall is through woman![36]

Women are impure, stupid, and dangerous. We see with some surprise that Persian Sufi poets allude in plain words to their impurity, comparing the greatest obstacles for the spiritual wayfarer to their menstruation, whether these obstacles be lust, or, much more frequently, miracle-mongering: the Eastern tradition says: 'Miracles are the menstruation of men',[37] since miracles bar the way to true union with God as much as a wife's impurity bars the possibility of true conjugal union.

[32] The importance of the *rites de passage* was first discussed by A. van Gennep in his book *Rites de passage* (van Gennep 1909).
[33] Thus *Mathnawī*, VI, 1222; see the examples in Schimmel 1975, Appendix II.
[34] *Mathnawī*, V, 2465.
[35] Ibid., VI, 2044–2129.
[36] Ibid., VI, 2799. There is no solution to this problem comparable with that expressed by Bernard of Clairvaux: *Sic vir non cadit nisi per feminam, etiam non erigitur nisi per feminam* (quoted by van der Leeuw 1956, 259).
[37] See *Mathnawī*, VI, 2935; for the miracles as 'menstruation of men' see Schimmel 1975, 212f. Khāqāni (d. 1199) says in a ghazal:

> From the female qualification with the water of manliness,
> Did we wash the menstruation of color and scent.
> (Khāqāni 1338/1959, 633).

The whole complex of fear of the demonic and impure side of the touching of body to body is reflected in a certain way in the idea that the bath, where one has to cleanse oneself from such acts, is regarded as the seat of devils and demons:

In the touching of body with body man needs a bath –
Where would be the necessity of a bath when the spirits touch each other?[38]

To see a bath in one's dream points to the dreamer's committing abomination.[39] It is not by chance that the hero of Rūmī's story about the repentance of Nāṣūḥ is a person employed in the public bath who, disguised as a woman, enjoys massaging the lovely ladies until in the moment of imminent life-danger he repents sincerely.[40]

One should also remember, however, the importance given to the bathing ritual for the breaking of the *nafs*: it was indeed one of the favourite practices of many Sufis to perform *ghusl* before every prayer, and Hamadhānī once performed the bath in the icy water of a Central Asian river for forty consecutive days after a pollution in order to educate his lower instincts.[41]

But woman is not only unclean and closely connected with powers that may hinder the wayfarer's ascent to higher spheres. She is also of little intelligence: to consult with women and then to act contrary to their

---

[38] Rūmī, *Dīwān*, no. 2207. Some other charming verses connected with the imagery of love and bath:

> This is even stranger that my eye which did not sleep from longing for you
> Went every morning to the bath due to the union with you!
> (*Dīwān*, no. 2234).

> The image of my friend came into the hot bath of my tears,
> The pupil of my eyes sat there as the watchman.
> (*Dīwān*, no. 3073).

Particularly interesting is the quatrain no. 285:

> This hot bath which is the house of the evil spirits
> And the private resting place of Satan:
> Yet, in it there is a fairy, someone with fairy-cheeks hidden.
> Much infidelity is certainly the ambush of faith!

I.e., just as the beautiful beloved goes to the bath, which is, in itself, a dangerous and unholy place, thus outward infidelity may also conceal true spiritual beauty. For the whole complex see Grotzfeld 1970.

[39] 'Abd ul-Ghanī an-Nābulusī, *Ta'ṭīr al-anām fī ta'bīr al-manām*, quoted by von Grunebaum 1966, 9.

[40] *Mathnawī*, v, 2228ff.

[41] See Schimmel 1975, 149; Teufel 1962, 69. Rūmī speaks in one of his ghazals (*Dīwān*, no. 158) of a 'lovely phantasy, nicely teasing, like a nightly pollution'.

advice is an oft quoted *ḥadīth* with the Sufis.[42] It was only the women who had spiritually reached an advanced stage, such as (the unmarried) Rābiʿa and (the married) Fāṭima of Nishapur, who were taken as man's peer, and could even freely converse with them, for 'if a woman walks in the Path of God, she cannot be considered a woman'.[43]

Some Sufis were immune to the other sex, and would have agreed with Kāzarūnī's statement that he would have married if there had been a difference, for him, between a woman and a pillar.[44] He prohibited his disciples from sitting with women and with unbearded young men, but advised them to get married if they could not restrain their lust.[45] As far as we can see most Sufis in early centuries followed this advice. After all, besides their preference for ascetic restriction, they had before them as a model the Prophet's *sunna* of getting married. But, even if they got married, or permitted marriage, they still found it dangerous, and certainly not advantageous for man. Ibrāhīm ibn Adham coined the famous sentence: 'When a man marries he boards a ship, and when a child is born to him he suffers shipwreck.'[46] Fuḍail ibn ʿIyāḍ's remark that family life is the greatest obstacle to religious life[47] is explained in a statement by Dārānī: 'The sweetness of adoration and undisturbed surrender of the heart which a single man can feel the married man can never experience',[48] as Saʿdī would say some 400 years later:

But in praying I can never forget:
What will my children eat tomorrow?[49]

Therefore it is small wonder that the sorrows of family life were

---

[42] The *ḥadīth* is quoted in *Aḥādīth-i Mathnawī*, ed. Furūzānfar 1334/1956, no. 74. Cf. Sulamī's remark: 'These with little intelligence are yet most clever in stealing man's intelligence!' and his quotation of ʿAli's alleged saying: 'The intellect of a woman is her beauty, and a man's beauty is his intellect' (Kister 1954, 51).

[43] For Rābiʿa see Smith 1928. About Fāṭima of Nishapur see Hujwīrī/Nicholson 1959, 120: although she lived in seclusion with her husband, on seeing Bāyezīd she removed her veil, and explained this to her husband Ibn Khiḍrūya: 'You are my natural spouse, but he is my religious consort. Through you I come to my desire, but through him to God. The proof is that he has no need of my society, whereas to you it is necessary.' See also ʿAṭṭār 1959, I, 285; Jāmī 1336/1957, 620. The same author also tells of women who participated in the meetings of Sufi Shaikhs; Abū Bakr al-Kattānī's daughter died during a sermon of Sumnūn al-Muḥibb (ibid., 623).

[44] Ed. Meier 1948, 36.

[45] Ibid., para. 158, line 22; para. 358, line 18; cf. Kister 1954, 51.

[46] Sarrāj 1914, 199.

[47] ʿAṭṭār 1959, I, 31. On the death of Miān Mīr (d. 1635 in Lahore) a poet wrote a chronogram in which he states that 'in his whole life he did not become fettered by the thought of a wife or the grief of children' (in: Qāniʿ 1956, 502).

[48] Ghazzālī 1289/1872, II, 222.

[49] Saʿdī, *Gulistān*, Bāb-i duwwum (Saʿdi 1342/1963, I, 73).

considered to be 'punishment for the execution of legally permitted lusts'.[50]

If the Sufi is married, he should better follow 'Alī's alleged advice: 'Let not your wife and children be your chief concern.' Did not even Abraham leave Hagar in her loneliness, and Moses the daughter of Shu'aib?[51] For 'if they are God's friends, God will look after them, otherwise, why care for them at all?' Such an attitude was quite common among the early members of the Chisti order in India, and K. A. Nizami's description of how some of these saints dealt with their wives and children displays a frightening hardening of the heart against any non-religious concern,[52] similar to the case of Fudail, who was seen smiling only once in thirty years – when his son died.[53]

Some Sufis would practice asceticism even though married, as early sources tell. One of the most famous, though legendary, stories in this respect is that of Ibn Khafīf who married four hundred women *tabarrukan*, for the sake of blessing, and then sent them away without having touched them. Of the forty who stayed with him none had ever seen him give in to his lust.[54] This version, told by Hujwīrī is certainly not accurate, for we know that he had at least one son; and he was well aware of the various pleasures of body and soul. The body, he says, has three pleasures: eating, sleeping, and sexual intercourse; the soul has three other pleasures: a beautiful voice, fragrance, and *nazar*, 'looking at beautiful individuals'.[55]

Marriage could also be understood as a kind of education: to be married to a talkative, misbehaving spouse was considered to be a substitute for hellfire and was therefore willingly accepted by quite a few Sufis, including Ahmad ar-Rifā 'ī (d. 1178) and Mazhar Jānjānān (d. 1781 in Delhi).[56] Or, based on the Koranic dictum, 'They are your garments'

---

[50] Jāmī 1336/1957, 185. Cf. also Rūmī, *Dīwān*, no. 195, where he warns people of too much sex because that will weaken them: 'for the cohabitation with something dead makes the body cold'. In another ghazal (*Dīwān*, no. 784) he describes the various people returning to their normal occupations after the festive days of the 'Īd: the true lovers have their business only with the bazaar of the Friend, but 'the lowly ones go to their parties, contracted to their private parts and their stomach'. That means, they are bound to follow their lust.

[51] Hujwīrī/Nicholson 1959, 74.

[52] Nizami 1955.

[53] Ghazzālī 1289/1872, IV, 282.

[54] Hujwīrī/Nicholson 1959, 247; 'Attār 1959, II, 128–9; but cf. Dailamī, 1955, Part II, para. 15, and the introduction.

[55] Ibid., Part XII, para. 1.

[56] See *Encyclopaedia of Islam, New Edition* (ed. Gibb *et al.* 1960), s.v. 'Ahmad ar-Rifā'ī'; for the family troubles of Mazhar Jānjānān, a leading Naqshbandi mystic of Delhi (1699–1781), see his *Maktūbāt* (Mazhar 1966).

(Sura 2:168), the Sufi might regard them as a garment on which to wipe his faults, as Maulānā Rūmī in *Fīhi mā fīhi*:

By enduring and putting up with the tyranny of women it is as though you rub off your own impurities on them. Your character becomes good through forbearance; their character becomes bad through domineering and aggression. When you have realized this, make yourself clean. Know that they are like a garment; in them you cleanse your own impurities and become clean yourself.[57]

But Rūmī knew also that patient desisting from lust will bring a good result, just as someone who has two wives may send one off and enjoy the other one all the more.[58]

On the whole, many Sufis seem to have led a rather normal family life: the touching story about Ruwaim and his little daughter,[59] the remarks about Ibn ʿAṭā and his ten lovely sons,[60] or some sentences by Najmuddīn Kubrā[61] point to a normal, if not happy, family life. And Junaid is reported to have said that he needed sex as much as food.[62]

That would be close to the line of some later Sufis, among them the members of the Naqshbandiyya, who taught to overcome lust by means of *dhikr*, but if they should fail to do so they should fulfill their desire as quickly as possible in order to return to work without too much delay.[63] This somewhat functional and loveless love-making is counteracted by the sayings or descriptions of some other Sufis who certainly did enjoy the pleasures of the body and of love. Among them the expressions of Bahāʾuddīn Walad, Rūmī's father, are remarkably outspoken. He considered the admiration of female beauty and the enjoyment of love as legitimate means of transcending worldly beauty and of reaching the vision of God and His creative power, quite contrary to an ethical maximalist like al-Muḥāsibī (d. 857) who had blamed the pious who looked at beautiful women in order to be reminded of the houris of Paradise.[64] Bahāʾuddīn Walad, however, sees the power of *shahwat* everywhere, recognizing in it the kindness or the *ladhdhat*, the enjoyment of God. Looking at the legs and backs of women he felt like enjoying 'God's wine which makes man unconscious and enables him to praise God more effectively',[65] and in an Arabic passage he claims that 'the . . . [the Persian editor has left out the relevant word "because of its indecency"!] of a lustful woman is the highest mosque for obedience to

[57] *Fīhi mā fīhi*, Arberry 1961, 98.   [58] *Dīwān*, no. 1340.   [59] Dailamī 1955, Part VI, para 1.
[60] ʿAṭṭār 1959, II, 68.   [61] Ed. Meier 1957, 51.   [62] Quoted by Bauer 1917, 26, n. 1.
[63] Quoted ibid.   [64] Meier 1976, 206.   [65] Bahāʾuddīn 1338/1959, 2; cf. 5.

the Lord',[66] expressions which are complemented by others but which are hardly translatable.[67] His son Jalāluddīn, then, describes the joys of love-making without inhibition, rather with apparent pleasure, in the story of the drunken *faqīh* and his dealing with a girl whom he treats 'as a baker treats the dough',[68] and also in the story of the young woman who became pregnant in spite of her father's advice.[69] The 'hand game of husband and wife'[70] is mentioned in his verse as is the feeling of the woman whose twenty children will always remind her of the happy moments of union.[71] Much later Khwāja Mīr Dard of Delhi (d. 1785) – the only major Sufi to write clearly: 'I love my wife and my children dearly'[72] – makes some remarks about the duty of women to decorate themselves in order 'that the work of begetting and procreating can be done frequently and nicely'.[73] The very fact that some of the leading Sufi masters had large families – Aḥmad-i Jām, 43 children; 'Abdul Qādir al-Jīlānī, 49 children – shows that the earlier ascetic habit was later practised only in exceptional cases.[74] Some of them might probably have excused their indulgence in sex by the feeling that man, after having renounced every pleasure of the *nafs* in the earlier stations of the Path, 'could stretch out his hand to everything without being damaged',[75] an idea that could doubtless lead to rather unsaintly excesses.

The general attitude towards the 'inferior' woman is complemented, to a certain extent, by the famous tradition according to which perfume and women were dear to the Prophet, and his consolation was in prayer.[76] Out of this tradition the school of Ibn 'Arabī developed the idea that 'love of women belongs to the perfections of the gnostics, for it is inherited from the Prophet and is a divine love'.[77] That is a far cry from earlier ascetic statements, but a foundation for the positive attitude towards sex in later times, perhaps also an excuse for all too frequent indulgence in human love.

For Ibn 'Arabī, woman was the place of manifestation of the divine names connected with forming and creating,[78] and Rūmī follows him in

---

[66] Ibid., 18.   [67] Ibid., 35; cf. 10.   [68] *Mathnawī*, vi, 3921f., especially lines 3946–3949.
[69] Ibid., v, 3716ff.   [70] *Dīwān*, no. 2003.   [71] *Mathnawī*, vi, 1804–1807.
[72] Dard 1308/1890, and 'Nala-yi Dard' in *Chahār Risāla* (Dard 1310/1892), no. 70.
[73] Dard 1308/1890, 523.   [74] Jāmī 1336/1957, 357; cf. Burton 1973, 207, about the Pir of Kingri!
[75] Meier 1976, 145, a quotation from Tirmidhī.
[76] This oft-quoted *ḥadīth* forms the basis for the concluding chapter, on Muḥammad, in Ibn 'Arabī's *Fuṣūṣ al-ḥikam*.   [77] Ritter 1955, 480.
[78] E.g., the names *khāliq, muṣawwir, muqaddir*. see Nicholson in *Mathnawī*, Commentary, vii, 155f., where he mentions also related theories by Najm ud-dīn Dāyā in his *Mirṣād ul-'ibād*. Ibn 'Arabī admitted of the possibility that women were among the group of saints called *abdāl* (see Jāmī 336/1957, 615).

this respect at least in one surprising passage of the *Mathnawī*.[79] The whole 'para-sexual symbolism of Ibn 'Arabī,' as Fazlur Rahman calls it,[80] belongs to this new approach to the feminine side of God as manifested in women. Lailā, the ideal of Majnūn, is the poetical metaphor of this love relation between man and God.

However, the appreciation of woman in this form is no more the rule in Sufism than is the full appreciation of conjugal life. Women were generally seen as the lowest rung of the spiritual ladder, as expressed in the well-known saying by Jamāl Hānswī: ṭālib ad-dunyā mu'annath, ṭālib al-ākhira mukhannath, ṭālib al-maulā mudhakkar: 'The seeker of the world is feminine, the seeker of the otherworld is a hermaphrodite, and the seeker of the Lord is masculine.'[81] Incidentally, the seeker of something besides God is classified as a hermaphrodite as early as in 'Aṭṭār's poetry,[82] and this type of person has been described in rather drastic verse by Rūmī.[83] For the true hero of Sufism is the 'man', *fatā*, *mard*, *jawānmard*, *er*.

This leads us to an aspect of love which is usually connected with the Sufi experience, that is, the 'love of the unbearded' and the whole problem of the mystical contemplation of a young beautiful male. The theories developed by the Sufis particularly in Iran and Turkey try to stress the perfect chastity of the lover, *la chasteté du regard*, claiming that looking at these beautiful forms may be a reminder of the prophets and angels whom one has seen in a vision.[84] Such a 'looking' in a society where decent female company was practically unobtainable outside wedlock was, of course, not always restricted to mere distant admiration.

---

[79] *Mathnawī*, I, 2437.

[80] Rahman 1966, 146: 'Adam, he taught, was really the first female for Eve was born from his inside, an act repeated by the second Adam, Mary, in generating Jesus. In the subsequent Persian Sufi poetry that blossomed so brilliantly, amorous images are employed in stark realism and many poets have been objects of controversy as to whether they were singing of spiritual love or earthly passion.'

[81] Invented by the thirteenth-century Indian mystic Jamāl Hānswī, see Ahmad 1968, 82. The saying has been very popular in Sindhi Sufi poetry up to our day.

[82] 'Aṭṭār 1339/1960b, ch. 20, par. 1.

[83] Rūmī, in a quatrain, addresses someone who does useless things (Rubā'iyāt no. 1784):
Oh, woe that you play the tamboura before the deaf,
Or that Yūsuf should live together with a blind person,
Or that you put sugar in a sick person's mouth,
Or that a catamite becomes the spouse of a houri!
See also *Dīwān*, nos. 2878, 2137, and 2280, the amusing ghazal where a hermaphrodite complains to a shepherd that his buck has gazed at him so strangely. The *ṭawāshī*, the eunuch as guard of the women's apartments, is mentioned once as 'eunuch of his grief' (*Dīwān*, no. 1405).

[84] Cf. Massignon 1922, 799. In Baqlī 1958, para. 79, Baqlī says: 'The face of Adam is the *qibla* of the lovers'. See also ed. Meier 1957, 221.

Therefore Hujwīrī utters the strong verdict that 'looking at youths and associating with them are forbidden practices, and anyone who declares them to be allowable is an unbeliever'.[85] As early a Sufi as al-Kharrāz (d. *ca.* 890) had a vision of Iblīs who boasted that he had at least one snare left to trap the Sufi, namely his association with the unbearded.[86] The numerous examples collected by Hellmut Ritter in the relevant chapters of *Das Meer der Seele*, along with his excellent commentary, show very clearly how important this issue was in Sufi history.

We cannot blame the orthodox who refused to accept the Prophetic tradition: 'I saw my Lord in the most beautiful shape' or, even more outspoken, 'I saw my Lord as a young man, with his cap awry.'[87] Yet, it was these alleged traditions which inspired Sufi poets to some of their most charming poems. As early as in ʿAṭṭār's verse the admiration for the *kach kulāh*, the young coquettish beloved with his silken cap awry occurs,[88] an admiration that has found its most well-known expression in Hasan Dihlawī's (d. 1328) verse:

Mā qibla rāst kardīm be-samt-i kachkulāhī
We have directed our *qibla* toward the quarter of the one with his cap awry.

Persian and Turkish poetry cannot be understood without this symbolism which led the mystics to see in the youth, preferably fourteen years old, a *shāhid*, a witness of God's eternal beauty, and which induced them to call him often an idol, *sanam* or *but*. The tension between the stern Islamic monotheism on the one hand, and the verbal idolworship of the Sufi poetry on the other gives a very special flavour to the poetical images, especially if we keep in mind that the idol was meant to represent Divine Beauty, *jamāl*, and at the same time God's *jalāl*, His Majesty. The beloved thus becomes a perfect mirror of the seemingly contrasting attributes of God, attracting the lover by his radiant beauty, but submitting him to unending affliction by the manifestations of his whims or his outright cruelty.[89] The whole store of images connected with this aspect of love reflects these two sides; they become particularly clear in the image of the Turk, the cruel, beautiful hero who drags the lover's head through the arena, inflicting wounds on him with arrow and dagger. That such a relationship was far from being only a literary device

[85] Hujwīrī/Nicholson 1959, 416.   [86] Qushairī 1330/1912, 9.   [87] See Ritter 1955, 445ff.
[88] ʿAṭṭār 1339/1960a, 26; Hasan Dihlawī's poem in Ikram 1953, 135.
[89] Schubart's classification (Schubart 1941, 193) of homoerotic relations as 'harmonious, without opaqueness and nightly awe' certainly does not work in the love mysticism of Persian Sufism; there his remark about homoerotic relations as an expression of 'hatred of heterosexual love' (ibid. 194) fits slightly better, though not completely.

is borne out by the numerous names of Sufis who indulged in *husnparastī*, worship of beauty as revealed in human forms, which entails every kind of suffering and eventually the annihilation of the lover in the beloved. The poets Fakhruddīn 'Irāqī (d. 1289) and Auḥaduddin Kirmānī (d. 1237) are best-known among them, but one could add hundreds of names, from Sarmad[90] in Mughal India to minor figures whose stories are often extremely weird.

The tension of a person afflicted by such a love could break all limits, and the sources frequently tell of people dying or swooning at the very sight of the beloved or when hearing a single word from him. Fritz Meier relates in this context an interesting story about Abū Sa'īd-i Abū'l-Khair, whose son was the object of a dervish's love. Being a good psychologist, he asked his son to feed his lover with his own hand and to give him sweetmeat, and the lover, in the explosion of his tension which had been soothed by this gentle act, immediately set out for pilgrimage. Abū Sa'īd sent his son to accompany him, but the dervish, cured by the very touch of the beloved, refused his company.[91]

Rūmī was apparently of a similar opinion, holding that a temporary fulfilment was more practical for a balanced and normal life than endless yearning. He simply put it somewhat more crudely when he was told that Auḥadduddīn Kirmānī's love for young boys was chaste (although he used to tear their frocks during *samā'*, dancing breast to breast with them). Rūmī's short remark about this kind of relation was simple: '*Kāsh kardī u gudhashtī*' (Wish he had done it and been done with it!).[92]

But it was not exactly the *kardan u gudhastan* that these Sufis wanted. For them the ideal was chaste love, as much as the admiration of the unbearded might often have degenerated into sheer pederasty. But the theoreticians of the movement always remained faithful to the alleged Prophetic tradition: 'Who loves and remains chaste and dies, dies as a martyr.' Rūzbihān Baqlī (d. 1209), whose statements about chaste love are

---

[90] For Fakhruddīn 'Irāqī and Auḥaduddīn Kirmānī see Browne 1921 and Rypka 1968. 'Irāqī's charming poetry has been edited by Sa'īd Nafīsī ('Irāqī 1338/1959). For Sarmad see 'Sarmad' in Hashmi 1933–4, and every history of Indo-Muslim literature. A particularly strange story about a Sufi who fell in love with a boy is told by Tattawī 1956, 112: the boy's father threw the dervish in the Indus, but some time later he was seen, happily riding on the waves, sitting on the millstone which the angry father had fastened around his neck! Poetical models of this relationship are mainly Maḥmūd (of Ghazna) and Ayāz, often praised in lyrics and in a considerable number of epics; Hilālī's *Shāh ū gadā* deals with a similar relationship, that of king and beggar, frequently mentioned in mystical works such as Aḥmad Ghazzālī's *Sawāniḥ* (Ghazzālī 1942, trans. Gramlich 1976), and related books. Amusing parodies of the style of such homoerotic poems can be found in the Turkish verse of the fifteenth-century Bektashi poet Kayğusuz Abdāl.
[91] Meier 1976, 223.   [92] Jāmī 1336/1957, 461.

probably the most impressive expressions of this experience (besides the writings of his elder compatriots Aḥmad Ghazzālī and ʿAinulqudāt Hamadhānī) remarks that 'the journey of the lovers is nothing but Reality, and the collyrium of their eyes is only the dust of the street of the *sharīʿa*', meaning that their eyes are brightened by the *sharīʿa*.[93] At the day of the primordial covenant (Sura 7:171) the souls flew in the world of heavenly love on the wings of human love. That is why Rūzbihān never ceases repeating that *ʿishqmajāzī*, metaphorical, that is, human, love is the ladder that leads toward the love of the Merciful: *al-majāz qanṭarat al-ḥaqīqa*.[94]

For Rūzbihān Baqlī, as for his friends in this school of love, human love means a pedagogic experience. It trains the soul to endure hardships and teaches man absolute obedience to the will of the beloved, and thus prepares him for obedience to God, the highest goal in life.

The reader of Persian mystical and mystically inclined poetry is well aware of the importance given by the writers to the experience of cruelty – Goethe, who had read but little Persian literature in translation, remarked that this cruelty as expressed in the image of ball and polo mallet as metaphors for the lover's heart in the beloved's curls is repugnant to our Western taste.[95] But the lover in the traditional strain, who derived his ideals from the *ḥubb ʿudhrī* as propounded by the Arabs and particularly as codified by Muḥammad ibn Dāʾūd aẓ-Ẓāhirī, as well as from the Sufi ideal of absolute surrender to the will of God, experienced the longing for pain and the hope for death as a martyr as an essential part of this love.[96]

Walter Schubart has correctly classified the close relation among tragic catharsis, mystical ecstasy, and erotic orgiastic rites, all of which aim at an outbreak of accumulated power into freedom.[97] Part of this experience is the polarity of pain and joy which, at the utmost end, become identical:

When pain reaches its limits it becomes remedy,

says Ghālib (d. 1869).[98] The overwhelming strength of the experience of an unfulfilled love manifests itself in longing for death as the only means

---

[93] Baqlī 1958, para. 112.

[94] Ibid., para. 4; para. 183. See also Baqlī 1966, ch. 182, para. 571: 'Love is the ladder to the pre-eternal roof of *tauḥīd*'. See also Corbin 1955.

[95] In *Noten und Abhandlungen zum West-Östlichen Divan* (see Goethe 1952), chapter entitled 'Despotie'.

[96] See the crude line in Amīr 1343/1964, no. 720:

> When a lover is killed because of love and passion,
> Then his blood is not the blood of martyrs, but the menstruation of women.

[97] Schubart 1941, 170.   [98] Mirzā Asadullāh Ghālib, *Urdu Dīwān*, refrain *hona* (see Ghālib 1969).

of being united with the beloved. The Sufis have stressed the importance of dying, of death as a lovely bridge between lover and beloved,[99] and, if their asceticism was some kind of sacrifice in order to attain something priceless, their wish of sacrificing themselves to the Beloved can be understood as the expression of the hope for complete liberation of the self from the limits of time and space.

The enjoyment of pain, rather the calling for pain, which permeates Sufi lyrics and prayers, is part of this process of liberation, which has unkindly been called 'mystical masochism'. The motif of the arrow that pierces the lover's body and soul reaches from allusions to it in early Sufi sayings to very concrete descriptions of the pain caused by it in late Sindhi folk poetry.[100] The predilection for the arrow motif may have to do with its underlying sexual symbolism. But we may also think of the numerous allusions to burning,[101] to the capacity of Sufis to inflict burn scars upon themselves without being aware of them, and of the whole imagery of the fire of love which is summed up in the experience that for the true lover, symbolized in Abraham, fire becomes lovely as a rose garden.[102] Perhaps the most outspoken mysticism of pain can be found in the verse of Shāh 'Abdul Laṭīf, the great Sindhi mystical poet of the eighteenth century, whose heroines, the suffering woman-souls, are afflicted with every conceivable pain, wandering through the burning desert heat, being drowned in the river, being tortured by the cruel ruler, and yet they call for more pain:

Let the knife be blunt that I may feel your hand longer![103]

This cry of the tortured human being is repeated time and again, and we may remember in this connection that, according to the school of Ḥallāj and his followers, Iblīs too enjoys being cursed and punished as long as he is sure that God looks at him while punishing him. The identification of the true lover and monotheist with Satan, not rare in medieval and modern writing, is part of this imagery.[104]

---

[99] For love and death cf. Schimmel 1975, 135.

[100] For the arrow motif in Shāh 'Abd ul-Laṭīf's poetry see Schimmel 1976, Part II. One should also think of the vision of Teresa of Ávila and her famous statue by Bernini!

[101] A beautiful description of the 'valley of love and its burning fire' in 'Aṭṭār 1961, 222. The instances are too frequent to be enumerated; among them, the 'ocean of fire' is most frequently used. Rūmī, Dīwān, no. 1657 sings:

> The school of education of the lovers is fire,
> I am day and night in this school.

[102] The story of Abraham and the rose garden was developed from Sura 21:70 and forms one of the favourite topics of Persian poetry.

[103] Shāh 1958, Sur Yaman Kalyān II, 12.   [104] For this problem cf. Schimmel 1976, 210ff.

The arrow motif as well as the fiery rose garden has led us to the world of symbolic expression of the experience of love in its various shades. Let us examine a few of them more closely.

Which lover in Persian poetry would not complain that his soul has come to his lips, that is, that he is on the point of dying, and that the beloved should grant him a kiss to quicken him? The idea of the kiss as an exchange of souls goes back to classical antiquity and has often been used by the poets of Greece and Rome, and by those of Europe who were acquainted with their works.[105] (The symbol of the Holy Spirit as the kiss between the Father and the Son in Greek Christian theology belongs here, too.[106]) Islam took over this imagery which was eased by the Koranic remarks about God's breathing into Adam in order to make him alive (Sura 15:29; 37:72), and also about the life-bestowing breath of Jesus (Sura 3:49, 5:110). Thus the kiss as the most tender expression of divine grace and inspiration offered itself comfortably to the Sufis. Even kissing the black stone of the Ka'ba might become a symbol for a higher reality, that is the real kiss, and thus, for inspiration, as in Rūmī's charming verse:

> The pilgrim kisses the black stone from his innermost heart,
> Because he feels the lips of his beloved in it.[107]

Related to this motif of the exchange of souls and the giving of life by means of a kiss is the motif of the reed flute which, touched by the lips of the beloved, is able to speak:

> If I would be joined to the breath of some companion,
> I would say everything that has to be said![108]

The favourite worship of the Sufis, the nightly prayer, was likewise connected with the imagery of love mysticism: a *ḥadīth qudsī* makes God say: 'He is a liar who claims to love Me, and when night falls he sleeps away from Me.'[109]

The sweetness of union during the *munājāt*, the nightly orison, has

---

[105] For the meaning of kissing cf. Heiler 1961, 321ff.; A. Schimmel, 'Kuss', in *Die Religion in Geschichte und Gegenwart*, 3rd. edn (eds. Campenhausen *et al.* 1957–65), IV, 189f. Besides such classical authors as Petronius and Catullus we find the motif also in John Donne's poetry ('So, so break off this last lamenting kiss') and in German classicism. The exchange of kisses in the church, the *philema hagion*, belongs here as much as does the widespread motif in legends and fairy tales that tell either of quickening by means of a kiss, or of God's taking away a saint's soul (for example, Moses) by means of a kiss.

[106] Cf. Segelberg 1960.   [107] *Dīwān*, no. 617.   [108] *Mathnawī*, I, 27.

[109] Hujwīrī/Nicholson 1959, 352; see also *Mathnawī*, I, 1989f. and Commentary, VII, 155.

often been described, and Dhū'n-Nūn's exclamation: 'In the crowd I call Thee "O Lord!", but in loneliness I call Thee "O Beloved!"'[110] points well to the experience of loving union during the lonely hours of the night when the soul receives the kiss of grace and touches the garment of the divine beloved.

It may seem amazing that even in a traditional setting where woman was usually referred to in rather deprecative remarks a kind of bridal mysticism could develop. An early Sufi said: 'The saints are God's brides, but only the close ones (mahram) can see the brides', for God is jealous of them, and not everyone has access to them.[111] Rūmī, on the other hand, may compare the mystical state (hāl) to the unveiling of the bride, and the longer lasting station (maqām) to the intimate time that the king enjoys with his bride in seclusion.[112] The numerous puns of the 'virgins', that is, 'deeper meaning', which should be given in marriage to the 'bridegroom', namely the 'word', belong here too; they are used, for instance, in the beginning of Ahmad Ghazzalī's Sawānih and in other mystical works.

Classical Islam had one symbol of the longing woman soul in the figure of Potiphar's wife, Zulaikhā, who, however, became 'purified' only in the Persian tradition. She is a noble model of the soul that is infatuated by the Divine Beauty, and the Koranic tale that the women who gazed at Joseph did not feel that they cut their hands instead of cutting the fruit (Sura 12:31) fits well into the general scheme of suffering in love without really being aware of it. A certain use of the feminine address to the loving soul in Niffarī's lyrics notwithstanding, it was only in one part of the Muslim world where an exact parallel to Christian bridal mysticism developed. That was in Indo-Pakistan.[113] The Indian tradition of the gopis as Lord Krishna's playmates has certainly contributed to the development of this image. It could also logically develop out of the image of the nafs as feminine: she now is no longer exclusively the nafs ammāra, the soul that incites evil (Sura 12:53), as is usually the case in classical Sufism, but develops through endless suffering into the nafs lawwāma (Sura 75:2) and finally becomes the nafs mutma'inna (Sura 89:28), the 'soul at peace' which can return to her Lord. The idea that God is able to cover the 'naked' disgraced woman with His grace, an allusion to His name as-Sattār, is very helpful in this connection, and the Pakistani

[110] Abū Nuʿaim 1932–3, XI, 332.   [111] Mathnawī, I, 428.   [112] Ibid., line 1435.
[113] Niffarī addresses his soul in some of his poems as yā bunayyatī, 'Oh my little daughter' (see Nwyia 1973). For the whole problem see Schimmel 1976, Part II, and Schimmel, 'Sindhi Literature', in ed. Gonda 1974, vol. 8, 4.

poets in the regional languages have most skilfully employed tales about brave and suffering women as they existed in the country to represent the soul on her various states of development until union is finally achieved. Sasuī who died in wandering, Sohnī who died in drowning, Hīr, and many others represent the fullness of mystical experience in the imagery of longing and yearning, of being punished for faithfulness, or for having indulged in the 'sleep of heedlessness'. In this poetry, the bridegroom is either the Lord Himself or, sometimes, the Prophet Muḥammad, for the later mystics hoped for union with the *ḥaqīqa muḥammadiyya*, the archetypical Muḥammad. Interestingly the same imagery has been taken over by the Isma'ili pirs in their *ginans*, the devotional songs that follow exactly the same pattern, only with the Imām as 'heavenly bridegroom'.[114] The development of these ideas could be helped by the use of an alleged Prophetic tradition, which was already quoted by Ghazzālī in the chapter on marriage in the *Iḥyāʾ ʿulūm ad-dīn*: 'If it were permitted that one should prostrate before anyone but God I would order that wives should prostrate before their husbands.'[115] The transition from such a saying to the application of the husband–wife symbol to God and the soul was, then, very easy.

The mystics did not hesitate to express their hope for complete union in very direct language. When Rūmī takes over Sanāʾī's lines 'I do not sleep with such an idol in a nightshirt',[116] he points to the necessity of complete denudation in front of the beloved. This imagery is not rare in his poetry. He asks the beloved to tear the garment off his body, and he wants to be embraced by the embrace of divine grace.[117] Similar expressions had been used by his father who spoke of 'sitting in the lap of Grace'[118] and compared the relation of man and God to that of a loving couple who see each other's most private parts and yet enjoy each other; thus the soul stands before God, naked, blushing partly from fear and partly from love, and waiting for his order,[119] for, as the Sufis of old said: 'When love becomes perfect the conditions of etiquette disappear.'[120] And Bahāʾuddīn Walad tells that he said to God: 'I am complaining like

---

[114] See Asani 1977.
[115] Ghazzālī 1289/1872, ii, 53; quoted also by ʿAndalīb 1310/1893, i, 578.
[116] *Mathnawī*, i, 138; taken from Sanāʾī 1341/1962, 488.
[117] Thus Rūmī, *Dīwān*, no. 551:

> I am better with you naked, I take off the dress of the body,
> So that the lap of your grace becomes a gown of my soul.

Further ibid, no. 2063, and, in a more metaphorical sense, ibid., nos. 314, 2555.
[118] Bahāʾuddīn 1338/1959, 28.
[119] Ibid., 139f.   [120] Abū Nuʿaim 1932–3, x, 288.

the loving bride, O God, do not deprive me of thy taste!'[121] One of the most outspoken remarks in this respect is found in Nāṣir Muḥammad 'Andalīb's (d. 1758 in Delhi) *Nāla-i 'Andalīb*, where he goes into the details of the love relationship between the maiden soul and her divine beloved: when the bride all of a sudden, after much pining and longing, experiences in the consummation of marriage the piercing of her body she is shocked; but the beloved consoles her by telling her that after showing his *jamāl*, his beauty and kindness, he has to show her his *jalāl*, his power and majesty (which is even more divine), and that this wounding of her body is nothing but the sign of highest love, of 'naked union'. All the motifs known from the earlier sources, longing, the twofold aspect of the divine beloved, the arrow motif, the necessity of suffering, nay, rather suffering as the fulfilment of love, are here harmoniously blended.[122]

It goes without saying that mystics who used the image of union so often and almost without restriction were also aware of the logical consequences, the pregnancy of the soul. This image is known to Hellenistic mystics such as Plotinus and Origen, and the metaphor is not unusual in Christian mysticism (Meister Eckhart's 'birth of Christ in the soul' comes to mind), either in a more abstract sense or in the very matter-of-fact fantasies of medieval nuns.[123] Of the Muslim mystical poets Rūmī, again, is most outspoken. Although he has a few descriptions of pregnancy with all its signs,[124] he usually sees the body as pregnant with the soul or the heart, or the soul as pregnant with the light of God's majesty. His numerous allusions to Mary, who represents the body, and Christ, the symbol of the soul which has to be born in everybody, belong to this tradition and are very close to medieval Christian ideas. In one place he even sees the spirit impregnating the body so that it can bring forth the burden of daily religious and secular works.[125] The imagery of the 'alchemical marriage', though barely mentioned by mystical poets in Islam, may belong to this group of symbols; the raw material of the soul is transformed into something higher by union with some mysterious substance. One should perhaps follow the traces of those Sufis who were credited with alchemistic activities, such as Jaʿfar as-Ṣādiq and Dhū'n-Nūn, and it seems more

---

[121] Bahāʾuddīn 1338/1959, 18, where also some other very strange remarks about sex and adultery can be found. Rūmī has likewise some verses about the Arabic saying: 'If you commit adultery, then with a free woman', *Mathnawī*, I, 2805.

[122] 'Andalīb 1310/1893, I, 560.   [123] Heiler 1961, 246f.

[124] Realistic descriptions: *Dīwān*, nos. 3070, 3090; 'The body is pregnant from the soul' no. 2285; further no. 2234. 'Everything under the sky is a mother of some sort', *Mathnawī*, III, 3362–3; cf. also ibid., I, 399.   [125] See also *Fīhi mā fīhi*, trans. Arberry 1961, 33.

than an accident that Rūmī married his beloved Shams-i Tabrīzī to a girl called Kīmīyā.

It is also Rūmī to whom we owe a rather dramatic description of the *hieros gamos*, where he sees himself as the earth and the beloved as the sky; with parched lips he waits for the rain of grace so that the earth may flourish with roses and gardens. But how could the earth know what is growing in her womb? God who has put the burden into her is the one who knows it best. Is not every atom pregnant with a different secret of God so that even out of these wombs the cries *ana'l-ḥaqq*, 'I am the Absolute Truth', and *subḥānī*, 'Praise be to me!' can emerge?[126]

In Rūmī this imagery leads logically to the imagery of children and their development until they, learning first metaphorical love by playing with dolls, eventually become acquainted in the fiery school of real love with the goal of life, and thus the imagery swings full circle.

There are still other areas that belong to the border zones between the erotic in the widest sense of the word and Sufi life. Schubart has rightly remarked that in ecstatic rapture the 'word becomes song, the step becomes dance',[127] and Goethe spoke of:

Das Doppelglück der Töne und der Liebe.

Taken from this viewpoint the numerous warnings of the sterner Sufis, let alone the orthodox, against the practices of *samāʿ* can be understood even better. It was not only the aversion of the sober to music and dance, but rather the perfectly correct feeling that in music and dance powers are at work which belong to that dangerous, uncontrollable zone of eros which the pious had to avoid or, at best, to strictly regulate. Indeed, the tearing of the garments of the dancers is one of the most objectionable aspects of Sufism and Sufi dance. Further, many a Sufi deemed the presence of a beautiful boy necessary for a perfect performance of *samāʿ*.[128] Again, Rūmī appears as an outstanding interpreter of these feelings in their totality: he who had given up his reputation for the sake of his love for Shamsuddīn and had begun to write poetry, to sing and whirl around in this frenzied love, has the richest possible imagery in musical terms. In addition there are the numerous ghazals that describe the *samāʿ* as a ladder to heaven or even as the force which originated with the first signs of life and which permeates everything created from the atom to the divine Throne.[129] The connection of the flute with the

[126] *Dīwān*, no. 3048.   [127] Schubart 1941, 139.
[128] Cf. Ritter's description of *samāʿ* in Ritter 1960, 249–70.
[129] For the whole imagery see Schimmel 1978, Part II, ch. 15.

breathing and the kiss, that is, the feeling of being quickened by divine grace, plays an important role in this connection. Or we may think of the image of the harp, an instrument that is caressed by the player's fingers and thus represents the lover's body longing for the touch of the beloved to lead him to ecstasy.

In a certain way the imagery of intoxication belongs to the same order. The connection of intoxication and sexual freedom is easily given, and the condemnation of sexual licentiousness and wine in the Koran goes together; but the 'spiritual wine' was rediscovered by the Sufis. Intoxication is an important step in the mystical path, although, according to the sober orders, it has to be overcome because it leads to the experience of all-embracing unity (*wahdat al-wujūd*), to cosmic love in the widest sense. The whole imagery of wine in Persian poetry could be comfortably combined with the love motif by introducing the young charming Zoroastrian or Christian cupbearer as the locus of divine manifestations, which brings us back to the 'love of the unbearded'.

Much rarer is the symbolism of sacred food in Islamic mysticism. To my knowledge the idea of taking the beloved into one's self (the *theophagia* of Christian theology), or to have communion with him, is barely mentioned; it would be worthwhile to look at the very extensive imagery of food in Rūmī's poetry from this angle. His use of the numerous allusions to *halwā*, sweetmeats representing the sweetness of the beloved's lips, or the sweetness of God's grace, certainly is part of this group of border images.[130] And maybe we can also explain from this viewpoint Rūmī's predilection for the use of *bū*, 'fragrance, scent', which is so ubiquitous in his verse. Although in general Islamic lore scent is connected with the scent of Joseph's healing shirt (Sura 12:94ff.) we cannot overlook Rūmī's verse in which he says:

> Who was yesterday your friend and bedfellow
> That the hot bath became full of musk due to his fragrance?[131]

Instances of similar lines could easily be multiplied.

The orthodox certainly approved neither of the practices nor of the poetical symbols of the Sufis. Schubart states that the further man is removed from the origins of religion the more he will deprive religion of

---

[130] A charming combination of food-and-kiss imagery in a verse by the Indian mystic Gēsūdarāz (d. 1422) (*Anīs al-'ushshāq* [n.p., n.d.], 87):

> Two three kisses, light, with a soft little biting
> Will be like sugar and *palūda* [a kind of pudding].

[131] *Dīwān*, no. 2409.

its eerie, weird, and frightful aspects until religion is dissolved into ethics, and the Holy becomes Moral Perfection.[132] The Sufis experienced time and again the *Urschauder*, the primordial rapture of love which they date back to the day of the Covenant, the *rūz-i alast*. They experienced it in a mixture of fascination and awe, whether this love was purely 'divine' or grew in connection with a human object. They went back beyond the institutionalized, rigorously legalistic framework of orthodox Islam into the darkness where the true Water of Life can be found.

The Sufis found various answers to the experience of the *Urschauder*; for some of them it proved too strong, and they tried to eliminate it completely by embarking on the hardest ascetic practices possible. Others gave themselves to music and dance, or even to limitless debauchery, obliterating the outward signs of established religion, thus following the example of Majnūn, the prototype of the frenzied lover who died in the desert far away from the city of reason. Or else they sublimated their overwhelming experience into a symbolic language which, even when watered down by frequent use in subsequent generations, still makes the reader feel how deeply spiritually shaken they were by the experience of the Holy, which can never be expressed in words but only in suffering. As Ghālib says, alluding to Ḥallāj's martyrdom for his alleged divulgation of the secret of divine love:

> The secret which is in the breast is not a sermon:
> You can say it on the gallows, but not in the pulpit.[133]

BIBLIOGRAPHY

Abū Nuʿaim al-Iṣfahānī (1932–3), *Ḥilyat al-auliyāʾ*, Cairo: Maktabat al-Khānjī; Maṭbaʿat al-Saʿādah.

Ahmad, Z. (1968), *The Contribution of Indo-Pakistan to Arabic Literature*, Lahore: Sh. Muhammad Ashraf.

Amīr Khusrau (1343/1964), *Dīwān-i kāmil*, ed. M. Darwish, Tehran: Intishārāt-i Jāwidān.

ʿAndalīb, Naṣir Muḥammad (1310/1893), *Nāla-yi ʿAndalīb*, 2 vols., Bhopal: Maṭbaʿ-i Shahjahānī.

Andrae, T. (1947), *I Myrtenträdgården*, Stockholm: A. Bonniers forlag; Eng. trans. (1987), *In the Garden of Myrtles*, trans. by B. Sharpe, Albany, NY: SUNY Press.

Arberry, A. J. (trans.) (1961), *Discourses of Rūmī*, London: John Murray.

Asani, A. S. (1977), 'The Motif of the Longing Soul in Ismāʿīlī *ginan* Literature', Honours thesis, Harvard University.

---

[132] Schubart 1941, 10.   [133] Ghālib 1969, IV, no. 83.

'Aṭṭār, Farīduddīn (1905-7¹; repr. 1959), *Tadhkirat al-auliyā*, A. Nicholson, London and Leiden: Luzac.

(1339/1960a), *Dīwān-i qaṣāʾid wa ghazaliyāt*, ed. S. Nafīsī, Tehran; Sanaʾi.

(1339/1960b), *Ushturnāma*, ed. M. Muhaqqiq, Tehran: University.

(1961), *Manṭiq uṭ-ṭair*, ed. M. J. Shakūr, Tehran: Kitābfurūshī-i Tehrān.

Bahāʾuddīn Walad (1338/1959), *Maʿārif*, vol. 4, ed. B. Furūzānfar, Tehran: Idāra-i Kull-i nigārish-i wizārat-i farhang.

Baqlī, Ruzbihān (1958), *'Abhar al-ʿāshiqīn*, ed. H. Corbin, Paris and Tehran: Adrien Maisonneuve.

(1966), *Sharḥ-i shaṭhiyāt: Les paradoxes des soufis*, ed. H. Corbin, Tehran and Paris: Adrien Maisonneuve.

Bauer, H. (1917), *Das 12. Buch von al-Ġazālī's Hauptwerk, Von der Ehe, übersetzt und erläutert*, Halle: M. Niemeyer.

Birge, J. K. (1937¹, 1965), *The Bektashi Order of Dervishes*, London: Luzac.

Browne, E. G. (1921), *A Literary History of Persia*, Cambridge University Press.

Burton, R. (1851¹; 1973), *Sindh and the Races that Inhabit the Valley of the Indus*, Karachi/New York: Oxford University Press.

Campenhausen, H. *et al.* (eds.) (1957–65), *Die Religion in Geschichte und Gegenwart*, 3rd. edn, 7 vols., Tübingen: J. C. B. Mohr (P. Siebeck).

Corbin, H. (1955), 'Sympathie et théopathie chez les fidèles d'amour en Islam', *Eranos-Jahrbuch*, 24, 199–301.

Dailamī, Abu'l-Ḥasan ad- (1955), *Sīrat-i Abū ʿAbdallāh ibn al-Khafīf ash-Shīrāzī*, Persian trans. Ibn Junaid ash-Shīrāzī, ed. A. Schimmel, Ankara: Türk Tarih Kurumu Basımevi.

Dard, Khāja Mīr (1308/1890), *'Ilm ul-kitāb*, Delhi: al-Maṭbaʿ al-Anṣārī.

(1310/1892), *Chahār Risāla*, Bhopal: Maṭbaʿ-i Shāhjahānī.

Furūzānfar, Badīʿuz-Zamān (ed.) (1334/1956), *Aḥādīth-i Mathnawī*, 10 vols., Tehran: University.

Gennep, A. van (1909), *Rites de passage*, Paris: E. Nourry; Eng. trans. (1960), *The Rites of Passage*, trans. by M. B. Vizedom and G. L. Caffee, University of Chicago Press.

Ghālib, M. A. (1969), *Dīwān-i fārsī, Kulliyāt*, 17 vols., Lahore: Majlas-e-Yadgar-e-Urdu.

Ghazzālī, Abū Ḥāmid al- (1289/1872), *Ihyāʾ 'ulūm ad-dīn*, 4 vols., Bulaq: n.p.

Ghazzālī, Ahmad (1942), *Sawāniḥ*, ed. H. Ritter, Istanbul and Leipzig: Brockhaus; German trans. (1976), *Gedanken über die Liebe*, trans. R. Gramlich, Wiesbaden: Steiner.

Gibb, H. A. R. *et al.* (1960), *The Encyclopaedia of Islam, New Edition*, Leiden: Brill.

Goethe, J. W. von (1952), *West-östlicher Divan*, vol. 2: *Noten und Abhandlungen*, Berlin: Akademie-Verlag.

Gonda, J. (ed.) (1974), *History of Indian Literature*, vol. 8, Wiesbaden: Harrassowitz.

Gräf, E. (ed.) (1968), *Festschrift Werner Caskel*, Leiden: Brill.

Gramlich, R. (1966), *Die schiitischen Derwischorden Persiens*, vol. 1, Wiesbaden: Kommissionsverlag Steiner.

Grotzfeld, H. (1970), *Das Bad im arabisch-islamischen Mittelalter*, Wiesbaden: Harrassowitz.

Grunebaum, G. E. von (1966), *The Dream and Human Society*, Berkeley and Los Angeles: University of California Press.

Hashmī, B. A. (1933–4), 'Sarmad: His Life and Quatrains', *Islamic Culture* 7, 1933: 633–73; 8, 1934: 92–104, Hyderabad: Deccan.

Heiler, F. (1961), *Erscheinungsformen und Wesen der Religion*, Stuttgart: W. Kohlhammer.

Hujwīrī, ʿAlī ʿUthmān al-Jullābī al- (1911[1], 1959), *Kashf al-mahjūb*, trans. R. A. Nicholson, London: Luzac.

Ibn al-Jauzī, Abū I-Faraj ʿAbd ar-Rahmān (1340/1921–2), *Talbīs Iblīs*, Cairo: Maṭbaʿat al-Saʿāda.

Ikram, S. H. (1953), *Armaghān-i Pāk*, Karachi: n.p.

ʿIrāqī, Fakhruddīn (1338/1959), *Kulliyāt*, ed. S. Nafīsī, Tehran: n.p.

Jāmī, ʿAbdur Rahmān (1336/1957), *Nafahāt al-uns*, ed. M. Tauhīdīpūr, Tehran: Kitābfurūshī-i Saʿdī.

Kadri, Yakup (1948), *Flamme und Falter: ein Derwischroman*, trans. A. Schimmel, Gummersbach: Florestan Verlag.

Karay, Refik Halid (*ca.* 1952[1]; 1964[2]), *Kadınlar Tekkesi*, Istanbul: İnkilâp ve Aka Kitabevleri.

Khāqānī (1338/1959), *Dīwān*, ed. Z. Sajjādi, Tehran: n.p.

Kister, M. J. (1954), *as-Sulamī's Kitāb adab aṣ-ṣuhba*, Jerusalem: n.p.

Kriss, R. and Kriss-Heinrich, H. (1960), *Volksglaube im Bereich des Islam*, vol. 1, Wiesbaden: Harrassowitz.

Lambrick, H. T. (1960[1]; repr. 1972) *The Terrorist*, London: Benn.

Leeuw, G. van der (1956), *Phänomenologie der Religion*, Tübingen: J. C. B. Mohr (P. Siebeck).

Littmann, E. (1951), *Ahmed il-Bedawī; Ein Lied auf den ägyptischen Nationalheiligen*, Wiesbaden: n.p.

Makdisi, G. (1974), 'The Hanbalite School and Sufism', *Humaniora Islamica* 2, 61–72.

Massignon, L. (1922), *La Passion d'al-Hosayn ibn Mansour Hallaj, martyr mystique de l'Islam, exécuté à Bagdad le 26 mars 922*, 2 vols., Paris: n.p.

Mayne, P. (1956), *Saints of Sind*, London: John Murray.

Mazhar, J. (1966), *Maktūbāt*, ed. A. R. Quraishī, Bombay: Alavi Bik Dapu.

Meier, F. (ed.) (1948), *"Firdaus al-murshidīyā fī asrār aṣ-ṣamadīya": Die Vita des Scheich Abu Ishāq al-Kāzarūnī*, Leipzig: Harrosswitz.

——— (ed.) (1957), *Die Fawāʾih al-ğamāl wa fawātih al-ğalāl des Naǧm ad-dīn al-Kubrā*, Wiesbaden: F. Steiner.

——— (1976), *Abu Saʿīd-i Abūl-Khair*, Leiden: Brill.

Naguib, N. (1972), 'al-Khurūj ilā as-sayyid al-badawī', in *Fikrun wa Fann: Zeitschrift für die arabische Welt*, eds. A. Theile and A. Schimmel, vol. 20, Hamburg.

Nizami, K. A. (1955), *The Life and Times of Shaikh Farīd Ganj-i Shakar*, Aligarh: Department of History, Muslim University.

Nwyia, P. (1973), *Trois oeuvres inédites des mystiques musulmans: Šaqīq al-Balḫī, Ibn ʿAṭāʾ, Niffarī*, Beirut: Dar al-Machreq.

Qāniʿ Mīr, Alī Shīr (1956), *Maqālāt ash-shuʿarāʾ*, ed. S. H. Rashdi, Karachi: Sindhi Adabi Board.

Qushairī, Abūʾl-Qāsim al- (1330/1912), *ar-Risāla fī ʿilm at-taṣawwuf*, Cairo: n.p.

Rahman, F. (1966[1]; 1979[2]), *Islam*, London and Chicago: University of Chicago Press.

Ritter, H. (1955), *Das Meer der Seele: Mensch, Welt und Gott in den Geschichten des Farīduddīn ʿAṭṭār*, Leiden: Brill.

—— (1960), 'Die Mevlânafeier in Konya vom 11. bis 17. Dezember 1960', *Oriens* 15, 249–70.

Rūmī, Maulānā Jalāluddīn (1925–1940), *Mathnawī-yi maʿnawī*, 8 vols., ed. and trans. with commentary, R. A. Nicholson, London: Luzac and Leiden: Brill.

—— (1336/1957–67), *Dīwān-i kabīr yā Kulliyāt-i Shams*, 10 vols., ed. Badiʿuz-Zamān Furūzānfar, Tehran: University of Tehran Press.

Rypka, J. (1968), *History of Iranian Literatures*, Dordrecht: D. Reidel.

Sadarangani, H. (1956), *Persian Poets of Sind*, Karachi: n.p.

Saʿdī, Muṣliḥuddīn (1342/1963), *Kulliyāt*, ed. M. A. Furūghī, Tehran: n.p.

Sanāʾī, A. (1329/1950), *Ḥadīqa*, ed. M. Razawī, Tehran: n.p.

—— (1341/1962), *Dīwān*, ed. M. Razawī, Tehran: Ibn Sina.

Sarrāj, Abū Naṣr as- (1914), *Kitāb al-lumaʿ fī t-taṣawwuf*, ed. R. A. Nicholson, London: Luzac; Leiden: Brill.

Schimmel, A. (1968), 'Sufismus und Heiligenverehrung im spätmittelalterlichen Ägypten', in ed. E. Gräf, *Festschrift Werner Caskel*, Leiden: Brill, 274–89.

—— (1974), 'Sindhi Literature', in ed. J. Gonda, *History of Indian Literature*, 8/4, Wiesbaden: Harrassowitz, 1–41.

—— (1975), *Mystical Dimensions of Islam*, Chapel Hill: University of North Carolina Press.

—— (1976), *Pain and Grace: a Study of Two Mystical Writers of eighteenth-century Muslim India*, Leiden: Brill.

—— (1978), *The Triumphal Sun: A Study of the Works of Jalāloddīn Rūmī*, London: East-West Publications.

Schubart, W. (1941), *Religion und Eros*, Munich: C. H. Beck.

Segelberg, C. (1960), 'The Coptic–Gnostic Gospel According to Philip and Its Sacramental System', *Numen* 7, 189–200.

Shāh ʿAbd ul-Laṭīf (1958), *Risālō*, ed. K. B. Adwani, Bombay, n.p.

Smith, M. (1928), *Rabiʿa the Mystic and Her Fellow Saints in Islam*, Cambridge University Press.

Subhan, J. A. (1960), *Sufism: Its Saints and Shrines*, Lucknow: Lucknow Publishing.

Tattawī, M. A. (1956), *Tuḥfat aṭ-ṭāhirīn*, ed. B. A. Durrānī, Karachi: Sindhi Adabi Board.

Teufel, J. K. (1962), *Eine Lebensbeschreibung des Scheichs ʿAlī-i Hamadānī*, Leiden: Brill.

Trimingham, J. S. (1971), *The Sufi Orders in Islam*, Oxford: Clarendon Press.

CHAPTER 16

The body in Sikh tradition

Eleanor Nesbitt

INTRODUCTION

Sikhs and the body

The word 'Sikh' conjures up a picture of a bearded man, his long hair covered by a turban. Physical form, uncut hair in particular, is an important indication of Sikh identity. The ideal of the physically whole saint–soldier is dramatically reaffirmed in every *amrit pahul*, the ceremony of initiation into the Khalsa (the community of Sikhs who adhere to the pattern required by their tenth Guru). In this chapter the extent to which a Sikh's physical form expresses rejection or affirmation of society – Hindu, Muslim, or Western, but particularly Hindu – is examined.

Sikh devotional behaviour can, it is suggested, be understood as a physical response to the exhortation, 'Every Sikh is bidden to accept the Granth as Guru.'[1] Contemporary cultic practice and, more generally, attitudes to the body will be explored in relation to the Gurus' insights and injunctions. The individual's bodily behaviour in worship, it is suggested, illustrates the relationship between Sikhism and surrounding Hindu society. As Sikh devotion continues in the framework of North Indian tradition, with parts of which the Gurus themselves took issue, this wider Hindu context also requires attention. Otherwise one will misunderstand both the emphases of the Gurus and the complexities of current practice and controversy. This study can focus on only a few elements in a continuing interactive process.

We shall first note the thrust of the scriptural teaching as it relates to the body, then examine the Khalsa initiation ceremony in the light both of this earlier teaching and of the physical requirements laid down by the tenth Guru. In doing so we note the implications of these for Sikh

---

[1] These words were first used in the *rahitnama* (code of discipline) attributed to Prahilad Singh (McLeod 1989, 36).

identity. Finally it is suggested that Sikhs express their belief in the scriptures as the manifest body of the Gurus (understood to be one in spirit) in the devotional idiom of wider Indian religious tradition. Apparent paradoxes, if they are to be understood, must be seen in this broad cultural continuum.

The Sikh community

Although the message of Sikhism is potentially universal and there are Sikhs now resident in many countries and on five continents, the sixteen million or so adherents are virtually all Punjabi in origin. Historically and emotionally rooted in the land of Punjab (literally five waters – i.e. the tributaries of the Indus), their mother-tongue is Punjabi and their traditions of dress and cuisine are Punjabi, shared by Punjabi Hindu and Sikh alike. The Punjab in its widest sense experienced numerous incursions from the West and, until the nineteenth century, Sikhism developed in a predominantly Hindu society which was dominated by Muslim rulers. Sikhs now identify with the fraction of Punjab which constitutes the post-1966 Indian state of that name.

The lives of Sikhs (literally 'learners') are, according to their religious teaching, to be guided by the Guru (teacher, spiritual instructor). For Sikhs the light of Guruship, supremely existent as God, shines in ten human Gurus and in the Guru Granth Sahib. Guru Nanak, born in 1469, was the first of the human masters and Guru Gobind Singh, who died in 1708, was the last. The Guru Granth Sahib is the 1,430 page volume of scripture, also known as the Adi Granth.[2] It is written or printed in Gurmukhi script and consists of the hymns of six Gurus and of saintly poets (*bhagat*) of whom some were contemporary with Guru Arjan Dev, the fifth Guru, and some predated Guru Nanak. The compositions of Guru Gobind Singh are not included in the Guru Granth Sahib, but some which are attributed to him are used in daily worship and in the rite of initiation to the Khalsa. Guidance and blessing from the Guru Granth Sahib are sought in every aspect of life.

Committed Sikhs also follow the *rahit* (code of discipline) associated with Guru Gobind Singh's creation in 1699 of a physically distinguishable community, the Khalsa. The relationship of the Khalsa to the *panth* (Sikh society as a whole) is discussed by McLeod (1989). In 1950 the Sikh Rahit Maryada was published and this is accepted as the authoritative

---

[2] In this essay Adi Granth references use the standard pagination unless English translations are specifically mentioned.

restatement of this code. (McLeod 1984, 71–86 provides a translation of this and parts of earlier *rahit-namas*). In practice there are many people who identify themselves as Sikh but do not choose to be initiated into the Khalsa. Of the *rahit* rules which they may observe, abstention from tobacco and haircutting are most decisive in conferring on males a strongly Sikh identity. Uncut, yet disciplined hair (and beard) indicate a disjunction with Hindu society and an affirmation of Khalsa identity. The term for a Sikh with uncut hair is *keshdhari*, and the importance of this is particularly clear in the definition of a Sikh provided by the Delhi Gurdwara Act 82 of 1971 (McLeod 1989, 98).

GURU NANAK'S PRIORITIES

The scriptures

The language of the Guru Granth Sahib is a vernacular akin to modern Hindi and Punjabi. The words *sharir*, *deh*, and *tan* all mean body in the sense of the physical vehicle for the *atma* (individual soul). *Tan* is particularly used in the formula 'tan, man, dhan' (body, mind, and wealth), but the terms for body do not in practice differ in their connotations, although *deh* has the original sense of 'covering' (Walker 1968, 162). On the basis of contemporary research Krause defines a *sharir* as especially relating to bodily drives and processes and the temporary aspect of a person, but part of a unity of *sharir* and *atma* (personal communication).

In the Guru Granth Sahib the body represents limitation from which God is free. Incorporeality distinguishes God from creation. According to mul mantar, the seminal statement with which the scriptures open, 'God is never born' (Adi Granth, 1). According to Guru Gobind Singh's Jap, repeated daily:

> God is without birth and death,
> without limbs,
> without form, colour, outline.
> (See Doabia 1980, 59–136)

Neither the particularity of the body nor its perishability are attributes of the divine, and the Hindu concept of God's descent (*avatar*) or incarnation in human form was not part of the Gurus' message, although Sikhs believe that the eternal Guru was incarnated in human form. As compared with the soul (*atma*) the body is transient. The soul is described as tenant of the body or as a bird perching on a tree (Macauliffe 1978, VI,

331). This being so, the display of grief at the death of a loved one should give place to remembrance of God and acceptance of mortality:

> This body, one thinks, will ever remain,
> This flesh which dissolves like a transient dream.
> (Adi Granth, 219; see McLeod 1984, 121)

However, what separated humanity from God most significantly, in Guru Nanak's view, was not body, but *haumai*, the self-centredness of those whose lives are responsive not to the Guru, but to the tendencies of *kam* (lust), *krodh* (anger), *lobh* (desire), *moh* (delusion), and *ahankar* (pride). The Gurus' challenge is to conquer not the body, but the *man* (a term meaning heart and mind, often in the sense of their capriciousness). So neither martyrdom nor mortification of the body can be the way to God:

> One does not reach truth by remaining motionless
> like trees and stones,
> Nor by being sawn up alive.
> (Adi Granth, 952)

The way to liberation and union with God, through the Guru's grace, is instead *nam simaran* (remembrance of God) in the midst of a life of active service. *Nam simaran* does not require rigorous asceticism, quite the contrary:

> Some there are who repair to the woods . . .
> Others freeze themselves like ice,
> Others besmear their bodies with ashes . . .
> Others keep their hair matted . . .
> Others wander about naked without dozing or sleeping,
> Others burn themselves in fire, limb by limb . . .
> Without the Lord's name their bodies are reduced to dust.
> (Adi Granth, 1285)

The Hindu context

Such penances were practised only by a minority of Hindus, the *siddha*, *yogi*, and *nath* ascetics. But Guru Nanak observed Hindu and Muslim alike demonstrating their religious allegiance through physical externals such as dress and ritual posture rather than through spiritual integrity. It is, in contrast, our twentieth-century concepts of holism and integration which better represent the Gurus' attitude to life in its inseparable aspects of body, mind, and spirit. This is significant in view of the polarities and hierarchies of Hindu tradition. Formative in the religious ecology of Guru Nanak's day were Hindu concepts which continue to find expression in the religions of India and to influence Sikhs' attitudes to the body. In accordance with centuries-old Brahminical precept, society was stratified with higher caste people avoiding all contact with those whose hereditary task was to dispose of excreta and dead animals. Thus abhorrence of bodily reality was institutionalized. Meat-eating was likewise condemned as incompatible with spiritual advancement. Ideally, in Hindu thought, human life consisted of four stages (*ashrama*) of which only the second (*grihastha*) allowed, and indeed required, sexual relationship, i.e. with one's spouse. Certain religious orders shunned family life and sought union with God by ascetic practices of the sort described by the Gurus. From the Guru Granth Sahib emerges a clear response to these beliefs and practices. They were false priorities which could not bring one any closer to the ultimate goal of being liberated from the cycle of rebirth. The insights of the Gurus and *bhagats* are conveyed not in didactic prose, but through an ironic use of imagery, rich in its portrayal of the human body.

The Gurus did not challenge the custom of marrying a member of the same caste, but made it clear that a person's status or caste had no relevance to spiritual progress. Kabir (a *bhagat*) emphasized this, enquiring:

> If blood runs in my veins
> Does milk run in yours?
> (Adi Granth, 1128)

A *janam sakhi*[3] story related that Guru Nanak cooked venison at a site held sacred by Hindus (see Cole 1984, 183). Whether or not this is apocryphal his words certainly put the *brahmans'* denunciation of meat-eating firmly in perspective:

> Man is first conceived in flesh . . .
> He seizes teats of flesh.
> You were produced from the blood of your parents
> But you eat no fish or flesh.
> (Adi Granth, 1289–90; see Macauliffe 1978, I, 48)

Vegetarians, too, may exploit others ('devour people in the darkness of night'). The Guru affirmed the physical, denouncing escapism as hypocritical.

Similarly Guru Nanak rejected the view that celibacy was essential for

---

[3] The *janam sakhis* are popular, hagiographic accounts of Guru Nanak's life. They do not have the canonical status of the Guru Granth Sahib.

spiritual development. Accordingly he did not confer Guruship upon the ascetic Sri Chand, his unmarried son, but upon a married follower whom he renamed Angad, a word meaning 'limb' or 'part of my body'. The Gurus did not require from their disciples total abstention from sexual intercourse, but the discipline of faithful married life. They regarded the *grihastha ashrama* (the married state) as the optimum for all.

Women

From this follow implications for the perception of women. Female sexuality has in Indian tradition been seen as seducing men from the spiritual ascent as well as jeopardizing their potency, which is diminished by the loss of semen (Aslam 1979, 133f; Carstairs 1957, 85). The Gurus' words are rightly understood by Sikhs to dignify women's status:

> It is through a vessel, the despised one, that we
> are conceived and from her that we are born.
> It is to a vessel that we are engaged and then married . . .
> Why denounce her from whom even kings are born?
> (Adi Granth, 473)

The Gurus also continue the metaphor of a woman's response to her lover for the response of the human soul to God. This simultaneously reinforces the notion of female submissiveness and encourages men to regard themselves not only as husbands, agriculturalists, or warriors (their masculine role) but, before God at least, as playing the feminine part in a spiritual relationship (see Nikky-Guninder Kaur Singh 1993, 90–117).

INITIATION

Seen in association with the Gurus' utterances, the *amrit pahul* (ceremony of initiation into the Khalsa) visually reaffirms the integration of physical and spiritual and the equality of all, even the low caste and the female (though in practice the *panj pyare*, those who administer the rite, are men[4]). The Brahminical obsession with pollution and purity, institutionalized in rules of commensality, is upended as candidates drink the *amrit* from the same bowl, finishing the remainder in reverse order. The bodies of initiates, male and female, all bear the same five required

---

[4] Enquiries during my 1992 fieldwork among Sikhs in Coventry elicited no hint of either male or female dissatisfaction with this limitation. For refutation of the suggestion that five uniformed women ('panj piarian') in a Hounslow procession were anything but a 'guard of honour' for the scriptures, see the British Punjabi weekly, *Des Pardes*, 4 December 1992, 11.

indications of commitment, the unshorn hair, comb, wristlet, short
sword, and *kachh* (cotton underwear) which together are called the *panj
kakke* (five items beginning with K in Punjabi).

The principles expressed by earlier Gurus have been transposed into a
self-evidently martial mode. All participants in the ceremony crouch,
with left knee raised, in the posture of military preparedness called *bir
asan* (See Singh and Rai 1984, 58).[5] The fifth and ninth Gurus had been
put to death by the Mughal authorities and the response of their sons,
Guru Hargobind and Guru Gobind Singh, was to arm. Guru Gobind
Singh required of his Khalsa self-sacrificial commitment and discipline,
spelled out in successive codes (*rahit*). (Khalsa can be translated literally
both as 'pure' and as 'owing direct allegiance to the Guru without
intermediaries'.)

The Khalsa Sikh must be both saint and soldier, *sant–sipahi*, prayerful
and ready for action against injustice. The five Ks are, for the initiated
Khalsa, no mere uniform or badge to be worn only at particular times.
The faithful Khalsa is not parted from his/her *kirpan* (sword) even when
bathing (Singh and Rai 1984, 52). The *panj kakke* are inseparable from the
whole person and, in the case of the *kesh* (uncut hair), organically part of
it. Physical fitness, encouraged specifically by the second Guru, has been
subsumed in physical wholeness symbolized by the hair. The *panj pyare*
are required to be whole in body (not maimed or deformed) as well as
conforming to the code of discipline. Guru Gobind Singh forbade
circumcision (Macauliffe 1978, v, 99) as well as the removal of hair from
any part of the body. Nor, he ruled, should the body be abused with
tobacco or intoxicants. The candidates for *amrit pahul* are committing
themselves to observe this code which can only be discussed so selectively
here.

The Five Ks

The five Ks, especially the *kesh*, have acquired profound meaning for
Sikhs. Each can be interpreted as condemnation of a norm in Hindu
society, just as the prohibition of smoking and *halal* meat are a
condemnation of Muslim practice. The Ks also symbolize and further
specific ethical principles. For example, the *kachh*, a stitched garment
which was more suitable in battle than the wrap-around garments of
Hindu men, comes to signify sexual restraint. The *kangha* (small wooden

[5] Photographs in this collection – of folk-dance, sword fighting, meditation, etc. – illustrate, better
than words can, the range of Sikh body language.

comb) represents soldierly hygiene and discipline, an obvious contrast to the matted, unkempt locks of Hindu renunciants. Awareness of context deepens Sikh understanding of *kesh*. Scholars also explore the historical context in their analysis of the five Ks. Uberoi sees in them the deliberate inversion of features of Hindu initiation: the *kesh* inverts the *mundan* (ritual head shaving) which is characteristic of Hindu initiation (1980, 38). Das (see 1977 and 1985) develops from this the view that:

It is the combination of opposition *in praesentia* [e.g. the steel bracelet with the sword] with oppositions *in absentia* [e.g. the long groomed hair of the Sikh with the matted hair of the Hindu ascetic] which succeeds in obliterating the categorical partitions between renunciation, kinship and householdership which obtained in the Hindu world. (1985, 194–5).

However, it may well be premature to assume that the physical marks of the Khalsa Sikh and of *keshdharis*[6] who have not been initiated signify a revolt against the body of society, or at least against established Punjabi norms, Hindu or Muslim. Before jumping to this conclusion, one has to consider McLeod's literary evidence that long hair was already customary for men of the Jat caste which was strongly represented in the Sikh *panth* (1976, 52). There is also Jagjit Singh's claim that men of other Hindu castes also kept their hair long (1985, 97). Hershman (1974) analyses the significance of hair in its many modes for Punjabis male and female, Hindu and Sikh. From this analysis it appears that Sikh women's hair behaviour is the same as Punjabi Hindu and Muslim women's, although a Sikh woman would not shave her head as Hindus may for religious purposes such as mourning. By contrast with Sikh females the unshorn male adopts hair behaviour which distinguishes him from other Punjabi men. He adopts the general female norm of uncut hair, but without the surrounding taboos on, for example, when it may be washed. The sexual meaning which Hershman reads into hair behaviour is far from the meanings of which Sikhs are conscious. It is likely that the meanings with which Sikh men invest their hair – and the other Ks – are various, and that these differ in emphasis from eighteenth-century perceptions.

Evidence of the emotive significance for male Sikhs of the *kesh* abounds. Women have never been under comparable social pressure to cut their hair. It is therefore the man's *kesh*, and by extension the turban, in North Indian terms the most dignified head-covering for men, which

---

[6] *keshdhari* – literally 'one who maintains uncut hair' – is the term used to denote a Sikh who observes Khalsa discipline in this respect.

have become for Sikh and non-Sikh alike the symbol of Sikh identity. The *janam-sakhi* story of a poor disciple selling his hair to purchase food for his Guru suggests that this was not always so (McLeod 1980b, 50).

Far better known by Sikhs is the story of the eighteenth-century martyr, Bhai Taru Singh, who was scalped rather than allow his hair to be cut. In his autobiography two centuries later Bhai Randhir Singh, a hero of the struggle for Indian independence, describes fasting in gaol because he could not eat without first combing his hair, and for this he required a particular oil (Trilochan Singh n.d., 383ff.). Many male Sikhs are *keshdhari* although they have not taken *amrit*.

Although many male Sikhs in Britain – mostly from the numerically dominant Jat caste – have, for practical reasons such as gaining employment, dispensed with their *kesh*, Sikhs rally in their thousands in defence of the right to wear the turban. Beetham (1970) provides detailed analysis of disputes over the right of Sikh bus crews to wear turbans. Subsequent protest by Sikhs against having to wear crash-helmets when riding motor-cycles resulted in legal vindication in the Motor-Cycle Crash-Helmet (Religious Exemption) Act 1976, cited by Sacha (1988, 38). Central to all these instances is the sanctity of the *kesh* as inseparable from Sikh identity. Thus when surgery is considered some Sikhs prefer death to the removal of hair from any part of their body (Bennett 1990). Since 1984, when Indian government troops stormed the Golden Temple in Amritsar, a frequent response to the perceived threat to Sikhism has been for short-haired, cleanshaven men to grow their hair and beard.

Conformity to the Khalsa code of discipline now signifies primarily a strongly Sikh identity rather than the deliberate segregation from Islamic society or a reversal of Hindu norms. Departure from the *rahit* carries a message which differs from one individual to another according to gender, caste, and circumstance. For a man to smoke would imply rejection of both a Sikh principle and accepted custom, whereas for a woman to smoke would in addition be a repudiation of a more widely held South Asian view of appropriate female behaviour. If a woman trims her hair or a man trims his beard they distance themselves from Khalsa ideals but not from the *panth* as a whole. If a male member of the Jat caste is clean-shaven and short-haired, his Sikh identity will usually not be questioned, whereas if a male Sikh from a family in a less solidly Sikh caste, such as the Khatri or Ramgarhia castes, dispenses with the *kesh* he is likely to be perceived as Hindu by other Punjabis. McLeod elaborates this further (1989, 111–12).

CONTEMPORARY PRACTICE: FURTHER ASPECTS

A glance at prevailing assumptions about the female body, and about health and diet, reveals that twentieth-century Sikh attitudes to the body continue to manifest the norms and presuppositions of Punjabi society.

Women

During the conflict of the eighteenth century, women took up arms. Remembering this and the Gurus' respect for women, an increasing number of female Sikhs now wear turbans. None the less what dictates a woman's physical behaviour – her dress and degree of contact with males – is not any precept of Sikhism, but the principle of *izzat* (honour) that dominates Punjabi society. This operates in tension also with the pulls of western society and feminist thinking. Some would argue that *izzat* is especially powerful in the Jat caste which is also most numerous in the Sikh community (Pettigrew 1972). *Izzat* means a sense of one's family status and reputation. This must be maintained, enhanced, and, when necessary, protected with one's life. Honour is most at risk from the immodesty or rumoured immodesty of female members of the family. A woman's body, particularly an unmarried woman's, is potentially the locus of shame for her many relatives. Pettigrew's account of her experiences in Punjab as a fieldworker, recently married into a Jat family, make this very clear (1981).

Disease

In the scriptures, as in Indian tradition more generally, no distinction is made between physical, mental, and spiritual disorder. All *dukh* (suffering) results from *haumai* (ego) and is healed by practising *nam simaran* (remembrance of God) (Atamjit Singh 1983). Many Sikhs would testify to the power of the *gurbani* (hymns of the Guru Granth Sahib) to heal their emotions. With this in mind the Sukhmani Sahib[7] is often read. Some would affirm the power of scriptural recitation in healing physical symptoms (Singh, Singh, and Brar 1979). Water which has been kept near the scriptures throughout a complete reading is popularly called *amrit* (nectar, holy water) and is felt to bring health and good luck. Not surprisingly, in view of the famous story of the healing of Rajni's crippled husband in the pool which later became Amritsar, bathing in the pools at

---

[7] Sukhmani Sahib is a hymn composed by Guru Arjan Dev.

sites associated with the Gurus is also believed by many to be therapeutic (Singh, Singh, and Brar 1980). Together, bathing and the recitation of scripture are further believed by many to release the soul from further rebirths, as is clear from an inscription at the Baoli Sahib gurdwara in Goindval, Punjab.

Punjabi culture inherits from Ayurvedic and Islamic medicine a widespread acceptance that illness results from the imbalance of the humours of the body. The body is not a separate entity from the rest of creation, in this view, but an ecology exhibiting the same processes as the wider physical environment. Nor is there a mind that can be treated in isolation from the body (see Kakar 1982 and Zimmerman 1987). Krause (1989) reports that for Hindu and Sikh alike the seat of 'mind' is not the head but the heart (*hriday*). Punjabis, irrespective of religious community, inherit the traditional belief that the cooling and heating effects of foods maintain or upset the physical balance (see Aslam 1979, 218–40; Beck 1969).

Diet

On the subject of diet – intrinsic to any discussion of the body – distinct attitudes interact within the *panth* (Sikh community), a community symbolized by *teg* and *deg* (sword and cooking pot). The tendency to eat more and different meats (for instance, turkey for Christmas in Britain) does not apparently contradict Guru Nanak's words cited above (Adi Granth, 1289–1290). But for many Sikhs it is as unthinkable as it would be for many Hindus that so holy a person as the Guru could have eaten flesh. Although Guru Gobind Singh is said to have prohibited only *halal* meat (animals slaughtered in accordance with Muslim requirement), *amritdhari* (initiated) Sikhs commonly feel committed to a diet free of eggs, fish, and meat of any kind. Contemporary movements within the *panth*, no less than earlier ones, are characterized by their ruling on non-vegetarian food. Strict vegetarianism is fundamental to the Namdhari (Kuka) sect. Devotees who have been influenced by spiritual teachers such as Baba Nand Singh of Nanaksar abstain from all non-vegetarian food and accordingly reinterpret accounts of the later Gurus' hunting (Doabia 1981, 100).[8]

---

[8] 'Baba Nand Singh Ji declared from time to time that the Gurbani strictly prohibits the eating of meat, fish, eggs . . . they used to assert, "some Satgurus did kill some animals, when sometimes they went for hunting. The Satgurus had and still own the power of infusing life in the dead. The object was not to eat meat. They did not eat meat. The object was to end their cycles of births and deaths." '

Devotion

In trying to understand present-day Sikh attitudes to the body and the bodily, one detects, even in the West, not so much the pressure exerted by Christian or western secular assumptions as a continuing interaction between elements from the older North Indian environment in which Sikhism emerged.

It is in the gurdwara, a term applicable to any place where the Guru Granth Sahib has been installed, that individually and corporately Sikhs give bodily articulation to this cultural interaction in the presence of the embodiment of the Gurus, the Guru Granth Sahib. According to a popular *janam-sakhi* story Guru Nanak at Mecca deliberately lay down with his feet pointing towards the *miharab* of a mosque (the niche indicating the direction of the Kaba, the revered hub of the Islamic world). (A nineteenth-century artist's impression of the scene is reproduced in McLeod 1991 as figure 7.) Even if this story originated as a claim by his followers that Guru Nanak was supreme, Sikhs today understand the story as making the point, obscured by the bodily orientation for Muslim prayer, that God is everywhere (Singh, K. 1963, 36). But religious faith always finds expression in posture and gesture, and contemporary Sikh practice is no exception. All who came into the presence of the Guru Granth Sahib cover their heads (if not already turbaned), remove footwear, and walk up to the Guru Granth Sahib. In front of this book all in turn kneel, touching the floor with their head in an action called *mattha tekna*. People sit cross-legged on the floor, so facing the scriptures without stretching feet out towards them which would be a sign of disrespect. They are always seated at a lower level than the Guru Granth Sahib which is installed on a special stand. If the scriptures are not present this code of physical behaviour does not apply.

The volume is supported on the *palki* or *manji* (palanquin or bed) by small cushions. When lying open, but not being read, it is covered by bright cloths called *rumalas*. Above is a canopy of wood or cloth. Whoever is in attendance on the Guru Granth Sahib waves over it a *chaur*. This whisk-like fan symbolizes princely authority, for princes and spiritual teachers were cooled in this way by their subordinates. The scriptures are 'laid to rest' (*sukhasan, santokh*) for the night. In some gurdwaras more or thicker *rumulas* are laid over the Guru Granth Sahib during the cooler months (Singh, I. P. 1961). Thus in considerable detail worshippers daily demonstrate respect for the scriptures as the Guru.

Plate 12   After a ceremonial reading in a Sikh home, the Guru Granth Sahib
returns to the gurdwara. As living Guru, it is borne, carefully wrapped, on a Sikh's
covered head. In front, water is sprinkled to cleanse the path of the Guru, and
behind, a boy waves the *chauri* as a mark of respect.

This is the expected norm which follows naturally – given the culturally
dominant Indian idiom of elaborate attention to the needs of the images
of deities in Hindu shrines – from belief that the volume of sacred hymns
is 'paragat guran ki deh' (the Master's body manifest). In an eighteenth-
century injunction ascribed to the tenth Guru the metaphor is elaborated.

The second [manifestation of the Guru] is the sacred scripture, the Granth. This
you must accept as an actual part of me, treating its letters as the hairs of my
body. (Nand Lal's *Prasan Uttar*, quoted in McLeod 1989, 53)

The way in which the scriptures embody the Guru is understood
differently by different Sikhs. For example Indarjit Singh writes:

When the tenth Guru said, 'Consider the Granth Sahib to be the future Guru',
he was clearly referring to the teaching, not to the physical paper and ink. He
was referring to the contents, not the container. In building increasingly lavish
'rest rooms' for the Granth Sahib in many of our Gurdwaras, are we not failing
to distinguish between legitimate reverence and superstitious deification?
(Singh, I., 1985, 27–8.)

A minority's interpretation

But congregations in some gurdwaras – in Britain notably in the Nanaksar gurdwara at Smethwick and Coventry – would see such practice as intrinsic to faith in the scriptures as 'paragat guran ki deh' (Nesbitt 1985). In these gurdwaras, where the congregations are regarded as heretical by many Sikhs because of the scale of devotion shown to a living leader, the scriptures are covered with *rumalas* the size of bedspreads. Food is offered three times daily. Readers have their mouths covered with a white cloth to prevent saliva dishonouring the Guru. In Nanaksar gurdwaras in India, the floor on which the Guru Granth Sahib is installed varies with the season to ensure that the Guru is enjoying the pleasantest temperature. The key to this is certainly not provided by Guru Nanak's disregard for convention at Mecca. It has much more to do with beliefs and practices in Sikhism's wider Hindu context, given the generally held Sikh belief that Guru Gobind Singh commanded, 'Guru maniahu Granth', i.e. 'Acknowledge the Granth as Guru' (McLeod 1976, 66, and 1989, 36).

Balbir Singh lists these details of devotional practice which stem from faith that the scriptures are literally the Guru's body (*deh*), and argues for such conviction from Hindu precedent where devotees' faith in an image was rewarded by God appearing (1983 Part 1, 85ff.). Similarly Baba Nand Singh's belief in the scriptures as 'paragat guran ki deh' had been so intense that Guru Nanak appeared before him as he meditated (see Doabia 1981). He placed food in front of the Guru Granth Sahib and fasted for many days before his faith was confirmed by the discovery that the food had diminished, i.e. been consumed by the Guru.

In Nanaksar gurdwaras, faith in the Guruship of the scriptures arguably leads to the acceptance of a view which is more Hindu than Sikh, that asceticism and celibacy are superior to *grihastha* (married life). The attendants on the Guru Granth Sahib in Nanaksar gurdwaras are called *bahingam*, from a Sanskrit word for bird which underlines their detachment from earthly matters. Baba Nand Singh was unmarried and celibacy is required from this nucleus of *bahingam*s (Doabia 1981, 19).

CONCLUSION

Fervent conviction within the *panth*, articulated as it is in the idiom of the wider North Indian tradition, is always open to criticism from within and without that it is 'too Hindu' or 'not Sikh'. Sikhism is a protestant religion, which is still to a great extent culturally embedded in older traditions whose priorities the Gurus challenged. These are continually surfacing in new combinations. In response, concerned members of the Khalsa are constantly striving to firm up the definition of who may rightly be called 'Sikh'. Khalsa-approved practice is itself strongly Hindu (in the older, wider sense of Indian) in its idiom. Nothing illustrates this better than Sikhs' cultic practices and intermeshed assumptions regarding the body.

BIBLIOGRAPHY

Aslam, M. (1979), 'The Practice of Asian Medicine in the United Kingdom', University of Nottingham, unpublished Ph.D. thesis.

Beck, B. E. F. (1969), 'Colour and Heat in South Indian Ritual', *Man* (n.s.) 4, 553–72.

Bedi, Sohinder Singh (1971), *Folklore of the Punjab*, New Delhi: National Book Trust.

Beetham, D. (1970), *Transport and Turbans*, Oxford University Press for Institute of Race Relations.

Bennett, O. (1990), *Listening to Sikhs*, London: Unwin Hyman.

Carstairs, G. M. (1957), *The Twice-born, a Study of a Community of High Caste Hindus*, London: Hogarth Press.

Cole, W. O. (1984), *Sikhism in its Indian Context 1469–1708*, London: Darton, Longman and Todd.

Das, V. (1977), *Structure and Cognition: Aspects of Hindu Caste and Ritual*, Delhi: Oxford University Press.
   (1985), 'Paradigms of Body Symbolism. An Analysis of Selected Themes in Hindu Culture', in eds. R. Burghart and A. Canthe, *Indian Religion*, London: Curzon, 180–207.

Doabia, Harbans Singh (rep. 1980), (trans.) *Nitnem*, Amritsar: Singh Brothers.
   (1981), *Life Story of Baba Nand Singh Ji of Kaleran (Nanaksar)*, Amritsar: Singh Brothers.

Douglas, M. (1973), *Natural Symbols*, London: Penguin.

Gideon, H. (1972), 'A Baby is Born in the Punjab', *American Anthropologist*, 64, 1220–34.

Hershman, P. (1974), 'Hair, Sex and Dirt', *Man*, N.S. 9, 274–98.
   (1977), 'Virgin and Mother', in ed. I. Lewis, *Symbols and Sentiments: Cross-Cultural Studies in Symbolism*, London: Academic Press, 269–92.
   (1981), *Punjabi Kinship and Marriage*, ed. H. Standing, Delhi: Hindustan Publishing Corporation (India).

Kakar, S. (1982), *Shamans, Mystics and Doctors: A Psychological Enquiry into India and its Healing Traditions*, New York: A. A. Knopf.

Krause, I.-B. (1989), 'The Sinking Heart: a Punjabi Communication of Distress', *Social Science and Medicine* Spring, 563–75.

Macauliffe, M. A. (rep. 1978), *The Sikh Religion*, I–VI, New Delhi: S. Chand.

McLeod, W. H. (1968), *Guru Nanak and the Sikh Religion*, London: Oxford University Press.

(1976), *The Evolution of the Sikh Community*, Oxford: Clarendon Press.

(1980a), *Early Sikh Tradition*, Oxford: Clarendon Press.

(ed.) (1980b), *The B40 Janam-Sakhi*, Amritsar: Guru Nanak Dev University.

(trans. and ed.) (1984), *Textual Sources for the Study of Sikhism*, Manchester University Press.

(1989), *Who is a Sikh?*, Oxford: Clarendon Press.

(1991), *Popular Sikh Art*, Delhi: Oxford University Press.

Nesbitt, E. M. (1985), 'The Nanaksar Movement', *Religion* 15, 67–79.

Oberoi, Harjot Singh (1987), 'The Worship of Pir Sakhi Sarvar: Illness, Healing and Popular Culture in the Punjab', *Studies in History*, N.S. 3/1, 50–3.

Pettigrew, J. (1972), 'Some Notes on the Social System of the Sikh Jats', *New Community* 1/5, 354–63.

(1981), 'Reminiscences of Fieldwork among the Sikhs', in ed. H. Roberts, *Doing Feminist Research*, London: Routledge, 62–81.

Sacha, G. S. (1988), *The Sikhs and their Way of Life*, 2nd edn, Southall: The Sikh Missionary Society (UK).

Sambhi, Piara Singh (1986/1987), 'A Survey of Religious Attitudes to Meat Eating', *The Sikh Messenger*, Winter/Spring, 27–31.

Singh, Atamjīt (1983), 'The Concept of Healing in the Sikh Scriptures', *Studies in Sikhism and Comparative Religion*, New Delhi: Guru Nanak Foundation, April, 53–7.

Singh, B. (1983), *Pragat Guran ki deh*, 3rd edn, Jagraon: n.p. (Punjabi).

Singh, I. P. (1961), 'Religion in Daleke a Sikh Village', in ed. L. P. Vidyarthi, *Aspects of Religion in Indian Society*, Meerut: Kedar Nath Ram Nath, 191–219.

Singh, Indarjit (1985), 'Sikhism a Philosophy for Today', *The Sikh Messenger*, Autumn, 24–9.

Singh, Jagjit (1985), *Perspectives on Sikh Studies*, New Delhi: Guru Nanak Foundation.

Singh, Joginder, Singh, Harcharan, and Brar, Baldev Singh (1979), 'The Sukhmani and High Blood Pressure', *Journal of Sikh Studies*, 6/1, Amritsar, 45–62.

(1980), 'Effect of Holy Dips in Treatment of Rheumatoid Arthritis and Osteo Arthritis in Believers', *Journal of Sikh Studies*, 6/1, Amritsar, 106–20.

Singh, Khushwant (1963), *A History of the Sikhs Volume I: 1469–1839*, Delhi: Oxford University Press.

Singh, Khushwant and Rai, Raghu (1984), *The Sikhs*, Varanasi: Lustre Press.

Singh, Nikky-Guninder Kaur (1993), *The Feminine Principle in the Sikh Vision of the Transcendent*, Cambridge University Press.

Singh, Trilochan (trans. and introd.) (n.d.), *Autobiography of Bhai Sahib Randhir Singh*, Ludhiana: Bhai Sahib Randhir Singh Publishing House.

Singh, Trilochan *et al.* (trans.) (1960), *Selections from the Sacred Writings of the Sikhs*,

UNESCO collection of representative works, London: G. Allen and Unwin.

Talib, G. Singh (1983), *Sikhism and Yoga*, London, Guru Nanak Foundation, U.K.

Uberoi, J. P. Singh (1980), 'The five symbols of Sikhism' in ed. L. M. Joshi, *Sikhism*, 2nd edn, Patiala, Guru Gobind Singh Department of Religious Studies, Punjabi University, 131–46.

Walker, B. (1968), *Hindu World*, vol. 1, London: Allen and Unwin.

Zimmerman, F. (1987), *The Jungle and the Aroma of Meats: An Ecological Theme in Hindu Medicine*, Berkeley: University of California Press.

Index